WORKS ISSUED BY
THE HAKLUYT SOCIETY

———

FRANÇOIS VALENTIJN'S
DESCRIPTION OF CEYLON

SECOND SERIES
NO. 149

ISSUED FOR 1975

Lt. 3. 61

OUD en NIEUW
OOST-INDIËN,

VERVATTENDE

Een Naaukeurige en Uitvoerige Verhandelinge van

NEDERLANDS MOGENTHEYD

In die

GEWESTEN,

BENEVENS

Eene wydluftige Befchryvinge der MOLUCCOS, AMBOINA, BANDA, TIMOR,
en SOLOR, JAVA, en alle de Eylanden onder dezelve Landbeftieringen
behoorende; het Nederlands Comptoir op SURATTE, en de
LEVENS DER GROOTE MOGOLS;

ALS OOK

Een Keurlyke Verhandeling van 't wezentlykfte, dat men behoort te weten van
CHOROMANDEL, PEGU, ARRACAN, BENGALE, MOCHA, PERSIEN, MALACCA,
SUMATRA, CEYLON, MALABAR, CELEBES of MACASSAR, CHINA,
JAPAN, TAYOUAN of FORMOSA, TONKIN, CAMBODIA, SIAM,
BORNEO, BALI, KAAP DER GOEDE HOOP en van MAURITIUS.

*Te zamen dus behelzende niet alleen eene zeer nette Befchryving van alles, wat Nederlands Ooft-
Indien betreft, maar ook 't voornaamfte dat eenigzins tot eenige andere Europeërs, in die Ge-
weften, betrekking heeft.*

Met meer dan thien honderd en vyftig Prentverbeeldingen verrykt.

Alles zeer naaukeurig, in opzigt van de Landen, Steden, Sterkten, Zeden der Volken,
Boomen, Gewaffchen, Land- en Zee-dieren, met alle het Wereldlyke en Kerkelyke, van
d'Oudfte tyden af tot nu toe aldaar voorgevallen, befchreven, en met veele zeer nette
daar toe vereyfchte Kaarten opgeheldert

DOOR

FRANÇOIS VALENTYN,

Onlangs Bedienaar des Goddelyken Woords in AMBOINA, BANDA, *enz.*

IN VYF DEELEN.

Te {DORDRECHT, {by {JOANNES VAN BRAAM, {Boekver-
{AMSTERDAM, { {GERARD ONDER DE LINDEN, {koopers.
MDCCXXIV.
MET PRIVILEGIE.

Fig. 1. Title page of *Oud en Nieuw Oost-Indien*

François Valentijn's
Description of Ceylon

Translated and Edited
by
SINNAPPAH ARASARATNAM

THE HAKLUYT SOCIETY
LONDON
1978

© The Hakluyt Society 1978

ISBN 0 904180 06 9

Printed in Great Britain
by Robert MacLehose and Company Limited
Printers to the University of Glasgow

Published by the Hakluyt Society
c/o The British Library
London WC1B 3DG

FOR MY PARENTS

Contents

List of Illustrations and Maps

MAPS

Preface

Through over two decades of study of Dutch overseas expansion of the chartered company period, I have had to consult continuously and fruitfully the many volumes of Valentijn's *Oud en Nieuw Oost-Indien*. I have become particularly familiar with the fifth volume which deals with the southern Asian region which has been my special interest over these years. I have referred to this volume frequently and have utilised its abundant material on Ceylon, Malabar and Coromandel, in my writings on the commerce and society of this region. My debt to Valentijn as a source book has indeed been great.

That a critically annotated edition of Valentijn's description of Ceylon (modern Sri Lanka) was a feasible proposition did not occur to me for a long time. I was perhaps put off by the enormity of its size (462 folio pages), its repetitiveness and its encyclopaedic character. The idea was put to me by my former colleagues and friends in the University of Ceylon (later Sri Lanka) who also suggested that it might become a volume in the publications of the Hakluyt Society. I took up their suggestion and made approaches to the Society and a proposal for a shortened one-volume edition of Valentijn's description of Ceylon was duly approved by that Society.

Immediately after starting work on the project, I moved from the University of Malaya to the University of New England, a move which caused an understandable delay in progress. When I resumed the work in New England, I had the benefit of generous research grants, support and encouragement of research by the University authorities and, above all, a congenial scholarly atmosphere in the University and the Department of History. The staff of the Dixson Library has always been helpful and co-operative as have also the staff of the other major University Libraries and the National Library of Australia. Work on this project had, however, to take third place, behind teaching and administrative tasks.

The task of editing Valentijn calls for expertise in a number of fields of study and a number of languages. Over and over again my own inadequacies in undertaking it have come home to me. I hope I will have the understanding and sympathy that the magnitude of the task requires.

The present edition consists of the first twelve chapters of Valentijn's description of Ceylon. These chapters bring the historical narrative up to the expulsion of the Portuguese from Ceylon and its environs by the Dutch East India Company. The following sections have been omitted from the text:

(i) p. 345 Extracts from the Instructions for Mr Jacob van Kittenstein, President and Head of the Hon. Company in Ceylon (Valentijn V. 1, pp. 128–35). The entire Memoir from which this section is extracted has been published in Dutch with an English translation in *Memoir of Joan Maatsuyker, 1650*. Ed. and Transl. by E. Reimers. Selections from the Dutch Records of the Ceylon Government No. 1 (Colombo, 1927).

(ii) p. 374 Considerations on Ceylon, given in the form of Instructions, according to the order of Their Excellencies, by the Hon. Commissioner Rykloff van Goens for the Governors of that island (Valentijn V. 1, pp. 148–54). These have been published in full in English translation in *Instructions from the Governor-General and Council of India to the Governor of Ceylon, 1656–1665*, Trans. by Sophia Pieters (Colombo, 1908).

While a number of people have helped by sharing their knowledge of various matters which impinge on the subject of this volume and in assisting in a wide variety of ways in the preparation of the final manuscript, I must record my special gratitude to a few among them. Professors Charles Boxer and James Cummins, both distinguished editors of Hakluyt publications and scholars of early modern European contacts overseas, have been a constant source of inspiration and encouragement. They have willingly given me their advice and their suggestions whenever I have turned to them with my problems. Mr Alan Treloar, my colleague in the University of New England, rendered valuable assistance in reading through the entire manuscript and suggesting stylistic revisions. Mrs M. Pittendrigh typed drafts at various stages of the work with her customary patience and accuracy. To them and to the numerous others in various parts of the world who looked up this and that reference, responded to my queries on a wide variety of matters and provided answers, or gave leads to solve a heap of problems—to all of them a sincere and deeply felt 'thank you'.

Abbreviations

Gk.	Greek
J.R.A.S.C.B.	Journal of the Royal Asiatic Society, Ceylon Branch
Mv	Mahāvamsa
Rv	Rājāvaliya
Sinh.	Sinhalese
Skt.	Sanskrit
Tam.	Tamil
V.O.C.	Vereenigde Oost-Indische Compagnie (United East India Company)

Introduction

The Author

François Valentijn was born in the city of Dordrecht on 17th April 1666, the son of Abraham and Maria Valentijn.[1] His father was a co-rector of the Grammar School at Dordrecht and his mother was a daughter of a Minister or *Predikant* of the Dutch Reformed Church. Abraham Valentijn belonged to an established middle class family which, as was evident from the subsequent career of François, had good connections with the Calvinist establishment, and even with the Netherlands-based official hierarchy of the Dutch East India Company (V.O.C.). François had a good early education at his father's school and continued his studies on a scholarship at the University at Leiden which he entered at the age of sixteen. He chose to study theology and progressed rapidly in his studies. When he turned eighteen, he had completed the prescribed examinations and had qualified as a Minister of the Reformed Church in 1684. His college studies gave him proficiency in the Classics (Latin and Greek), some Hebrew and possibly some Arabic. The early completion of these studies indicated application and intelligence, and the ability to cope with the demands of an education to qualify for the clergy at an age barely out of adolescence. At the end of 1684 he was appointed Minister to the East Indies and taken into the service of the East India Company. He was given a five-year contract and the Directors appointed him to the parish of Victoria Castle on the island of Amboina.

[1] The details of François Valentijn's early life and career are from the following sources: *Encyclopaedie Van Nederlandsch-Indie* Deel IV ('s-Gravenhage, 1921), pp. 493–8, *Nieuw Nederlandsch Biografisch Woordenboek* Deel V (Leiden, 1921), p. 989, C.A.L. Troostenburg de Bruijn, *Biographisch Woordenboek van Oost-Indische Predikanten* (Nijmegen, 1921), pp. 434–44, S. Kalff, 'François Valentijn', *De Indische Gids* Vol. 22, pt. 11 (1900) pp. 907–39, *Van en Naar Indie. Valentijns eerste en tweede Uit- en Thuisreis*, Voorafgegaan door Busken Huets, opniew uitgegeven door A. W. Stellwagen ('s-Gravenhage, 1881) and F. Valentijn, *Oud en Nieuw Oost-Indien* (Dordrecht, 1726) *passim*.

He was just nineteen when he boarded ship to sail to the East Indies. He sailed in the yacht *Moerkappel* which left the South Holland port of Hellevoetsluis on charter to the Rotterdam chamber on 13th May 1685. François' career as an observer and recorder of events was launched on that day. For from then on began his habit of keeping a diary and describing daily events on board ship which was later embodied in the accounts *Van en Naar Indie* (From and to the Indies) which was to be incorporated in volume four of his monumental work *Oud en Niew Oost-Indien*.[1] Thanks to this travelogue, we know what went on in this journey and how François spent his time. He was a lover of music and apparently took on board with him his violin and his accordion. Thanks to this travelogue, we know today every discomfort on that and other journeys, every cold, seasickness and other illness he had, and every hazard that his ship and its passengers had to undergo. One of his fellow passengers was a 'black' servant called Anthony who was returning to the east from the Netherlands. This Anthony had been a slave of Cornelis Speelman, an officer of the Company who had held many distinguished posts in the east, including Governor of Coromandel (1663–1665), Director General (1678–1681) and Governor General (1681–1684) at Batavia. Anthony had been taken by Speelman to Holland where he had left him with his son and now Anthony was being repatriated. Valentijn does not say what nationality Anthony belonged to, but it may be presumed that he was either an Indian Christian or a Malay who had become a Christian under Portuguese rule. Anthony was proficient in Portuguese and Valentijn, with his customary diligence, set about learning Portuguese from him, knowing that proficiency in the language was going to be very useful to him in the east where, even almost half a century after the eclipse of the Portuguese power, the Portuguese language remained something of a *lingua franca*.[2]

After a short stop at the Cape where all East Indiamen called for rest and recreation for the crew, refreshments and provisions, and repairs to ships, Valentijn proceeded on his journey to the Indies through the Straits of Sunda. The ship arrived in Batavia on 30th December 1685. Valentijn was immediately introduced to Dutch–Asian society

[1] Valentijn, Deel IV Stuk 2, pp. 95–166. This has been edited with a critical introduction by Busken Huets and published as *Van en Naar Indie. Valentijns eerste en tweede Uit- en Thuisreis* ('s-Gravenhage, 1881).
[2] Valentijn IV. 2, p. 101.

and life styles in the capital city. He made the acquaintance here both of the civilian officials of the Company and the clergy of the Reformed Church in the east. His first impressions of Batavia were good. He was offered hospitality on all sides. The prominent Dutch citizens of the town and members of the Council of the Indies, the highest governing body of the V.O.C. in the east, received him warmly. He received hospitality in the house of the Reverend Theodorus Zas, Mr. Dionys Kelk and the Reverend Isaac Hellenius, the Minister to the Malay congregation, all of whom entertained him one after the other. They all invited him to stay with them and he decided to lodge at the Reverend Hellenius' residence during his stay in Batavia. Of the life style of Batavia he says:

> I found Batavia exceptionally relaxing, and the means of living there entirely courtly, magnificent, friendly—the men very sociable and especially very hospitable, by which I had opportunity to be received, often very elegantly, by many of the most important people there.[1]

One of the members of the Council of the Indies who befriended him was Rijckloff van Goens jnr., the previous Governor of Ceylon (1675–1679) and now in Batavia from 1684 as a Councillor. The Governor General Johannes Camphuis received him in audience and later invited him home for dinner. Here he had his first taste of eastern cuisine—Japanese, Chinese and Malay dishes tastefully prepared and served by an array of servants—and was initiated into the experience of eating with chopsticks.[2] He began to learn his first Malay words and to observe and acquire some of the customs of the land. He showed his adaptability by learning quickly these strange habits of the east, to which many of his countrymen had been acclimatised. He learned to like eastern cooking with its assortment of spices and he took to the eastern habit of chewing betel.[3]

Among the friends François made in Batavia was Reynier de Vos who had served in Ceylon in the 1670's as Senior Merchant and Dissava[4] of Matara. Later he was Commander of the Return Fleet in which Valentijn left for Holland in 1694.

[1] Valentijn IV. 2, pp. 105–6.   [2] Valentijn IV. 2, p. 106.

[3] The betel leaf is chewed with dried arecanuts and other spicy ingredients. This was a popular social habit spread throughout south and southeast Asia.

[4] A Sinhalese office of Governor of a province or district. The nomenclature was retained by the Portuguese and the Dutch.

His colleagues on the establishment of the Reformed Church were also most agreeable. He presented his credentials on 31st December 1685 to the Church Council of Batavia and, as the record of that meeting states:

> His Honour was heartily welcomed and
> took his seat in this Gathering.[1]

On 21st January 1686, the Council of the Indies appointed him Minister to Amboina to be stationed in Victoria Castle, the seat of the Governor and administration of that island. At the meeting of the Church Council on 21st February 1686 he was given a pleasant farewell and the blessings of the gathering.[2] He left Batavia for Amboina via the central Javanese port of Japara a few days later in the ship *Voorschoten* and arrived there on 30th April.

Amboina was then under the administration of Governor Robert Padbrugge. It was one of the earliest of the East Indian islands to come under complete Dutch control which had been established there by the 1630's. It was the chief seat of Dutch power in the Moluccas and controlled the subordinate islands. A Christian community with a relatively long history existed on the island. The earliest conversions had taken place under the Portuguese in the 16th century and these were consolidated by the Ministers of the Dutch Reformed Church. Victoria Castle, because of its long history and its strong roots in the island, had developed many Dutch social institutions making life pleasant for the Dutch settler colony. Malay was of course an important language of communications. The island of Amboina, together with other islands of the Moluccas, had an abundant variety of sea life and this attracted the interest of some of the Dutch officials stationed there. The most famous of these who was active on the island, despite his blindness, was the great naturalist and collector Georgius Everhard Rumphius[3] who was to play an important role in Valentijn's career as a writer.

The initial circumstances augured most favourably for a happy stay in Amboina. The Governor Padbrugge took to the young Minister

---

[1] J. Mooi, *Bouwstoffen voor de Geschiedenis der Protestantsche Kerk in Nederlands-Indie*, Derde Deel (Batavia, 1931), p. 664.

[2] Mooi, *Bouwstoffen* . . . , III, p. 673.

[3] There is an abundant literature on Rumphius. For a comprehensive survey of his career and work, see *Rumphius Gedenkboek 1702–1902* (Koloniale Museum te Haarlem, 1902).

immediately and a firm friendship was sealed between the two.[1] His senior colleague, the Reverend Cornelis van der Sluys, took him under his wing and saw him through the early phase of his professional duties. Then there was the erudite Rumphius, always willing to share his vast knowledge of Ambonese history and natural science, and very knowledgeable in Malay. Under the expert instruction of Rumphius and Jan de Ruyter, François set about the study of Malay in earnest and, within three months of his arrival in Amboina, was able to deliver his first sermon in Malay.[2] Because of his progress in Malay, his salary which was initially 80 Guilders a month was increased to 100 Guilders and later to 120 Guilders. Such salary increases were used as an incentive for Ministers to learn Asian languages in the various Asian comptoirs of the Company.

The European community in Amboina was quite comfortably installed. They had an active social life of dinner parties and afternoon tea parties, and Valentijn seems to have been drawn into this society. His musical talents were useful in organising entertainment and he was also drawn into the activity, common among Ambonese Europeans, of collecting various specimens of plant and sea life that abounded in the island. It could reasonably be conjectured that Rumphius would have aroused this interest in him. This period also saw the beginnings of serious study of the Malay language and specifically his early efforts at translation into Malay of the Bible and of some missionary literature.

The beginnings of such a pleasant life were interrupted by a cloud on the horizon, the first of a number of disputes with the civil authority in the east. In July 1687, the Ambonese Council selected him for a vacancy in the Reformed Church in the Banda Islands. He protested against this appointment on the ground that he had been appointed from Holland for service exclusively in the island of Amboina. But his protest was of no avail and he was told that he had to obey the orders of the Ambonese government or be sent back to the Netherlands without pay. The appointment of officials, including clerical officials, in the east was the total responsibility of the civilian administration and no conditions entered into at home held good in the Indies. So Valentijn bowed to the authority of the government and betook himself to the Banda Islands. He arrived there on 8th August and remained in this post for 10 months.[3] He detested this posting as it involved a good deal of travelling on inspection tours to Christian

[1] Valentijn IV. 2, p. 110.   [2] Valentijn IV. 2, p. 110.   [3] Valentijn IV. 2, pp. 114–17.

communities on three islands—Neira, Lontor and Pulo Ai—in the chain of Banda Islands. Valentijn was always averse to sea travel and he missed the expansive life of European society in Victoria Castle. Thus he was most relieved to be able to come back to Amboina in May 1688. His Malay was now much improved and he appears to have begun to undertake a systematic translation of the Bible into Malay from 1689.

In this period François, who had come out alone to the east, had members of his family joining him in Amboina. A sister and a brother joined him in the first two years. In 1692 François married Cornelia Snaats, widow of Hendrik Leydekker, a private Dutch citizen of Amboina. Leydekker had been the Captain of the Burghers of Victoria Castle and a member of the settlement's *Raad van Justitie* (Court of Justice). He had been besides a merchant of some wealth and had had his own ships that sailed the Moluccan waters. From all the evidence, Cornelia inherited a substantial fortune after her husband's death, which was now available to François, making his life henceforth one of affluence and style. She had four children by her previous marriage— two sons and two daughters—and François fathered two children, Maria and Cornelia. Evidently Cornelia Snaats came from an old East Indian family and was probably born in the east. She was very proficient in Malay and could read the Jawi script. It could be presumed that she would have been a great asset to her husband in his Malay studies. The marriage was thus in every way a great boost to François' station and ambitions and went a long way in helping him to achieve what he did in the field of scholarship, by providing him with financial independence and research assistance. One of Valentijn's step-daughters, Cecilia, was also noted as a linguist. A document exists in the University Library at Leiden, a letter from the Sultan of Bachan written in Malay in Jawi script, which had been translated by Cornelia Valentijn—almost certainly the wife of François Valentijn.[1]

Some time after his marriage, François wanted to return to the Netherlands. His five year contract of service had expired in 1692, though he could have continued to serve longer if he wished because of the great shortage of Ministers in the east. He had a completed manuscript translation of the Malay Bible which he now wanted to have published in the Netherlands. But it was only in May 1694 that

[1] Leiden Ms. No. 1625. Cited in C.A.L. Troostenburg de Bruijn, *Biographisch Woordenboek* . . . , p. 438.

a successor was appointed and he could relinquish his post. His daughter Maria had been born recently and this too had increased his desire to go home. He left Amboina on 7th May with his wife and five children and was almost shipwrecked when the ship struck a reef on St. Mathew's Island near Tucan Besi. He arrived in Batavia on 7th June. Early in December, François and his family boarded the *Waddinxveen*, one of the ships of the Return Fleet to Holland. He arrived there on 24th August 1695.

He was received with honour by the city of his birth, Dordrecht, as a hero returning home with glory after spreading the Word in the heathen east. He established himself there and renewed contacts with his old friends. Evidently he did not take a post in Dordrecht but led a life of ease and comfort, among his documents and writings, his Malay translation projects and his sea-shell collection, which was always his pride. After his first visit to the east, he already had a reasonably good collection of Moluccan sea products which he displayed in a cabinet of which the doors opened at set times. Apparently there was a club of collectors which met periodically at each other's houses and studied and admired each other's collections. Valentijn records with regret that he presented this cabinet to an influential gentleman in the hope of getting a post for a relative in the Indies but that this did not materialise. It contained a number of rare items which he could not replace.[1]

In 1705 he was again appointed to the Reformed Church in the east and decided to go for another term of duty there. On his departure he preached a farewell sermon on 8th March 1705 in the Great Church at Dordrecht. He said on this occasion that he was going out east again 'on the earnest insistence of some powerful gentlemen and good friends'.[2] This sermon was published as a parting gift to Valentijn by the members of the Dordrecht parish.[3] Again he was appointed specifically to Amboina by the Directors. On his departure, the Committee for Indian Affairs of Amsterdam presbytery wrote to the Church in the Indies that they 'should receive him with upright love' and attested to the

worthiness of this man who is known for his virtue, friendliness, modesty, and of very agreeable companionship which the Christian

---

[1] Valentijn III. 1, p. 537. [2] Valentijn III. 1, p. 95.
[3] F. Valentijn, *Afscheidsrede van Dordrecht* (Dordrecht, 1705).

Synod of North Holland also emphasises, ... [and declared that] he was further provided with many gifts which are recognised in a faithful servant of the word.[1]

During this period when he was in Europe, he had evidently tried to influence the Company's authorities into publishing his translation of the Bible. He was having no success in this because there was at this time a rival work by the Reverend Melchior Leydekker of Batavia (no relation of his wife's first husband) who was making his own translation which was more favoured by the Batavian authorities. In 1698 he published a short book in Holland, *Deur der Waarheid* (Door to Truth), setting out his reasons why the Bible should be translated in Low Malay rather than in High Malay.[2] His own translation, he felt, was in Low or colloquial Malay that could be understood by all, while a translation into High or literary Malay could only be understood by a few and would not be very effective in winning souls to Christianity. He was not immediately successful in getting a decision on the publication of his translation and the question was left open when he returned to the east.[3]

On 10th May 1705 he boarded the ship *'t Hof van Ilpendam* which left Texel for the east. He was accompanied by his wife, five children, a servant maid and some relatives. This proved a very difficult journey, the seas were rough, many fell sick and some died. They were all relieved to reach the Cape in September, where a prolonged rest and refreshment made them fit for the second half of the journey. The journey from the Cape to Batavia was also very uncomfortable, and he and the family were in no condition to travel further when they landed in Batavia. They arrived in Batavia on 27th December 1705, and Valentijn asked to stay there for a few months to recover completely from the effects of the journey. During this period he attempted to get the backing of the Batavian Church Council for his Malay Bible.

This time circumstances were not so favourable to him in Batavia as during his last visit. His friendly patron, Camphuis, was no more the Governor General. The Director General was Abraham van Riebeeck,

---

[1] Van Boetzelaer van Asperen en Dubbeldam, *De Protestantsche Kerk in Nederlandsch-Indie* ('s-Gravenhage, 1947), p. 231.

[2] F. Valentijn, *Deure der Waarheijd* (Dordrecht, 1698).

[3] For a discussion of the controversy surrounding Valentijn's translation of the Bible, see G. H. Werndly, *Maleische Spraakkunst* (Amsterdam, 1736), pp. 241–9.

brother-in-law of the Reverend Leydekker, his rival in Malay translation. At this time a Dutch military expedition was setting out from Batavia to the eastern part of Java. The Dutch had become involved in the politics of the Javanese kingdom of Mataram. There was a disputed succession in Mataram after the death of Sultan Amangkurat II in 1703. His only son and heir was bitterly hostile to the Dutch and they decided to support a pretender, the young Sultan's uncle. He had been installed on the throne by Dutch troops in 1705 and was now facing an attack by the former Sultan's supporters who had mobilised an army in east Java and were joined by Surapati, the Balinese guerrilla leader.[1] In 1706 the Dutch decided to send an expedition against these combined forces and the Reverend Feylingino was appointed army chaplain. Feylingino had suddenly fallen sick and the Batavian Government decided to appoint this Minister recently arrived from the Netherlands in his place.

Again this was in violation of the conditions of his appointment by the Directors. And he was particularly distressed because he was not yet in good physical condition after the long voyage. He was at all times a man who desired a restful, comfortable life and he dreaded the rigours of long marches, camping in uncomfortable surroundings, the features of life with an army expeditionary force, and he felt he would not have the energy to last this expedition. He feared very much for his life. Besides, he had brought a large family with him to the east and was distressed at having to part from them before he could see that they were well settled. The Batavian authorities set aside the Directors' conditions almost with relish when Valentijn waved them before their faces. The Director General van Riebeeck, who was responsible for appointments of personnel, told Valentijn

> The Gentlemen in the Fatherland decide matters as they think fit but we do here what we decide and judge is best. Do what you will and run around to all the Gentlemen [of the Council of the Indies]; you shall yet go on this expedition or otherwise return to the Fatherland without pay.[2]

These decisive words left Valentijn with no choice and he left with the troops as army chaplain to east Java on 22nd June 1706. Valentijn

[1] For a history of these events, see H. J. de Graaf, *Geschiedenis van Indonesie* ('s Gravenhage, 1949), pp. 238–41.
[2] Valentijn III. 1, p. 101.

felt later that the rough treatment he received was partly because of his dispute with the Reverend Leydekker over the Malay translation of the Bible, and that van Riebeeck was taking revenge on him on behalf of his brother-in-law.[1] The hostility between the two was to last longer and, when van Riebeeck became Governor General in 1709, he was in a position to do further harm to Valentijn.

While on the army expedition, Valentijn's worst fears were confirmed. It was a difficult expedition, constantly harrassed by Surapati's guerrillas, and hence forced to be on the move constantly. Valentijn fell seriously ill, with fever and dysentery, suffered bitterly from the uncomfortable conditions and had to be sent back in the middle of November 1706. One of the letters of the time speaks of him as the 'impotent Predikant'.[2] Despite these discomforts, the observer and recorder in Valentijn was not stifled. He kept a diary of events and on the basis of this he described the expedition in his section on Java in his voluminous work. He not only provides interesting descriptions of army camp life but also fascinating sidelights on Javanese court life and on Javanese society.[3] On his return he stayed in Batavia until February 1707 to recuperate his health.

It was during this time that he entered into discussions with the Batavian Church Council in an effort to get them to adopt his manuscript translation of the Bible. Up till this time Valentijn had sought to do this through Church and Company authorities in Holland. When this was not successful he turned his attention to Batavia. The Church Council of Batavia had not seen the translation and requested to be provided with a copy. Valentijn let them have a copy of his manuscript and the Council instructed the Reverends van der Vorm, Coldehon and van der Sluys to examine it. They went over it and suggested some revisions which Valentijn agreed to make. He left Batavia on 17th February 1707 in the ship *Slooten* for Amboina with his family. He arrived there in mid-March and settled down in Victoria Castle. His old friend Adriaan van der Stel was Governor but many things had changed. The city had expanded and was now more attractive. Rumphius, the scientist, had died in an earthquake in 1702, his great work on Ambonese natural history unpublished. Two of Valentijn's step-children married into the Rumphius family and it appears that, because of this relationship, Valentijn was able to secure

---

[1] *Ibid.*   [2] Valentijn IV. 2, p. 98.   [3] Valentijn IV. 1, p. 55ff.

access to innumerable manuscripts belonging to Rumphius which were very useful in the preparation of his great work.

During this second residence in Amboina, Valentijn fitted in easily into the life of European society in Victoria Castle. He was very affluent now, being in charge of the Leydekker legacy inherited through his wife, and had large amounts of capital available to him. He used to lend large sums of money to the Company's administration. But he had problems in his relationship with the administration as well as with the Batavian Church Council. He had disputes with the Governor over the appointment of a catechist as well as over the appointment of a Catholic as supervisor of the poorhouse. He wrote bitter letters to the Batavian Government complaining about the Ambonese administration and even asked to come to Batavia to speak to the Governor General about these complaints. This request was not granted to him. During this period he also took to writing contentious, and sometimes insulting letters to the Batavian Church Council over various matters, but especially on the dispute over the Malay translation of the Bible.[1] He was extremely dissatisfied with the conditions of service in Amboina and requested to be repatriated to Holland.

The Batavian Government decided to take him to task for his serious allegations of misconduct against the Ambonese administration. The Council of Indies decided, by resolution of 29th December 1711, to summon him to Batavia to be questioned on these allegations. On 25th May 1712 he left Amboina with his family for Batavia. The Governor General van Riebeeck was obviously hostile and went out of his way to pin him down. Valentijn was asked to provide further elucidation and evidence of these allegations which he did in a written statement. The Council was not satisfied with this statement, refused his request for repatriation and decided by resolution of 18th October 1712 to put the matter in the hands of the Advocate-fiscal. The Advocate-fiscal gave his opinion that Valentijn be proceeded against by law for not substantiating allegations made from Amboina. The Council decided to file action against him in the *Raad van Justitie* which heard the case early in 1713. He was given a conditional acquittal by the court.[2]

In the meantime the post of Minister at Ternate became vacant with

---

[1] Van Troostenburg de Bruijn, *Biographisch Woordenboek* . . . , pp. 435–53.
[2] A. K. S. Gijsberti Hodenpijl, 'François Valentijns laatste verblijfsjaren in Indie', *De Indische Gids*, 38 (1916), pp. 168–75.

the death of the Reverend Petrus Beterkooper and in December 1712 the Government appointed Valentijn to this place. Now Ternate was looked upon by the Ministers of the Church as a hardship station. A volcanic island, it had poor road communications and was sparsely provided with water. There were two live volcanoes on the island and it was liable to earthquakes. The heat of the day and the cold of the night took a heavy toll among Europeans in sickness and death. Besides there were, what Valentijn dreaded, obligatory tours of inspection around the island in small native boats. European Ministers usually shied away from an assignment there and, in a period of eighteen years, only two had been sent to this community. The Christians there were generally ministered to by native schoolmasters and catechists. Valentijn refused to go to Ternate, again brandishing the conditions of his original appointment by the Directors; and he repeated his request to be repatriated to Holland. Again this was of no avail, the Batavian Government insisting that he go, on threat of dismissal from service and repatriation without pay and allowances. With his acquittal by the *Raad van Justitie* and the death of van Riebeeck on 17th November 1713, he was permitted to go back to Holland, though not reinstated in service.[1]

On 25th November 1713 Valentijn boarded the ship *Engewormer* with his wife and two children. Again the journey was rough and Valentijn suffered much from seasickness. His daughter Maria was much worse and reached Holland in a very weak condition and it took over six months for her to recover completely. The ship stopped at the Cape for about two and a half months and Valentijn and his family were boarded in the house of a Dutch burgher. He had to spend a great deal of money here for the sustenance of the family and, as he was without pay, he had to fall back on his wife's fortune. Starting from the Cape on the second part of the journey on 10th April 1714, the party arrived in Holland on 4th August 1714 at the port of Hellevoetsluijs. On the way Valentijn relates that he saw a sea-monster wearing a grey cap on its head, which he describes as a mermaid. He enthusiastically describes mermaids and mermen in his book with pictures and shows himself a believer in their existence.[2]

He was extremely relieved and thankful to Providence at the safe return of the whole family to the fatherland. The trip had been particularly difficult, with personal and professional problems. At

[1] *Ibid.*, pp. 175–7.　　　　[2] Valentijn III. 1, pp. 330–5.

the end of the journey, out of a sense of relief, he presented a bottle of Cape wine and some pickled foodstuffs to the crew, a gesture which he regretted later because of the high value of the former.[1] His misfortunes continued: the Company's authority in the harbour detained two chests from among his luggage on the grounds that it was in excess of his entitled luggage space. Valentijn suspected that this was on the order of the Governor General Riebeeck.[2] Presumably these contained more of his papers and documents and one shudders at the thought that his work would have been expanded even further had these been released.

In Holland his patrons among the Directors, the Van Dams and Advocate Schot, had died. There was no one among the Directors who could intercede on his behalf in his quarrel with the Governor General Riebeeck. He wrote to the Directors complaining about this and about the detention of his chests but he could get no redress. He finally appealed to the Chairman of the Directors, the Burgomaster Hoofd, from whom he obtained an evasive reply: the detention of the chests was by order of the previous Court of Directors, and he could not help him now. Valentijn talks very bitterly about this whole incident.[3]

He proceeded immediately to his birthplace, Dordrecht, and established himself there. From then on his life was devoted to working on the numerous papers he had accumulated, corresponding with a number of people who had served in the Indies, and preparing the manuscript of *Oud en Nieuw Oost-Indien* (Old and New East Indies) for the press. The only relief from this was the study and enjoyment of his Neptunus-cabinet, which housed his collection of sea shells, coral and the other sea-products he had brought with him after his second stay in the east. This was a larger and richer collection than the one he had brought with him on his first visit. Valentijn was proud of his collection. He says that he had 300 more varieties of horns and shells than Rumphius. Other ex-Indies hands came together to study and admire each other's collections. Six of these friends had formed themselves into a club which met on the first Wednesday of each month at each other's houses to study their respective collections.[4]

The first part of the manuscript of *Old and New East Indies* must have been submitted to the press before 1724 when the first volume came out. The material in the volumes shows that he was continuously

---

[1] Valentijn IV. 2, p. 165. [2] Valentijn III. 1, p. 104. [3] *Ibid.*
[4] S. Kalff, 'François Valentijn', *De Indische Gids*, 22, 11 (1900), 933-4.

working on these one after the other until 1726 when the last volume appeared. During this period he also wrote some religious tracts and linguistic texts in Malay: Malay Psalms, a Malay Catechism, a Malay Dictionary, a Javanese Dictionary and a Description of the Muslim religion. His Malay translation of the Bible was never printed. After the completion of this work, Valentijn moved to the Hague. He died in the Hague the following year, on 6th August 1727. His body was brought to Dordrecht and ceremoniously buried there on 12th August, as the death register records, 'with six carriages more than the usual number'.[1]

Oud en Nieuw Oost-Indien

It is not for his services as a Minister of the Dutch Reformed Church in the east that Valentijn is remembered by posterity. There have been others more distinguished and more dedicated in the eastern service of this Church. Others have made more lasting contributions to the spread of the Christian faith in the diverse settlements of the Dutch in Asia. Valentijn's career as a Minister in the east was, by comparison, devoid of substantial achievement and was marred by continuous disputes with the civil authority, and even with the religious establishment. As an evangelist among non-Christian communities he made no marked progress. But Valentijn has overshadowed all his other co-workers in the Dutch Reformed Church and imprinted his name firmly in historical memory wholly through the publication of his *Oud en Nieuw Oost-Indien*. The work is in five volumes published in eight folio parts. The full title of the work was: *Oud en Nieuw Oost-Indien, Vervattende een Naaukeurige en Uitvoerige Verhandelinge van Nederlands Mogentheyd In die Gewesten ... Met meer dan thien hondred en vyftig Prentveerbeeldingen verrykt. Alles zeer naaukeurig, in opzigt van Landen, Steden, Sterkten, Zeden der Volken, Boomen, Gewasschen, Land-en Zee-dieren, met alle het Wereldlyke en kerkelyke, van d'Oudste tyden af tot nu toe aldaar voorgevallen, beschreven, en met veele zeer nette daar toe vereyschte Kaarten opgeheldert Door François Valentyn, Onlangs Bedienaar des Goddelyken Woords in Amboina, Banda, enz. In Vyf Deelen.*

[1] Cited in Kalff, *op. cit.*, p. 935.

[Old and New East Indies, embracing an exact and detailed treatment of Dutch power in these quarters. .... Enriched with more than ten hundred and fifty printed illustrations. Everything very accurately described, in respect of lands, cities, ports, customs of the people, trees, products, land and sea animals, with all secular and religious matters that happened there from the earliest times to the present, and elucidated by very accurate maps required for this purpose by François Valentijn, lately servant of God's word in Amboina, Banda, etc. In five volumes.][1]

Volume 1 is in two parts with an introductory description of the establishment of Dutch power in the East Indies in the first part and then a description of the Molucca islands and of North and East Celebes. Volume 2, also divided into two parts, is a description of the Amboina territory. Volume 3 is in two books the first of which is local church history and natural history of Amboina, the second deals with Banda, Timor, Solor, Macassar, Borneo and Bali, as well as with Tonkin, Cambodia and Siam. Volume 4 is also divided into two books, the first dealing with Java which is continued into the second book, which is followed successively by a Description of Surat, Lives of the Great Moghuls, Description of China, Formosa and finally Valentijn's outward and homeward journeys. Volume 5 is also in two books, the first dealing successively with Coromandel (along with Pegu and Bengal), Persia, Malacca, Sumatra and Ceylon, the second dealing with the Malabar coast, Japan, the Cape of Good Hope and Mauritius. There are thus in all eight books of folio size with a total of 4,631 pages and over 1,050 illustrations.

A glance at this list of contents shows the very far-reaching territorial embrace of the work but also its disorderly nature. Valentijn has not worked to a geographic plan of arrangement. Indo-China is lumped together with Borneo and Bali, Sumatra is put between Malacca and Ceylon, Java is followed by the Great Moghuls who are again followed by China. The homeward journey is inserted in the middle of the work. Part of this is explained by the history of the planning and publication of the work. A Dutch contemporary monthly literary periodical *Boekzael der Geleerde Werelt* records the first prospectus announcing the publication of this work in its issue of December 1722. This

[1] Te Dordrecht/Amsterdam by Joannes van Braam, Gerard onder de Linden, MDCCXXIV.

prospectus promised five folio volumes at a subscription price of $70\frac{1}{2}$ florins and a small number on superior paper at 80 florins.[1] As it went to the press, the number of books increased to eight; the number of prints and maps was much larger. It is obvious that Valentijn threw into the press whatever material he had in an undigested form. Even a continuous pagination was not possible; in many of the volumes the pagination is broken up into parts.

Valentijn himself provides the evidence, in his preface to some of the volumes, of the enlargement of the work from its original conception. In the *Preface to the Discerning Reader*, introducing the first volume, he says that the forerunner of this work was an account of the Dutch achievements and activities in these quarters.[2] He implies that this aim was considerably widened with the acquisition of more material and the work became not merely one on *Nieuw* ('new') East Indies but also of the *Oud* ('old') East Indies. This point is further confirmed in his preface to the third volume where he writes thus, for the *Information of the Discerning Reader*:

> When we first decided to publish this work, we estimated that it would amount to about one thousand sheets. But after the world saw what matters were included in it, many gentlemen of importance now came forward, some at my request, others of their own accord, to enrich this work by providing this and that Indies material in their hands.[3]

Thus it appears that the enlargement of the work went on even after the publication of the first volumes. It is reasonable to assume that the Amboina part of the work and the extension of Dutch power there was the section that was first conceived. This was what Valentijn had been working on from a very early stage. The addition of other regions, particularly those outside the southeast Asian area, was largely caused by the ready availability of material at a later stage of the preparation of the work. As new material came in, the original plan was expanded, both territorially and chronologically, to squeeze in this material.

It must be noted here that Valentijn's travels took him to the Cape of Good Hope, Batavia, East Java, Amboina and Banda Islands but

[1] Cited in *Encyclopaedie van Nederlandsch-Indie* IV, 505.
[2] Voorreden tot den Bescheyden Lezer, Valentijn I, pp. 1–4.
[3] Voor Bericht van den Schryver aan den Bescheyden Lezer, Valentijn III. 1, pp. 1–3.

to no other places in the east. He had not been to Sumatra, Malacca, Ceylon or to the Indian mainland. The description of these places are thus based on existing travel descriptions and on documentary evidence from the Company's papers, and from material collected from his many friends and acquaintances who had been in those parts. It is significant that many of those named by Valentijn, and thanked for substantial assistance, are Company officials who had served in South Asia, an area of which Valentijn had no first-hand knowledge. These are Matheus van der Bourke (Malabar and Bengal), Elias van der Bourke (Coromandel), Daniel Bernard (Coromandel), Adam van der Duyn (Malabar and Ceylon), Joannes van Steeland (Coromandel) and Cornelis Joan Simons (Ceylon).[1] Valentijn was particularly close to the van der Stel family. Simon van der Stel, who was Commander at the Cape of Good Hope on his first journey out, seems to have taken kindly to him and treated him lavishly as a house guest. His sons, Adriaan and Willem Adriaan, served for long in the east and the whole family, both by themselves and by marriage, had extensive eastern connexions. Another influential family, whose acquaintance Valentijn made, was the van Goenses, father and son, who had served with distinction in Ceylon. On his journey out of Batavia to Japara, on the way to his first tenure at Amboina, Valentijn reports meeting two ensigns, Michiel Ram and N. Lamsweerde, who had been Dutch ambassadors to the court of Kandy in 1685.[2] He appears to have struck up an acquaintance with them also. All these willing (and even unwilling) sources seem to have been assiduously tapped to gather material on those parts of the east of which he had no first-hand knowledge.

As soon as the work was launched it proved a great success. When the subscriptions were opened, they were all taken in eight to ten days' time and the 2,200 copies the publishers had planned were all sold out, as they state in a Further Notice to the Reader.[3] They say there that, because of the excellent reception the work has had from a 'newsgreedy' public, they have thought it advisable to print more copies. Soon after the enlargement of the work from five to eight books and an increased number of illustrations, the pre-publication price was increased from $70\frac{1}{2}$ florins and 90 florins to 90 florins and 120 florins respectively for the two types of imprints. This was later

---

[1] Valentijn III. 1, pp. 1–3.   [2] Valentijn IV. 2, p. 108.
[3] Nader Bericht aan den Lezer, Valentijn 1 (n.p.).

increased further to 116 florins and 150 florins respectively. Copies of this work in later years were not so rare as some other contemporary works. Even today it is possible to buy a full set of the first and only edition, but the marked price in a Martinus Nijhoff catalogue of 1973–1974 was 1,775 florins.

Perhaps because of its immense size the work was never published in a subsequent edition. Interest in it was always there and it was treated as an encyclopaedia on the Dutch east. In the 19th century there were plans now and then to bring out abridged, modernised versions of Valentijn. In the early part of the century the Amsterdam Booksellers Johan van der Heij and Son opened subscriptions for a reprint of the work in six octavo volumes. They could not find sufficient takers to begin the venture.[1] A subsequent effort met with success. In 1856–58, Dr S. Keijzer edited and abridged *Oud and Nieuw Oost-Indien* in three octavo volumes.[2] These three volumes were intended as the first part of the publication and contained Valentijn's account of that part of the East Indies still ruled by the Dutch in the 19th century. The second part which was to have contained the remainder of the work never appeared. Dr Keijzer's intention was to provide some material for the Dutch colonial administrators of his day and to give them some familiarity with the regions they were called upon to administer.[3] The text was modernised, thus losing much of the quaint Valentijn charm of expression, but at the same time making it easy reading. Valentijn's description of his outward and homeward journeys, *Uit- en- 'thuis reijzen,* was published in 1879 by Conrad Busken Huets, the Dutch man of letters, in his *Litterarische Fantasie,* and in 1882 it was published separately by A. W. Stellwagen from the Hague.[4] Busken Huets, one of the greatest Dutch literary critics of his time, was most impressed with this piece of descriptive writing. He says in his introduction:

Valentijn's first and second outward and homeward journeys deserve to live and should be placed in the hands of the coming generation

[1] Van Troostenburg de Bruijn, *Biographisch Woordenboek . . .,* pp. 440–1.

[2] *François Valentijn's Oud en Nieuw Oost-Indien. Met aantekeningen, volledige inhoudsregisters, chronologische lijsten, enz.* Uitgegeven door Mr. S. Keijzer (Amsterdam, Wed. J. C. Van Kesteven en Zoon, 1862).

[3] Keijzer, *François Valentijn's . . .* Foreword.

[4] *Van en Naar Indie. Valentijns eerst en tweede uit'en' thuisreis.* Voorafgegaan door Busken Huets. Litterarische-Critische studie over François Valentyn opniew uitgegeven door A. W. Stellwagen ('s Gravenhage, Henri J. Sternberg, 1882).

to be received with gratitude. . . . [They] ought to be placed in the library of Dutch classics. They conclude in a worthy manner the series of the old Dutch ship-journals.[1]

In 1859 Mr R. H. Major edited, for the Hakluyt Society, the *Early Voyages to Terra Australis, now called Australia* in which was included the *Voyage of Gerrit Thomasz Pool to the South Land,* translated from Valentijn's *Beschryvinge van Banda.*[2] The most recent occasion for a Valentijn edition was the publication in 1971 by the van Riebeeck Society in Cape Town of his description of the Cape of Good Hope.[3]

Wydluftige Landbeschryvinge van 't Eyland Ceylon

The first book of the fifth volume of *Oud en Nieuw Oost-Indien* embraces a miscellaneous assortment of countries and regions. It begins with a Select Description of Coromandel, Pegu, Arakkan, Bengal and Mocha, all of which occupy the first 198 pages. It then goes on to a description of the Dutch comptoir of Persia in pages 199 to 307. From page 308 follows an Exact Description of Malacca which is carried on till page 360 followed by a Description of the island of Sumatra where a separate pagination is used. Sumatra occupies 46 pages and then begins what Valentijn obviously intended as the core of this particular volume—A Wide-ranging Geographical-Description of the Island of Ceylon. It occupies 462 pages and, next to Amboina and Greater Java, receives the most copious and the most detailed coverage of all the countries and regions dealt with in the entire work.

The account of Ceylon in Volume V was known to many writers on Ceylon but has never been published subsequently in Dutch or in translation. Short extracts were translated by A. E. Buultjens and published in a Ceylonese journal *Orientalist* in 1885–86, 1888–89 and

[1] *Van en Naar Indie* . . . Voorafgegaan door Busken Huets. Opniew Uitgegeven door A. W. Stellwagen, p. 37.

[2] *Early voyages to Terra Australis, now called Australia.* Edited with an Introduction by R. H. Major, Hakluyt Society. First Series No. 25 (London, 1859), pp. 75–6.

[3] François Valentyn. *Description of the Cape of Good Hope, with the matters concerning it* (Amsterdam, 1726). Edited and annotated by Prof. P. Serton, Maj. R. Raven-Hart, Dr. W. J. de Kock. Final Editor Dr. E. H. Raidit. Introduction by Prof. P. Serton. English Translation by Maj. R. Raven-Hart, Part 1, Second Series, No. 2, Van Riebeeck Society (Cape Town, 1971).

1891.[1] In the early years of British rule in Ceylon, when there was a great deal of interest among British administrators in Dutch sources on Ceylonese society and economy, an English civil servant, Andrew Armour, began to translate Valentijn's account of Ceylon. Sir Alexander Johnston, Chief Justice of Ceylon (1806–19), was well known for encouraging the accumulation of indigenous traditional, as well as Portuguese and Dutch sources on Ceylon.[2] Armour wrote to Johnston informing him of this project:[3]

> To: The Honourable Alexander Johnston Esq
>   Second Member of His Majesty's Council
>   and Puisne Justice of the Supreme Court
>   of Judicature in the Island of Ceylon etc. etc.

Your personal knowledge of the Island of Ceylon induces me to signify to your honour that I have it at present in contemplation to prepare a translation of its History by the Reverend François Valentijn, which History your Honour is particularly acquainted with, and have been pleased to recommend it, as the best yet existing. The abilities of the Author seconded with the best Sources of information, cannot fail in giving a superiority to the work itself, and I shall endeavour, and take care as much as possible that it loses nothing in coming through my hands. It is my intention to make occasional illustrations in marginal notes with regard to points coming within my knowledge, and if possible I shall add something by way of an appendix concerning the religion of the Cingalese and some of the Natural productions of the country.

> Honourable Sir,
>   Your Honour's most obedient and humble servant
>   A. Armour.

In all probability this was the translation that Johnston presented to the Royal Asiatic Society of Great Britain, in whose collection the

---

[1] François Valentijn, 'The Dutch in Ceylon', tr. by A. E. Buultjens, Orientalist (1885–86), 201-8, 3 (1888–89), 9–17, 4 (1891), 50–7.

[2] On Sir Alexander Johnston as a collector of historical material on Ceylon, see E. Upham, The Mahavamsi, The Raja-Ratnacari and the Raja-Vali. Sacred and historical books of Ceylon. (London, 1833) 1, pp. VI–VIII. Also H. W. Tambiah, 'The Alexander Johnstone [sic] Papers', The Ceylon Historical Journal, III, 1 (1953), 18--30.

[3] Andrew Armour to the Honourable Alexander Johnston, reproduced in P. E. Pieris, Sinhale and the patriots (Colombo, 1950), p. 440.

manuscript now rests. Sir Emerson Tennent, Colonial Secretary of Ceylon (1845–49), and a prodigious writer on the history and geography of that island, quite rightly calls it a 'very incorrect and imperfect translation', like so many other translations of Dutch material lying in the Johnston papers.[1]

Among early British administrators in the east, Valentijn's work came to the attention also of Colonel Colin Mackenzie, an officer in the Indian army from 1783 to 1821. He was also a noted collector of Indian and Southeast Asian historical documents and among his collections are translations of very extensive selections of Valentijn's voluminous work.[2] There are translations of the whole section devoted to Affairs of Religion in the Island of Java (Mackenzie Manuscripts: Private 63), of the first part of Volume 1 entitled Dutch power in the East Indies (Mackenzie Manuscripts: Private 64.I), of the whole section devoted to the Molucca Islands (Mackenzie Manuscripts: Private 64.II and 64.III), of The Ecclesiastical Affairs of Amboina (Mackenzie Manuscripts: Private 64.IV), of the description of Macassar, Borneo, Bali and Siam (Mackenzie Manuscripts: Private 64.V), of sections of the description of Ceylon (Mackenzie Manuscripts: Private 78.2), of the entire section dealing with Coromandel (Mackenzie Manuscripts: Private 89) and of the Lives of the Great Moghuls (Mackenzie Manuscripts: Private 87).[3]

In the quality and quantity of information provided, the coherent and flowing narrative and the total picture painted of the island's history, geography, society and institutions, this Description of Ceylon ranks with Valentijn's treatment of Amboina and the Moluccas. The 462 pages of narrative and extracts from original records are divided into 17 chapters. An Introduction defines indigenous terms for officials and caste groups of the island. The rest of the book is divided into three parts. The first part consisting of three chapters and running to 58 pages, is subtitled Description of Ceylon. These chapters are a geographic and ethnic description of the island, where the reader is taken on a tour of the entire land, identifying the cities, towns, villages, rivers, mountains, forests, wasteland, reefs and the

---

[1] Emerson Tennent, *Ceylon* (Fifth Edition, London, 1860), 11, 32.
[2] For a sketch of the career of Col. Mackenzie, see *Mackenzie Manuscripts*, 1, Ed. T. V. Mahalingam (Madras, 1972), pp. i- xxii.
[3] C. O. Blagden, *Catalogue of manuscripts in European languages belonging to the library of the India Office. Vol. 1. The Mackenzie Collections Part I* (O.U.P., 1916), pp. 201, 202, 228–9, 250, 252.

like, and an attempt is made to describe the people, their customs and the languages. With Chapter Four begins the second part which consists of 12 chapters (4 to 15) and occupies 307 pages. It is subtitled Particular Affairs of Ceylon (*Bijzondere Zaaken van Ceylon*). It is a historical treatment of events from the earliest colonisation of the island by the Sinhalese. This history continues in desultory fashion until 1724. The third part is subtitled Matters of Religion in Ceylon and occupies the last two chapters of 155 pages. These chapters are devoted to the major religions of Ceylon, Buddhism, Hinduism, Islam, Catholic and Protestant Christianity. The material on Ceylon is as profusely illustrated as the other volumes. There are thirty-one illustrations of which one is a large map of the island, 17 inches square, and the rest are charts of forts, churches and cities, and pictorial illustrations of social life and of historical events which are described in the text.

The Preface to the Reader explicitly states the aims of the work which are always implicit through each of its sections. The original work was devoted to the rise and growth of Dutch power in the East Indies and it was from this that voluminous accounts of individual regions grew, with the accumulation of sources and information. The original work was intended as a tribute to the Netherlanders serving in the east, to show that their generation was true to the ideals of the founders of the republic and the eastern empire.[1] This nationalistic aim pervades the whole work and a pride in the achievements of his countrymen appears on every page. The account of the history of Ceylon is interspersed with remarks which show his conviction that the exploits of the 'gallant Batavians' in Ceylon were far greater than those of the Portuguese and of other preceding periods in the island's history.[2] This nationalism is further emphasised by the publisher Johannes van Braam in the presentation of the work. In verse and prose, in Latin and in Dutch, the greatness of the Fatherland, of the city of Amsterdam, of the Company and its Directors and of the author Valentijn is sung repeatedly, and the book is dedicated to the burgomaster of the city of Amsterdam and a Director of the Company, Egidius van der Bempden.[3]

In this respect Valentijn's work is the last of the genre of Dutch works on the east which reflect the period of greatness and glory. Valentijn's stay in the east belongs to the tail-end of that period and,

[1] Valentijn I. Voorreden . . . , pp. 2–3.
[2] See for example Valentijn V. 1, Ceylon, p. 462.   [3] Valentijn I, Opdragt, pp. 1–5.

even during his second term, stagnation and decline of the Company's affairs in the east were not readily visible. This Dutch nationalism does not interfere directly with large parts of the work on Ceylon which deal with the periods before Dutch contact. And the abundance of sources used by Valentijn and their diverse character very often counteract the nationalistic bias. It is, of course, true that the account is always narrated from the point of view of the Dutch rulers but it was too early to expect anything different.

Another feature expressly stated in the Preface also acts as a counter-influence to Valentijn's nationalism. This was his great interest in the languages and cultures of eastern people and even more a lively desire to be seen and recognised as an expert Orientalist. In his Preface, Valentijn proclaims to all and sundry his knowledge of the languages of the lands in which he had travelled. He proclaims the obvious superiority of the linguistically proficient traveller over the non-proficient when he comes to describe his experiences. He makes a sweeping claim when he says he understood soundly these languages but refers especially to his proficiency in Malay and his ability to read the Arabic script in which it was written.[1] He probably had some slight acquaintance with the major language families of the east. Malay and Javanese gave him access linguistically to a large area in Southeast Asia. In South Asia, he does not seem to have known any language but he was certainly familiar with the linguistic complexity of the area and knew of its linguistic distribution. He knew that Sanskrit was the parent of many of the Indian languages and comments critically on the lack of Sanskrit knowledge of Rogerius and Baldaeus who had written on India.[2] He had some acquaintance with the Sanskrit Vedas and their antiquity. He stressed the necessity of Christian ministers working in South Asia learning the Sanskrit language.[3] He seems to have been familiar with the extant literature and the contemporary authorities on eastern philogy and language. He was familiar with the work of the noted Dutch linguist Dr Adrian Reland, Professor of Oriental Languages and Ecclesiastical Antiquities at Leiden University. Reland was the author of *Dissertationes Miscellaneae*, published in 1716, in which he dealt with the grammar and script of a number of Asian languages—Malay, Sinhalese, Tamil, Javanese, among others. He provides a vocabulary of these languages and discusses the origins

[1] Valentijn I, Voorreden . . . , pp. 1–3.   [2] Valentijn V. 1, Choromandel, p. 72.
[3] *Ibid.*

of some words—information which Valentijn appears to have utilised in his work. It made him familiar with Sinhalese and Tamil, the two languages dominant in Ceylon, and enabled him to understand and appreciate the meanings of place names, words and phrases that he would have come across in his many sources. He also knew of Thomas Hyde, the English philologist and Regius Professor of Hebrew at the University of Oxford. He says of him: 'If Mr Hyde, the Professor of Eastern Languages in Oxford, had lived longer, there was hope of obtaining more knowledge of the Vedas and opening the door to heathenism.'[1] He knew the difference between the Sinhalese and Tamil languages of Ceylon and was familiar with the early beginnings of European linguistic work on these two languages by Ministers who worked in Ceylon after its conquest by the Dutch. The most notable among these were the Reverends Philippus Baldaeus (1656–62), Johannes Ruell (1692–1701), Conradus Cronenburg (1692–1700), Adrianus de Meij (1690–99) and Simon Kat (1671–1704). But it cannot be said that he had any deep knowledge of Sinhalese or Tamil which would have enabled him to go to the original sources and thus increase the value of this part of his work.

Despite the highly disorderly arrangement of the whole book, Valentijn seems to maintain an inner ordering in his presentation of each section. This ordering he sets out in the preface as

> ... first an accurate description of the lands, thereafter follows an exposition of events happening in each land, and finally an orderly account of matters relating to religion.[2]

This three-part division Valentijn has maintained, at least as far as Ceylon is concerned. The Ceylon account shows that Valentijn could write narrative history, in which respect he compares favourably with many of his contemporaries. One must, however, qualify this by saying that the narrative is very often interspersed with lengthy documents, the contents of which are not integrated into the discussion or condensed meaningfully. But this was typically the Valentijn style and indeed he took pride in this when he said:

> Here one comes across some selected documents, seldom or never used by any other writers ... which I have had to collect from so many lands...[3]

[1] *Ibid.*   [2] Valentijn I, Voorreden..., p. 2.   [3] *Ibid.*

This is, of course, Valentijn's *forte* and his greatest value to subsequent generations of researchers.

The papers of the Company were secret and confidential and its officers were not permitted to keep official documents, diaries or reports of any sort in their personal possession. This prohibition also extended to maps, charts and other illustrations. It was frequently broken, however, as were many other dictates of the Company, and very many returning officers kept duplicates of official papers. After Valentijn announced his intention of writing a history of the East Indies, many of them, listed by him, came forward to offer their papers, motivated perhaps by an altruistic wish to further objective writing, and perhaps by the likelihood of getting their names into Valentijn's history. On Ceylon, Cornelis Joan Simons, Governor of Ceylon 1703–06, and apparently a good friend of Valentijn, has given him papers from the time of Rijckloff van Goens (1670's) onwards.[1] In fact this period is copiously documented, sometimes with rare and valuable documents, not the least of which relates to Simons' own times. Simons had settled in Utrecht on his return to Holland and died in 1727. Valentijn had corresponded regularly with him on his work and had also discussed matters relative to Ceylon with Rijckloff van Goens the younger, Governor of Ceylon 1675–79, after his return to Holland in 1680.[2] Another ex-Ceylon hand with whom Valentijn was closely associated was Adam van der Duyn who served from 1699 to 1708 in Ceylon in many positions and rose to the rank of Commander of Jaffna. He retired to Holland in 1709 and lived till about 1723. He had given some maps and other information to Valentijn. In particular, five excellent charts of the port Trincomalee and its environs were given by him.[3]

Besides papers given to him by others, he deserves credit for the good deal of research that he must have done in the papers of the V.O.C. Perhaps because of his influence with the Directors, he seems to have had access to the Letter Book (*Brieven Boek*) and Daily Register (*Dag Register*) of the Company. There is ample evidence of work done among these papers either in Holland or in Batavia. The account of Ceylon has benefited by such research. The treatment of early Dutch relations with the Kings of Kandy through the frequent exchange of letters between them is invaluable to modern students of

[1] Valentijn III. 1, Voor Bericht . . . , pp. 203.   [2] Valentijn III. 1, p. 309.
[3] Valentijn, V. 1, p. 366.

that period. Valentijn paraphrases a number of letters written by the Governors Joan Maatsuycker (1646–52) and Jacob van Kittensteyn (1650–53) to Raja Sinha, the king of Kandy. Some of these letters are no longer extant; others are available only in the Hague Archives. A contemporary historian has relied heavily on them in his study of the diplomatic relations between the Dutch and Kandy in the 1650's, though he advises caution in their use because of the selective character of the extracts.[1] Commenting on Valentijn's published extracts of these letters, he says:

> Of these [letters] only a few are available at the Rijksarchief at the Hague or (as far as I know) any where else. On account of this, Valentijn's extracts and summaries are invaluable.[2]

It appears that Baldaeus, who writes on the same events, has not had such extensive access to this correspondence or, if he did, does not use them in such a detailed manner. Equally valuable is the access he has had to memoirs of departing Governors to their successors, documents that are extremely important as sources because of the depth and sweep of their concerns. This is one of the major reasons for the enormous prestige that Valentijn has enjoyed in academic circles well into the 20th century. Research students have used Valentijn as a public archive from which to write interpretative treatises on their subjects of research. Until the publication of the *Dag Register* of Batavia,[3] and De Jonge's admirable series of documents on the *Opkomst van het Netherland Gezag in Oost-Indie*[4] and the more recent Coolhaas volumes on the *Generale Missiven*,[5] Valentijn has contained the only sources on the V.O.C. that were readily available to the scholar.

For a person who had not set foot on the island, Valentijn has been able to describe the country and its inhabitants with admirable accuracy and penetration. This is largely due to Valentijn's excellent sources and his search after them with uncanny enthusiasm. His introduction

---

[1] K. W. Goonewardena, *The foundation of Dutch power in Ceylon 1638–1658* (Amsterdam, 1958), p. xv.

[2] Goonewardena, *op. cit.*, p. 134.

[3] *Dag Register gehouden in 't Casteel Batavia*, Ed. J. A. van der Chijs (to 1677), F. de Haan (from 1678). 31 vols. ('s Gravenhage—Batavia, 1896–1931).

[4] J. K. J. de Jonge *et al.*, *De Opkomst van het Nederlandsch gezag in Oost-Indie*, 17 vols. (The Hague—Amsterdam, 1862–1909).

[5] W. Ph. Coolhaas, *Generale Missiven der V.O.C.* 5 Vols. ('s Gravenhage, from 1960).

and the first three chapters contain a lot of accurate ethnological and topographical material which Valentijn could have secured only by working hard on his sources. His excellence as a sharp and critical observer has been acclaimed by many. His description of the Moluccas, which he knew better by direct observation, has been widely acclaimed. The Governor General Baron van der Capellen (1819–25), while on a tour of the Moluccas, was greatly impressed by the accuracy of Valentijn's description, even a hundred years after its publication.[1] As late as the end of the 19th century, ships' captains sailing these waters would keep Valentijn handy as a book of reference.[2] These powers of observation and his natural curiosity would have led him to build up a reasonable storehouse of contemporary information on Ceylon. He used to question officers who had served in Ceylon whom he met while travelling on board ship or in Batavia and other places where he resided. In this respect his is comparable with another great historical and topographical work on Ceylon written in Portuguese in the 17th century. Father Fernão de Queyroz, like Valentijn, had not set foot on the island but had, on the basis of documentary material and the use of informants, written the *Conquista Temporal, e Espiritual de Ceylão* ('Temporal and Spiritual Conquest of Ceylon') in 1687, but published for the first time only in 1916.[3] Among sources used by Valentijn, are the travel journals of the 17th century voyagers, some of which were published in that period. Specific mention may be made of the ship's journal of Joris van Spilbergen, Admiral of the Dutch Fleet that sailed east in 1601,[4] and of the writings of Jan Huyghen van Linschoten. Spilbergen went on an embassy to the King of Kandy and this journal is an invaluable record of the interior of the island, the first information by any Dutchman of that part of the country. The Journal was first published in Holland in 1604; there were subsequent impressions of it in 1605, 1617, 1644, 1648 and

[1] Troostenburg de Bruijn, *Biographisch Woordenboek . . .* , p. 443.

[2] Dr. C. W. Th. Baron van Boetzclaer van Asperen en Dubbeldam, *De Protestantsche Kerk in Nederlandsch-Indie* ('s Gravenhage, 1947), p. 248.

[3] Fr. Fernão de Queyroz, *Conquista Temporal, e Espiritual de Ceylão Com muytas outras proveytoças noticias perfencentes a disposicao e governo do Estado da India* (Colombo, 1916). An English translation was published in 1930.

[4] First published as:
't Historiael Journael | van 't ghene ghepasseert || is van wegen dry Schepen | ghenamt den Ram, Scheep ende het Lam | ghe- || varen uit Zeelande vander Stadt Camp-Vere naer d'Oost-Indien | onder t' beleyt || van Ioris van Spilbergen, Generael | Anno 1601 || Blz 67.
An   annotated edition was published by the Linschoten Vereeniging in 1933.

1652, and Valentijn made copious use of its descriptions. Linschoten's encyclopaedic work, *Itinerario* . . ., written after five years' residence in Goa (1583–88), was of enormous value to his contemporaries and was utilised in planning the first Dutch eastern voyages. The section *Van't Eylandt Seylon* has been used by Valentijn as indeed other parts of this voluminous work have been referred to by him in his other regional descriptions.[1]

Besides using documentary material and notes from discussions with first-hand observers, Valentijn has relied very largely on a number of previous authors on Ceylon. In the first part of the work he ostentatiously parades his classical knowledge even to the extent of introducing words in Greek script in his text. On a closer examination these are found to be taken direct from Diogo de Couto's *Decadas*.[2] Valentijn's blatant plagiarism from this and other authors will be discussed later with examples. Diogo de Couto was a Portuguese gentleman who lived in the Portuguese city of Goa for long periods of time from 1559, his first arrival there, till his death in 1616. He served the Portuguese Crown as soldier, chief keeper of the Records in Goa, and official chronicler of India. He wrote the history of the Portuguese eastern empire, beginning from the date (1526) where a previous chronicler, João de Barros, had concluded his work. His *Decadas Da Asia* was written and published intermittently from 1602 onwards and Decadas IV, V, VI, VII and VIII would have been available to Valentijn in printed form.[3] The classical allusions to Ceylon and the identity of Taprobane, as well as the collection of much later material on Ceylon by Couto in his fifth *Decada* have been extensively used by Valentijn in his account.

Valentijn was also aware of the work of João de Barros, the Portuguese historian who preceded Couto and whose work he was con-

---

[1] *Itinerario, voyage ofte schipvaert van Jan Huygen van Linschoten naer oost ofte Portugaels Indien 1579–1592* (Amsterdam, 1596). An edition was brought out by the Linschoten Vereeniging in 2 volumes in 1910 and another in 3 volumes in 1955–57. The Hakluyt Society brought out an English translation in 1885.

[2] This was first discovered by D. W. Ferguson who translated and edited the sections of Couto's *Decadas* dealing with Ceylon. *The History of Ceylon, from the earliest times to 1600 A.D. As Related by João de Barros and Diogo de Couto.* Transl. and Ed. by Donald Ferguson, *Journal of the Royal Asiatic Society, Ceylon Branch*, XX, 60, 1908 (Colombo, 1909).

[3] For an analysis of Couto as a historian, see J. B. Harrison, 'Five Portuguese Historians', in C. H. Philips, ed. *Historians of India, Pakistan and Ceylon* (London, 1961), pp. 155–69, and C. R. Boxer, 'Three Historians of Portuguese Asia', in *Boletim do Instituto Portugues de Honkong* (Macau, 1948), I.

tinuing. Three *Decadas* of Barros' history of the Portuguese in Asia appeared in Lisbon in 1552, 1553 and 1563.[1] In his third *Decada*, Book II, Chapter I, Barros deals with classical references to Ceylon from which Valentijn has drawn. Another Portuguese writer with whom Valentijn was familiar was João Ribeiro, a Portuguese soldier who lived in Ceylon for 18 years from 1640 to 1658. He completed his *Fatalidade Historica de Ilha de Ceilão* ('Historical Tragedy of the Island of Ceylon') in 1685. The strength of this work, like that of Robert Knox, lies in the author's first-hand knowledge of the subject described and in many ways complements Knox's account of Sinhalese life and customs.[2] The full text of this was not published till 1836 but an abridged French translation was published by Abbé le Grand in Paris and Amsterdam in 1701.[3] Valentijn would have used this French translation.

Among Dutch writers, three important authors on South Asia preceded Valentijn: Abraham Rogerius, Philippus Baldaeus and Daniel Havart. Rogerius' *De Open-Deur tot het Verborgen Heydendom* ('Open Door to Hidden Heathendom') was published in 1651 and provided what was, for that period, a plausible account of Hinduism as practised in South India.[4] It is clear that Valentijn has picked up a great deal of his knowledge of Hinduism from this book. The Sanskritic terms he uses are the Tamilised form in vogue in South India as are also those of Rogerius (e.g. *Vedam, Grantham*).

Baldaeus published his *Beschrijvinge der Oost-Indische Kusten Malabar en Choromandel ... als ook het Keijserrijck Ceijlon* ('Description of the East Indian coast of Malabar and Coromandel, the bordering kingdoms and the Empire of Ceylon') in 1672.[5] This work has a

---

[1] *Asia de Joam de Barros, dos fectos que os Portugueses fiʒeram no descobrimento & conquista dos mares & terras do Oriente*, 3 Decadas, Lisboa, 1552–1563.

[2] For an appraisal of this work, see C. R. Boxer, 'An Introduction to João Ribeiro's "Historical Tragedy of the Island of Ceylon" 1685', *The Ceylon Historical Journal*, III (1953), 234–55.

[3] Captain João Ribeiro, *Histoire de L'isle de Ceylan ...* Traduite du Portugais par Monfr. L'Abee Le Grand (Paris Amsterdam, 1701).

[4] Abraham Rogerius, *De Open-Deure tot het Verborgen Heydendom* (Amsterdam, 1651). Republished in an annotated edition by W. Caland for the Linschoten Vereeniging in 1915.

[5] Philippus Baldaeus, *Beschrijving der Oost-Indische Kusten Malabar, en Choromandel, der selver aangrensende Koninckrijcken, en Vorstendomme als ook het Keijserrijck Ceylons nevens de Afgoderije der Oost-Indische Heijdenen* (Amsterdam, 1672). It was translated and published in Vol. 3 of Churchill, A. and Churchill, J. *Collection of voyages and travels* (London, 1704). The translation is not very accurate. The section on Ceylon was published

great deal of similarity to that of Valentijn and their relationship should be carefully considered. It has been far more useful to Valentijn than any other work on the area as a model. It is divided into three parts: the first part deals with Malabar and Coromandel, the second with Ceylon and the third is a sketch of 'heathenism' or popular Hinduism as practised in South India and Ceylon in Baldaeus' time. The section on Ceylon covers much the same ground as Valentijn was to do later and deals with similar themes of geography, topography, social life and the background of historical events. Valentijn generously compliments Baldaeus' work as the 'most detailed and the best' written on Ceylon and goes on to say:

> We thank his Reverence, as he has in general written very well on these matters and has given me much enlightenment in many respects; though this only applies mostly to the coastal places conquered by us.[1]

Baldaeus had the advantage of knowing Malabar, Coromandel and Ceylon at first-hand, having served there as a Minister from 1656 to 1665. Valentijn refers to Baldaeus frequently, relies on him substantially but also improves on this work in many parts.

Valentijn's geographical and topographical descriptions are superior to Baldaeus' and extend to the interior of the island while Baldaeus has almost totally restricted himself to the coast. Similarly, Valentijn has had access to superior sources for his account of the early history of the island up to the arrival of the Portuguese. Baldaeus' history begins with the coming of the Portuguese to the island in 1506 and from this point onwards his account of Sinhalese politics and the wars with the Portuguese is detailed and valuable. He has had access to Portuguese sources and perhaps to some Portuguese versions of Sinhalese sources. He is also able to interpret and use more effectively his Sinhalese sources which he could have had clarified and explained to him during his residence in Ceylon. On these events, the accounts of Valentijn and Baldaeus are very similar, a feature which may lead one to the conclusion that Valentijn has copied these parts wholesale from Baldaeus. But a few differences in the treatment of events, and

---

in English translation with an Introduction by S. D. Saparamadu as Vol. VIII of *The Ceylon Historical Journal* (Colombo, 1960). The section on Hinduism was edited and published by A. J. de Jong for the Linschoten Vereeniging in 1917.

[1] Valentijn, V. I, p. 19.

the fact that Valentijn is able to trace these events further back beyond the point at which Baldaeus begins, shows that Valentijn also had access to sources of a kind used by Baldaeus and has not relied solely on Baldaeus for a knowledge of these events.

The dissimilarity in the two accounts is also seen in the treatment of the expanding Dutch conquests in Ceylon. After the fall of Galle to the Dutch in March 1640, Baldaeus skips over the events of the next 15 years and picks up the story at the final assault of the Dutch on the Portuguese in 1655, though he comes back to it many chapters later with a sketchy account of these intervening years. Valentijn, however, proceeds chronologically to give a connected account of the Dutch–Portuguese wars and of Dutch–Kandyan relations of this period, with the use of Dutch records, to which obviously Baldaeus has not had access. Baldaeus, however, having been with the Dutch forces in the last stages of their attack on Portuguese positions in Ceylon, is more detailed and informative on this last phase of the struggle.[1] Also, he worked more intensively in the northern Tamil areas of the island and is therefore more knowledgeable on the Tamil people and their country. Baldaeus' description of the caste system among the Tamils is better than that of Valentijn, who has, however, a much superior description of Sinhalese castes. The personal experience of the country comes through in Baldaeus, with the relating of a number of anecdotes and quaint details of personal life.

On the extension of Protestant Christianity into Ceylon and on the areas of contact with Hinduism and Hindu society, Baldaeus is decidedly superior to Valentijn. Baldaeus lived for long among Hindus of north Ceylon and south India and made some efforts at evangelism among these people. He had some knowledge of the Tamil language and of the literature of Hinduism.[2] It has, however, been established that he plagiarised extensively from unpublished Portuguese missionary writings on Hinduism.[3] He seems to have had access to these after the Dutch conquest of Cochin. Valentijn seems to have secured his knowledge of Hinduism and Hindu literature from

[1] Baldaeus, Chapters 22 to 43, pp. 55–157.

[2] On Baldaeus' pastoral work in Ceylon, see S. Arasaratnam, 'Reverend Philippus Baldaeus: His pastoral work in Ceylon', *Nederlands Theologische Tijdschrift*, XIV, 5 (1960), 350–60.

[3] Jarl Charpentier, 'The British Museum MS. Sloane 3290. The Common source of Baldaeus and Dapper', *Bulletin of the School of Oriental and African Studies*, III (1923–25), 413–24.

Rogerius and Baldaeus, though he has supplemented this by the writings of later Dutch missionaries on the island.

Another Dutch work, with which Valentijn was familiar, was Daniel Havart's *Op- en Ondergang van Cormandel* ('Rise and Fall of Coromandel') published in 1693.[1] This work, which is a first-hand account of the Dutch on the Coromandel coast by a physician of the Company who served in those factories, helped to instruct Valentijn on the southern Asian area. He has relied on this work very much for his description of Coromandel in the second part of Volume Five.[2]

A work that was useful to Valentijn in filling in gaps in his knowledge of the island was Robert Knox's *An Historical Relation of the Island Ceylon* published in London in 1681.[3] This was a singular work of its kind that soon made its mark, even in a century that abounded in travelogues. What made this work so penetrating and so authentic was the fact that the author had lived in the interior of Ceylon as a prisoner of the King of Kandy for a period of 19 years (1660–79). It differs from all the other works of this period on Ceylon in that it is a view of the island from the interior, a perspective that was denied to most other travellers. A Dutch translation of the work was made by S. de Vries and published at Utrecht in 1692.[4] Valentijn recognised the value of Knox and relied on him for a view of the interior of the island. He was aware that the relative ignorance of conditions in the interior was a weakness in other writings on Ceylon, and noted it particularly in Baldaeus who had almost nothing to say on the Kandyan provinces. Valentijn tried to redress this imbalance by borrowing heavily from Knox and supplementing it with evidence from the reports of Dutch ambassadors sent to Kandy. Valentijn's topographical, zoological

[1] Daniel Havart, *Op- en Ondergang van Cormandel* (Amsterdam, 1693).

[2] S. Arasaratnam, 'François Valentijn's Description of Coromandel', *Professor K. A. Nilakanta Sastri Felicitation Volume* (Madras, 1971), pp. 1–10.

[3] There is a substantial literature on Knox. The following is a selection. D. W. Ferguson, *Captain Robert Knox: the twenty years captive in Ceylon ... Contributions towards a biography* (Colombo, 1896–97); D. W. Ferguson, 'Robert Knox's Sinhalese vocabulary', *J.R.A.S.C.B.* XIV, 47 (1896), 150–200; E. F. C. Ludowyk, *Robert Knox in the Kandyan Kingdom* (O.U.P., Bombay, 1948); C. R. Boxer, 'Ceylon through Puritan eyes. Robert Knox in the Kingdom of Kandy 1660–1679', *History Today* IV, 10 (1954), 660–67; K. W. Goonewardena, Some Comments on Robert Knox and his writings on Ceylon', *University of Ceylon Review* XVI, 1 and 2 (1958), 39–42; R. Knox, *An historical relation of Ceylon*, Ed. by S. D. Saparamadu (*The Ceylon Historical Journal*, 1958), Introduction.

[4] *T' Eyland Ceylon, in sijn binnenste of 't koningrijck Candy; geopent ... door Robert Knox*. Vertaeld door S. de Vries (Utrecht, 1692).

and anthropological notes of the Kandyan kingdom are borrowed from Knox and much of the knowledge he exhibits of Sinhalese social life is taken directly from him. Valentijn has also borrowed a number of Sinhalese words, particularly of plants, animals and birds, from Knox. The two accounts offer an interesting contrast in styles and in the intellectual approach to the subject. Knox's is anecdotal and rich in personal experiences that throw far more light on Sinhalese society and culture of the 17th century. His descriptions of the country are more vivid in respect of villages and regions he lived in and travelled through. Valentijn's is a bookish account, very cartographic and scientific; rivers are chartered in all their twists and turns, mountains are identified and many more villages are located and named. It is an overview of the whole area, more factual but less colourful.

Valentijn's is one of the most accurate accounts of the pre-European period of Ceylon history up to his time. He devotes two lengthy chapters to a sketch of the early history of the island from the mythical origins of the Sinhalese dynasty and its establishment in Ceylon up to the arrival of the Portuguese. In none of his other descriptions of South Asia—Coromandel, Malabar, Bengal—does he attempt an account of traditional history. The fact that he chose to do so with regard to Ceylon and did it quite successfully is due to the authenticity of his sources. The Portuguese writers had pioneered in this in some way, though the best of these accounts, that of Queyroz, was not available to Valentijn. Couto, the first Portuguese historian who wrote briefly on the 'antiquity of the island of Ceilao; of the beginning and origin of its kings',[1] narrated the legend explaining the origins of the Sinhalese in Ceylon, namely Vijaya and his banishment to the island. Then he leaps forward about 1700 years to the 13th century. Baldaeus is also weak on these aspects, repeating the myth of the Chinese as the first settlers, his real history beginning with the arrival of Lourenço de Almeida to Ceylon.[2] Knox is even less knowledgeable in this respect, being content with repeating a popular version of the Vijay legend that he had obviously picked up from the common people.[3] Queyroz and Valentijn are outstanding in the depth and accuracy of their treatment of this subject and in the provision of a list of Kings of the Sinhalese dynasties. Both Queyroz and Valentijn and to some extent Couto must have had access to the historical traditions of the Sinhalese in some form or other. Couto claims to have had

[1] Couto, *Decada* V, Bk. 1, Chap. V.   [2] Baldaeus, Chap. 1, pp. 2–3.   [3] Knox, p. 61.

access to a traditional history, probably a version of the *Rājāvaliya*, through some Sinhalese princes living in Goa.[1] It has been indicated by Fr. Georg Schurhammer, a scholar of Portuguese colonial historiography, that he may have had this knowledge through an Augustinian priest, Father Agustinho de Azevedo, who had done considerable researches on traditional society.[2]

Queyroz and Valentijn had access to more complete versions of this Sinhalese chronicle. It does not appear that either of them knew of the *Mahāvamsa*,[3] another chronicle enshrining a version of the Sinhalese tradition. Their lists of kings differ markedly from those in the *Mahāvamsa* and are closer to the *Rājāvaliya* in one of its versions. With a few exceptions all the names on Valentijn's list can be identified through the *Rājāvaliya*.[4] Now the *Rājāvaliya* was a chronicle written by a number of persons, each of whom kept on adding to its original contents and consequently the manuscript kept on expanding with each addition. Some copies end with the time of the arrival of the Portuguese, others with the Dutch conquest of Colombo (1656), and a few are even brought down to the beginning of the 19th century. Manuscript copies of this work were common in Ceylon and were found in many temple libraries and the text of most of them was corrupt in varying degrees.[5] Both the Portuguese and the Dutch, in their curiosity about the traditions of the Sinhalese, secured access to some of these copies. In translation the corruption was compounded, especially of names of persons and places. Fr. Francisco Negrao, an Italian Franciscan missionary working in Ceylon, seems to have procured translations of Sinhalese chronicles and made up a list of Kings of Ceylon. Fr. S. G. Perera, who edited Queyroz's manuscript, has stated that Queyroz relied on this writer for events prior to 1612.[6] Among the Dutch, Rijckloff van Goens, the elder, was very keen on the accumulation of the traditions of the Sinhalese to assist in the orderly administration of the Sinhalese people. Adriaan van Rheede,

---

[1] Couto, *Dec.* IV, Bk. VIII, Chap. XIV. Ferguson's translation, p. 101.

[2] Georg Schurhammer, S.J., *Franz Xaver, Sein Leben und seine Zeit, 11, Asien 1541–1549,* (2) *Indien und Indonesien, 1547–1549* (Freiburg, 1971), pp. 448–53.

[3] *The Mahavamsa.* Ed. by Wilhelm Geiger (London, 1908).

[4] *The Rājāvaliya or a historical narrative of Sinhalese Kings from Vijaya to Vimala Dharma Surya 11.* Ed. by B. Gunasekara (Colombo, 1900).

[5] C. E. Godakumbara, *History of Sinhalese literature* (Colombo, 1955), p. 128. Don Martino de Zilva Wickremasinghe, *Catalogue of the Sinhalese manuscripts in the British Museum* (London, 1900), p. 74 ff.

[6] Queyroz, I, p. 14.

who was sent as Special Commissioner to Ceylon in 1677, also had much traditional information on Sinhalese society collected through local officials, which he incorporated in his lengthy report on the condition of the island.[1] Joan Simons was also engaged in the collection of the laws and customs of the country. It is from these sources that Valentijn must have secured translated extracts of the *Rājāvaliya* tradition.

The list of kings provided by Valentijn is much more authentic and more complete than that of Queyroz. Valentijn names 78 kings as compared with Queyroz's 52 in the pre-Portuguese period. Queyroz's names are, in many cases, mutilated beyond recognition and sometimes bear no relation to kings known to have existed from other records. Valentijn's names, though also largely transmuted, are recognisable and identifiable with the kings listed in the version of the *Rājāvaliya* edited by H. M. Gunasekara. The sequence is reasonably accurate and corresponds to the *Rājāvaliya* tradition. Now and then names appear—such as Sagoeganatissa, Goloeumbera, Beminitissa, Chorawa Rajoe, Tomo, Nalabissava, Elunna, Asnopa Raja, Senam Raja, Lamini Tissa, Amlan Heranam—which are not to be found in this version of the *Rājāvaliya*. Interestingly enough, some of these names are identifiable in the *Mahāvamsa* list. Thus Valentijn appears to have had access to a superior version of the *Rājāvaliya* or to more than one Sinhalese tradition. He provides the names of kings who reigned for brief periods of a few months, names which appear to have been omitted from many Sinhalese and Pali texts. There are frequent differences in regnal years attributed to kings by Valentijn from those in the *Rājāvaliya*. Also, there are incidents referred to by Valentijn but not to be found in the *Rājāvaliya*. Valentijn's sources seem to have also drawn on some independent traditions then extant in Ceylon. This source of information comes to an end with Dos Raja.

This list is very useful for a student who seeks to reconstruct the political history of early Ceylon. Some of the names are probably extant only in the form given by Valentijn. There is, however, a yawning gap in his chronological sequence of kings. After Dos Raja, whose rule brings the chronology down to about the 8th century, he crosses seven centuries to come to Ruccule Parākrama

---

[1] *Consideratien van de Heer van Rheede over Ceylon,* overgegeeven aan de Heer Maatsuyker en Raaden, 1677. Lengthy extracts from this Report are published by Valentijn, V. 1, pp. 247–85.

Bāhu who ascended the throne in A.D. 1453. He solves this problem, or at least his sources solve it for him, by postdating the accession of Vijaya to A.D. 106, which other traditions date at the year of the Buddha's enlightenment, 543 B.C. Then he goes on to construct a chronological sequence with great attention to precise details of years and even months a king or queen reigned and thus brings the list down to Raja Sinha's death in 1593. He is aware that he has missed out many kings and mentions the tradition of '2007 years which they ascribe to the Emperors'.[1] This would seem to be reasonably accurate, assuming that the tradition was recorded somewhere in the end of the 15th century or the beginning of the 16th.

An interesting feature of Valentijn's early history of Sinhalese settlement in Ceylon is his version of the Vijaya legend. According to this version Vijaya was descended from the kings of Tenasserim, which is a province of Lower Burma, and his account speaks of the kingdoms of Pegu, Siam and Cambodia as the environs in which the incident he relates of Vijaya's ancestry took place. 'This Vigea Raja,' he says, 'sprang from the kingdom of Tillingo, bordering on Tanassary, formerly named Ajota and standing under Siam, of whose king he was a son.'[2] Here Valentijn combines two traditions, one which implies that Vijaya was from the Telugu country (Tillingo) in east-central India where Kalinga was generally placed. The other tradition traces the origin of Vijaya to the Southeast Asian mainland and appears to be a later one which took root in Ceylon and was widely known about this time. This tradition is repeated by other writers writing about this time such as Couto and Queyroz. The Mahāvamsa tradition places the lands in which Vijaya's ancestors lived on the Indian mainland and refers to place names that can be located on the western and eastern parts of the sub-continent. At some point in the history of the Sinhalese the identification of Kalinga, Ajota and other places connected with the origin of Vijaya seems to have been transferred to the mainland of Southeast Asia.[3] It is this tradition that was available to Couto, Queyroz and Valentijn in their accounts of the Vijaya legend.

The accuracy and immense value of Valentijn as a source increases as he approaches the period of European contact with Ceylon. Here he has a number of sources available to him. There were the Portuguese

[1] Valentijn, V. 1, p. 83.
[2] Valentijn, V. 1, p. 61.
[3] S. Paranavitana, *Ceylon and Malaysia* (Colombo, 1966), p. 101.

writings, the account of Baldaeus, but most important of all the continuation of his Sinhalese traditional sources. There is no doubt that, for the history of the period 1453 to the final Dutch success in Ceylon in 1658, in respect of indigenous political and dynastic struggles, Valentijn has had access to the most accurate, most detailed and most vivid sources then available. His account of this period is more factual than any which preceded him and many which succeeded him till well into the 19th century. In fact many British writers on Ceylon in the 19th century, as will be demonstrated later, used him as their primary, and sometimes only, source for their accounts of that period.

In relating the events of this period, Valentijn not only speaks of the major kings but also refers to minor kings and feudal lords, and mentions some events and incidents for which today he is the only source. He speaks, for example, of the invasion of Ceylon by the King of Canara (probably Vijayanagara) which was repelled by King Parākrama Bāhu VI.[1] Again he talks of a Ceylonese expedition to Adriampet (Adirampattinam) in retaliation for the seizure of a Ceylonese ship laden with cinnamon.[2] The account of the exploits of Alakēswara, the commander-in-chief of Bhuvanēka Bāhu,[3] seems to be based on the contemporary work of *Alakēsvara Yuddhaya,* antecedent to *Rājāvaliya* and to which, or at least to its material, Valentijn seems to have had access.[4] Similarly, the exploits of Taniyan Valla Bāhu, Prince of Mādampe and Sakalakalā Valla, Prince of Udugampola, are related in Valentijn in greater detail than elsewhere, also pointing to some access to contemporary sources, not now extant, and even then not readily available to others.[5] The political events of Ceylon after the Portuguese involvement are related with a lot of detail, but these have been available to some others, including Couto, Baldaeus and Queyroz, who mention substantially the same facts. The conflict between the Portuguese and the Sinhalese is related with a sympathy for the Sinhalese side which reflects both the Dutch stance on these matters at that time, as well as the reliance on the *Rājāvaliya* which was a chronicle written from the Sinhalese point of view.

One of the most remarkable aspects of Valentijn is the glossary

[1] Valentijn, V. 1, p. 72.   [2] Valentijn, V. 1, p. 72.   [3] Valentijn, V. 1, pp. 71-3.
[4] *Alakēsvara Yuddhaya* (Sinh.), Ed. A. V. Suraveera (Colombo, 1965). I am indebted to Professor T. B. H. Abeyasinha of the University of Sri Lanka, Colombo, for this suggestion.
[5] Valentijn, V. 1, pp. 74-6.

of native official terms and, more importantly, of castes and sub-castes.[1] So comprehensive and detailed is this list that it is far in advance of what any other western writers on Ceylon knew and has since become a standard source for all those who try to write on the Sinhalese caste system. In fact a modern sociological study of the Sinhalese caste structure relies on it to a large degree for a historical perspective.[2] Valentijn gives many subdivisions of castes which are not recognisable today but must certainly have existed at that time. Compared with him Knox is an amateur on this subject, giving the names of only fifteen of the major occupational castes.[3] Not only does Valentijn provide an outline of the structure of the main occupational castes, he goes further and describes the subdivisions within each caste, their status relationships and the obligatory services to be performed by each to others. The *Karāva*, or fisher caste, are subdivided into nine sub-castes and each of these is distinguished by the mode of fishing they adopt, their obligations, the status symbols that are due to them and the officials who exercise control over them. The *Chandos*, or *Durāvē* (*toddy-drawers*) are subdivided into ten sub-castes and are similarly described. As the *Durāvē* are subject to many types of obligatory service to the village and to individuals, these are meticulously described. Then comes a description of the artisan castes or *Navandannayō*, who are also distinguished occupationally, followed by the *Goigama* whose many grades are distinguished. Then a number of other sundry castes are listed and described, right down to the lowest caste of untouchables, the *Rodiya*. In modern times almost all the sub-castes have merged, simplifying caste divisions, and the information about sub-castes and terms given here are a valuable document of social history. Valentijn's knowledge extends even to Tamil castes, though here it is not as extensive. Three types of *Chetties* (merchants) are distinguished. Even amongst *Veddas* or hunting tribes, two types are distinguished which corresponds with the best anthropological knowledge of the Vedda people. The account of taxes and dues with which this section concludes is another very enlightening piece, together with the major *baddē* or departments under the royal administration. The material here is comparable to D'Oyly's *A Sketch of the Constitution of Kandyan Kingdom,* though D'Oyly is

[1] Valentijn, V. 1, pp. 1–12.
[2] B. Ryan, *Caste in modern Ceylon* (New Brunswick, 1953), pp. 65–79.
[3] Knox, pp. 66–71.

much more centred on the Kandyan Kingdom and its institutions.[1]
The sociologist, Ryan, lists caste names provided by a number of
authorities both traditional and European, right down to the end of
the 19th century, and there is no doubt that Valentijn provides the
most comprehensive list.[2] It is as full a list of Sinhalese castes as one
will get anywhere. It was probably drawn from lists specially prepared
for the Dutch by their subordinate officials, the Sinhalese Mudaliyars,
to help them in the administration of service tenure. It is much more
detailed than textual accounts such as the 15th century *Janavamsa*,
which is a description of caste status among the Sinhalese.[3]

For a man who has not set foot on the island and was unfamiliar
with the Sinhalese, Valentijn makes some pertinent observations of
Sinhalese society and character.[4] He is able to do this because he has
had the advantage of a number of Dutch reports that make comments
on Sinhalese society as well as of the excellent work of Knox. He
follows Knox very closely in describing the character of the Sinhalese,[5]
which he does candidly and without malice, pointing out the favourable
and the darker sides of what he believed was their character. Together
with many other European writers he describes them as friendly but
conceited, generous but avaricious, esteeming virtue but doing little
to practise it, superstitious, quick-witted, quick to understand,
cunning, crafty and clever, and very similar to the Portuguese. Also
like many other Europeans, Valentijn tries to distinguish between the
Sinhalese of the low country and those of the mountains, the former
gentle and pleasant, the latter rough and hard-hearted, though
courteous and genteel in speech. In respect of the social life of the
people—laws, marriage customs, food habits, domestic life and the
like—Valentijn is a condensation of Knox whose work far more
centrally deals with these themes. Valentijn is far less knowledgeable
about Tamil society, and, rather strangely, takes up the limited space
he devotes to them in describing the Tamils of the Vanni south of
Jaffna, occupying the border country between Dutch and Kandyan
territories rather than describing the central homelands of the Tamils
in Jaffna and Batticaloa. On the Veddas he repeats what was stock

---

[1] John D'Oyly, the Principal Accredited Agent of the British Government in the
Kandyan Kingdom, 1810–15, wrote *A Sketch of the constitution of the Kandyan Kingdom*,
which was published in 1835 and 1925.
[2] Ryan, *op. cit.*, pp. 65–71.
[3] Cited in M. B. Ariyapala, *Society in medieval Ceylon* (Colombo, 1956), pp. 290–1.
[4] Valentijn, V. 1, pp. 43–50.   [5] Knox, pp. 63–5.

knowledge to the Europeans of the time, including an account of a particular custom that appears over and over again in western travel literature on Ceylon. This is that, when the Veddas want arrows or weapons to be made for them by the village blacksmith, they come by night and leave a sample of the weapon to be made with a loin of venison in payment. They return after a few days and take the new weapons which the blacksmith would have made and left for them outside his house. This singular custom is related by Ribeiro, Queyroz, Knox, Valentijn and Tennent among others.[1]

Valentijn who fancies himself a naturalist devotes some attention to the description of Ceylon's fauna and flora.[2] But again his treatment is restricted by his not having visited the place, unlike Amboina where he devotes several pages to natural history.[3] Here again, in the description of trees that are peculiar to Ceylon, such as the *talipot* palm and the *kitul* tree, he relies very much on Knox. But he is more knowledgeable on the cinnamon tree on which there is a good deal of Dutch literature which he has read and digested. Access to the trade journals of the Company has made it possible for him to give long and comprehensive lists of articles of the export and import trade, coins current in trade here and the standards of weights and measures.[4] He winds up the chapter on society and administration with some useful sketches of the tax system, a view of the official hierarchy of the Kandyan Kings and their nature and methods of warfare. Here and there one gets a rare insight, a flash of light, which Valentijn is able to provide through his wide and varied sources. But by and large this section is a rehashed version of Knox, written up in the ponderous literary style for which Valentijn has become well-known.

Two chapters of geographic description of the island are a commendable effort.[5] They are not taken from one obvious source, as none of the works that he has consulted gives such a detailed description. Beginning from the south-western port of Galle, he takes the reader northwards, mile by mile as it were, naming and sometimes describing every town and village, every river and creek, every mountain and jungle. Coastal towns where the Dutch had settled in numbers and had administrative headquarters are meticulously

---

[1] Ribeiro, Chap. XXIV, p. 171, Queyroz I, p. 17, Knox p. 62, Valentijn V. 1, pp. 9–10 and Tennent, *Ceylon* I, p. 593.

[2] Valentijn, V. 1, pp. 50–5. [3] Valentijn III. 1, pp. 1–586.

[4] Valentijn, V. 1, pp. 55–6. [5] Valentijn, V. 1, Chapters I and II, pp. 12–42.

described. For the larger cities and forts, such as Colombo, Galle, Matara, Negombo, Trincomalee, Batticaloa and Jaffna, excellent maps have been drawn, based on charts which were lent to him by officials who served in these quarters. What is remarkable is the mapping of the interior parts of the country, province by province, district by district, town by town and even village by village. Unfortunately, some of these names have been so mutilated by Valentijn or his sources as to be unidentifiable in modern maps. The evidence is invaluable to the historical geographer of the island. Valentijn makes a manful attempt at the difficult task of describing the island's central highlands and in fact prides himself on it. But here the information is less reliable, more confused, and it is obvious that large parts of the country have been left out. One fascinating feature is the description of the Mahāveli Ganga, the largest river in the island, which is traced from source through all its twists and turns till it falls into the sea near Trincomalee.

Valentijn's topographical description provides a reasonably acceptable outline of the contours and regions of the island. It has proved the most difficult part of the text to edit. The shift in towns and villages, the mutilation of names and the ambiguity in directions and distances have made a few of the places mentioned by him unidentifiable. Valentijn, on his tour of the island, mentions a multiplicity of place names, rivers, jungles and mountains, some important, others very minor, a few totally unidentifiable. In general, the names along the west coast and in the Dutch occupied territories are easily identified. These are places that featured often in the turbulent events of the 16th and 17th centuries. It is when Valentijn talks of the interior of the country, particularly the territories of the Kandyan kingdom and the eastern and southeastern coast, that problems of identification arise. Valentijn provides more place names in the Kandyan kingdom than does Knox and reveals a passable knowledge of the topography of its mountainous regions. He names more places and provides more topographical details than any other European writer down to contemporary times. The historical geographer can see what the settlement patterns of the 17th century were, can trace some of the abandoned towns and the dried up river beds by carefully following up Valentijn's evidence. Valentijn is also quite strong in locating shoals and reefs near the coast and on the depth of lagoons and coastal waters on which, of course, there would have been abundant Dutch evidence. It is not known whether there was one comprehensive and detailed geographic description of Ceylon from which Valentijn drew all his information, and the identity of which he does not reveal, or whether it was brought together by him from very many sources. The latter was more probably the case. There were a number of Dutch reports and travel diaries available to him with geographical information. Spilbergen's journal seems to have provided some information on the Kandyan kingdom. Van Goens' two reports had a wealth of geographical information and seems to have been relied on heavily.[1] And there were some reports of inspection tours of particular regions by subordinate officers.

Mapping of the island had progressed with good results during the 75 years of Dutch occupation and much advance had been made on Portuguese knowledge of the island. The Directors were repeatedly ordering the administration of Ceylon to prepare detailed maps of the whole island and especially of those parts under Dutch jurisdiction. The measurement and mapping of the Dutch-held territory was done with reasonable accuracy. During the second Governorship of van Goens (1664–75), efforts were made to measure and map the entire coastline. The results of these surveys are found in the statistics of distances between points given in his memoirs and in the reports of succeeding officials. Valentijn has used all these statistics and provides a table of distances, as well as incorporating them in his description. As Governor Simons admits in his memoir, the Dutch maps of the coast were not exact, particularly as regards bays and inlets.[2] The inaccuracies were most seen in the remote south-eastern and the north-eastern coast. Consequently the circumference of the island is given by Valentijn as 886½ miles as compared with an actual distance of 1100 miles. This is caused by under-estimating some distances between points on the eastern coast. Some of the other measurements are, however, reasonably accurate, e.g. length of the island (Valentijn) 247½ miles, (actual) 271½ miles; breadth (Valentijn) 135 miles, (actual) 137½ miles.[3] This also applies to the distances between places given by Valentijn in his description of the geography of the island.

[1] Valentijn, V. 1, pp. 160–83, 204–46.
[2] *Memoir of Cornelis Joan Simons . . . for his successor Hendrick Becker 1707.* (Colombo, 1914), p. 5.
[3] The German mile in which Valentijn's distances are given was during this period equivalent to approximately 4.5 English miles. Valentijn's distances have been converted on this basis. But as these are approximate equivalents, no exact comparisons with modern measurements can be made.

For a century and a half there was admiration and amazement at the gigantic mass of information and source material assembled by Valentijn; but with the beginning of an intensive investigation of aspects of the V.O.C.'s past, these sentiments towards Valentijn began to diminish. As researchers went to the original sources, it was noted that Valentijn often had only partially published his source and that he was not always the best judge of what was important and what was not. More significantly, as work advanced on 16th and 17th century writers and texts, it was realised that Valentijn had plagiarised outright from some of his predecessors in a manner that was damaging to his integrity and honesty. But to put this criticism in its proper perspective, it should be noted that plagiarism was a common practice in that period; authors thought nothing of using material that had appeared in print, copying large parts of it and putting it into their own work. Scholars have already drawn attention to the extensive and unscrupulous plagiarism by Valentijn from the work of his friend Rumphius.[1] During his second tour in Amboina, Valentijn had become a wealthy man and was thus a patron of many Dutch families there. After Rumphius' death he seems to have looked after Rumphius' children and in fact his two stepsons married two daughters of Rumphius after the father's death. Through this relationship, Valentijn seems to have secured control of the papers of Rumphius. Among these were various writings of Rumphius on Amboina: *Ambonsche Landbeschrivinge* ('Description of the Land'), *Ambonsche Historie*, *Herbarium Amboinese* and *Ambonsche Dierboek* ('Ambonese animals'). From all these works Valentijn seems to have extracted entire sentences and incorporated them in his description of Amboina in Volume I of his work. Both in the botanical and zoological sections as well as in the historical parts, Valentijn has copied from the work of this great pioneer of Ambonese studies. It has been noted that he has tried to cover this up by deliberately and needlessly changing the chapter division and by leaving out Rumphius' name altogether in those parts where he follows most closely the work of Rumphius.[2] It is the opinion of some scholars that the same may also be the case with his much-vaunted Malay translation of the Bible.[3] The Batavian Church Council

---

[1] Dr. F. de Haan, 'Rumphius en Valentijn als geschiedschrijvers van Ambon', *Rumphius Gedenkboek 1702–1902* (Haarlem, 1902), pp. 19 ff; *Rumphius Memorial Volume*, Ed. by H. C. D. de Wit (Baarn, 1959), *passim*.

[2] de Haan, 'Rumphius en Valentijn', pp. 20–2.

[3] *Encyclopaedie van Nederlandsch-Indie*, IV, pp. 501–2.

had been surprised when Valentijn claimed to have completed the translation of the Bible within a short period of having started the work. The Reverend G. H. Werndley, writing a few years after the publication of Valentijn's work, asserts that Valentijn came into possession of the papers of the Reverend Jacobus de Bois who had been Minister at Banda from 1681–87. Among these papers were presumably some translations into Malay presented to the Minister by the Reverend Simon de Larges who was noted for his proficiency in the language.[1]

It would appear that this criticism of Valentijn is also substantiated by the use he has made of some sources in the account of Ceylon as well. This plagiarism is most marked in his treatment of Couto's *Decadas da Asia*. Valentijn begins his description of Ceylon with what appears to be a learned discourse on the classical knowledge of Ceylon. He sets out to 'prove' that Ceylon was Taprobane, with many citations from classical and later authorities and one is left in admiration at his profound learning. In fact this entire section and the learned discussion of the identity of Taprobane is taken almost *verbatim* from Couto's Fifth *Decada*, Book I, Chapter VII, entitled: *Of the various opinions that have existed amongst geographers as to what was the Taprobana of Ptolemy; and of the reasons that were given for it being that island of Ceilao; and of the names that its cinnamon bears amongst all nations.*[2] Introducing his first chapter Valentijn says: 'Here we deal with it in greater detail, *narrating different opinions of geographers on Taprobana of Ptolemy, with reasons which we give that this is no other than the island of Ceylon; and also of the different names given to its cinnamon by different people.*'[3] Then follows an exact translation of Couto. It should suffice to give one sample paragraph to illustrate this:

[1] G. H. Werndley, *Maleische Spraakkunst* (Amsterdam, 1736), pp. XIV–XVI.
[2] Couto, pp. 80–90. This and all subsequent references are from the Ferguson edition.
[3] Valentijn, V. 1, p. 14 (Italics added to show similarity to Couto).

Couto[1]	*Valentijn*[2]
Pliny, speaking of Taprobana, says that it is six thousand stadia in length and five thousand in breadth, and that it was in a way considered a new world, and that it was discovered in the time of the emperor Claudius, and that a king of that island sent ambassadors to him, and that the ships that used to go there were not directed or steered by the stars, because they did not see the poles.	Pliny, speaking of Taprobane, says that it was 6000 stadia in length and 5000 in breadth, that it was believed to be a new world and was first discovered at the time of the Emperor Claudius to whom the King of this island also had sent ambassadors, but the ships which went there were not steered by the stars as they could not see the Pole.

It goes on in this fashion for the next 4½ folio pages or about 3,500 words.

In transcribing from Couto, Valentijn has made a few revisions of his own, some of which are erroneous. Micer Poggio, the Florentine author of the journey of Nicolo de Conti, becomes Michael Poggius; Hector de Laguna, the translator of Dioscorides becomes Lagena; *Bom Jesus*, a ship which was lost at sea in 1590 on its return journey from Goa to Lisbon, becomes *Bon Tehis*; Ramnusio becomes Ramutius. Again Couto, speaking of Arrian's description of elephants, refers to the superiority of the Ceylon elephant of 'which we have experience every day in this city of Goa among those that the king employs in his dockyard from different countries'.[3] Valentijn disingenuously repeats this, saying 'as one sees here daily in the city of Goa among elephants which the king has brought to his stall from different lands.'[4] Again he makes a tell-tale error in plagiarism in copying Couto's reference to Jambulus, a writer, mistakenly thinking this word refers to an island. In this way, the entire section relating to classical references to Ceylon and the arguments intended to establish that Taprobane is Ceylon are a straight copy from Couto. Another section of Couto's work from which Valentijn has made extracts, but with acknowledgment, is the description of Adam's Peak in the Fifth *Decada*, Book IV, Chapter II. Again he has translated

---

[1] Couto, p. 80.   [2] Valentijn, V. 1, p. 14.   [3] Couto, p. 86.
[4] Valentijn, V. 1, p. 16.

this account, with a few original mistakes of his own in the transcription, providing in sum a curious mixture of accuracies and errors.[1]

The borrowing from Knox, though not as direct as from Couto, is nevertheless unmistakable. Here he has taken the sense of Knox's account and paraphrased it in his words. While the ideas are those of Knox, the words are not an exact copy as in Couto. This is particularly so with regard to such things as the life styles, customs and manners of the Sinhalese, and the flora and fauna of the interior country, about which he did not have much Dutch evidence.

The plagiarism from Couto is somewhat puzzling, considering that Valentijn has had training in the Classics, was able to read and understand Latin and Greek and shows considerable familiarity with many classical authors. In other parts of the work, particularly in the introductory section in Volume I, he has copious references to these very authorities whom he has copied from Couto and shows familiarity with their work, their arguments and the problems of geographical identification and historical interpretation in their works. The fact that he should have in this way copied *ad verbum* from a secondary source facts which he could have derived from the original shows the attitude of the times towards plagiarism and borrowing from others. The printed word was public property and it did not matter if one repeated what someone else had said or where he got one's material.

Valentijn's map of Ceylon is superior to that of both Baldaeus and Knox. Dutch cartography was at this time the most advanced in the world and even Knox's map bears traces of Dutch origins. The house of Van Keulen, a famous family firm of marine atlas and pilot book publishers, published a series of *Zee-Atlasen*. Each of these Sea-Atlases had a large folded map of Ceylon.[2] The V.O.C. appointed a cartographic consultant very early and from 1633 onwards from this office corrected and revised manuscript charts were issued to the Company's pilots. The information was incorporated into the published maps of Amsterdam. In the early 18th century Van Keulen published a six volume sea atlas called *De Niew Groote Ligtende Zeefakkel* (The New Great Shining Sea-torch).[3] This work has a

---

[1] Couto, pp. 108–18, where the editor has drawn attention to these errors in footnotes.

[2] For example, *De Groote Nieuwe Vermeerderde zee Atlas ofte Water-Werelt* (Amsterdam, 1681), Map No. 27—Pascaert van't Eyland Ceylon.

[3] *De Nieuwe Groote Ligtende Zee-fakkel* door Claas Jansz Voogt. Gerard van Keulen (Amsterdam, 1728). Tweede Boek. 'De Beschryving van de Zee kusten van het Eyland Ceylon', pp. 20-5.

description of the sands, shoals, reefs, water depth and anchorages round the island of Ceylon which may well have been used by Valentijn. The map of Ceylon in this volume looks very similar to Valentijn's map and is an improvement on the maps of the Knox/ Baldaeus period. Valentijn's map provides *kōralē* and district boundaries and attempts to name all these. Valentijn's map also provides more details such as names of villages and small towns, and traces mountain ridges. He also provides economic details like cinnamon woods, elephant *krals,* salt pans, and pearl banks. Valentijn also shows the southern tip of India, with the Kingdom of Madura and the principality of Rāmnād.

The present edition concludes with the first twelve chapters of Valentijn's *Beschrijvinge van Ceijlon.* Valentijn brings the story here up to the expulsion of the Portuguese and the establishment of Dutch hegemony. Three more chapters deal with the Dutch administration of Ceylon till 1724 (showing that Valentijn was writing his last volumes after the early ones had gone to press). Though very substantial in length (they together take up 211 folio pages), these chapters are constituted largely of extracts of reports, memoirs and instructions of Dutch officials in Ceylon. In fact, out of these 211 pages, 190 are taken up by these extracts, leaving only 21 pages of Valentijn's own narrative. This narrative is consequently broken up and patchy and quite unlike the narrative in the first twelve chapters. This last section has been obviously put into press hurriedly, out of material that came to hand in the later stages of his research. Many of these memoirs and instructions have been published by the Ceylon Government Archives in its series of Dutch records. For this reason, because of the constraints of space and because of the doubtful value of the narrative, these chapters are omitted from this edition.

At the end of the fifteenth chapter, Valentijn begins the third and last part of the work, entitled Particular matters of Religion in Ceylon. This consists of two chapters, 16 and 17, and covers ninety-six pages. Chapter 16 deals with the traditional indigenous religions—Hinduism, Buddhism and Islam. Chapter 17 describes Roman Catholicism and Protestant Christianity on the island. Colonel Mackenzie had the description of indigenous religions translated which is to be found in the Mackenzie Collection: Private 78.

Valentijn first describes Buddhism and the religious practices of the Sinhalese to which he devotes 17 pages.[1] Here he gives two versions

[1] Valentijn, V. 1, pp. 366–83.

of the life of the Buddha. These appear to be drawn from Sinhalese versions of the Pali Buddhist literature that record a number of these stories in the Buddhist canon. The date of the Buddha's birth which he gives as 622 B.C. agrees with the Sinhalese tradition, as opposed to the Indian which dates this event a good 60 years later. The linguistic terms used also show the sources to have been unmistakably Sinhalese. He records the suggestion that has been made at various times that Buddha was a fugitive Syrian Jew, an Israelite, a disciple of the Apostle Thomas, but he dismisses this on the grounds of impossible chronology. He misquotes Couto as asserting that Buddha was the prophet Joshua and dismisses this assertion as a foolish one.[1] Valentijn has some inkling of the Brahmanical religion that had been fused into Sinhalese Buddhism when he says:

> Besides Buddha, the Cingalese recognise seven other sacred beings or Vice-Gods, to each of which they ascribe a particular attribute and form.[2]

He is, however, able to name only one which he calls *Candea Suanim*, a mutilated form of Kandaswamy, the Hindu deity, son of Siva, worshipped by the Sinhalese under the Sanskritic name of Skanda.

He identifies some important places of pilgrimage. One of them is what he calls the 'Mountain of the Three Pagodas' or Trincomalee where an ancient and famous Hindu shrine was the object of worship. On Trincomalee, he records a tradition that prevailed in contemporary times of a prophecy that had been inscribed on stone on the history of this shrine. As he translates it:

> Manica Raja has built this temple to the honour of the God Videmal in the year 1300 B.C. But a certain nation, called Franks, will come and destroy it and there shall come a king who will rebuild it.[3]

Queyroz also refers to this tradition but his version substantially changes the latter part of the prophecy and says: '. . . and there will be no king in this Island to rebuild it anew'.[4] Valentijn then goes on to

[1] Valentijn, V. 1, p. 374. Couto was really commenting on the similarity between the Buddha legend and the legend of Barlaam and Josaphat. Couto, p. 113.
[2] Valentijn, V. 1, p. 375.   [3] Valentijn, V. 1, p. 367.
[4] Queyroz II, p. 67. This is a singular and very strange tradition in Ceylon history. The stone on which this inscription was engraved was later used in the construction of Fort Frederick on the Trincomalee rock. Early in the 20th century, the Ceylon Epigraphist read this inscription as follows: 'The Portuguese shall take the holy edifice built by

describe in detail Adam's Peak, a place which was the scene of pilgrimage by Buddhists, Hindus and Muslims.[1] He devotes eight pages to a description of this mountain, the shrines on it, the famous footprint embedded in the rocks and the beliefs of the people associated with it. A large part of this description is, however, a translation of Couto's account in *Decada* Five, Book VI, Chapter II, but this time he does it with acknowledgment as an extract from this work. There are some errors in the translation, errors which have crept into subsequent works which have relied on Valentijn. Valentijn has utilised other sources as well for his description. One of them is an anonymous description of images and figures which are to be seen on the mountain of Mokeregelle (Mulgirigalle), otherwise named Adam's Mountain.[2] This account gives detailed measurements of images and shrine rooms of a temple on this mountain. The other is a letter written to the Governor Simons by an officer, G. Helmont, who describes the same place after a tour undertaken in the company of some others including a Minister of the Reformed Church. It appears from this that there were two places in Ceylon known to the Europeans of that time as Adam's Peak or Mountain and that Valentijn confuses these two. One is the well-known Adam's Peak, known to the Sinhalese as Samanalakanda and Tamils as Sivanolipadam, where the only centre of attraction is a large footprint believed by Sinhalese to be that of the Buddha. There was another mountain shrine, also known as Adam's mountain, but by the Sinhalese as Mulgirigalle which was an old Sinhalese temple, dating back to the 5th century A.D., in the southern district of Hambantota. It is this temple and the statuary that are described in these two reports quoted by Valentijn. The same confusion is noted in Couto, who describes Adam's Peak (Samanalakanda) in great detail in Chapter Two of the Sixth book of the *Decada* Five and refers briefly to the pagoda of Adam's Peak (probably Mulgirigalle) in the next chapter as one of the principal pagodas in the island.[3]

Valentijn narrates an interesting episode in Ceylonese history, the

---

Kulakoddan of ancient times, O King hearken! After the cat's eyed one, the red-eyed one, the smoke-eyed one have gone, there will be that of the northerner.' He thinks this prophecy was an intelligent forecasting of Ceylon's colonial history. It is dated about the end of the 16th century. [H. W. Codrington, 'The Inscription at Fort Frederick, Trincomalee', *J.R.A.S.C.B.*, XXX, 80 (1927), 448–51.]

[1] Valentijn, V. 1, pp. 375–83.   [2] Valentijn, V. 1, pp. 376–8.   [3] Couto, p. 118.

Portuguese capture of what they believed was the tooth relic of the Buddha.[1] His account of this is rather sketchy. Couto provides a more detailed account of how this relic was captured in Jaffna when that city was attacked by the Portuguese in 1560. It was presumed to be among the treasures taken by the Sinhalese prince Vidiyē Bandāra when he fled north to the kingdom of Jaffnapatnam. The Portuguese took this relic to Goa where the king of Pegu, a Buddhist kingdom with long ties with Sinhalese Buddhism, offered a huge sum as ransom for it. The Portuguese civilian authorities would have dearly liked to trade it in for the money but the Archbishop of Goa intervened and had it publicly burnt and the ashes thrown into the sea. Van Linschoten, who visited Goa soon after this incident, recorded it in his *Itinerario* and this was probably Valentijn's source for his account. He goes on to say that a 'vile *benjaan*', probably *banya* or merchant, had obtained another monkey's tooth, which he had exchanged for a false one destroyed by the Portuguese. He sold this tooth to the King of Vijayanagar for a large sum of money and a large number of pilgrims now flocked to his land to see this tooth, as they had previously done in Ceylon.[2]

Valentijn then goes on to speak of the origin of 'Biruma, Vistnoe and Uritram', that is Brahma, Vishnu and Rudra or Siva.[3] This appears to be a statement of popular Hindu beliefs on the origin of the universe, the attributes and function of the three elements of the Hindu God-head and of the many incarnations that these gods took on earth. It is a potted version of the vast corpus of Hindu mythology as found in the Puranas and which have been put in the form of a simple statement, probably by a Brahmin priest or a person learned in Hindu literature in the Tamil areas either in South India or North Ceylon. The terms are all Dravidian or Tamilised forms of the original Sanskrit.

Valentijn gives translated extracts from a number of old texts, mostly from Tamil literature.[4] Some of these he identifies wrongly. They are mostly ethical and moral treatises written in the Tamil language and dating back to the earliest beginning of Tamil literature. Valentijn appreciated the significance of the moral codes and the standard of social conduct they represent and in introducing them, comments thus:

---

[1] Valentijn, V. 1, pp. 374–5. The incident is also mentioned by Couto, pp. 190–2.
[2] Linschoten, *Itinerario* (1910), pp. 190–2. [3] Valentijn, V. 1, pp. 383–6.
[4] Valentijn, V. 1, pp. 386–99.

So that one may not have all too low an opinion of the Cingalese and the Malabars [Tamils] living on this island, even though they were such wild and unashamed heathens, we have deemed it necessary to append here some of their moral lessons. . . .[1]

He notes that these are in the 'Grantham language' which is the mixed old Tamil and Sanskrit script in which some old Tamil religious literature was written.

The selected extracts consist mostly of moral maxims from Tamil ethical works. Three of these are works attributed to a poetess of the 9th century, Auvai. They are *Attisudi, Konrai vēndan* and *Mūdurai*; there are rather lengthy extracts of the first two and a short piece from the third. There are also some extracts from some lexical and grammatical works. There is a brief version of the history of Sirutondan from the *Siruthonda Purānam*, a history of one of the Saivite Saints of the 7th century. These extracts appear as such without any attempt to integrate them into the body of his description. They are more an index to the efficiency of the collector of rare and valuable items than to any merit in understanding or the interpretation of their contents. Finally there is a very interesting list of Tamil works consisting of 65 items, each of them briefly identified and described. This is an exhaustive and largely authentic list of the major literary works in Tamil spread out over 15 centuries. On one of the most celebrated Tamil poets, Thiruvalluvar, the author of *Thirukkural* who lived about 3rd century A.D., Valentijn's entry reads thus:

Tiriwalluwir. One of their best prayer books, composed in clear and concise verses by Thiruwalluwer. Those who can read and understand him, can also understand the most difficult poets. This writer, according to the writings of Seneca, lived over 1500 years ago at Mailapore or San Thome.[2]

These extracts and the annotated list of literary work in Tamil show that Europeans in South Asia were beginning to have access to the vast store of indigenous literature of the societies of this region. Considering the fact that this was a period of decadence in literary activity and that many flourishing institutions of local learning had decayed in the absence of royal patronage, this amount of familiarity with indigenous traditions is an index to the curiosity and inquisitiveness of some European administrators, merchants and clergymen.

[1] Valentijn, V. 1, p. 386.   [2] Valentijn, V. 1, p. 400.

The Catholic missionaries of south India had done a good deal of pioneering work in the study of Indian languages and literatures. They had collected a number of these sources of Indian tradition but were generally averse to publishing them for theological reasons. They kept them in manuscripts in their monastic libraries to which members of the order had access and which were to be of use to them in their missionary activity. The Dutch were keen publicists, and, with their well developed printing industry, put into print whatever they could acquire and would in their view be useful and of interest. Baldaeus was one of the first to publish an attempted grammar of the Tamil language together with the Tamil script in Rotterdam, and a number of cardinal features of Christian belief and worship such as the Lord's Prayer, the Ten Commandments and the Articles of Faith were translated and published as an appendix to his major work.[1] Dutch missionaries continued the work begun by their Catholic predecessors in language study and the collection of sources. By the end of the 17th century, two seminaries providing some form of higher education, one in Tamil, the other in Sinhalese, had been established in Jaffna and Colombo respectively. The serious study of these languages and their literatures had begun and a number of Dutch specialists emerged. The Reverends Simon Kat and Johannes Ruell were scholars of Sinhalese; the former compiled a Sinhalese Dictionary and the latter a a Grammar of the Sinhalese language. This latter manuscript was sent to the Directors of the Company who published it after his death in Holland in 1708.[2] The Reverend Adriaan de Meij, the Rector of the Malabar (Tamil) Seminary, was a scholar of Tamil. There were also a number of young Sinhalese and Tamils who acted as informants on their literature and tradition. In this way the Dutch Ministers began to acquire some of this material that was lying unknown through neglect and ignorance and may be said to have initiated the beginnings of interest in them that was to bear fruit in the 19th century. Valentijn is thus one of the early channels through which this knowledge seeped down to the European literati.

Valentijn continues with his exposition of Sinhalese and Tamil religion.[3] He talks more of Buddhist institutions and practices than

---

[1] Baldaeus I, pp. 195–7. 'Malabaarsche Spraakkunst'.

[2] Pieter van Dam. *Beschrijvinge van de Oost-Indische Compagnie* Vierde Boek (The Hague, 1954), pp. 218 ff; Johannes Ruell, *Grammatica of Singaleesche taalkunst* (Amsterdam, 1708).

[3] Valentijn, V. 1, pp. 402–8.

those of Hinduism because he deals with the latter in his account of Coromandel. He describes Buddhist *vihāres* and *devāles* and shows an understanding of these two types of religious edifices in which Buddhists worshipped. He also talks of the Buddhist clergy, again distinguishing the hierarchy among them, as also the difference between the *bhikkhu*, the priest of orthodox Buddhism, *kapurāla*, the priest of the *devāle*, and *kattādiya*, the devil dancer and exorcist. He describes the rituals performed by each of these specialists and also attempts an account of the major festivals. He gives a description of the *perahera* which is to this day a festival of pageantry and colour among the Sinhalese. Similarly he gives brief descriptions of ceremonies on Adam's Peak and at the Mahābodhi tree or Sacred Bo Tree in Anuradhapura and of other annual festive occasions. He concludes this section with an account of the ceremonies of swearing on oath and for apprehending thieves among the Sinhalese.

Valentijn makes this very interesting observation while commenting on Sinhalese religion:

> We should say more here, if one could find among the Cingalese those who were in a position to decipher accurately for us this and that old Cingalese letters which one sees here and there deeply inscribed in stone; but so far no-one has been found suitable for this.[1]

He is referring here to the innumerable Sinhalese inscriptions of ancient and medieval Ceylon which were written in an old script which Valentijn's contemporaries could not read. The reading of these inscriptions, in the 19th century after the development of the study of linguistics, opened new doors towards the study of Sinhalese history.

Valentijn does not speak very much of Hinduism in this chapter, not because he does not have material on this subject. He has reserved this for that part of the book which treats of Coromandel where Hinduism was the major religion.[2] The brief reference to Islam is partly because of the smallness of the Muslim community in the island and also because he has dealt copiously with Islam in the earlier volumes dealing with the archipelago.

[1] Valentijn, V. 1, p. 408.
[2] Valentijn, V. 1, Choromandel, pp. 71–125.

Valentijn and succeeding writers

Valentijn's work on Ceylon was certainly known to Dutch officials in the island after its publication. But it would not have been indispensable, as most of the documents he reproduced would have been available in the Company's archives in Colombo. Governor van Imhoff makes a critical reference to him in his Memoirs, accusing Valentijn of inaccuracy and prejudice against the Company, without identifying these specifically.[1]

When the English captured Ceylon in 1796 from the Dutch, and set about establishing an administrative system, they were looking for information on the country, its history, institutions, customs and manners, and the obvious sources from which they sought such information were the records and writings of the Dutch, their immediate predecessors. It has already been noted that Alexander Johnston, the first English Chief Justice of Ceylon, was a foremost pioneer in the collection of Dutch and Sinhalese sources.[2] It was at this time that Valentijn, as a compendium of original material on Ceylon unavailable anywhere else, became widely read, studied and quoted. The English connexion with Ceylon immediately produced a rush of writings on the island, topographical and historical descriptions, and travelogues. The expansion of the English in the east had created interest among the educated and literate public in these strange new lands, over whose destinies the English had now been called upon to preside.

John Pinkerton (1758–1826), antiquarian, collector, and editor of travelogues in many languages, published his multi-volume work: *A General Collection of the best and most interesting voyages and travels in all parts of the world; many of which are now first translated into English* (London, 1812). Volume XI of this work is devoted to southeast Asia and here Valentijn's work is used extensively. The translator observes thus, in a note:

> The inestimable work of Valentijn, to which the reader is so frequently referred, is scarce even in Holland. It consists of five large folio volumes, containing upwards of one thousand copper-

---

[1] *Memoir of Baron van Imhoff*, 1740 (Colombo, 1911), p. 93.
[2] See above, pp. 20–21.

plates. The translator is in possession of a copy, which he procured at much pain and expence; and would his limits allow of it, he would be more copious in his extracts from it, as it is a treasure locked up in a chest, of which few have the key, no translation having ever been made of it.[1]

Those writers who attempted a connected history of the island found themselves relying very heavily on Valentijn, with or without acknowledgment. The Reverend Fellowes who wrote a *History of Ceylon from the earliest period to the year 1815*, under the pseudonym Philalethes, was heavily indebted to Valentijn. In his preface, he declares his great esteem for Valentijn's work thus:

The great Dutch work of Valentijn, the long concealed merits of which I have studiously laboured to bring to light in the course of the present history, has enabled me to exhibit a full and faithful picture of the mythological system and religious doctrines of the Sinhalese.[2]

Later on, in reconstructing the early history of the Sinhalese, he says:

I shall exclusively follow the authority of Valentijn in his famous work on the East Indies, which is but very little known, either in this country, or on the Continent, but which probably contains a mass of more valuable matter on the subjects of which it treats than any other publication which has appeared.[3]

Having said this, his first fourteen chapters are a straight translation from Valentijn, retaining even his chapter divisions and his outline headings at the beginning of each chapter. He also translates the excerpts from indigenous moral and ethical literature that Valentijn has published in his account of Buddhism and Hinduism.

William Knighton in his *The History of Ceylon from the Earliest Period to the Present Time* has utilised Valentijn, particularly for his account of the Portuguese and Dutch wars in Ceylon.[4] It appears, however, that he has used Philalethes' version of Valentijn, rather than the original itself. Philalethes' use of Valentijn was commended

[1] J. Pinkerton, *A General collection* . . . , XI, 263.
[2] Philalethes, *History of Ceylon* . . . (London, 1817), p. VIII.
[3] Philalethes, *op. cit.*, pp. 13–14.
[4] W. Knighton, *The history of Ceylon* . . . (London, 1845), pp. 245–78.

by Sir George Barrow who published *Ceylon Past and Present* in 1857. He says:

> The anonymous author has availed himself of the great Dutch work of Valentijn—a sealed book to most English readers; and he is thus able to illustrate the fabulous age of the island, and its various aspects under European domination.[1]

Another writer who has used Valentijn was Charles Pridham, author of *An Historical Political and Statistical Account of Ceylon and its dependencies* (London, 1849). He compares Valentijn with the information subsequently made available on Sinhalese history by the work of the pioneering Pali and Sinhalese scholar George Turnour.[2]

Perhaps the historian who benefited most from Valentijn as a source book was Emerson Tennent who in his *Ceylon. Account of the Island, Physical, Historical and Topographical* provides us with a critical evaluation of this work relating to Ceylon.[3] He was the first scholar who saw Valentijn for its real worth and described it as a much overrated work. In his judgment 'the portion which treats of Ceylon seems to be scarcely worthy of the high reputation of the work.... As to the general information supplied by Valentijn himself, it is both meagre and incorrect.'[4] Tennent was probably over-critical of Valentijn, and in any case, it can be seen from his copious references to the work in the course of his historical description that he did not really think too badly of it after all. In fact he relies on Valentijn heavily for his treatment of Portuguese and Dutch relations with Ceylon and judging from his copious references to Valentijn in his footnotes, it appears that he does treat him as something of an authority.

After a substantial corpus of writings on Ceylon in the English language had come into existence, the interest in Dutch sources and therefore in Valentijn ceased in the second half of the 19th century. To students and writers of the succeeding periods Valentijn was a closed book, partly because of the language problem and partly because of the vanishing interest in Sinhalese institutions of earlier centuries. It is only in the 20th century when the Ceylonese produced their own

---

[1] Sir George Barrow, *Ceylon Past and Present* (London, 1857), p. 1.
[2] Charles Pridham, *An historical*... (London, 1849), p. 26, pp. 99 ff.
[3] James Emerson Tennent, *Ceylon*..., Fifth Edition (London, 1860), II, 32.
[4] *Ibid.*

historians, desiring to know of their past heritage, that Valentijn was rediscovered and subjected to a closer examination as a source book on the 16th and 17th centuries. Today no scholar researching on that period can afford to ignore the documents and the commentaries of Valentijn.

Conclusion

A proper assessment of Valentijn's work, of his attitudes and their significance in the history of western approaches to non-western societies is a task fraught with complex problems. The material to be surveyed is formidable and for any valid study of these aspects one must go beyond the small section of the work printed here and wade through the hundreds of thousands of words he has written. The very varied sources he has used and the blurred distinction between what is his and what is borrowed from others complicates the problem further. The kinds of subjects that he deals with are also so diverse that it makes it difficult to pursue common attitudes through a common body of material. Because of these problems any attempt at passing judgments of Valentijn has to be tentative, cautious and the results are sometimes contradictory.

Valentijn does afford some assistance in such an assessment by the manner in which he, now and then, intrudes through the narrative in a personal manner. During these occasions, he comes through with a personal comment, observation or judgment. One is able to take a peep, through all this verbiage, at what one presumes is the real Valentijn. It is largely on the basis of these that the following comments are made.

One may first get the passionately held attitudes and obvious prejudices out of the way. They are there for all to see. The first of these is the Dutch nationalism and pride in the achievements of Dutch empire-builders. Valentijn shares a contemporary belief in the destiny of the Dutch as colonisers and does so with a greater conviction and sense of purpose than the customary attitude of an empire for commerce only. In this respect he shares the enthusiasm for empire of the Portuguese and Spanish writers of the 17th century, an attitude that comes much later to the northern Europeans. Valentijn betrays this enthusiasm far more than does Baldaeus for example, and in English writings this is even later in making its appearance.

A second obvious attitude flows from his Calvinistic religious background and vocation. It must be pointed out however that in Valentijn this takes second place to his Dutch nationalism. This is quite a contrast to Baldaeus who is primarily an evangelist and his evangelical interests keep coming through on every page of his writings. But there is a sense in which Valentijn is more narrowly sectarian than Baldaeus and that is in his anti-Catholic prejudices. These surface very often and sometimes even cloud his judgments on events and personalities. More understandable and equally obvious are his prejudices against non-Christian religions. This is something common to all missionary writing of this period.

A combination of his political and religious attitudes leads him to a very strongly anti-Portuguese position. The Portuguese were the enemies of the Dutch for a great part of the period he is describing and their successful Catholic missionary activity was also not something about which a Dutch protestant *padre* could be enthusiastic. This anti-Portuguese bias enables him, however, in the context of Ceylon events, to take a less subjective approach to the Portuguese–Sinhalese wars. Throughout the narrative he is aware of the Sinhalese side of the story and takes up positions critical of the Portuguese and favourable to the Sinhalese. By adopting this anti-Portuguese line he is able to arrive at judgments of events and personalities considerably fairer than those of contemporary Portuguese writers. A clear example of this is his assessment of Vimala Dharma Sūrya I (whom he consistently calls Don Jan), a life-long opponent of Portuguese colonialism in Ceylon. He provides a pen-sketch of his complex and fascinating personality that would stand up to the canons of modern historical criticism.

Some of the attitudes that Valentijn exhibits, both explicitly and implicitly, may be considered in the context of European approaches to non-western societies in his time. From about the second half of the 17th century, there was a growing curiosity and even an inquisitiveness about the strange new lands which many of them had visited and from which an increasing array of products were now available for sale in Europe. This desire to inform others who had not been there was keenly felt and resulted in a rash of travelogues describing the 'curious' east. Though Valentijn tried deliberately to dissociate himself from this amateur travelogue-writing, his work has a great deal of similarity to such writings and indeed has drawn substantially on one of the greatest of them.

The image of eastern society reflected in the travel literature of Valentijn's age was a combination of the exotic, the bizarre, the revolting and the fascinating. There is a good deal of the bizarre and the revolting in Valentijn's description, a number of occasions when he reacts adversely to what he is describing, obviously disapproves of it and intrudes into the east the values of an alien culture. But when Valentijn and other observers of his age are not revolted by what they see, their instinct for the curious and the exotic takes over and they then become objectively interested in something different from what they have experienced before. Robert Knox is the classic example of this type of curiosity and the empathy which it produces with the strange phenomena that are being observed and reported. Consequently Knox produced one of the most sympathetic observations of a complex Asian society by an outsider who has tried to view it from inside. We can see some of its liveliness even when it comes through Valentijn's cumbersome prose.

Valentijn did not have the first-hand experience of society in Ceylon that Knox or Baldaeus had. But he lived in some eastern societies and experienced enough of eastern culture to recognise some of its characteristics and to appreciate its essential difference from the west. He, more than Knox, came into contact with the 'high' culture of some eastern societies whereas Knox's familiarity was with the peasant or popular culture. He was more educated than Knox and had enough intellectual snobbishness in him to be drawn towards this 'high' culture. Whatever part of Asia attracted his attention—Moluccas, Java, India or Ceylon—he was deliberately looking for the literate society, for what could be discovered of the elements of philosophical thought, religious ideas, for the ways people were governed and who governed them.

The instinct of curiosity and the interest in 'high' culture combine to tone down and even eliminate the value judgments and the prejudice. Not infrequently Valentijn advances rational explanations of what to a westerner would be bizarre customs. The naturalist in Valentijn also contributes towards this attitude. The knowledge of diverse types of physical geography and ecological systems leads to an appreciation of differences in life styles between peoples. The fact that Valentijn chose to inform himself on many different regions of Asia added to this appreciation of cultural differences. Someone who chose to study and describe societies as varied as the Ambonese, the Bandanese, the

Javanese, the Malaccan, the Sinhalese, the Tamil, the Malayalee and the Bengalee, could not but have moved towards a position of appreciation of cultural differences, could not but have moved away from a position of Europe-centricism.

Valentijn lived and wrote a few decades before the Age of Enlightenment in Europe. But in two respects his work points to the attitudes that were characteristic of this age towards non-western culture. There is firstly his enthusiasm, inquisitiveness and thirst for knowledge of unknown lands and peoples. He had this interest very early in his career and began accumulating such information as he could from his very first contact with the east. Secondly there is his interest in the characteristics of civilisation among these people, his inquiry into what are the elements of the literary culture of these societies. These two features combine to produce in him the early beginnings of cross-cultural understanding. Thus he has in him some of the ingredients that go towards the formation of the attitudes of the Enlightenment towards non-western cultures.

A Note on the Translation

This translation tries, as far as possible, to be faithful to the text and to reproduce the language and spirit of the cumbersome Dutch prose of François Valentijn, while at the same time endeavouring to make it intelligible to the modern reader. The long sentences and the inter-linking of many ideas, the irregular punctuation and the frequent parenthetical clauses have sometimes been rationalised, though generally the framework of the original Valentijn sentence has been maintained.

Valentijn prefaces each chapter with a lengthy abstract of contents, which abstract he uses as sub-headings at the side of each paragraph of the text as he goes along. These abstracts and sub-heads have been reproduced in translation.

The somewhat irregular procedures for italicisation and capital-isation in the Dutch text have been rationalised. Non-Dutch words used by Valentijn have been italicized where they have been re-produced as such. The excessive use of capitals, usual to Germanic languages, has been reduced and the rules of English prose-writing generally applied.

Place names have been reproduced in the form used in Valentijn's text. There has been a good deal of inconsistency in spelling, caused largely by the fact that Valentijn was writing from a number of texts of diverse origins and talking of places with which he was not personally familiar. Thus, for example, Trincomalee, the well-known east coast harbour of Ceylon, is spelt variously as Trinkenemale, Trikoenmale, Trikoenemale, Tricoenemale, Tricoenmale. There are thus a number of such inconsistencies, sometimes in the same paragraph. Similarly, proper nouns, however distorted they may be, are reproduced in the original Valentijn spelling. The modern equivalents of these place names and proper names, wherever the identification is clear, are listed in italics in the index, opposite each entry.

Omissions from the text have been of portions that have been printed already and are noted by a short space and continuing asterisks: *****. As all these omissions are documents which Valentijn has reproduced, they do not interrupt his narrative.

The Text

Names of the Native Officers in the Villages of Ceylon

CORALE[1]   A Coraal[2] is something like an overseer of a Corle[3] or Province, who has under him as deputies 2, 3, or 4 Attacoreleas,[4] according as the Corle is large and subdivided, as in a Corle there are sometimes 3 or 4 Pattoes[5] or divisions. Also he has under him 6 to 8 Lascarines,[6] Pamideas[7] or messengers; and the Attacoreleas must perform what is ordered by the Corale.

CARIECORANNO[8]   or Majoraals.[9] These are petty chiefs of a village. In some there are 1 or 2, and sometimes up to 6 and more, according as the village is large and developed as well as well populated. They must pay their Deccum[10] yearly; they also must endeavour to have the sowing and harvesting in the village done in the proper season and to give a proper account to the Lord of the Land or the owner yearly of these and other benefits to be found in the village; and if the Lord of the village comes into the village they must see that a good residence at a suitable place is kept for him and that it is covered with white linen and that it is further provided with bed and chairs which are similarly covered. Also they should bring Adreckes[11] or cooked food and Peyndoes[12] or uncooked food twice a day as the Lord of the village desires for as many days as the village is accustomed to

---

[1] *Kōrāla* (Sinh.).

[2] There was a frequent confusion in the spelling of this word by the Dutch, the forms used being *Corale, Coraal, Korale, Coralea*.

[3] *Kōralē* (Sinh.).   [4] *Atukōrāla* (Sinh.).   [5] *Pattu* (Sinh. and Tam.).

[6] From *Lashkari* (Persian and Hindi) meaning 'soldier'. Portuguese used it in corrupted form of 'lascarin' to mean indigenous Indian soldier and this usage was taken over by Dutch and English.

[7] *Panividea* (Sinh.).   [8] *Kāriyakarannō* (Sinh.). Literally, those who perform tasks.

[9] *Maioral*. A designation given by the Portuguese to village headmen in Ceylon.

[10] *Dakum* (Sinh.). A tax, traditionally paid as a present on seeing the king or lord.

[11] *Adukku* (Sinh.). A tax paid in the form of cooked food for the Lord's table.

[12] *Pahidum* (Sinh.). A tax similar to *Adukku* paid as uncooked provisions.

and according to its size and suitability, be it 3, 4 or 6 days for one village. These Majoraals are of five sorts, the one somewhat more important than the other, such as the Hitihamis,[1] Japamis,[2] Pati Rannearae,[3] Gamneralearoe,[4] Vitarannearoe.[5]

LIANNO[6]   He is like a writer of the village who records everything that is harvested and gathered therein and must give account of it to the Lord of the village.

CANGANEME[7]   He mobilises the people if there is any work in the village and calls them together.

MANANNA[8]   A grain-measurer who must divide all the grain, if there are different share-holders, after it has been harvested. Also he must specially measure out the tax.

GAMHEWAJA[9]   A village-lascarine, who at the order of the petty chief or Vidaan[10] of the village summons the people and must warn them from house to house on what day and time they must come. Also he runs messages.

HAINDES[11]   They must perform the work that there is in the village and by turns must also work for the King or the Lord of the Land.

COELIS[12]   Bearers of all kinds of burdens, goods and *andols*[13] or palanquins. These coolies are of the caste (or race) of Bellales[14] who appeared during the time of the Portuguese. Before this time there had been no coolies of the Bellale caste but only of the low castes.

---

[1] *Hitihāmī* (Sinh.).   [2] *Yāpahāmī* (Sinh.).   [3] *Patirannahē* (Sinh.).
[4] *Gamarāla* (Sinh.).   [5] *Vitāranna* (Sinh.).   [6] *Liyanna* (Sinh.).
[7] *Kankānam* (Sinh.), from *Kankāni* (Tamil).   [8] *Manannā* (Sinh.).
[9] *Gamhevāya* (Sinh.).   [10] *Vidānē* (Sinh. and Tam.).   [11] *Naindē* (Sinh.).
[12] *Kūli* (Sinh. and Tam.). A word which has come into the English language to mean hired labour.
[13] *Randōla* (Sinh.).
[14] *Vellāla* (Tam.). A Tamil caste of agriculturalists. They were probably taken prisoners in the Portuguese wars in north Ceylon and brought as labourers to the south.

THE KING SOERIEVANKSE[1] This signifies that he is descended from the sun or from Vigia Raja,[2] the first King of Ceylon, by whom was granted to all the following castes the honour of washing,[3] and so on, as is mentioned in the following under each caste, which has thus been in use from that time till today, beginning with 2 special castes, first the Carrea Caste[4] or the Fishers and Chiandes[5]; under the Carrea Caste are nine different sorts, namely

1. Caraeuw[6]
2. Baroedel-Caraeuw[7]
3. Dandoe-Caraeuw[8]
4. Moroe-Caraeuw[9]
5. Kespe-Caraeuw[10]
6. Cadoel-Caraeuw[11]
7. Tock-Keulo[12]
8. Godo-Keulo[13]
9. Indimal-Keulo[14]

These nine sorts of Carreas have each a special type of fishing gear, each must strictly adhere to this as has been laid down as of old and is shown in greater detail below.

CARAEUW These are the most important fishermen, whom they also make their chiefs, according as they are expert in war. Among them there are also Modeljaars,[15] Mohamdirens,[16] Araatsjes,[17] Cangenys[18] and other important officials. They may sail in their *thonies*[19] or boats with their fishing gear deep into the sea but may not fish with angle or line.

BAROEDEL-CARAEUW They may not use anything other than throw-nets, called Baroedel[20] or Wisoedel[21] by them, in sea and in the rivers.

---

[1] *Sūriyavamsa* (Sinh.). The sun dynasty. [2] Vijaya.
[3] The right of having one's clothes washed by a caste of lower status is one of the important caste privileges.
[4] *Karāva* (Sinh.), Karaiyār (Tam.). [5] *Chandō* (Sinh.). A Caste of toddy tappers.
[6] *Karāva* (Sinh.). [7] *Barudel Karāva* (Sinh.). [8] *Dandi Karāva* (Sinh.).
[9] *Moru Karāva* (Sinh.). [10] *Kespe Karāva* (Sinh.). [11] *Kadul Karāva* (Sinh.).
[12] *Tok Kevulu* (Sinh.). [13] *Goda Kevulu* (Sinh.). [14] *Indimal Kevulu* (Sinh.).
[15] *Mudaliyār* (Sinh. and Tam.). [16] *Muhāndiram* (Sinh. and Tam.).
[17] *Ārāchchi* (Sinh. and Tam.). [18] *Kankāni* (Sinh. and Tam.).
[19] *Thōni* (Tam.). [20] *Barudel* (Sinh.). [21] *Wisudel* (Sinh.).

DANDOE-CARAEUW   They may fish in the sea but with angle rods made by them from small bamboos with which they go deep in the sea.

MOROE-CARAEUW[1]   They have nets of hemp and go to the sea to catch sharks from whose fat they make oil which they sell; they may not catch any other fish.

KESPE-CARAEUW[2]   They go into the sea with their large nets to catch turtles by which they must subsist.

CADOEL-CARAEUW   They make a reddish brown dye from the bark of the *cadoel*[3] tree with which they dye the sails of their *thonies* in which they are accustomed to fish in the river.

TOCK-KEULO   They may not go to sea except to salt water inlets, or to the mouth of the river. They have another kind of net, to which two long cords are bound and to which young *olas*[4] from the *jaggery*[5] tree (in Cingalese[6] called *Talgas*[7]) are fastened on one end and the other end hangs in the water; stretching the cords on both sides of the net they keep their *thonies* opposite the open side, then beat with a stick on an edge of the *thony* and go away till the net is hauled up. In this and in no other way may they catch fish.

GODDE-KEULO   They may not go to the sea but fish in the river, and at the mouth or in the salt water inlets. They have also a special fishing gear such as a foursided net which they spread under the water on the ground with 4 stones; also on the four corners are four wooden props, where at the end sit four persons each with a towing cord in the hand, all stretching away further from the four props or cords, to which young *olas* (or leaves of trees) are tied, to

---

[1] *Mōri* (Sinh.)—shark.   [2] *Kespe* (Sinh.)—turtle.

[3] *Kaduru* (Sinh.)—*Cerbera manghas*.   [4] *Ola* (Sinh.), *Olai* (Tam.)—a leaf.

[5] Probably a Portuguese form of *sakkarai* (Tam. and Malayālam) meaning a coarse brown sugar made from palm juice. Though Valentijn refers to this tree in Sinhalese as *talgaha*, it cannot be the palmyrah palm because: (i) Palmyrah does not grow in that part of the country of which he is speaking; (ii) The palmyrah leaf cannot be used in the way described. The tree referred to here is probably the coconut palm or the *kitul* palm.

[6] Modern 'Sinhalese', the language and ethnic group of the majority community inhabiting Sri Lanka (Ceylon).

[7] *Talgaha* (Sinh.)—*Borassus flabellifer*. A variety of palm.

which [fishes] are chased by other persons at the end of the rope, but sometimes not, according to the situation. And if the four persons observe that there are fishes in the net then they haul it up quickly.

INDIMAL-KEULO   They make coir ropes from the coconut husk and also nets from it which they sell to the fishers. They also catch fishes in the river with baskets and small nets, but on their festivals they may not use the flowers or *Majang*[1] (the first shoots of the fruit) of the coconut tree, but only date palm flowers which they call *Indimal*.[2]

These three last types of fishers are the lowest caste among them, with whom the others will not eat or intermarry.

The most important of them have half as much honour as the Ballales,[3] namely, the washers are obliged to work for them for payment; also they must decorate their *Mandoeves*[4] on their festivals with white linen and spread white linen where they eat, on the bed and around it and also wrap white linen round their *adackes*[5]; they may also carry a torch or a flambeau (called by them *Dawalpandam*).[6] They also have a white flag with a fish in the middle as an emblem which they call *Addealancody*[7] and the fish *Maghere*,[8] which honour the higher among them do not permit to the lower, nor can they blow the *chank*[9] shell.

At their festivals the following castes may eat together: the Hinnewas,[10] Radewas,[11] Berrewajas,[12] Halys,[13] Hangeneme,[14] Uliya,[15] Kinnereras,[16] Pallis,[17] and other low castes, but the Smiths or Navadannajo,[18] Annalio,[19] Taylors, Panickers[20] or Barbers will not eat with the fishers.

The fishers may also carry a *talpot*[21] or *satys*[22] but the *satys* must be

---

[1] *Majang* (Malay)—young shoot of arecanut or coconut tree.
[2] *Indimal* (Sinh.)—Flower of *Phoenix ʒeylanica*.   [3] *Vellāla*. See p. 66 n. 14.
[4] *Mandapa* (Skt.)—hall.   [5] *Adukku*. See p. 65 n. 11.   [6] *Davalpandama* (Sinh.).
[7] *Adaikalankody* (probably Tam.)—*kodi*—flag.
[8] *Makara* (from Skt.)—a mythical fish. From a legend in traditional *Karāva* mythology.
[9] From *sanku* (Tam.)—a sea shell found in south Indian, Ceylonese waters.
[10] *Hinnāvō* (Sinh.). This and the castes that follow are described later in the text.
[11] *Radāvō* (Sinh.).   [12] *Bēravā* (Sinh.).   [13] *Hāly* or *Halāgama* or *Salāgama* (Sinh.).
[14] *Hangarannō* (Sinh.).   [15] *Olī* (Sinh.).
[16] *Kinnarā* (Sinh.).   [17] *Palī* (Sinh.).   [18] *Navandanna* (Sinh.).
[19] Probably *Hannālio* (Sinh.).   [20] *Panikki* (Sinh.).
[21] *Talapata* (Sinh.). *Corypha umbraculifera*. Here refers to leaf of the *talapata* (talipot) palm carried as a sunshade or umbrella.
[22] The word is unidentifiable. *Satykka* (Sinh. and Tam.) means nutmeg. The meaning here is an umbrella or frond made from the leaf of the talipot palm.

red at the edge. Also within their limits they may have white linen spread for their feet.

They have also a militia under them such as Modeljaars, Mahandirems, Araatsjes, Canganes and Lascarines, and now there are even those who occupy the position of Adigar[1] after they have earned this by their cleverness. Also they have been honoured with titles by the King or the Lord of the Land and may also be carried in palanquins (but the palanquins have no curved bamboo), with the beating of tomtoms (or drums) carrying a double or *Irette Talpat*,[2] a painted shield, a *dawalpandam* or torch burning by day and even elephants and even more honours that each most deserves.

Among the fishers are still other chiefs, besides these, and important persons, as also those in servitude such as:

Pattabendas[3]
Tottehewajas[4]
Nanajancarajos[5]
Hannedas[6]
Baddatoeras[7]
Coelis[8]

Pattabenda. Signifies one titled, such as are among the chiefs of the fishers; for, if they are not titled, they are named Baddas.[9]

Tottehewaja. Is a messenger but the word itself signifies a Lascarine of the pass.

Nanajancarajo. Are among the people of standing on whom no service whatsoever is imposed, except some important service which must be performed or some very light service, in which case they are expressly charged with it.

Hannedas. Are people who go with *thonies* to the sea.

Baddatoera. They must deliver fish to the landlord free twice a day as also to the chiefs of the others.

Coelis or *Nilecareas*.[10] They must carry all kinds of burdens. The most

---

[1] *Adigār* (Sinh.). Explained later in text. See below p. 82.   [2] *Irattai* (Tam.)—double.
[3] *Patabandā* (Sinh.).   [4] *Tottehēvayā* (Sinh.).   [5] *Nanayakkāra* (Sinh.).
[6] *Hennadi* (Sinh.).   [7] *Badaturu* (Sinh.).   [8] *Kūli* (Sinh. and Tam.).
[9] *Badda* (Sinh.)—a body of taxpayers.   [10] *Nilakāraya* (Sinh.).

important will not eat or intermarry with them. But in Mature[1] and its dependencies there is little difference. Also there are among the fishers Deccum Careas[2] or those who pay a yearly poll tax.

Chiandes Caste or *Tappers*. These, called Doerawo[3] in Cingalese, consist of 10 types, called Dahadoerawo[4] who subsist by tapping trees, though each type has its distinctness, especially in custom and different rank. Their names are as follows:[5]

1. *Magoel Doerawo*. These are the most important and are used for the capturing and taming of elephants, and also as lascarines and in other important services, and as woodcutters, and are tappers of coconut trees.

2. *Nattanbowo*.[6] They are a grade below the first and there is little difference between the two types, just as each of the following is consequently lower in rank.

3. *Niello*. They tap the *jager* trees[7] and may not carry a wooden hook but put their *majang*[8] knife in a case which must be bound with a rope round the middle, as also their pots in which they put the *suri*[9] (or coconut juice). But the earlier mentioned castes carry a wooden hook. This caste must hang a small bell around their waist to make known their caste and so that the Bellale caste passing under trees on which they have climbed could avoid them.

4. *Oesanno*.[10] They are also tappers who tap *jager* trees, cannot use anything other than what the Niellos use and must also hang a bell around the waist and besides must do coolie service in carrying things as directed.

5. *Weedy*. They are also tappers though a grade lower than the last but there are none in the island.

6. *Cottoe*.[11] They are one grade lower still than the last and are not now found in the island.

7. *Coetang Wolle-etto*.[12] They are dancers, both men and women,

---

[1] Mātara in south Ceylon.   [2] *Dakumkāraya* (Sinh.).   [3] *Durāvō* (Sinh.).
[4] *Daha Durāvō* (Sinh.)—Daha—Ten.
[5] Many of these subcastes were extinct even in Valentijn's time. Modern investigators have not been able to trace any of them (Ryan, *Caste in Modern Ceylon*, p. 111).
[6] *Natambuvō* (Sinh.).   [7] Probably *kitul* tree from whose juice jaggery sugar is made.
[8] *Majang* (Malay)—knife.
[9] *Suri* (Skt. and Hindi)—intoxicating liquor, here refers to toddy.
[10] *Usannō* (Sinh.).   [11] *Cottu* (Sinh.).   [12] *Cutary Wolle-etto* (Sinh.).

of the temple and also do whatever else they are ordered, being a grade lower than the last sort.

8. *Arambeo.* They are also dancers of the temple Iswarredevi Cowille[1] and they will dance nowhere but in this temple, but are a grade lower than the last sort.

9. *Ackerammo.*[2] They make coir (or coconut yarn) and are also required to blow the bellows in the smithy and strike with the fore-hammer and to work at the timber yards with the augers and other things, being a grade lower than the last sort.

10. *Agoenmady.*[3] This is the last sort of the islanders and also the lowest, with whom none of the others shall eat or intermarry, though they also tap. Also they do not enjoy as much respect as the former; they have a special type of musical instrument, such as an earthen pot round as a ball with a hole on one side on which they hold one hand and on the other side is a neck which is open with an iguana skin drawn over it on which they play with the hand.[4]

The first two of these 10 types enjoy the honour of white linen and washing by washermen like the Careas but they may not have the *chank* shell blown. They also have an *Addealanchody*,[5] or a flag with a red lion in the middle painted on a white background. The most important among them will not concede any more honours to the others than they please, which thus decreases with the lower categories. And with these people also will such castes eat as with the Careas or fishers, among whom are Araatjes,[6] Canganes,[7] Lascarines, Writers, Dureas,[8] Panikeas,[9] Coirnaikers,[10] Decumcareas,[11] Annekeas,[12] Gonbadocaneas,[13] Oeloewadaeas,[14] Wittanannes,[15] Cammelcaneas[16] and Nilecareas.[17]

Of the Chiande[18] caste a part belong to the temple of Dondra,[19]

---

[1] *Isvaradēvi Kōvil* (Sinh. and Tam.).   [2] *Akerannō* (Sinh.).   [3] *Agunmady* (Sinh.).
[4] A percussion instrument used in folk music both by Sinhalese and Tamils.
[5] See p. 69 n. 7.   [6] *Ārāchchi* (Sinh. and Tam.).   [7] *Kankāni* (Sinh. and Tam.).
[8] *Duraya* (Sinh.). Headmen of the lower castes.   [9] *Panikiya* (Sinh.).
[10] *Horanacāraya* (Sinh.). They are defined in the next paragraph.   [11] See p. 71 n. 2.
[12] *Anikiyā* (Sinh.).   [13] *Gonbadukārayā* (Sinh.). Defined below.
[14] *Uliyakārayā* (Sinh.). One liable to obligatory service.   [15] *Vitārana* (Sinh.).
[16] *Kammalkārayā* (Sinh.).   [17] *Nilakārayā* (Sinh.).   [18] *Chāndō* (Sinh.).
[19] The southernmost tip of the island. Sinhalese called it Devundara. The temple is the Vishnu Devalē, a well known place of worship.

a part to the Matura Ettelle,[1] a part to the Etbandanne[2] and also here and there in the villages where they live, and are obliged to tap and some to work in the smithy and others under Vidanes.[3]

Under the temple of Dondra belong:

Dureas or Overseers, as among the woodcutters, Deccumcareas (or payers of life tax).

Gombadoe Careas, or those who drive the draught animal and go back and forth, who also have their Dureas.

Aneckeas, or those who procure people for the smithy.

Cammalcareas, or those who draw on bellows and work with the fore-hammer.

Cottanno are woodcutters or choppers who cut down trees at a distance and chop them into logs.

Zingaran Careas,[4] or drum and tom-tom beaters and others whom they call Mached or Mohandirems.

Kornecareas or shawm[5] blowers.

Conboecareas[6] or tooters.

Under the Mature Ettele, or the elephant stable of Mature, belong:

Araatsje or one who attends to the stable, seeing that the animals are always given leaves, brought water in time and what is further necessary in the stable.

Lianna, writer who notes the names of the workers of the stable and the beasts and also the leaves which the grass cutters must bring.

Cangany, or one who also looks after the stable.

Panickeas or those who tame the elephants.

Coirnackeas[7] or servants of the Panickeas who must tie up the animals, untie them and bring them to work.

---

[1] From *atto* (Sinh.)—people.
[2] *Etbandenna* (Sinh.). The department in charge of trapping elephants.
[3] *Vidānē* (Sinh. and Tam.)—headman.   [4] *Simhakkārayō* (Sinh.).
[5] A reed musical instrument.   [6] *Kumbakkārayō* (Sinh.).
[7] *Kurunāyaka* (Sinh.).

Lascarines, Panniwedas[1] or messengers.

Witarannas, the collectors of the Deccum.

Deccumcareas, who pay yearly capitation tax.

Anneckeas, who procure people for the smithy.

Cammelcareas, who work in the smithy.

Hoedoehacoereas,[2] who must bring the white sugar for the Lord of the village.

Under the Etbandene or the Elephant hunt belong:

Araatsje, the Sergeant among them.

Lascarines, Panniwedas, being messengers.

Dureas, Overseers, also called Manquedans.[3]

Cournakeas, who look after the newly captured elephants.

Deccumcares, who pay the yearly capitation tax.

Thereafter follow 18 low castes called by them *Dahate Nagarame,*[4] beginning with the most important:

Navandannajo,[5] or Craftsmen who, though practising different crafts, yet are of one caste in rank. Half of them may be honoured with white linen on their festival of Mandoe, which they also spread out where they sit, display a flag where the ape, named Anoemante,[6] is painted, also have a torch burning by day and have been also honoured by the King with titles according to their caste. But the fishermen shall not eat with this caste nor go to their festivals or elsewhere with them. They give them white linen but will not tie it and the next lower caste also will not eat with them except the Oleas[7] and Kinneneas.[8]

Achiary[9]—Smiths.

---

[1] *Panividea* (Sinh.).   [2] *Hudahakkura* (Sinh.).

[3] Origin of this word is obscure. Probably Portuguese; an officer who had police and security powers over a group of labouring people.

[4] *Dahahatē Nagarama* (Sinh.). Dahahata—eighteen.   [5] *Navandannō* (Sinh.).

[6] *Hanumān* or *Anumān*, the monkey god in the Rāmāyanā.

[7] *Oli* (Sinh.)—devil dancers.   [8] *Kinnāru* (Sinh.)—mat weavers.   [9] *Ācāri* (Sinh.).

Baddallo[1]—Silversmiths.

Waddoewo[2]—Carpenters.

Liane wadowo[3]—Turners.

Ridiale Ancarao[4]—Engravers who engrave silver and gold.

Adatketeancarao[5]—Ivory and cabinet makers.

Galwadoewo[6]—Stone cutters.

Ratneenderecarao[7]—Stone polishers.

Iwadoewo[8]—Pike-shaft makers and japanners.

Sittereo[9]—Painters with lacquer and dye.

Locoeroewo[10]—Coppersmiths.

These craftsmen eat together, and intermarry. They come under the temple, Cattal[11] and Audebadde.[12]

Hannalio.[13] Tailors who must work for the Lord of the Land. The washers will wash for them but will not eat with them. Also they do not enjoy the honour of linen except with the consent of the King.

Hommaroe.[14] Shoemakers. They are to be found only in Candi. The washers will wash for them but they do not enjoy the honour of linen.

Ambetteo.[15] Barbers. One of them must go everywhere with the Lord of the Land. The washers wash for them, but they do not eat with them, though they enjoy the honour of white linen.

Coebello.[16] Potters. They are subject to the temple and to the village, and must also make earthenware pots for the landlord. They have also their Dureas and pay Decum or capitation tax. The workers work for them but do not eat with them and they do not enjoy the honour of white linen.

Weenawo.[17] Are like the Baddanas[18] or elephant catchers. They search

---

[1] *Badallu* (Sinh.).
[2] *Vaduvō* (Sinh.).
[3] *Liyana vaduvō* (Sinh.).
[4] *Ridiceto Ancaruvō* (Sinh.).
[5] *Atdatkatayankārayō* (Sinh.).
[6] *Galvaduvō* (Sinh.).
[7] *Ratneendekārayō* (Sinh.).
[8] *Ivaduvō* (Sinh.).
[9] *Sittaru* (*hittaru*) (Sinh.).
[10] *Lokuruvō* (Sinh.).
[11] *Kottalbadda* (Sinh.)—Artificer's department.
[12] *Handabadda* (Sinh.).
[13] *Hannāliō* (Sinh.).
[14] *Hommaru* (Sinh.).
[15] *Ambattayō* (Sinh.).
[16] *Kumballu* (Sinh.).
[17] *Weenavō* (Sinh.).
[18] *Baddannō* (Sinh.), literally, those subject to a tax.

them out, chase them into the *kraal*[1] and if there are any defects in them they kill them with their large *assegai*.[2] The workers work for them but do not eat with them nor do they enjoy the honour of linen.

Haly[3] or *Chalias*. Cinnamon peelers. They must peel cinnamon for the Lord of the Land and deliver it according to their tax. They have 2 vidanes, namely Mahabadde[4] on the side of Bellitotte[5] and Roenebadde[6] in the Mature district. This caste has also its militia, such as Mohanderems who are chiefs over one or two bands of lascarines. They have also their Araatsjes (or Sergeants) Canganies (Corporals), lascarines (or soldiers). The Vidane has supervision over a part of the people of the delimited villages. They also have Dureas (such as Manquedans[7] or those who control the people), Liannas (or writers), Decum Careo or those who pay capitation tax and Nilecareo[8] Coolis or carriers. For them the washers do not wash, though they have others called Hinnevo[9] who do this for them. Nor do they enjoy the honour of white linen.

Hangarema[10] or the tappers of *jager* trees, named Kitaelgas[11] by them from whose sap sugar is made. Among them there are also those who smelt iron and are called by them Jamano.[12] They must also give *rotangs*[13] to bind the elephant *kraal*. Their caste is under 2 Vidanes, one Malidoewepitegawe,[14] and the other Canoemaaldimpitigava[15] among whom are also Dureas, Canganys, Lascarines, Decumcareas and Coolies as under the Chalias. They also have no honour of washing (except by the Hinnevo) nor of white linen.

Hoenno[16] or Chinamberos.[17] Lime burners among whom are different sorts and services such as the Hoenoedewea,[18] their chief, who customarily plasters the walls and directs the people.

---

[1] From Portuguese word *corral* meaning 'enclosure'.

[2] A spear or lance of hard wood pointed with iron. From Arabic word through Portuguese *aʒagaia*.

[3] *Hāly* (Sinh.). In modern Ceylon this caste is known as Salāgama.

[4] *Mahābaddā* (Sinh.).

[5] Place names are listed in the index in their modern form.   [6] *Ruhunabadda* (Sinh.).

[7] Valentijn spells this word variously as 'Manquedans' and 'Mancquedams'. See p. 74 n. 3.

[8] Nilakārayā (Sinh.).   [9] Hinnāvō (Sinh.).

[10] *Hangarammu* (Sinh.). In modern Ceylon this caste is called Hakurō.

[11] *Kitulgas* (Sinh.)—the *kitul* tree: *Caryota urens*.   [12] *Yamannō* (Sinh.).

[13] *Ratan* (Malay)—cane.   [14] *Malidūva Pitigāya* (Sinh.).

[15] Probably *Kanumūldeni Pitigāya* (Sinh.).   [16] *Hunnō* (Sinh.).

[17] From *Chunnāmbu* (Tam.)—lime.   [18] *Hunudēvea* (Sinh.).

Duneas,[1] being their Mancquedams, who must go into the woods with the wood cutters to cut down trees; also he must whiten the house of the landlord once or twice a week for which they have special whitewashers under them. Also he or the Durea must provide fine purified lime for betel-chewing.

Deccum Careo.[2] They pay a yearly capitation tax. Also they must make the lime kiln, set it on fire and take care of it till it is completed. They enjoy no honours of linen, nor of washing but the caste of Pallys[3] wash for them.

Hoenoe Kattanno,[4] are woodcutters who cut all kinds of trees in the woods and must buy the coconut trees for the lime kilns and in time of war carry the gun powder.

Hoenoegambadoe[5] are cattlemen who provide the draught cattle and also have a special Duria.[6]

Among this caste are also coolies who live in the village and also some who do Baddanas[7] service at the elephant hunt but they are not on this side.[8]

Radaeuw[9] are washers who are obliged to work for the most important castes and also for the Careas and Chiandes and will eat with them but do nothing further. Though they also work for the craftsmen, tailors, potters and barbers, they shall not eat with them nor go to their festivals. They enjoy no honour of white linen and wash for themselves. Among the washers are also Sayacareas[10] or dyers and they pay deccum as also do their militia.

Berreways,[11] *Tablinjeros,* or Tambourin players, among whom also are dancers, charcoal burners, grass cutters, and deccumcareas; they have their Mancquedams whom they call Oeliwalia.[12] Like the washers, they will not eat with the low caste and are stationed under Vidanes. They do not enjoy the honour of linen nor of washing which the Pallys do for them.

Heeri[13] are woodcutters. They have their Vidane and have to cut all

---

[1] *Duraya* (Sinh.).
[2] *Dakumkārayā* (Sinh.).
[3] *Palī* (Sinh.).
[4] *Hunakattannō* (Sinh.).
[5] *Hunugonbadu* (Sinh.).
[6] *Duraya* (Sinh.).
[7] *Baddana* (Sinh.)—a caste tax.
[8] Probably meaning, on the Dutch side of the island.
[9] *Radau* (Sinh.).
[10] *Sāyacarea* (Sinh.). From *sāyam* (Tam.)—dye.
[11] *Berevayō* (Sinh.).
[12] *Hulavāliyā* (Sinh.).
[13] *Hiyāri* (Sinh.).

sorts of trees, to carry the gunpowder in time of war, to cut open the paths, though this caste is not to be found in the lowlands but in Kandy. They enjoy no honour of washing or of white linen but the caste of Gangavo[1] wash for them.

Olias[2] are dancers, who provide the landlord with oil for the lamps and sweep his house and grounds clean every day and must look after the elephant stable and apply medicines as necessary. Among them are also Dureas who fill the place of Majoraals in the villages and come under the Vidanes of Gattere.[3] This caste has no honour of white linen and the Gangavos wash for them.

Pally[4] are washers for the abovementioned lime burners and Berrevais.[5] They are not on this side but rather in the land of Kandy. They have no honour in the world, nor do the four following.

Hunniwo[6] are washers of the aforementioned Chalia caste; they must also bring leaves for the elephant stable and they are under the Vidanes of Gattere.

Gangawo[7] are washers of the castes Heery[8] and Olias.[9]

Padoewo[10] have among them Dureas or Nancquedans,[11] Deccumcareas, lascarines and coolies and are placed under Vidanes.

Palleroe[12] are forest rovers who live in the woods and in or under the earth; the four last enjoy no honours whatsoever.

The Hiene Jaty[13] and *Antere Jaty*[14] } Two castes who have no esteem whatsoever in the world, being not reckoned among the other castes and held as the lowest of all.

The first of these two, also called Kinneas[15] belong under Vidane, weave fine mats or *Ballales*[16] out of which they pay their Deccum.

The second sort, called Rodias,[17] are the lowest in rank, have no Vidanes or chiefs and live in the *Caepajeme*,[18] being a type of house

---

[1] *Gangavō* (Sinh.). [2] *Oliyō* (Sinh.).
[3] *Gattara* (Sinh.). A low caste probably descended from Tamil captives.
[4] *Palī* (Sinh.). [5] *Berevāyō* (Sinh.). See p. 77 n. 11.
[6] *Hināva* or *Hinnivō* (Sinh.). [7] *Gangavō* (Sinh.). [8] *Hiyāri* (Sinh.). See p. 77 n. 13.
[9] *Oliyō* (Sinh.). See n. 2. [10] *Pāduvō* (Sinh.).
[11] Misprint for Mancquedans. [12] *Pallaru* (Sinh.).
[13] *Hīna Jāti* (Sinh.). Literally 'low caste'. [14] *Antara Jāti* (Sinh.).
[15] *Kinnaru* (Sinh.). [16] Probably a misprint for *kalāla* (Sinh.), a mat woven from hemp.
[17] *Rodiyā* (Sinh.). [18] Probably *kupāya* (Sinh.).

which has neither walls nor posts at the corners as both roofs come to the ground and have only a half roof so that one side rests on the ground, and they may not live in any other type of house. They may not play a tambourine or tom-tom covered on both sides but only on one side. They eat dead animals and make cords of cow and buffalo hide into snares to catch elephants, etc. They may not have even the smallest bit of white linen on their head and must tie up their hair above in the middle of their heads.

Mantris. Counsellors. These give counsel in matters of importance and otherwise, being next to the King in administration, on whose death such a Mantri is also the next to take on the administration in place of the son (if he is yet a minor) and if there is no son he rules with the other counsellors till another King is installed.

From them also come their priests, temple officials, doctors, surgeons, teachers or *Ragegoeroe*,[1] soothsayers, astronomers, pilgrims and hermits.

Welinde[2] or *Chittys*[3] are merchants and, as soon as there is something to be traded in, a Paele Chitty[4] is called in who has to transact business even for the King both by sea and by land. But among these merchants are four different castes who earn a living each by dealing in particular goods, namely:

1. *The Chittys.* They deal in all kinds of medicines, cloth, ships and also sail, each according to his ability.
2. *The Caver Chittys.*[5] They deal in gold and silver, also assaying and valuing them.
3. *The Comety Chittys.*[6] They deal in all kinds of fruits, grains, vegetables and cooked food.
4. *The Waligi Chittys.*[7] They deal in all kinds of corals, finger and arm rings made of *chank,* glass, earth, lead, tin, copper or any other metals.

These four sorts of merchants have one script and language and are

---

[1] *Rājaguru* (Sinh. and Tam.)—royal priest.
[2] *Vēlanda* (Sinh.).   [3] *Chetty* (Tam.).
[4] There are a number of subcastes among the merchant caste of *chetty*. This particular one is unidentifiable.
[5] *Kāveri Chetty* (Tam.).   [6] *Kōmatti Chetty* (Tam. and Telugu).
[7] Cannot be identified. Probably *Vadugai Chetty* or *Balija Chetty.*

not native to Ceylon but are from the opposite coast and in time have multiplied.

These four types of Chittys will not eat with each other, nor even intermarry, that is, the higher caste not with the lower, except that some do it for wealth. But the lower will eat with one who is higher and also take his daughter in marriage.

Goy[1] or *Bellales*.[2] They are two words which signify one and the same thing, namely an agriculturalist. The first word says it in Cingalese and the latter in Tamil. The word Handaeroevo,[3] that is honourable or pure, is also added to it. Among this caste are different sorts, each of whom knows what its work is, of which the four most important are:

1. *Bandares*[4] or *Adassing*,[5] being those who are at court as courtiers, counts or even princes of the royal family.
2. *Mantrioenoe*,[6] who are next to the King as highest counsellors at the court and serve as deputies.
3. *Maendellyperoe*.[7] They become Modeljaars, Adigars and Dessaves, though they are mostly in the militia.
4. *Goyperoe*.[8] They are found both in the militia and as cultivators.

Besides this there are still nine other sorts of Bellales who are obliged to work for their King both at court and in the Gabadas[9] or dispense villages (called Batgamme[10] by them) but to no other service (as one sees below).

1. *Wanneweddes*[11] are wild hunters, living in the forest, with their own princes as they do on the island of Ceylon in the land of the Wanny,[12] though they are under the King and now under the Company, but they are obliged no further by agreement than to contribute yearly and appear with tusked elephants. Among them are two sorts of Weddas: the one who wear leaves on their bodies, and the other called Ritipatte[13] or wildmen of the trees

---

[1] *Goviyā* or *Goyigama* (Sinh.).   [2] *Vellāla* (Tam.).
[3] *Handuruvō* or *Hamuduruvō* (Sinh.).
[4] *Bandāra* (Sinh.).   [5] *Adahasin* (Sinh.).
[6] *Mantriunnē* (Sinh.).   [7] *Mudali pēruva* (Sinh.).   [8] *Goviya pēruva* (Sinh.).
[9] *Gabadā* (Sinh.). *Gabadagam*—a royal village.
[10] *Batgama* (Sinh.). Dispense villages were villages where the cultivated produce was taken for royal consumption.
[11] *Vanavadda* (Sinh.).   [12] Vanni, in north-central and north-eastern Ceylon.
[13] *Rittapatta* (Sinh.). Bark of the Ritta tree.

because they wear the bark of trees, being beaten soft, round the body and have houses fully made of leaves of trees, both men and women eating nothing but the flesh of elk, deer, etc. which they keep in honey in a hollow tree. Their weapons consist of bow and arrows and, when they are in need of arrows, they bring as much iron as is required with a loin of elk's flesh or of venison and a model of the arrow which they want and place these in the night before the smith's door and after waiting 3 or 4 days, as they reckon it will be ready, return with yet another leg of wild flesh to the former place and, if they find their arrow lying there complete, they place the leg there by night and depart quietly without speaking to anyone. But if the smith neglects this they will do him all possible harm.[1]

2. *Diegaranno*,[2] are those who search for precious stones from rivers and springs where they are found.

3. *Mallacarao*.[3] They are suppliers of flowers with which they should provide the court daily.

4. *Dala Moerecareo*[4] are betel or arecanut suppliers.

5. *Hoenkiricareo*.[5] They are milk suppliers with which they should provide the court daily.

6. *Dadeweddes*[6] are hunters.

7. *Goddegarranno*[7] who search for precious stones of the land out of the ground.

8. *Batgamwelle Etto*.[8] They are sowers of the Royal Gabaddas or dispense villages.

9. *Gombadoecareo*[9] are herdsmen who look after the cows and bring grain and other wares with them for the King.

Though these are now divided into so many sorts, they constitute but one caste, Bellales. But the most important and those who are but one grade higher will not eat with the lesser in their festivals or elsewhere, nor give them their daughters in marriage. But a lesser one will take the daughter from a superior one. They sow and mow and all their distinction consists only in the service they have at the court of the king, though they sometimes look to wealth in their marriage.

[1] This piece of Vedda social history was recorded by many contemporary writers on Ceylon. See Knox p. 62, Ribeiro p. 171, Queyroz I, 17.

[2] *Diyagarannō* (Sinh.). [3] *Mālākārayō* (Sinh.). [4] *Dalamurukārayō* (Sinh.).
[5] *Hunukirikārayō* (Sinh.). [6] *Dadavadda* (Sinh.). [7] *Godagarannō* (Sinh.).
[8] *Batgamvelle Ettō* (Sinh.). [9] *Gombadukārayā* (Sinh.).

When a King is crowned, then all the four most important castes must be present, such as *Raja, Bronne*[1] *Welende* and *Goy*, by which four persons of different caste the royal crown is taken and set on the King's head.[2]

According to their wealth and qualifications, the two aforementioned castes may enjoy royal honours, except the adorning of white linen, the white sombreiro (or umbrella) called Moetoekanda[3] by them and adorned from below and above with white linen, either in a *Catapaenel*[4] or otherwise, which honour belongs only to the King, and such others as he will permit on their festivals.

Besides these there are Bellales who are subject to 5 or 6 different services, down to coolies who are of low and poor origins. But the rich and most important attain all kinds of great offices at the court according to their conducting themselves and according to the faithful service of their forefathers to the King.

The officers under the Dessavaship of Mature are the following ten:

1. *Adigar.*[5] He is as a second to the Dessave who does everything the Dessave orders and gives him first-hand information of all matters. He attends to the welfare of the land everywhere, taking care that no one is oppressed by the lesser chiefs, of which the Dessave himself must take note, as he also should to similar activities of the Adigar. Also the Adigar must look after all the necessities for the service of the Lord of the Land.

2. *Modeljaar.*[6] He is like a Captain, having under him 3 or 4 *nantjes*[7] or bands of lascarines, each of which *nantjes* consists of 1 Araatsje, 2 Canganes and 24 lascarines or native soldiers, who must be always ready for war and relieve each other from their guard-duty every 14 or 30 days.

3. *Mohotirales*[8] or *Mahatiaars*[9] are certain writers at the court, of the sort that there are now 4 in Mature under the Dessave,

---

[1] *Bamunu* (Sinh.)—Brahmin.
[2] This is the Sinhalese version of the Brahmanical four *Varnas*: Brahmin, Kshatriya, Vaisya and Sūdra.
[3] *Mutukuda* (Sinh.)—the pearl umbrella, royal insignia.
[4] Probably from an Indian language, through Portuguese, meaning a large, open boat.
[5] *Adigar* (Sinh.). In the later Kandyan system, the *adigār* is a superior officer to the Dissava, being something like a chief minister to the king.
[6] *Mudaliyār* (Sinh. and Tam.).   [7] Probably of Portuguese origin.
[8] *Mohotirālē* (Sinh.).   [9] *Mohotiār* (Sinh.).

of whom Attepatte Mahatiaar[1] must continuously be with the Dessave to write all *olas*[2] or papers, acts, letters, *placaats*[3] and ordinances that come up, for which he gets his payment. Also the other Mahatiaars must always be present, though each has his own special service and, what their special service is, is seen in the following:

Attepatte Mahatiaar has under him the roll of the maintenance allowance to all the chiefs and lascarines, as also of craftsmen in the District of Mature and what each of them enjoys from the Lord of the Land, as also their freely given Parvenies[4] which they possess hereditarily. This Mahatiaar must always be ready for the exchange of such *olas* as may happen in the Mature Dessavany.

Of the other Mahatiaars should one (apart from him who must write for the Dessave) collect the Mahanadapoe[5] and Marale[6] (certain taxes), another the Madapo[7] and Faros,[8] and the third the Araak[9] (all being taxes of the land). Every year particular Mahatiaars are chosen by the Dessave to investigate the annual difference as they are not to be trusted too much.

4. *Toepairale*[10] or the interpreters of the Dessave of Mature, who translate to him all the complaints and other native matters.

5. *Apohamis.*[11] This is actually not an office but they are sons of the black chiefs who were named Apohamis. They go to the court also as young courtiers and there are among them those who have 2 bands of lascarines under them who are Mohemdirems and must do guard duty.

6. *Mohemdirems.*[12] They are chiefs who have 2 bands of lascarines under them, do guard duty and must go wherever they are ordered in war.

7. *Badde Corene*[13] or *Cornerale.*[14] He is like a Cangany of the Adigar under whom he is; has 2 bands of lascarines and must do guard

---

[1] *Attapattu Mohotiār* (Sinh.).   [2] *Olai* (Tam.)—palm leaf used for writing.
[3] Dutch—an edict or proclamation.
[4] *Paravēni* (Sinh. from Tam.). A heritable piece of landed property.
[5] *Mahānadappu* (Sinh.). A tax paid by village headmen to the king.
[6] *Marala* (Sinh.). Death duty.   [7] Probably *Nadappu* (Sinh.).
[8] Probably *Foros*, a Portuguese tax or quit-rent collected in Ceylon.
[9] *Arecanut.* A portion of the nuts produced by the areca tree was due to the king as tax.
[10] *Thupahirālē* (Sinh.). *Thupahi* from *Dubash* (Hindi)—two languages.
[11] *Apuhāmy* (Sinh.).   [12] *Muhāndiram* (Sinh. and Tam.).
[13] *Baddakarana* (Sinh.).   [14] *Karanarālē* (Sinh.).

duty and also attend to everything that the Adigar orders and must also stand ready with his men to proceed at the slightest command.

8. *Araatsje*, like a Sargeant, each one having one band of lascarines under him, though they stand under their superiors.

9. *Canganys* or corporals coming under their Araatsjes.

10. *Lascarines* or messengers, being native soldiers who enjoy some maintenance and because of this must always be ready.

The taxes of the land also have different names among the Cingalese, such as:

Mahanadapoe, that is the great incomes of the land such as from the Dolosdas Corle which is called thus.

Nadappoe. Another tax of the land which is collected like the former but this is from the Billigam[1] and Morrua Corle.[2]

Marale. This is a tax of the Lord of the Land where he claims a third of the goods of one deceased on account of the deceased having possessed the lands from the King or the Lord of the Land, which is now collected by the Company for itself from all who live in the district of Mature, though not from Christians and only from heathens.

Basnaicke,[3] the first spokesman of the language.[4] He was called Cangany in Cingalese, among whom there are bonded and free. He is the head of the Pagoda at Dondere called Devinouere, that well known holy city. The subject people of all sorts must pay yearly their head and life money, except those who are bonded to the temple, as at Mature, which tax is called in Cingalese Dewallebadde.[5] Besides this obligation and the obligatory service there are still others placed under 18 Vidanes, from old times, as at Mature, and which will be seen hereafter in the description of the lesser castes.

Sabandoe,[6] or the Sjahbandaar like the one at Beligam who is chief of this place, having under himself 3 writers who must give account of the monthly feudal dues at Mature, where he himself must appear every month and all people in his jurisdiction.

---

[1] *Weligam Kōralē.*   [2] *Morawak Kōralē.*   [3] *Basnāyaka* (Sinh.).
[4] In the sense of Chief Interpreter.   [5] *Devālēbadda* (Sinh.).
[6] From *Shahbunder* (Persian), a collector of dues at the port. The term was Sinhalised to *Sahabandu.*

Gaginaicke,[1] the head of the Mature elephant stables, under whose supervision are the animals and the provision of sufficient fodder which is looked after by the servants appointed thereto and they are under the Vidanies of the Mature *ettele.*[2] He must also look after the animals stationed in Dekwelle and elsewhere and moreover he must show annual account of the incomes, occupying now the position of Wedderale.[3]

Etbandenne[4] or Elephant-children, that is the elephant trappers. They belong to the elephant hunt to which all these people belong as under the other Vidanies, also Deccumcareas or those who pay life tax. They must provide a certain number of elephants yearly.

The further big and small Vidanies, the land taxes and those of the villages, and their names are as follows:

Kottalbadde[5] or *Audebadde*[6] are Vidanies of the smiths who are now served by a Vidani under which belong all iron smiths who are required to work for the Lord of the Land among whom are also Deccumcareas.

Dewalebadde, a Vidani which comes under the temple called Dewondere,[7] called Dewalebadde in Cingalese, from the word Dewale which means a temple. To this belongs not only all subject to service but also all sorts of craftsmen, both high and low-castes and Deccumcareo.

Roenebadde,[8] that is the taxes of the interior under which Vidani belong the Chalia caste of cinnamon peelers who do not have one place or village but different villages where they live.

Wellalesaroe[9]
Adigaar-saroe[10]
Matere Magisaroe[11] They are also taxes on the land which the
Reyganbandegesaroe[12] inhabitants must pay yearly.
Oenoenchivillesaroe[13]
Gongebadesaroe[14]

---

[1] *Gajanāyaka* (Sinh.).   [2] *Attala* (Sinh.). A place where elephants are kept.
[3] *Vedarāla* (Sinh.).   [4] *Etbandenna* (Sinh.).
[5] *Kottalbadda* (Sinh.).—Artificers' Department.
[6] *Handebadda* (Sinh.)—Department of Carpenters and Weavers.
[7] Devundara or Devinuvara in Dondra.   [8] *Ruhunabadda* (Sinh.).
[9] *Vellalesāru* (Sinh.). Saru—tax.   [10] *Adigārsāru* (Sinh.).
[11] Unidentifiable, probably *Mātara Magisāru.*   [12] *Rayigambandagēsāru* (Sinh.).
[13] Unidentifiable. Probably *Ununchivillesāru.*   [14] *Gangebadasāru* (Sinh.).

Vidanes are the overseers of the villages who must see that no inhabitants suffer any oppression and that the land is sown in time and everything is harvested, of all of which they must give the Lord of the Land account in respect of his revenue.

Patticareo Deckme.[1] They are herders of cattle who milk the animals, called Bojeros by the Portuguese. They pay yearly Deccum or life tax and, if the Lord of the Land will have milk instead, they must give it.

Caraeu Deckme.[2] This is a tax on Betel[3] gardens of Mature which is paid yearly.

Polwatte Piedie.[4] This is a tax on Mature coconut gardens within the four gravettes[5] by which annually half a stuyver[6] is collected for 10 fruitbearing trees.

Malidoewepittigay,[7] being the tax from a special low caste, called Hangereme[8] who tap the *jager* or *Niepere*[9] trees, but they do not live in one place and are spread out here and there in the villages and Corles.

Canoemoeldenie Pitagawa,[10] being a tax from the land like the former.

Radebadda,[11] being a tax which the washers pay yearly.

Sajakarabadde.[12] They are also washers, but they dye and paint cloth and some also wash and they pay deccum yearly.

Oedoegangattere[13] and *Welligamgattere.*[14] They are two Vidanies under whom are also certain people who must pay annual life tax.

Kinnerebadde.[15] This is one of the lowest castes which must pay Deccum of fine mats or *caleles*[16] which they weave or otherwise must pay yearly a certain sum of money.

From this then one sees described in detail the most important officers who are in the District of Mature.

---

[1] *Paticārayō Dakum* (Sinh.).   [2] *Saruva Dakum* (Sinh.).

[3] Gardens of the betel vine from which leaves are taken to chew with arecanuts: *bulath* (Sinh.).

[4] *Polvatta Pīdi* (Sinh.). Pol—coconut.   [5] Four districts adjoining the Mātara fort.

[6] Dutch copper coin, 16 of which make a Guilder or Dutch florin.

[7] *Malidūva Pitiga* (Sinh.).   [8] *Hangarammu* (Sinh.).

[9] *Nipah* (Malay) *Nipa fruticans*. A variety of palm whose sap was used for making toddy and vinegar.

[10] Unidentifiable.   [11] *Radabadda* (Sinh.).   [12] *Sayakārabadda* (Sinh.).

[13] *Udugangattara* (Sinh.).   [14] *Weligamgattara* (Sinh.).

[15] *Kinnarabadda* (Sinh.).   [16] *Kalāla* (Sinh.)—mat.

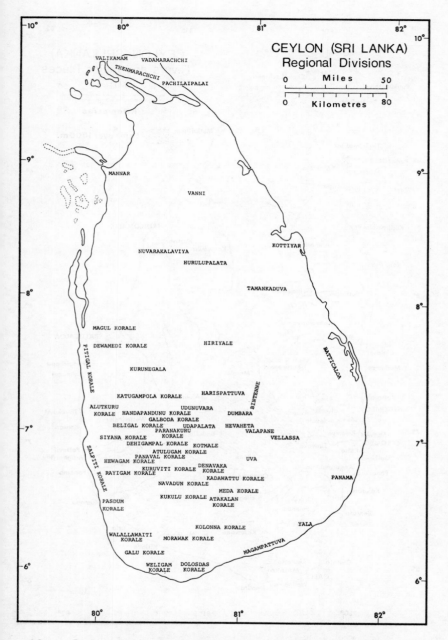

Map 1. Ceylon, sketch map showing district divisions of the 18th century

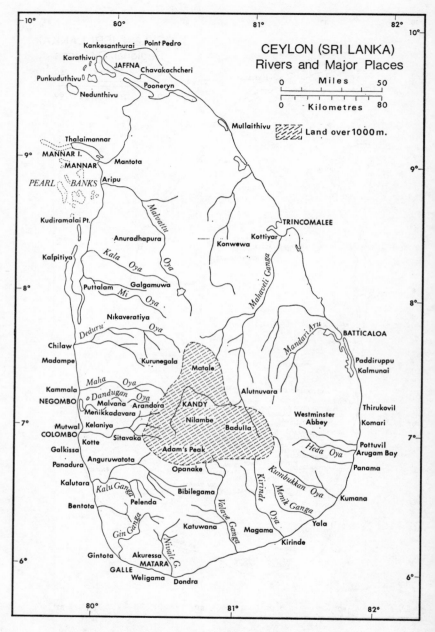

Map 2. Ceylon, sketch map showing major ports and towns

DESCRIPTION OF THE ISLAND
CEYLON: EIGHTH BOOK

First Chapter

[Geography]

Description of the island Ceylon. Arrangement. Name of the island. Ceylon proved to be Taprobana of the ancients. Latitude and Longitude. Boundaries. Shape. Size. Various writers on Ceylon. Among whom Baldeaus and Knox are outstanding. Also Joan Ribeyro. Ceylon divided into different Kingdoms. Their names. And Princedoms, Earldoms, Marquisates and Domains. Modern division into six Kingdoms. Their names. Names of the Princedoms. Earldoms, Marquisates and Domains. The 34 major districts. And 33 lesser districts. Coastal towns on the east side. Three great cities of the interior. Smaller interior cities. Rivers. Land form. Wonderful seasons there. Earthquakes. Map of Ceylon. City of Gale described and two maps of it. Gindere, a market town. Bakwelle and Gannegamme. Kosdoewa. Reygam. Madampe. The towns Billitotte and Maplagam. The villages Bentote. Alican. Verberin Island. Makoene town and Pelando village. The Fort Caleture. Angretotte and Panadure. Galkisse town. Cotta. Colombo city. Governor's house and other buildings in Colombo, shown in map. Governor and other officers described. Malwana, Reygamwatte, Groewabli and Matuwaal. Nigumbo Fort. The towns Camel, Arrunderi, Alanha, Marabel and Medampe. The town Chilauw. The town Corinde Coanwatte. Calpentyn Island. With the villages Maripo and Televari. The town Navacar. And the Calpentyn Fort. The towns Portaloan and Caddaumatris. The village Golgom. The island Grudumale. The town Aripen. The village Musalipatte. The island Manaar. The Fort shown in a map. Villages there. Manaar City. The villages Tottevalli, Eckelampatti, Carcel, St. Peter, Peixala, Tellemanaar, Peringale, Vellipatta, Palicoera and Calimoni.

Description of
the island
Ceylon

As Ceylon is one of the largest islands of the East Indies, it is also one of the most important and first governments which the Company has there and possesses by force of arms.

Arrangement of
description

To get a correct knowledge of it, we shall describe the island with the utmost detail, so far as is known to us, thereafter the events that have happened there from ancient times under the Cingalese, and further under the Portuguese and under us.

The name of
this island

The island is now called by us Ceylon (by some Seylaan and Zeylan[1]), by the Persians and Arabs Serindib, also sometimes Serandib, Serandive and Selandive[2] (which means the island of Ceylon, as the word Dive[3] means an island) and by the ancients Taprobana.[4]

With regard to the last, namely Taprobana, we have already spoken of it in the introduction to our work *Old and New East Indies*.[5] Here we deal with it in greater detail, narrating different opinions of geographers on Taprobana of Ptolemy, with reasons which we give that this is no other than the island of Ceylon; and also of the different names given to its cinnamon by different people.

Ceylon shown
to be Taprobana
of old

Many have stated that the island of Sumatra was the Taprobana of old.

Pliny,[6] speaking of Taprobana, says that it was 6000 stadia in length and 5000 in breadth, that it was believed to be a new world, and was first discovered at the time of the

---

[1] Dutch variation of 'Ceylon'.

[2] Arab versions of their name for Ceylon. Probably derived from Sinhala dīpa—island of the Sinhalese. Ibn Battuta, the famous Arab traveller who visited Ceylon in 1344, called it Serendib.

[3] *Dvīpa* (Skt.), *Dīpa* (Pali), *Thīvu* (Tam.).

[4] The classical Greek and Roman name for Ceylon. This name is discussed later in the text in great detail.

[5] Valentijn I, Chap. IV, pp. 42–7.

[6] From here till p. 174 Valentijn has relied extensively on Diogo do Couto's *Decadas da Asia*. Portuguese text in *Decadas da Asia. Escritar per Diogo do Couto*. Tome 1, Que Contem as Decadas IV and V. Offerecidas Ao Thomas da Silva Teller, Lisbon MDCCXXXVI. Decadas Quinto—Livro Primeiro Capituto VII, pp. 312–17. English translation of the section on Ceylon in Donald Ferguson. Transl. and Ed. *The history of Ceylon, from the earliest times to 1600 A.D. As related by Joao de Barros and Diogo de Couto. Journal of the Ceylon Branch of the Royal Asiatic Society*, 1908. XX, 60 (Colombo, 1909). The sections from which Valentijn has borrowed are on pages 80–90. See Introduction to present work pp. 44–6. Subsequent references are to the Ferguson edition.

Emperor Claudius to whom the King of this island also had sent ambassadors, but the ships which went there were not steered by the stars as they could not see the Pole.[1]

Strabo, speaking of Taprobana, describes it to be as big as does Pliny.[2]

Onesicritus, one of the captains of Alexander the Great who sailed the coast of India, says that Taprobana is 5000 stadia large, without saying if it was long or broad, and that it is separated by Prasis[3] above the Ganges, a sailing of 20 days, and that between it and India are many other islands but that it lies more to the south than all other islands.[4]

Arrian,[5] in his treatise on Indian navigation, says that those who depart from the coast of Comora[6] and Poduca[7] have to go to an island, situated to the west, called Palla Simonda[8] and by the ancients Taprobana, which they held for a new world and was very well known in their time and that the largest elephants of India were born there.

Eratosthenes,[9] a Greek author, says that the island Taprobana is in the eastern sea, between East and West on the border of India and situated 20 days' journey from Persia.

Ptolemy,[10] in his Tables, places the island Taprobana on the coast of India, opposite the Cape Comori, which he puts at $13\frac{1}{2}$ degrees north and *Pliny* calls it the promontory of

---

[1] Roman historian Pliny (A.D. 23–79) described Taprobana, generally accepted as referring to Ceylon, in his *Naturalis Historia*, VI, C22 (24). See *Ancient India, as described in Classical Literature*. Translated and copiously annotated by J. W. McCrindle (Westminster, 1901), pp. 102–6.

[2] Strabo (Greek geographer and historian, b. *circa* 63 B.C.), *Geographica* I, 63 xv 690, McCrindle, *Ancient India* ... pp. 20, 90.

[3] To classical geographers, the central plains of Hindustan along the banks of the Ganges was known as Prasii or Prasiaca.

[4] Onesicritus, Alexander's admiral, is quoted by Strabo. McCrindle, *Ancient India* ... p. 20.

[5] Arrian, Greek historian and philosopher (A.D. 96–180). Author of *Indica*. See R. C. Majumdar *The Classical Accounts of India* (Calcutta, 1960), p. 5.

[6] Kumari or Cape Comorin on the southern tip of India.

[7] Identified as Pondichery on the southeastern coast of India.

[8] Ceylon was known to the early classical writers by the name Palae Simondu. Its origin is obscure, but a plausible explanation is that it was derived from Pārasamudra, by which name it was known in Sanskrit literature.

[9] Greek astronomer, geographer and mathematician (c. 276–192 B.C.). Author of *Geographica*. Arrian's *Indica* was based on this work which is no longer extant.

[10] Claudius Ptolemy's *Guide to Geography* VII. 4 (2nd century A.D.).

Colaicum[1] and says that it was formerly called Sunoda.[2] But in his time it had the name Salica[3] and the natives were called Selim,[4] the island having a length of 930,000 stadia or 210 Portuguese miles. Also he says that there was much rice, honey, ginger, precious stones, hyacinths and other sorts and also metal here, all of which are to be found only in the island of Ceylon.

There are also geographers who hold that Sumatra is Taprobana.

Michael Poggius,[5] the Florentine, private secretary to the Pope and a very learned man, has described, on the order of the Pope, the journey of Nicolaas de Conti, a Venetian, through the entire Indies to Cathay and has stated there that this Venetian had been to the island of Sumatra, the Taprobana of the ancients.

Maximilian of Sevenbergen,[6] private secretary to the Emperor, remarks in a letter to the Cardinal of Salzburg, where he gives an account of the first voyage of the Portuguese to India, that they had been to the coast of Calicut and that from there they had left for Sumatra, named Taprobana by the ancients.

Benedictus Bardone,[7] in his description of the island says that the island of Madagascar or that of St. Laurens is 1300 thousand stadia to the west of Ceylon and 1800 thousand stadia to the south of Taprobana, all of which we find in more geographers whom we now pass over.

Joan de Barros,[8] a very learned geographer, says of the

---

[1] Probably the port Colchi near Cape Comorin.

[2] Couto has Simonda, a more accurate version.

[3] A later classical name for Ceylon. Probably derived from Sihala.

[4] Couto has Salim.

[5] Couto has Micer Pogio. Poggio Bracciolini (1340–1459), the Papal Secretary under Pope Eugenius IV. Nicolo di Conti, the 15th century Venetian traveller, was ordered by the Pope truthfully to relate his travels to the Papal Secretary Poggio. Poggio published a monumental *Historiae de varietate fortunae.* The fourth book contains the Travels of Nicolo Conti in the East.

[6] Maximilian I (1597–1651), Duke of Bavaria and Lord High Steward of the Holy Roman Empire. Couto has Maximilian Transylvanus.

[7] Benedetto Bordone, Venetian author of *Insulari di Benedetto Bordone nel qual si ragiona de tutte l'Isole del mondo,* Vinegia, 1528.

[8] João de Barros (1496–1570). Portuguese nobleman who held several offices in the colonial service, but not in the east. Author of *Asia de João de Barros dos*

island of Ceylon that it is the Taprobana of Ptolemy, as he in his map of the world shows in greater detail, which has disappeared after his death, and is to be deemed a great loss.

The authority of this writer alone is enough to prove that Ceylon is Taprobana, adding to this that Ptolemy has placed the island from the Ganges inwards on the coast of India, which cannot be taken to be Sumatra which is so far out from the Ganges.[1] We will also show further that they all speak of Ceylon and not of Sumatra.

Pliny[2] says that Taprobana is 6000 stadia in length and that it was discovered at the time of the Emperor Claudius by a freed slave of Annius Ploclamius[3] who, sailing along the Arabian coast in a ship driven by the west winds, was brought in 15 days along Caramanien[4] and finally arrived in Taprobana, where he was well received by the King of the island, to whom he presented some minted Roman coins on which the Emperor's image was imprinted, and that on his departure this King sent some ambassadors with him to the Emperor. Now it remains for us to show further that Ceylon is this island.

With regard to the size of the island, it is the same as Ptolemy gives as he puts it in his map as two degrees south of the Equator. For it appears that in his time it was that size and the natives confirm and hold this for certain from their writings that this island had been so large, that it was united to the Maldive Islands and that the sea has in time cut it off on this side, covering it with water in the position in which one sees it today. And that the higher ports are separated into many islands as they now lie in a great stretch behind one another, which stretch the sailors generally call the south-east and the northwest where they say are more than 13000

---

fector que os Portuguesos fizeram no descobrimento & conquista dos mares & terras do Oriento, published in Lisbon in 1552 to 1563.

[1] Barros discusses this issue in Decada III Bk. 11, Chap. i, subtitled: In which is described the position and things of the island of Ceilam which the ancients call Taprobana. See Ferguson, pp. 29–32.

[2] McCrindle, *Ancient India* . . . pp. 103–4. This whole section is an exact translation of Couto. See Couto pp. 82–4.

[3] Annius Plocamus, as correctly stated by Couto.

[4] Carmania. The south coast of Persia.

islands[1] (though by others are reckoned 11000, formerly having been united to each other[2]) and even in Ptolemy's time (who flourished in A.D. 143) it appears that the sea had begun to cause destruction because he says that in the region of Taprobana were 1368 islands.[3] And the freedman of Annius, having sailed with the wind in 15 days from Arabia to Taprobana, is clearly seen to speak of Ceylon which lies 500 miles from the Arabian coast which is more than one can sail in 15 days. Also this island is on the Indian coast beyond Caramanien, and Sumatra is outside the whole of India and many miles beyond the Ganges and one needs another 15 days to go only from Ceylon to Sumatra even though one sails always with the wind.

Apart from all these reasons, we find in Ceylon remains of Roman buildings from which it appears that they have had intercourse with this island. Also there are coins, brought by the freed slave, to be found here. For in the time of Joan de Mello de Sampay, Captain of Manaar (in the island of Ceylon) A.D. 1574 or 1575,[4] some buildings were excavated there on the other side in the lands of Mantotte, which shows till today very large ruins and pieces of a Roman building or marble work, from which the workmen shifted a stone from below on one part of the foundation, and on turning it over they found an iron chain of such a wonderful and stately make that there is in the whole of India no artisan who can dare to undertake to make one similar. They also found three copper coins, one entirely worn out and one of gold entirely worn out underneath. On the other side they discovered a portrait of a man from the breast upwards with a part of an inscription on the side and in the beginning the letter C, but the rest of the contents effaced, and an inscription round the side in which could still be seen the letters R.M.N.R.

This chain and medal were brought to Joan de Mello who valued them very highly and took them with him to Portugal to give them to the King. But he perished on the homeward

---

[1] Couto has 30,000 islands.

[2] This parenthesis is a Valentijn original, not to be found in Couto.

[3] Couto has 1378 islands.

[4] An error in Couto reproduced by Valentijn. João de Mello was Captain of Mannar in the 1580's.

journey in A.D. 1591 with the ship St. Bernardo together with the ship Ban Tehis[1] on which was Manuel de Souza de Coutinho who had served out his time as Viceroy.

Now it is possible that these medals were those which the freed slave of Annius had brought there and that in the period of 6 months when he was in that island had given orders to build this building in the Roman style and in the foundation had thrown the medals, a custom that is common in Europe.

Diego de Couto,[2] chronicler of the Kings of Spain, having seen these medals and many other inscriptions, was of opinion that the letter C is the first name of Claudius and that the faded part was Keyser, for the remaining R.M.N.R. appear to say clearly Der Romeynen.[3]

Another coin was found in the Indies of Castilians,[4] or the Philippines, which Pedro Colon discovered (according to the narrative of Lucius Marinus, the Sicilian,[5] in his book of the Memorable Things of Spain, in the Lives of Catholic Kings[6]) when uncovering similar marbles, with the portrait of Emperor Augustus.

This coin was held by Don Joan Rufo, Bishop of Cuenca[7] and he sent it to the Pope from which Lucius Maximus[8] concludes that the Romans had sailed to all these parts of the world.

If it is true, as Hector de Lagena[9] says, that in the time of Pope Paul a piece of cinnamon wood was found (which was preserved by the Romans as something valuable) which appears from its inscription to have been there at the time

[1] Couto has *Bom Jesus.*

[2] Diogo de Couto, Portuguese historian of Asia. See Introduction, pp. 28–9.

[3] Couto pp. 83–4. Valentijn spoils the whole argument of Couto who interprets this inscription to mean Imperator Romanorum. He says the word 'Imperator' has faded away and R.M.N.R. is the abbreviation for Romanorum.

[4] That is, the Spanish Indies.

[5] Couto has Lucius Marinaeus Siculus. This is Lucio Marineo, the Sicilian (1440–1536).

[6] The work referred to is *Obra conquesta pur Lucio Marineo coro nista d'sus majestades de las cosas memorables de Espana,* MDXXXIII.

[7] Couto has Dom Joao Rufo, Archbishop of Cuenca.

[8] Error for Marinaeus, see n. 5 above.

[9] Both Couto and Valentijn are in error here. The reference is to Dr. Andres de Laguna (d. 1560). Author of *Pedacio Dioscorides Anaçarbeo, acerca de la Materia Medicina,* Salamanca, 1566.

of Emperor Arcadius, son of Theodosius, who was living in A.D. 397 which is 126 years after the time of Claudius, it could well be that it was brought by the above mentioned ambassadors as a present to the Emperor when they came to Rome with the freed slave.

Leaving Pliny, let us go over to Onesicritus.

He says[1] that Taprobana was of 5000 stadia and that it was separated from Prasis above the Ganges by a voyage of 20 days and that between India and it there were many islands but that it lay more to the south than all the others.

As far as its size is concerned, he agrees with Ptolemy. That it was separated from the Ganges by a 20 day voyage and that there were many islands between it and India, shows clearly that he speaks of Ceylon. For there are as many sailing days from the Ganges, it is to the south of the whole coast of India and the many islands of which he speaks are Mamale[2] (or the Maldives) and everything else to which Ptolemy refers, while Sumatra is east of India, separated from it by a great distance.

Arrian,[3] by saying that one leaving from the coast of Camare and Poduce westwards will arrive at Taprobana, very clearly speaks of Ceylon. For Ptolemy puts Camara and Poduce on $14\frac{1}{2}$ degrees on the coast of India from Cape Comorin inwards, which appears to be St. Thome[4] or Nagapatnam.[5] For those departing from this coast to find Ceylon must sail westwards and to Sumatra eastwards and one knows that Ceylon has the largest elephants in India, as Arrian also testifies. It is true that all other elephants recognise its great superiority, so that on seeing a Ceylonese elephant they run away terrified, as one sees here daily in the city of Goa among elephants which the king has brought to his stalls from different lands.[6]

[1] Arrian, Chap. 10, Sec. 5. McCrindle, *Ancient India* . . . p. 20.

[2] Maladivu or Maldives, about 500 miles southwest of Ceylon. Some authorities think that Portuguese used the term Mamale to mean Laccadives, nearer to the west coast of India.

[3] Majumdar, *Classical accounts* . . . p. 5.

[4] San Thome, about four miles south of the modern Madras.

[5] South of San Thome on the Coromandel Coast.

[6] This statement is based on the personal experience of Couto, a Portuguese who lived many years in Goa, which Valentijn has directly copied. The state-

Eratosthenes, a Greek writer, says that Taprobana is in the eastern sea between east and west and that it is separated from Persia by a journey of 20 days opposite the coast of India.

He speaks more clearly of Ceylon, that it lies 8 degrees to the north between east and west and that with a strong wind and light ship it takes not more than 20 days journey from north of the Strait of Persia to come to Ceylon, which makes out 500 miles.

Now Sumatra lies not in the eastern sea but below the Equator, from which we have shown clearly that Ceylon is rightly Taprobana of the ancients.

Let us go over to the contemporary writers who make Sumatra of Taprobana. They all, seeking this island Taprobana below the Equator, where Ptolemy put it (because, as we said, he in his time placed it two degrees on the southern side) and running through the whole coast of India up to the Ganges and finding nothing other than Sumatra, have made it Taprobana without any further consideration. Likewise they have also placed the River Indus at the mouth of Cambay which error we shall demonstrate later.[1]

Benedictus Bardon[2] refutes Pliny, speaking of Taprobana, where he says that the north is not seen, that is that the North Star or North Pole is not seen in Taprobana, because he says that those who live in Taprobana beside the cape of Colaicum see this star rising 13 degrees and that according to the elevation in which those of this island live they see it rising but that those who live below the Equator can see neither the one Pole nor the other. By this he contradicts himself in making Taprobana Sumatra. The Equator cuts the island of Sumatra through the middle and the island extends no further than 5 degrees towards both Poles. Therefore those who live on the corner of Daja,[3] which is the northernmost,

---

ment sounds absurd, coming from Valentijn, as the Portuguese had left Ceylon in 1658 and therefore elephants were not shipped to the stalls of Goa. Couto, p. 86.

[1] Valentijn repeats this promise of Couto (Couto p. 86), but neither writer fulfils this promise.

[2] Benedetto Bordone, see p. 92 n. 7.

[3] Couto has Daya. The place is unidentifiable. Could it be Acheh? But Valentijn would have been familiar with the correct name of this place.

see this star rise no more than 5 degrees. In the same way those who live on the other extremity on the south side hardly see it, while the opposite is true of Ceylon. For those who live on the extreme corner of Jaffanapatnam[1] see the North Pole rise 8½ degrees and those on the Point Gale (being the southernmost) see it rise 5 degrees. From which it is clear that this last is Taprobana, that it at that time extended up to 2 degrees to the south and that the promontory of Coelaicum of Pliny and of Comorin[2] of Ptolemy is the Cape Comorin. For we must assert without doubt that in this time and for many years thereafter the Kingdom of Ceylon was the greatest of the whole of Malabar and stretched up to the reef or rocks of Chilauw and that as the Cape Comorin was under this kingdom and one of the most famous in the world it was called by Pliny the promontory of Colaicum, or the promontory of the kingdom of Ceylon. And it can well be that Ptolemy called it the promontory of Cori,[3] after Toetoecoryn that was then a great place and visited by many foreigners for which reasons Ptolemy gave to this promontory its name.[4]

For this and other reasons which we pass over, it appears to us that the island of Ceylon is also the same as Sambolo,[5] of which Diodorus Siculus[6] speaks in his second Book of his abridged History[7] and which Baptista Ramutius[8] and others also make out to be Sumatra.

It has given us no small trouble to investigate from what

---

[1] Northernmost point of the island of Ceylon.

[2] Ptolemy has Comori. Kumarimunai or Kanyākumari.

[3] Couto has Titi Cori.

[4] This interpretation which Valentijn copied from Couto (p. 87) is most improbable. Cori was probably derived from Kumari, the Tamil name for the promontory on the southern tip of India. Tuticorin (Valentijn's Toetoecoryn) is a Portuguese version of Thūthukudi, a Tamil name for a port a few miles from Cape Comorin.

[5] Valentijn makes the mistake here of interpreting Couto's Jambulus to mean the name of an island. Couto was referring to an author of that name (p. 87).

[6] Greek historian who lived in the second half of the 1st century B.C.

[7] Diodorus Siculus' *Bibliotheca Historica*.

[8] Couto has Baptista Ramnusio. This is probably Giovanni Battista Ramusio, the editor of a number of volumes of travel accounts, who lived in mid-16th century.

the name Taprobana has its origins, as in the entire island of Ceylon there is not one bay, port, city, village, promontory, spring nor river known by this name or anything similar.[1] Also there is nothing in the chronicle of the Cingalese nor in those of the Canarese, nor in any of their languages is this name known, from which it appears to us to be a Greek name, coined by Ptolemy, which describes some greatness or quality of that island, for which reason also the name of Ceylon was given to that reef on which the Chinese were wrecked near this island, which has become so famous since up to this time, that the island was not called by its own name but by that of the reef. For as the Persians and Arabs sail with difficulty to this island past this reef, they always had it in their minds, saying they went to or came from Cinlao,[2] which means nothing else but that they went to or came from the reef of the Chinese, which letter having changed somewhat in time, there grew the name of Ceylaon or Ceylon.[3]

And since we have been able to uncover, as often as we get the opportunity, the great corruption which time has brought to the proper names of cities, kingdoms, rivers, mountains, herbs, spices and other things of these lands, we will therefore, while we are still on this island, begin here also and show all the different names which the Greeks, Latins, Persians and Arabs have given to the cinnamon of this island, as also all the names which the people of the east have given, from which a great confusion has arisen among the specialists of medicine.

The cinnamon of this island, being the best of the entire east, is called Corundo Potra,[4] that is Bark-tree, for which

[1] Valentijn is of course in error here. There was an ancient port on the west coast of Ceylon called Tambapanni from which Taprobana may have been derived. While there is a great measure of agreement among scholars today that the classical Taprobana was Ceylon, this controversy is by no means dead. At the Sixth International Conference of Asian Historians at Jogjakarta in August 1974, Professor Jean Filliozat of the Ecole Francais de L'Extreme Orient, Paris, presented a paper which sought to identify Taprobana as Sumatra.

[2] Cin-lao. *Lao* (Chinese)—Torrent, breaking of waves.

[3] Both Couto and Barros have this interpretation which seems fanciful (Barros p. 33, Couto p. 88).

[4] *Kurundu patta* (Sinh.)—cinnamon bark.

reason the Malabars call the bark Caroa[1] which the Cingalese call Corundo[2] and the Arabs Caufa[3] for which our medicines use the corrupted name of Querfe or Guirfa.

The Persians call it Dar-Cin,[4] that is Chinese wood, since the Chinese were the first to have transported it and all other eastern goods to the Gulf of Persia, from where they were brought to Europe with the same name which the Persians had for them and not with their proper names by which they were known in the lands where they were found. It is hence that Serapio[5] calls this Dar-cin a Chinese tree, because he thought that this cinnamon bark was found in China. Thus Arrian also deceives himself in saying that Cassia and Senquin,[6] which are certain types of cinnamon, grew in a certain part of Troglodyta[7] and that the merchants transported it from there to Greece.

The same error is also made by Pliny who says that the cinnamon grows in Ethiopia, bordering on Troglodyta and that this district, because it stretched up to the Equator, was called by writers Cinnamon-growing as it grew there. That the same cinnamon came to our hands by the Red Sea, through Arab merchants who lived in that part of the Troglodyta and, as in Greece it was not investigated any further where the cinnamon really grew, they have thought that it grew in the land of the Arabs who brought it over to them.

Similarly some old writers, thinking that cinnamon came from Aleppo, have called it Aleppo cinnamon. Through these multitudinous errors even till today it is not known what sorts of spices are Duaca,[8] Monotto,[9] Magla[10] and

[1] Karuvā (Tam.)—cinnamon.

[2] *Kurundu* (Sinh.).

[3] Couto has carfa. The proper Arabic word is *qirfa*.

[4] From *daru* (Skt.)—tree or wood.

[5] Couto has Serapion. Saint Serapion. Author of *Liber Serapionis aggregatus in medicum simplibus*.

[6] Couto has zinguir, more correctly. Probably related to *χingiberis* (Gk.)—ginger.

[7] Classical term for country in the region of Ethiopia.

[8] *Daucum* (Latin), a plant used in medicine.

[9] Couto has mocrotto. *Mocrotou* (Gk.)—a kind of frankincense.

[10] Gk. A kind of spice.

Easiply[1] to which Arrian refers, saying that they grow in Arabia and Ethiopia. Also one does not know what to make of Nicabo-Gabalio[2] and Tarro[3] which Pliny calls Arabic drugs, and why we have no more knowledge of frankincense, storax and myrrh which possibly Pliny means. In the whole of Ethiopia there is no other drug except ginger and that is very bad, and this too only in the kingdom of Damute.[4] To return to cinnamon, the Malays call it Cajoe Manis,[5] that is sweet wood, which is the same as Caisman or Casmanis[6] of the Greeks, from whom they appear to have borrowed this name and to have corrupted it still further by calling it Cassia Lignea, a name which we do not find among any people in the east. Physicians appear first to have named it Cais Lignea, the wood of Cais, for in former times, before the kingdom of Ormuz moved to the island of Gerum[7] (where it presently is), the island of Cais[8] was the capital and emporium of the entire Persian Gulf from Ormuz inward and as the merchants of Europe persisted in coming to that island, as now they go to Ormuz, taking from there cinnamon which the Chinese brought from the island of Cais, they have therefore named it Cais Lignea.[9]

With regard to the naming of this island among the inhabitants themselves, they call it Langkauwn[10] which some say means the world, others that it means a Paradise.

Pliny and Ptolemy say that in olden times it was called Simondi, Palai Simondi[11] and Salike[12] and that the inhabitants were called Salai.[13] Also Ptolemy places it among the five islands, called by him Borusse,[14] giving to this one the name

---

[1] Couto has asiplij. *Aspalathos* (Gk.)—a tree whose roots were used to make perfume.

[2] Couto has Nicato, Gabalio. *Gaballium* (Latin). An aromatic drug from Persia.

[3] *Tarum* (Latin), aloe wood.   [4] Damietta or Dimyat in Lower Egypt.

[5] *Kaju manis* (Malay). Literally, sweet wood.   [6] Couto has Caesmanis.

[7] Hormuz is a tiny island at the entrance to the Persian Gulf and there is a larger island of Qeshm next to it. There is a place called Jahrum but it is a few miles inland in Persia.

[8] Qais, an island west of the entrance to the Persian Gulf.

[9] The close reliance on Couto ends here.

[10] Lankāva (Sinh.).   [11] See p. 91 n. 8.   [12] See p. 92 n. 3.

[13] Probably derived from Sihala.   [14] *Barussae Insulae* in Ptolemy.

Panigarensis.[1] After him the Arabic writers call it Sisuara, Tenarisis and Nanigeris.[2]

It lies off the Cape Comoryn, or with its northernmost part opposite the Coast of Choromandel.

Point Gale, called Gale by us, lies on the longitude 102 degrees and 30 minutes.[3]

The island extends to the north from 6 degrees to 10 degrees latitude and has to the north a part of the coast of Choromandel, to the east the Gulf of Bengal to the south the great open sea, such as shows itself between the island of Sumatra and the Maldive Islands, and in the west the Maldives itself.

The shape of the island is like a large ham, for which reason our people have named the Fort of Ceys,[4] situated near Jaffanapatnam, not improperly Hammenhiel,[5] after the shape of the island at that place.

In olden times it was (as some confidently say) 400 miles in circumference, but to the north side from time to time the sea had encroached much and it is felt, not without reason, that it had been in very olden times attached to the mainland of the Choromandel coast by the island of Manaar, where Adam's Bridge now appears with the island of Ramancoil[6] (which lay 12 miles from each other), and that the sea has separated them over the ages.[7]

Actually, according to our most accurate measurement its length from north to south is 55 miles, in breadth from east to west 30 miles, at Panoa and Cotjaar 18 miles, at the Lagoon

---

[1] *Nanigeris* in Ptolemy.

[2] None of these names is identifiable. Susuara and Nanigeris are islands located by Ptolemy east of Taprobana.

[3] Galle lies 80° 13′ east of Greenwich. Valentijn's longitude measurement seems to be based on the Prime Meridian of Ferro in the Canary Islands, which many contemporary maps used.

[4] The modern Kayts, in Tamil Ūrukāthurai.

[5] Dutch, heel of a ham.

[6] Rāmēsvaram. Rāmancovil is the famous Hindu temple on that island. India and Ceylon were formerly joined together but were separated by sea, probably in the Miocene period.

[7] This view is generally accepted by geologists. The present circumference of the island is 1100 (English) miles and the figure of 400 German miles (1800 English miles) is 700 miles more than the present distance. Valentijn's distances are in German miles; 1 German mile is equal to approximately 4·5 English miles.

of Jaffanapatnam 7 miles and in its entire circumference 197 miles, as can be seen from looking at the following list.[1]

	Distance in Miles
Tricoen-male from Punto das Pedro[2]	30
Oostenburg, a fort of Tricoen-male	$\frac{1}{2}$
Dwaars in de weg, an island (off Oostenburg)	$\frac{1}{2}$
Cotjaar from Tricoen-male by sea	3
but by land 18	
Enkelansine, a fortress lies $\frac{1}{2}$ mile further	$\frac{1}{2}$
Baticalo from Cotjaar by sea	14
but by land 18	
Soratjan Condawa from Baticalo	5
Apretotte[3] from Soratjan	12
Komboken from Apretotte	7
Jale from Komboken	5
Koekelamalagamme from Jale	5
Waluwe from Koekelemalagamme	10
Nielewelle from Waluwe	8
Mature from Nielewelle	5
Gale from Mature	10
Bentotte from Gale	12
Caliture from Bentotte	4
Colombo from Caliture	4
Nigombo from Colombo	6
Chilauw from Nigombo	10
Calpentyn from Chilauw	10
Man-Aar from Calpentyn	10
Jaffanapatnam from Man-Aar	24
Punto das Pedras from Jaffanapatnam	2
	$197\frac{1}{2}$

[1] Compare Valentijn's measurements with the exact distances. Length (Valentijn) $247\frac{1}{2}$ miles (Actual) $271\frac{1}{2}$ miles. Breadth (Valentijn) 135 miles (Actual) $137\frac{1}{2}$ miles. Circumference (Valentijn) 889 miles (Actual) 1100 miles. Dutch surveys had acquired a reasonable measure of accuracy, though there were some inaccuracies in some of the distances given in Valentijn's table below.

[2] The Portuguese name for the place today called Point Pedro.

[3] Apperetotte. A distorted version of Appuratōttai.

Various writers
on Ceylon

Various learned and ignorant men have written on Ceylon in former times and, according to their times, very well. But in my opinion in general they could have put it in better order, besides theirs is not a description of the entire island.

Among whom
Baldaeus

The most detailed and the best of those who have written on Ceylon is Mr. Philippus Baldaeus, who had been minister of the Gospel there.[1] He has particularly enlarged on the siege of Colombo and other conquered towns and fortresses there as well as on church matters and religions of the heathens.

We are grateful to his Reverence as he has in general written very well on these matters and has given me in many respects great enlightenment. But this is seen only regarding the coastal places conquered by us.

And Cnox excel

Robert Cnox has no knowledge of the coastal places but only of the interior of the island and that only of the places he had seen (which were very few), of which he says many things which are good. But he does not set it out for us in that order as it ought to be, namely by a special description of each district, and not always as we would wish it.[2]

Nonetheless, he tells us many things which were otherwise unknown to us and which are worthy of note which we shall utilise as occasion arises, as also of Mr. Baldaeus.

Also Joan
Ribeiro

Joan Ribeiro, a Portuguese Captain, also writes of the island but in a very confused manner, though he is best on Portuguese matters which he knew best.[3]

Besides these there have been more but we shall refer to what they have said when we speak of particular matters that have happened in Ceylon at the proper place and therefore not mention it here.

Ceylon divided
into different
kingdoms

The island of Ceylon has been divided according to some in former times into 9, and by others into 7, kingdoms

[1] Philippus Baldaeus. *Beschryving der Oost-Indische Kusten Malabar en Choromandel, derzelver aangrezende Rijken, als ook het Keijzerrijck Ceylons* (Amsterdam, 1672). See Introduction, pp. 29–32.

[2] Robert Knox. *An Historical Relation of the Island Ceylon* (London, 1681). See Introduction, pp. 32–3.

[3] João Ribeiro. *Fatalidade historica da Ilha Ceilão* (Lisbon, 1836). The edition available to Valentijn was an abridged translation into French by L'Abbé Le Grand published in Paris in 1701. See Introduction p. 29.

which, however, come under one sovereign. The names of
the kingdoms are these:

Cotta, whose king was honoured as Emperor of the *Their names*
whole island
Denuaca
Oeva
Candi
Sitavaca
The Seven Corles, and
Chilauw.

Today there are but 6 kingdoms and the land, besides, *Modern*
is divided into different princedoms, earldoms, marquisates, *division into 6*
and domains, of which, since the rule of Raya Singa,[1] one *kingdoms*
has begun to obtain the correct knowledge for the first time,
because this haughty King was very proud and particularly
attached to these titles of honour, which he seems to have
borrowed both from the Portuguese and from us, and knew
very little of these previously.[2]

The names of the kingdoms are these: *Their names*

Candi, also Candia, or Conde Ouda,[3] that is, the high
mountain, in Cingalese
Cotta
Sitavaca
Dambadan
Amorayapoere
Jaffanapatnam

Besides these kingdoms there are also 6 princedoms, *How many*
12 earldoms, 4 marquisates and 9 domains from which Raja *princedoms,*
Singa used to derive his titles. *earldoms,*
marquisates and
domains

[1] Rāja Sinha II, king of Kandy 1629–1687.
[2] Valentijn has used European feudal territorial terms and it is difficult to
translate them into their Sinhalese counterparts and identify the distinctions.
Besides, he has subsumed the divisions of many periods of traditional history
into one. At the time Valentijn was writing, the administrative divisions were
simplified into Dissavāny (principality or province), Ratta (smaller province),
Kōralē (district) and Pattu (division).
[3] *Kanda uda* (Sinh.).

Names of the Princedom	The princedoms[1] are these: Oeva Mature Denuaca, otherwise called Two Corlas Four Corles Seven Corles Matale
Earldoms	The Earldoms[2] are these: Trinkenemale, properly Tricoenmale Baticalo Vellase Bintene Drembra Panciapato Veto[3] Putelam Vallare Gale Billigam
Marquisates	The Marquisates are these:[4] Duranure Ratienure Tripane Accipate
Domains	And the Domains[5] are these: Alican Colombo Nigombo Chilauw Madampe Calpentyn Aripo

---

[1] These would be Dissavanies. Some could be called princedoms because they were governed by members of the royal family.

[2] Some of these are Dissavanies, others Ratta and others Pattu.

[3] Vahittha or Mahāvetta. [4] These are Ratta. [5] These are all coastal ports.

ManAar
The Pearl Fishery

Besides these above named divisions, the land in the interior is in general divided into 34 particular Corles or Districts, among which as one goes from Gale in the south, along the sea, northwards, are the following:[1]

Gale Corle

Walalawitte Corle
?asdum Corle
Reygam Corle
Salpitti Corle
Hewegam Corle, somewhat landwards or to the east
Hina Corle   do.
Pittigal Corle
Migonne or Mangul Corle

When one goes directly northwards from Billigam in the south, one comes across these districts:

The land of Mature, extending eastwards
Billigam Corle[2]
Dolasdas Corle, east of Billigam
Koekele Corle[3]
Naudum Corle
Saffragam Corle[4]
Morawa Corle,[5] east of Saffragam
Denkelvaca[6] or Two Corles, north of Morawa
Korne Corle,[7] east of Morua Corle
Vitte Corle,[8] situated near Adam's Peak
Attacolan Corle,[9] east of Denuaca
Kuruwitte Corle,[10] north of Saffragam
Attulagam Corle,[11] north of Vitte Corle
Four Corles, or Panaval Corle, north-east of Attulagam
        Corle and just north of Adam's Peak

[1] Most of the kōralēs (districts) are reasonably accurately named.
[2] Weligam Kōralē.   [3] Kukulu Kōralē.   [4] Sabaragamuva Kōralē.
[5] Morawak Kōralē.   [6] Probably Denavaka.   [7] Probably Kolonnē Kōralē.
[8] Probably Kuruviti Kōralē, though Valentijn repeats it later.
[9] Attakalan Kōralē.   [10] Kuruviti Kōralē.   [11] Atulugam Kōralē.

Mende Corle,[1] east of Adam's Peak
Dehegampala Corle, north of Kuruwitte Corle
Hina Corle,[2] north of Sitavaka
Happittigam Corle, east of Hina Corle
Seven Corles, north of Hina Corle
Billigal Corle,[3] which lies well to the north of Seven
    Corles
Gampele Corle,[4] east of Billigal
Tun Corle, north of Billigal
Houtera Corle[5] ⎱
Hat Corle   ⎰ east of Chilauw

And 33 lesser districts

Besides the above named 34 large districts there are yet
33 other of lesser rank, named thus:

The 9 Nevayas[6] in the south, situated east of Billigam
    from where we again go northwards
Jale in the southeast, south of Cadduatta Corle[7]
Malwana, near Colombo
Balane, in the Four Corles
Deleswage, just north of Adam's Peak
Coetemale, north of Deleswage
Panoa to the east, and north of Jale
Oedipollat, somewhat north of Coetemale
Hewahette, northeast of Oedipollat
Jatti, northwest of Hewoyhatty and just south of Candi
Goddaponohay, east of Jatti
Jotta Kinde, east of Hewahette
Tunponahoy, west of Candi
Horsepot, north of Candi
Porcipot, east of Candi
Vallaponahoy, east of Porcipot
Vilacen, northeast of Vallaponahoy
Matecalo[8] ⎱
Baticalo   ⎰ in the east near Baticalo
Maetale, northeast of Candi

---

[1] Meda Kōralē.   [2] Siyana Kōralē.   [3] Beligal Kōralē.
[4] This must be Galboda Kōralē.   [5] Hatara Kōralē.
[6] Probably Levāya, the salt districts of the southeast.   [7] Kadawattu Kōralē.
[8] This is a distorted form of the old Tamil name of Batticaloa: Maddakalappu.

Palavi, somewhat east of Calpentyn

Bintene, near the city of this name on the Trinkenemale River

Newecalawa or Neucalawa in the middle of the country north of Hotcorla

Tommakod, somewhat south of Cotjaar

Cotjari ⎫ in the east together, not far
Trinkenemale ⎭ from the east coast

Hoerli, north of Newecalawa

The land of the Weddas, east of Trinkenemale

The land of the Wannias

Four special territories of Jafnasapatnam, being:

Welligamme
Timmoratie
Warmoratie
Pachealapalie

In this mighty island, there are also, both along the coast and in the interior, various important cities which deserve to be specially mentioned. *Coastal cities on the west side*

On the western coast lay, from south to north, these cities:

Point Gale on 6 degrees 5 minutes north lattitude
Caliture
Columbo
Nigumbo
Medampe
Chilauw
Portaloon or Putelan
Calpentyn, on an island of this name
Aripe or Aripo
Mantotte
Manaar, on an island of this name
Jafnapatnam, on an island of this name, right in the north

To the east side of the island, there are these cities: *Coastal cities on the east side*

Trinkenemale
Baticalo

Large inland cities

In the interior are three large cities, namely:

Ceita-vaca, on the Colombo River[1]

Candi, on the Trinkenemale River or Mawielliganga River[2] in the middle of the land, near Colombo

Vintana,[3] on the same river but lower in the middle of the country and nearer Trinkenemale.

Smaller inland cities

Besides these three great interior cities there are still other smaller cities, namely:

Harsipotte in Cockele Corla[4]

Panetotte ⎫
Oedibod[5] ⎬ situated near Corna Corla[6]
Katwane ⎭

Wallagodde in Corne Korla

Dinavaca in the Two Corlas

Tammegamme[7] ⎫ East of Dina-Vaca
Bibligam ⎭

Batugedra, west of Dina-Vaca

Jemature[8] south of Dina-Vaca

Cambevolle,[9] north of Attagalan Corla

Malpitte in Menda Corla

Collegom north of Adam's Peak

Coetemale situated in Coetemale

Pool Pite, somewhat west of Coetemale

Badaule,[10] east of Pool Pite

Manicramare, just east of the Colombo River, in Happitigan Corla

Nilobe, formerly a capital city, 14 miles south of Candi

Elledat, near Nilobe, between Eudanoer and Hewoohatty

Dietlige, a later capital city than Nilobe, situated in Goddaponahoy

Laleluja,[11] near to and somewhat east of Candi

Sigelis,[12] north of Porcipot and east of Horsepot

[1] Kelani Ganga.   [2] Mahāveli Ganga.   [3] Bintenne or Alutnuvara.
[4] Kukulu Kōralē.   [5] Probably Udabadda.   [6] Probably Kolonnē Kōralē.
[7] Tangama?   [8] Unidentifiable. Could be Divitura, near Galle.
[9] Probably Kumbalvella.   [10] Badulla?   [11] Probably Haloluva.
[12] Unidentifiable. Contemporary maps locate a town called Sigelis of Safalocki on the Mahāveli Ganga south of Alutnuvara. Could be Simbella.

Bonder-coos-wat, north of Horsepot
Nicavar, north of Bonder-coos-wat
Parroah, north of Nicavar
Vellas, somewhat west of Baticalo
Hondopoal,[1] north of Parroah
Colliwilla,[2] north of Newecalawe
Anarogdburro, north of Colilwilla

And other similar cities and towns[3] which are found still further in the interior not all of which are well known.

This island is full of steep mountains and abounding in water. There are many large and some ordinary rivers. The largest of all is the Mavela Ganga.[4] It has its origin in Adam's Peak, a mountain, in the middle of the country, situated on the latitude of Colombo or at $6\frac{1}{2}$ degrees. It runs from there to the north, winds about three-quarter miles from Candi, runs then to the east some miles to the royal city of Digaliga, where it runs again to the north, flowing through the city of Bintana, from where it winds gradually to the northeast and flows into the sea near Cotiaar or in the Bay of Trinkenemale. It is about a musket shot broad, rather rocky (like all rivers here) and therefore dangerous.

Rivers of Ceylon

Besides this river, there are on the west side those of Kosdoewa,[5] near Gale (which has its origins from the Hoyberg), of Alican[6] and of Panture[7] which are not very large, of Colombo[8] which is reasonably large and also has its origins in Adam's Peak, like that of Calture.[9] Further there are those of Negumbo,[10] of Caimel,[11] of Chilauw,[12] of Caula Woya[13] and of Aripen, named Cononda Woya.[14]

---

[1] Handapola or Ambanpola? [2] Probably Kaluvila.

[3] Valentijn used the terms *stede* and *vlek* which have been translated as 'city' and 'town' respectively. The distinction seems to be largely one of size, the bigger urban settlements being referred to as *stede* and the smaller ones as *vlek*. Some of the places referred to as *vlek* are very small indeed but it is possible that they were townships of some size in the past and hence so referred to in Valentijn's sources. For villages, Valentijn uses the term *dorp*.

[4] Mahāveli Ganga. Valentijn spells the name of this river in different ways.

[5] Kosdūva. The name of the river is Gin Ganga. [6] Bentota Ganga.

[7] Mahā Oya. [8] Kelani Ganga. [9] Kalu Ganga.

[10] Dandugan Oya. [11] Mahā Oya. [12] Deduru Oya.

[13] Kalā Oya. [14] Kurundu Oya or Malvattu Oya.

On the east side there is the Berbero or Cutiale river,[1] north of Trinkenemale, as also that of Cotiar or of Trinkenemale,[2] that of Baticalo,[3] Sengare,[4] Heddelon,[5] Koebekan Oye,[6] the river of Jaleput,[7] Cerinde Oye,[8] the Walauwe River[9] in the south, also having its origin in Adam's Peak, and that of Mature,[10] besides other small streams.

Shape of the country

As this land is full of mountains, even up to near Jaffnapatnam, except for a few plains, so it is also full of jungle everywhere, excluding the Princedom of Oeva and the small districts of Oedipollat and Deleswage or Dolusbag which not only serve to divide the earldoms and provinces from each other but also especially to strengthen the security of the country, for which reason no one may on pain of death thin out or cut down the trees or make the paths wider more than enough for just one to go through, it being impossible for anyone to penetrate further.[11]

Astonishing seasons here

The seasons on this island are very different; for when it is the rainy season on the west side and the west wind blows through, then on the east side it is the dry season and very clear beautiful weather. And when it is the monsoon rain on the east side, then to the west side it is the eastern monsoon and clear weather. This change begins near the centre of the island. There is however on the mountains above more rain than below, but the driest weather is to the north side of this island.

Occurrence of Earthquakes here

There are now and then some earthquakes here, sometimes reasonably severe with some shock everywhere, as all warm lands are mostly subject to this, though it occurs in one country more severely than in another.

After these remarks on this island in general we will pass over to a particular description.

Map of Ceylon

To do this with some order, we shall use a new map prepared by ourselves, which we here give under P.Q.[12]

[1] It is not known which river is meant. There is a place called Kuchaveli about 20 miles north of Trincomalee. There are a number of rivers in that area.

[2] Mahāveli Ganga. [3] Mandari Āru? [4] Sangaratōpu Āru.
[5] Heda Oya. [6] Kumbukkan Oya. [7] Menik Ganga.
[8] Kirindē Oya. [9] Valavē Ganga. [10] Nilvalā Ganga.
[11] Cp. Knox Pt. 11, Chap. 111 (p. 70) where the same point is made.

[12] This is Valentijn's alphabetical index of his maps, charts and pictures. This map is reproduced here. See p. 374.

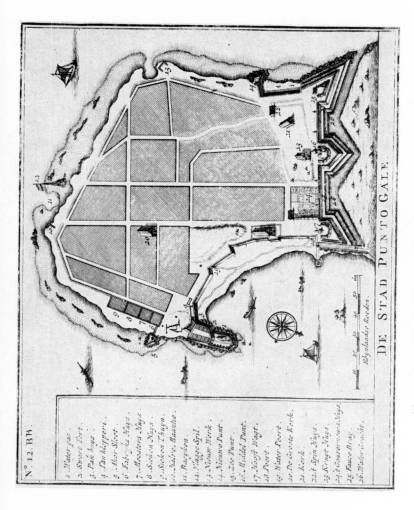

DE STAD PUNTO GALE.

Rhedlandse Reeden.

Map 3. City of Galle (Valentijn V. 1, facing p. 22, No. 12BB)

Map 4 City of Jaffnapatnam (Valentijn V. 1, facing p. 30, No. 13)

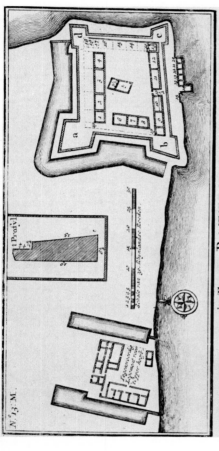

Map 5. Batticaloa Fort (Valentijn V. 1, facing p. 32, No. 13M)

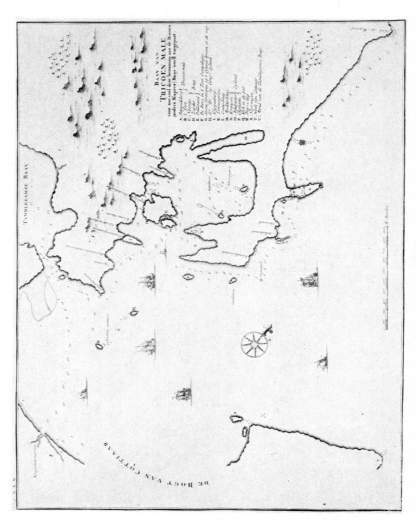

Map 6. Bay of Trincomalee (Valentijn V. 1, facing p. 360, No. 12 NAN)

We then make a beginning with the Earldom of Gale and the City Point Gale which is situated on the southwest side of this island, on the longitude of 102½ degrees[1] and on the northern latitude of 6 degrees, and then describe all the coastal places right round the entire island first. The city as it shows itself on the sea side can be well seen in Baldaeus's work.[2] But here we portray it very beautifully from the land side in No. 12B and No. 12B.B. in flat ground in 1663.[3]

The city of Gale described and 2 maps of it

Gale embraces in circumference within the wall about half a mile, with very broad and high walls on three sides on the land side, besides a moat which is very deep and about 18 feet broad. It has really only 3 firm bulwarks, the Sun, the Moon and the Star, between which is the city gate, after which are other points, namely Mariner Point, Utrecht, the Flag Rock, Venus, Mars and Aeolus.[4] On the east side there is only one gate named the Sea or the Water gate and beyond lies the city on the sea side quite open. But it is so strongly provided by nature with many rocks that it is impossible to come there or nearby without a pilot, without running into the utmost danger. Therefore it is customary to fire a gun every half hour as one approaches the city to receive the pilot.

In order to avoid this, a shot is fired from a rock which lies just outside in the sea from which the flag of the Hon. Co.[5] flies to warn ships not to sail further and there a pilot comes on board, who brings the ship in along the side of the immense rocks which must be passed narrowly through an opening which is an half an hour wide. Also there is a strong current at the entrance which seems irresistible.

One cannot come into the bay without passing by the Fort which is seen on a rock or high ground and the Water-gate which is fortified with 6 metal twelve pounders, where is also the house of the Commander of the city and the main guard and one sees the sea beating against the city walls.

[1] See p. 102 n. 3.   [2] Baldaeus, p. 63.
[3] Here Valentijn gives two illustrations, a double page drawing of Galle seen from the harbour and a half page ground plan of the fort area. The latter is reproduced here. See pp. 112–13.
[4] The names of the bulwarks.
[5] The Honourable Company—the formal way of referring to the Dutch East India Company.

Close by is built a promenade on poles some paces into the harbour which is made out of planks and covered with a roof, the wood is named *Wambays*,[1] along which it is very pleasant to walk.

As one approaches the Fort which appears on the rock, on the left is the Hospital and further towards the city the bastion Akkersloot, where there are 8 pieces of cannon which can defend the Bay. In the Bay a ship can lie the whole year freely and many ships could remain there in safety, but, if it blows strongly, the sea is open and lively and the ships can be affected by the intense rolling, unless skilful mariners learn to moderate it by weighing an anchor.

On the right, to the land side, there is besides the high city walls and a draw bridge over the moat, the Middlepoint, a stronghold on which are 10 pieces of cannon which partly command the main guard (where there is a force of 60 to 70 men) and partly the city walls, below which is also a half moon battery.

The Seapoint is the last on the land side where also most artillery is placed and where the whole night a corporal with 6 men must keep guard.

Between the Seapoint and a new work which is erected on the storehouse, one sees a beautiful stream of fresh water springing out of the side of the rock, despite the sea washing against the rocks but a pace from there.

Within the city, which is built with regularity and neatness, but is about half as big as Batavia, there are many moderately wide streets (some of earth, some with grass growing), many beautiful stone buildings, some moderately large churches, beautiful wells in most houses and outside the city (as also here and there within it), very beautiful gardens and courtyards with a beautiful view of the mountains east of Coekele Corla,[2] Harsipot and Hoyberg. Among the buildings that of the Commander of Gale is exceptional, which stands opposite a very large arsenal and has very beautiful apartments. There is also a church serving the Dutch in the morning and the Cingalese in the afternoon, at the end of the

---

[1] Probably *wammutu* (Sinh.), a type of wood used in construction.
[2] Kukulu Kōralē.

Commander's beautiful dwelling. There are those who assert that this city lies on swampy ground, while on the contrary it is situated on a beautiful hill and is very airy, being continuously cooled by the fresh sea breeze or by the pleasant land breeze.

It has a beautiful view to the sea side and is, like a seaport city, generally full of life and swarming with people, flourishing from a strong traffic and trade with many quarters, besides generally the Fatherland Fleet which departs from Ceylon is loaded here and leaves for Holland on the 25th December annually. I shall not tarry to say when this city was conquered as that will be done later.[1]

The city was the seat of the Governor of Ceylon till 1656

Here we have our second comptoir in Ceylon, where for the Company there are a Commander as Head, a *Koopman* as second and some other officials who together constitute a Council. There is also a sizeable force here with the necessary military officers such as a Captain, Lieutenant and Ensign, but of especial importance is the administration of the outstations over which a Dessave[2] or sheriff has authority.

When one goes 2 miles northwest, one comes across a small town Gindere,[3] somewhat northeasterly and landward about two miles away lies Bakwelle (which is as far from Gindere) and Gannegamme which is just south of the River of Kosdoewa[4] which originates from the Hoyberg, about 4 or 5 miles northeastwards and further north of that river a little higher than the village of Bakwelle is the village Kosdoewa also about 2 or 3 miles landward.

Gindere, a town

Bakwelle and Gannegamme

Kosdoewa

Two large miles[5] north of Gindere one sees the village of Reygam along the sea, and as one goes as far northeast one sees just on the side or south of a small stream the village

Reygam

---

[1] This is one of the best contemporary descriptions of the city of Galle under the Dutch, much superior to that of Baldaeus.

[2] A Dissāva, as described by Valentijn in his Introduction, was a provincial Governor. This office in the Sinhalese administrative system was taken over by the Dutch, through the Portuguese. There were thus many Dutch Dissāvas throughout the country.

[3] Gintota. The distances are in German miles, each approximating 4.5 English miles.

[4] Gin Ganga.

[5] The German mile had three divisions of small, medium and large and there was a difference of about 2,500 feet between each.

Madampe, and just north of this stream the town Billitotte, and about 4 or 5 miles landwards the village Gedewelewitte, just north of the river of Kosdoewa and opposite is the town Maplagam, south of that river but lying on a new, separate eastward flowing stream about a couple of miles from Hoyberg, being a solitary and reasonably high mountain in itself with yet a small one besides.

As one goes northwards from Billitotte where there are various forests in front and to the east, one comes into the Walawitte Corla[1] or the Earldom (for this is the meaning of Corla) of Walawitte though it stands with us for a special district of this name, which borders on Pasdun Corla[2] to the north and the Cockele Corla[3] to the east, which are both ordinary provinces.

Fully three miles from Billitotte there is the village Bentotte just south of a small stream, to the east of which about 2 to 3 miles is a large forest called Peliwatte which appears for some miles on all four sides as a boundary between Walawite, Pasdun and Cockele Corlas.

When one goes 8½ miles north of the Bentotte stream and even north of the River of Alican, one comes to the village of the same name, to the north of which in the Pasdun Corla again there are some forests which stretch further to the east, almost up to Naudum Corla.[4] A little in the sea is the island Verberin[5] which is very small in circumference.

Full two miles to the north of Alican is the town Makoene between which and the village Pelando about 3 or 4 miles to the east landwards is a large forest.

Three miles to the north is the Caleture Fort on a beautiful large river which flows down from Adam's Peak where it falls into the sea.[6] It lies 8 miles from Colombo and is about a day's journey from Point Gale.

It is a beautiful structure of double earth walls and is occupied by a reasonable force and is generally held to be one of the most important fortresses and a particularly strong refuge but otherwise has nothing special. On the land side it

[1] Walallawiti Kōralē.   [2] Pasdum Kōralē.
[3] Kukulu Kōralē.   [4] Navadun Kōralē.
[5] Known later as Barberyn, near Hikkaduwa.   [6] Kalu Ganga.

has four redoubts lying opposite one another which are provided with thick palisades. The walls are so high that not a house inside can be seen and there is only one way inside as it lies on a high hill.

Just to the north, about 4 or 5 miles inland to the east on the same river there is the village Angretotte in Reygam Corle and in the middle of a forest about 12 miles from Colombo. It is a beautiful, strong place where some men are in occupation and is provided with some pieces of cannon, as also of all kinds of eatables and, because of the nearness of the river, also an abundance of fish, turtle, etc.

The village Angretotte

Somewhat north of the River of Caleture is a small lagoon that extends from this river to the Paneture river about 4 or 5 miles distant and discharges itself in it or unites with it.[1]

Paneture

To the south of the River Paneture[2] is a village of the same name, to the east of which 3 or 4 miles inland some hills appear.

From the River Paneture is a separate stream that extends northwards about 2 miles distant up to near the town Galkisse and is named Clantete.[3]

The town Galkisse

This district is called Salpiti Corle in which there is Oclomme[4] and especially to the east in the interior a large cinnamon forest.

Just north of Galkisse one sees the old remains of the palace of the old kings of Cotta and of the city where they used to hold court, which borders on the Hewagam District and is separated by a forest.

Cotta

Four or five miles north of Galkisse is the ancient and famed Colombo.

The city of Colombo

This is a beautiful city situated on a beautiful large river which originates from Adam's Peak[5] and at its mouth is called Motoaal and higher up Colombo and, by the Cingalese, oil.

It lies at about 6 degrees 95 minutes on the north latitude and on the longitude of 102 degrees and 10 minutes.[6]

---

[1] Bolgoda lake.   [2] Mahā Oya.   [3] Probably Kolontota.
[4] Unidentifiable. Is it Hōmagama?   [5] Kelani Ganga.
[6] From the prime meridian of Ferro Island.

It gets its name from a mango leaf, which is named in the Cingalese language, Cola Ambo,[1] as *Ambo* means mango fruit and *Cola* a leaf from which the Portuguese and we after them have made up Colombo.[2]

It used to be much larger when the Portuguese occupied it but we have reduced it considerably on conquering it (1656) and Mr. van Goens[3] had ordered many alterations to be made near Points Victoria, Kandy, Raja Singa, etc. in his Considerations over Ceylon and especially to strengthen the frontier posts of Malvane, Hangwelle and Anguratotte and by no means to abandon them.[4] At this time also many of the large and beautiful houses were broken down and the city strengthened on the land side with a beautiful moat of fresh water.

It had been formerly open entirely on the sea side. It had 8 bulwarks all round, besides another four-sided outer work in the northeast which used to be joined to two bulwarks. But as this required too many troops, now its strength consists mainly in the Fort which is situated in the west on the sea side. It has four gates, namely the Gale gate, the Delft, the Nigombo and the Watergate. Inside the Fort are some streets and also some flowering trees. There is also a fine arsenal for all war materials, a beautiful warehouse and an elephant stable which is close behind the church. Beneath the water-pass (of which we shall speak presently) there is a saw mill and above it near the Gale gate a powder mill. At present the city has only 5 bulwarks named Victoria, Constantia, Concordia, Haarlem and Enkhuysen.

[1] *Kola* (Sinh.)—leaf; *amba* (Sinh.)—mango.

[2] This is a folk etymology of Colombo of doubtful validity. It was, however, widely held in Ceylon. Knox (pp. 1–2) gives a similar version. A more likely derivation is *kolamba* (old Sinh.)—breach in bank of river or tank.

[3] Commissioner and Admiral of the East India Company. Governor of Ceylon 1662–1663 and 1664–1675.

[4] Commissioner van Goens delivered a policy statement to Adriaan van der Meyden, when he was appointed Governor of Ceylon in 1661. This document entitled 'Consideratien over Ceylon, by Forme van Instructie opgesteld, na de Ordres van haar Edelheden voor den Gouverneur van dat Eyland, door de E. Heer Commissaris, Rykloff van Goens, 21 Juni 1661, has been published in English translation by the Ceylon Government Archives (Trans. Sophia Pieters, Colombo 1908). Valentijn has published some extracts from this (V. 1. pp. 148–54).

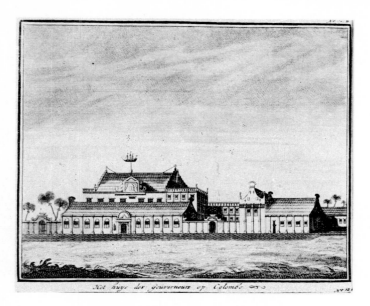

Fig. 2. The Governor's house
(Valentijn V. 1, facing p. 24, No. 12D)

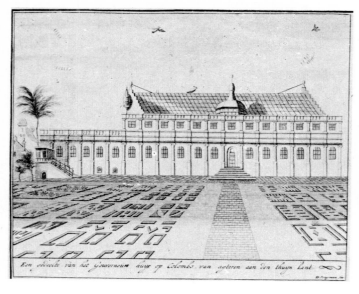

Fig. 3. Another view of the Governor's house from the rear
(Valentijn V. 1, facing p. 24, No. 12E)

Fig. 4. Outhouse of the Governor
(Valentijn V. 1, facing p. 24, No. 12G)

Fig. 5. Pleasure-house of the Governor
(Valentijn V. 1, facing p. 24, No. 12F)

Among the beautiful buildings, which are found in Col- The Governor's
ombo, the house of the Governor excels over others as it house
reveals itself in the Fort. It is a wonderful building and may
be reckoned among the best in the whole Indies.

We show it from the front in No. 12D, on the side it has
three instead of two stories and its view to the shore is
lengthened by a piece which must come to the side. No. 12E
shows this beautiful house from behind on the garden side of
which only a small part is seen here.

We add here in No. 12F a pleasure house on the sea side Another
standing before the entrance hall before which on Sundays building in
the parade usually takes place. Colombo shown
in Print

Further we show in No. 12G the outhouse of the Governor
from the front, before which the trees which hindered the
view are taken away.

And in No. 12H is seen this house from behind with a
building on pillars extending into the Motuaal river.

And finally we show No. 12I the flat ground of the garden
which lies behind the Governor's house in Colombo, and
is well worthy of being seen by a connoisseur as it is divided
into very beautiful flower beds.[1]

In the city there is also a fine hospital and a beautiful
orphanage and in the centre is the church yard which is
surrounded by a wall and near which is also a Malabar[2]
school, and also outside the church yard is a large market
where everything is sold by the Moors, Persians, Cingalese
and others.

Outside the Nigombo gate stood the so-called Moors
quarter (on Company land) where Governor Simons[3] had
the old street cleared in order to root out the kissing and
coquetry of all kinds of rabble living here outside streets
without their evil being discovered, and made it 5 Rhineland
Roods[4] broad and had yet another new street built through
this disorderly quarter and commanded the Moors to build

---

[1] Valentijn gives six plates of drawings of the Governor's house and gardens
from various angles. Four of these are reproduced here. See Illustrations 2, 3, 4
and 5.
[2] Tamil.   [3] Cornelis Janszoon Simons, Governor of Ceylon 1702–1706.
[4] A rood was about 6 to 8 yards.

their houses with their fronts to the street in an orderly fashion, which was accordingly done.

Also there is a great headland in the sea which curves to the west and with the southwest bulwark makes a harbour, though the ships there lie as in the open sea exposed to the northwest monsoon, besides they are also obliged to lie half a mile away from the shore. On the left of this head there is also a beautiful water-pass on which several pieces of cannon are placed to cover the harbour which the southwest bulwark also can do.

Colombo is in its circumference about an hour distant, has strong walls all round, many beautiful streets, many fine stone buildings, but all are here (as also in Gale and elsewhere) only one storey high and the best houses are from the time of the Portuguese who used to make everything firm and strong.

The new city is divided from the old by a barrier, and there is one also just outside the old city. Also the new city is smaller than Batavia but with the old is larger, though not so well built.

Here is our chief comptoir on the island where the Governor has his residence with an *Opperkoopman* as second in Colombo (though not of the government, which is the Commander of Gale), with the most important officers of the Company most of whom live in the Fort. Here there is also a fiscal (who till 1713 was independent, none of his successors received such power[1]), a Storekeeper, a Military Paymaster, Cashier, Private Secretary of the Governor and Council and many other minor officers.

Also here is the Great Council of the Ceylon Government also called Political Council, being the first and most important and under which are all the other comptoirs of this island, thus also the two Commanders of Gale and Jaffanapatnam, with all their officers.

Here is also a Court of Justice which judges not only the cases of this city but which is also supreme over all lesser comptoirs by way of appeal (in respect of this government),

[1] Till 1713 the Fiscal in Ceylon was independent of the Ceylon Government and took his orders directly from Batavia. He was called Independent Fiscal.

though one can appeal from this court to the Court of Justice at Batavia, as the highest in the Indies.

There is also a Council of Small and Matrimonial Matters, an Orphanage Council and everything else that there is generally in a government, and many other officers, according to the circumstances of this country, to manage the cinnamon which is found here.

Here is also a Captain or Commander of the military, a Lieutenant, Ensign and a substantial force, both for the Fort and for various outposts belonging under it.

The Governor is of such importance that he generally is also an Ordinary Councillor of the Indies,[1] and is generally held to be one of the first Governors of the entire Indies.

The Governor and other officers here

He administers the entire island, with his Council, up to the coastal territories under our possession and lives there with an uncommon pomp and station, as his income is large and in keeping with the income of all other governors in respect of his monthly salary and other known extra benefits which we have seen under the subject of Amboyna.[2] But the unknown and secret profits are not to be calculated, though it is certain that they become wealthy in two or three years, just as it is with the Commanders of Gale and Jaffanapatnam (though with one difference, that they should know how to keep in the favour of the Governor and to give and take with a mature judgment).[3] He is however under the Supreme Government of Indies at Batavia to whom he is responsible in everything, though there have been times when this has not been so closely followed.

Even now, just as it is with the Governor in respect of his pay and other benefits, so also is it with all other officers stationed here who, just as in other governments, have their fixed work here and among whom are certain permanently appointed members of the Political Council, out of whom and from some Burghers[4] are again appointed the members

[1] That is, a full member of the council of the Indies, the highest policy-making body of the Company in the east which sat in Batavia.
[2] Valentijn II *Beschrijvinge van Amboina*, pp. 272–88.
[3] Valentijn is referring to the many opportunities for illegal advancement through private trade, tax and revenue farms, cooking the books and so on.
[4] Dutch settlers in the colonies not in the Company's service.

of the Court of Justice and of the smaller Councils.

The comptoirs belonging to this Head-comptoir are: Mature, Calpentyn, Manaar, Jafnapatnam, Trinkenemale, Cotjaar, Baticalo, Panua, The Salt pans, Magamma, Point Gale, Nigombo, various outstations under Colombo, Toetecoryn and Point Pedro.

In 1672 Ceylon had a revenue of f683058.14.14 but the expenses of the fortification, which in 1664 were 866000 gl., had in 1672 increased to f1156371.13.5, so that this Comptoir was still f473312.18.7 in arrears.[1]

Also we must observe here that Malabar stood under the Government of Ceylon till 6 September 1669, but then it was placed separately under a special Commander. Similarly the trade from here to the Maldive Islands belongs to this government.

And it is most important that we think it necessary to leave here the City of Colombo. For if we were to speak so extensively of the other cities of Ceylon as we have done of Amboina and Batavia, the description of Ceylon should alone require a large volume. Therefore we will let it rest here.

Malvana,
Reygamwatte,
Goerbevele and
Matawaal

Landwards to the south of the Colombo river is a small jungle clad district or place called Malwana with two small villages or hamlets without name, and a mile higher up to the east round the river also the village Reygamwatte, and another two miles eastwards the village Goerbeville, also one sees on the sea side, a mile north of Colombo, the village Matuwaal on one side of the river on an oblong island that stretches from the Colombo river to the north up to the Nigombo river and along a lake that runs from this river into the Nigombo river.[2]

A great mile from the shore from Matuwaal a large shoal is seen which stretches from there to Nigombo and is about a mile broad being at most 10 to 12 fathoms deep, though on the north side it is only 7 fathoms. Between Reygamwatte and the Nigombo River is the great town of Maguhare, and some jungle, especially to the east side and around the village

---

[1] All figures are in Guilders (florins), Stuivers and Pence.
[2] Dandugan Oya.

Kalone,[1] which is about 2 miles inland and south of the Nigombo River.

The Nigombo Fort (which comes under Domains) is five hours by sea from the City of Colombo and 6 hours by land from there. It is a beautiful fort and a particularly strong place chiefly designed to cover the cinnamon lands. It has four points or bulwarks, two to the sea side named Hoorn and Enkhuyzen, and two to the land side named Delft and Rotterdam, and a beautiful earthen wall, 22 feet broad with 8 pieces of cannon on each bulwark. It has a land and a water-gate and had in former times within it another separate fort of two bulwarks named Middelburg and Amsterdam at the foot, with four large square stones drawn up very high and furnished above with an earthen parapet and surrounded with a moat in the middle of which, for greater strength, there was also a firm and well laid out palisade. But after Colombo was conquered, everything up to the stone bridge or Fort was levelled and abandoned to save the expenses of a large force.

The Nigombo Fort

Here there is also a *Koopman*[2] as Chief who has some officers under him to manage the affairs of the Company. How many they are and how strong is the administration there, is unknown to me.

This Fort has not only a beautiful outlook to the sea side but also to the land side where to the east is the Hina and Happitagam Corles and to the north Pitigal Corle and there is a beautiful wide-stretched plain, also there is a moderately large river which bears the name of this Fort. Hereabouts there are very beautiful cinnamon lands which used to be formerly in the Cotta Kingdom.

Two miles from Nigumbo on a small river lies the town Caymelle in a district named Alutcoer,[3] to the sea side, as in the land side within a mile or two is Pitigal Corle.

The town Caymele

If one goes further to the east, one comes to the Seven Corles and into the Billigal and Gampele Corles.[4] Above this

---

[1] Probably Kolonnāwa.

[2] A grade in the service of the Dutch Company, comparable to Merchant in the English E.I. Company.

[3] Alutkuru Kōralē. [4] Katugampola Kōralē.

small river lies Tun Corle and about 4 or 5 miles inland at the
place where this river originates are the towns Arunderri
and Alanha or Alauw.

Arunderi,
Alanha

When one goes north from this river along the coast two
miles from Caymelle, there is the town Mirabel, from which
to the town Medampe is a large plain and a large jungle full
of buffaloes which gives this place the name jungle of
Medampe. Also in this town Medampe is a harbour or bay
into which small vessels can sail.

Mirabel and
Medampe

To go from Medampe to the city of Chilauw, one has to
cover two miles. It has the name of a Domain, though it is
not less than lordly[1] and is but a native town or a miserable
nest, where is seen nothing but bad native houses or huts.
It lies on a small stream, which runs southeast from the
great Chilauw river (which divided itself in the east at
Hattera Corla,[2] 3 or 4 miles inland, into two streams).[3]

About 3 miles from the coast, between Chilauw and
Medampe, lies a small shoal of a mile in circumference with
only 3 fathoms of water.

To the north of the Chilauw River one comes into the
Kingdom of Candi, to the east are some forests and on the
coast 3 or 4 miles from this town several salt pans appear
and 3 miles inland lies the town Corinde Cornwatte in the
middle of a forest.

The town
Corinde
Coanwatte

From the Chilauw river the land curves northeastward to
the furthest salt pans. Also there is right in front of this
river a small shoal which stretches to the northwest. It is
called Lama Vermelha[4] and from there to the pearlbank of
Manaar is water of 60, 70 and 80 fathoms. But within it is
hardly 19 to 20 fathoms deep or less.

A mile north of this river, and also about a mile away
from the coast appears an island and the Domain of Calpentyn
that stretches from south to north about 5 or 6 miles and is
about a mile broad. On it are two villages, namely Maripu[5]
almost on the southwestern point and Tellevari[6] situated

The Calpentyn
Island

The village
Maripu and
Televari

---

[1] Appears to be a misprint for 'much less than lordly'.
[2] Hatara Kōralē or Four Kōralēs.
[3] Mahā Oya.   [4] A name given by the Portuguese.
[5] Probably Māmpuri.   [6] Probably Talaivillu.

about the centre and to the west side. Also there is here the town Navacar[1] on the east side, about 2 miles from Maripu and on the north side of the island, on the east about a mile from the point (where it divides itself into three as in the south end it is divided in two) lies the Calpentyn Fort which is reasonably strong and provided with a reasonable force.

The town Navacar and Fort Calpentyn

Between the island and the mainland coast in the south and especially in the north are many rocks and catacombs.

Five or six miles from the Chilauw river going north along the coast is the town Portaloon in the district of the same name, just south of which is the Palawi district where there are many forests.

The town Portaloon

From Portaloon to the town Caddaumatris[2] situated about 5 miles away are very thick mountains continuously for about a mile or two till the Coedremale mountain. Also there is between Portaloon and Caddaumatris, Mangul Corle or Migonne[3] and about 3 miles east of Portaloon, the village Golgom.

And Caddaumatris

The village Golgom

From the mountains near Caddaumatris and near this town there is a beautiful large stream, Caula Weya,[4] mostly flowing east which falls about four miles eastward from the interior into a small river called Hembolonggom Weya.[5]

Two miles above Caddaumatris is the Coedremale mountain, between which place and the mountain a mile from the coast is a small island Coedremale (also called Caradia).

The island Coedremale

From the mountain of Coedremale, where there are more difficult rocks, the land curves into a protruding bay for a mile or two, turning gradually to the east (where there is a large lowland plain) first up to the village Aripo (which lies on the River Coronda Weya[6] and is 4 miles from the above-named mountain) and from Arippu to the town Matotte[7] in the district of the same name, with a large flat inner bay about 4 miles distant, without meeting any villages between the two except only the village Moesilipatte hardly a mile from Aripo.

The village Aripo

The village Moesilipatte

---

[1] Probably Nāvatkādu.
[2] Unidentifiable. Could be Kaduruwēgama.
[3] Probably Mīgamuwa.
[4] Kalā Oya.
[5] Siyambalagaha Oya.
[6] Kurundu Oya. [7] Māntota or Māntai.

In the village Aripo is also a Fort and station of our people where are generally placed four field pieces and a Sergeant and 24 men.

Here there are many Malabars[1] everywhere who have many cattle, milk, butter, chickens, pigs, eggs, etc. for sale, whereby this garrison (which is stationed here for the security of the Pearlbank so that no one except those authorised by the Company could fish here) is supplied for so little, as one can buy an ox there for half a Rix Dollar.[2]

The place is very unhealthy for which reason many people die there and the force is relieved every four months and replaced with fresh people from the island of Manaar.

Between Aripo and Matotte, about 2 miles from the coast, lies the Pearlbank of Manaar which stretches northwest and southeast about 2 miles distant, being at a guess, a mile broad. On it there are many catacombs.

The island Manaar

About a mile to the northwest, from Matotte the land runs flat to the island of Manaar making an acute angle where is seen the island Manaar, about a mile from the coast and stretching to the northwest about 5 miles in length, 2 miles broad including the salt river which runs into it and thus is 14 miles in circumference.

The Fort represented in Print

It lies 9 degrees north of the Equator and is provided with a beautiful, large Fort named Manaar which is shown in No. 12C.[3] It is situated in the east and has very fine bulwarks and a deep moat and a large garrison of 100 men and all war materials. The word Manaar means in the Malabar language a sand river.[4]

To the southeast side of the island only small vessels can sail through between it and the mainland coast. Between the island and the coast of Ceylon on the east there is a shoal of 3 miles which has here and there catacombs, decreasing towards the north and becoming smaller.

The villages there

On it there is a city of the same name and the villages Tottevali, Carcel, Erkelampatti, St. Pieter's Village, Peixale and Tellemanaar.

---

[1] Tamils.　　[2] Dutch silver coin worth about 2½ guilders.
[3] A half page diagram of the Mannār Fort.
[4] *Man* (Tam.)—sand, *Āru* (Tam.)—river.

The city of Manaar, situated somewhat south of the Fort, is but an open town and not large. There are a few beautiful houses there, an attractive church in the north and a beautiful plantation of trees on the east and south side. Similar plantations are there along the sea side both in the south up to almost the end of this side of the island, and to the north from the northeast corner on and following the salt river more than half way up the north side of the island. In the northeast is a place, Browerswyk, and in the southeast one called Bakenburg.[1]

The village Tottevali lies a little west of the city on the north side of the island and not far from the salt river which is more like a great creek. There is also a church there.

Erkelampatti, also a small village, lies on the north side of the island, just north of the salt river or the creek, about a great mile from the northeast corner, it being also provided with a church.

The village Carcel lies near the middle of the island but somewhat to the east surrounded by a beautiful plantation and like the other village provided with a church.

St. Pieter, where most of the fishermen live, lies to the north side in the middle and almost an hour's journey west of Erkelampatti.

A half hour to the west lies the village Peixale, in the same group to the north side of the island and about 2 large miles further to the west side, about a mile from the southwest, lies the village Tellemanaar.

Between Peixale, Tellemanaar and the south side of the island there are many moderately high hills that are also very jungle-clad.

West of the island Manaar are some shoals stretched lengthwise along the west, of which one is joined to this island and again to another shoal. Between the latter which is 3 miles long like the former and about a mile broad is a gap of a half mile both to the east and to the west side, after which follows yet another small shoal of a mile long and about as broad and there is a similar gap named the Cross Channel, to the west of which is the island Ramannacoil,[2]

[1] These names given by the Dutch have not survived.　　[2] Rāmēsvaram is meant.

which is about 2 miles long and one mile broad and on which there is a famous temple, between which island and the mainland coast of Choremandel[1] (or properly of the Teuver[2] or the Nayak of Madure[3]) there is again an opening found named the Tear Channel[4] or Pembenaar.[5]

These shoals together up to the island Ramannacoil make up, in my guess, about 13 miles and have the name Adam's Bridge, because the natives think (though without the least ground) that Adam and Eve lived hereabouts and that Paradise would have been here.[6] We shall speak of this in more detail in dealing with Adam's Peak.[7]

One is of the opinion, with much probability, that this Adam's Bridge was attached to the shore of the Madure Coast[8] and also to the Manaar island which again was attached to the island of Ceylon, but that by the massive irruption of the sea, here and there a breach was made and that gradually it was totally separated.[9]

The island is full of cattle, birds and very rich in fishes and specially well provided with trees and fruits.

In old times Manaar was very well known by its Pearlbank and the pearl fishery and became very rich thereby as the Portuguese have shown well enough by the prestigious buildings and their churches and monasteries there. But before this island fell into our hands, the banks had not been fished for 11 or 12 years, or rather not much was caught, because of which the place had begun to be impoverished markedly. But as soon as we became masters of the place,

---

[1] The east coast of India has come to be known by the Europeans as the Coromandel coast, a derivation from Cholamandalam, or the territory of the Cholas, one of the most powerful south Indian dynasties.

[2] Thēvar, a feudatory ruler of the principality of Rāmnad who had become virtually independent.

[3] The ruler of the south Indian kingdom of Madura, originally a feudatory of the Vijayanagar Emperor but independent from the early 17th century.

[4] Valentijn uses the words *Gat van Tear*. The meaning of *Tear* here is unclear.

[5] Pāmban Āru or Pamban Channel.

[6] This was an Arab belief that can be dated back to the 13th century.

[7] In Chapter 16 where he discusses religious beliefs, V. 1, pp. 375–6.

[8] The coast of south India directly opposite Mannar.

[9] This is a sound geological view. The separation of Ceylon from south India is held to have taken place in the Miocene Period of the Tertiary Era.

fishing began here again in 1666 and has gone on since then with great success.

Now that we have described the island of Manaar so far, we return again to the mainland of Ceylon where going from Mantotte first northeast and then again north we come to the land of the Wannias[1] or the Malabars,[2] which is generally called Wanni.

About 4 miles from Mantotte, not far from the coast where the shore bends first northeastward and then again north, we come across the village Peringale, north of which one first comes to a forest, and about 5 or 6 miles from there the district of Coelang[3] and further north from there that of Sette[4] where again there are some jungles.

The village Peringale

Between Peringale and Coelang there are three small islands seawards and two more near Coelang and about 2 miles south of Coelang a small river.

Villipatta, Palicoera & Calmonie

Three miles north of Sette is the village Villipatta and 2 or 3 small streams between both, just as there are 3 others between Villipatta and the village Palicoera situated five miles north between 2 forests.

From Palicoera the coast turns somewhat north by west, decreasing gradually till near the channel of Jaffanapatnam it is not more than a mile broad; from Palicoera to the village Calimonie (which is on the northwestern end of this stretch of land in the north) is about 5 miles.

Here the sea breaks in with an opening (called Chawatzeri) of a half or quarter mile, between the coast of Jaffanapatnam and the small strip of land on the west side, such that it runs into the land about 8 or 10 miles southeast up to the Fort Calireaw,[5] situated on the east side of the island, being a mile broad in the middle but hardly half a mile at the end, where also the country of Jaffanapatnam is joined to the mainland of the land of Ceylon or the land of the Veddas by a small strip.

[1] Vanniar, the people occupying the jungle-clad lands of the north, below the Jaffna peninsula. [2] Tamils.

[3] Probably *kulam* (Tam.)—tank or pond. This area was full of these tanks but each was known by a name with the suffix *kulam*. [4] Cheddikulam.

[5] Unidentifiable. There is a place now called Elephant Pass in this area whose Tamil name is *Ānai Iravu*. *Ānai* (Tam.), *Ali* (Sinh.)—elephant. Could *ānai* have been transformed by Valentijn's source to *ali*?

Second Chapter

[Geography (contd.)]

The Kingdom of Jaffnapatnam, divided into four Districts. The Fort and City described and map. Also the Church of the Cross. The villages of Welligamme. Warmoratie, Timmeratie. And those belonging to Pachelapali. The islands west of Jaffanapatnam. Amsterdam, Leyden, and their villages. The Fort Cais or Hammenhiel. The islands Delft, Middelburg, Hoorn, etc. The land of the Weddas or Bedas. The Fort of Tricoenmale. The town Cotjaar. The town and Fort of Baticalo. The city of Baticalo at a distance. And a map of the Fort. Various towns and villages. The towns Mature and Billigam. Toetoecoryn. The interior of Ceylon described. Reasons why not much can be said of the interior. From Gale northwards one comes to the town Mapulagam, etc. Adam's Peak. The town Anguratotte and Saffragam. The towns Malvane and Balane. The city Sitavaca. The Fort and town Ruanelle, etc. The city Manicramare. The Fort Ganoor. Various towns and villages. The city Elledat and Dietlicke. Also Nilobe and Candi. Various towns and villages. The city Bintene. The town Anaragiepoer. Other towns and villages. The cities Jale and Vellas.

The kingdom of Jaffanapatnam

We go on now to describe the Kingdom of Jaffanapatnam. This country is in the north 6 or 7 miles broad, and not much less to the south, though somewhat smaller to the west side. But on the southeast side it narrows to a small stretch of land which is about 3 miles broad at Cattinai, gradually becoming smaller till at the port Calieraw[1] it is hardly half a mile broad, but from Rundelau[2] in the southeast to Tancora[3] on the

---

[1] Unidentifiable. Probably Ānai Iravu or Elephant Pass. See p. 129 n. 5.
[2] Unidentifiable.   [3] Unidentifiable. Could it be Thenkudā?

island Amsterdam[1] it is 12 to 13 miles long east to west, at its broadest 4½ miles and at its narrowest near Pachele Pali 2 miles.

Formerly it was a very famous kingdom by itself, but now, apart from the great Fort, it is divided into 4 districts, Welligame, Warmoratie, Timmeratie, and Pachelepali.

Divided into 4 districts

The first lies right in the north by west, the second in the northeast, the third in the southwest and the other in the southeast at the end of this stretch of land.

The Fort or Castle of Jaffanapatnam lies on the south side of the Welligame district, has four strong bulwarks and 2 round towers of white coral stone, a counterscarp, a deep moat, a beautiful waterpass and has also a much larger garrison than the Castle of Batavia.

The fort and city described

It also serves as a residence for the Commander, the deputy and other officials of the Company as we have a large comptoir here.

The Commander has authority over the Fort and the city situated beside it which is very large and very neatly built. We show the city in No. 13 and the Fort in No. 13O and the fine church in No. 13P.[2]

There are in the city (which is a mile large and is entirely open) very fine streets, beautiful buildings, a moderately large church, a beautiful hospital and other public residences which give this city a very good prospect. Inside and outside it are also beautiful gardens.

And Maps, as also of the church

All round outside the city there are many passes or inner and outer watches such as the Pass-Pyl (in memory of the Governor Pyl[3]), the Pass-beschutter, the Elephant Pass and Point Pedro, but built in later times (as we show elsewhere) situated 21 miles from Manaar, 3 from Jaffnapatnam, 5 from Cais and from Point Pedro.

If all the villages in this great country are added up they will total a large number.

---

[1] Kāraithīvu.

[2] Valentijn presents a double page plan of the city and two half page drawings of the fort and the church. The plan of the city is reproduced here. See Map 4.

[3] Laurens Pyl, Commander of Jaffna 1673–1679 and Governor of Ceylon 1679–1692.

The villages of
Belligamme

In Bellegame there are only four, namely Navacoela, east of the Fort, Achiavelli, north of it, Oudewil and Telipole situated in the northeast and north. However there are several other such as Batecotte, Paneteri, Manipay, Mallagam and Mayletti which lie stretched from the southeast corner to the northeast corner.

Those of
Warmoeratie

In the district of Warmoeratie, there are in the northwest the village Pareriturai, and to the west and southwest some jungle. But outside this there are other villages such as Tondemanaar in the north, Catavelli lying more to the southwest and more inland away from the sea side, then there is the Fort Point Pedro which lies right on the northeast point. Thereafter follows, to the west and along the coast, the village Vergammoni[1] which lies one mile from Pareriturai or Point Pedro. Then Calcoelang, Urepoetti, Coerette, Amban, Nagarcojel, Illondi[2] and Matuwaal, which villages are situated to the west each a mile from the other and each separated from the other by a forest.

Timmeratie

Thereafter follow the villages belonging to the district of Timmeratie such as Tsjenbaimpatti, Coedorep, Waranne, Martenni[3] and Poenretton,[4] southwest on the northside of the land, each also a mile from the other and separated from each other by jungle. But to the south side of the land are the villages Chavatzeri, near a salt creek, and a mile southwestwards Catehay,[5] another mile southwestwards St. Jago, and near the sea on the bay there is the pass of Catehay.

And under
Pachelepali

In the southeast are the villages which belong under the Pachelepali district. To the northwest side Aliancelle, Oeretura, Wettilegemi,[6] Mogommale (a little further inland) and Coenrengoeture,[7] each a mile from the other and separated by jungle, and to the south side round to the southwest and then further east from there is Mulipatto, a mile further Poelepolay, and two miles further Tambamme. These are the most important but not all the villages and large hamlets which (there) are in this jungle country as there are in all 160 in number.

[1] Probably Veeramānikkatēvanturai.
[2] Probably Villūndi.
[3] Unidentifiable.   [4] Poonakari or Poonery.
[5] Probably Kachchai.
[6] Unidentifiable. Probably Vettilaikamam.
[7] Unidentifiable.

North of Welligamme, about 3 miles out in the sea is a small shoal where there are 4 to 5 fathoms of water in the north and 7 fathoms to the south. Also to the northeast of Point Pedro is a shoal about 3 miles in length and 1 mile in breadth stretching mostly northeast and southeast, as there is another shoal in the sea off Pareriturai with 7 or 8 feet of water.

West of Welligamme and the Jaffanapatnam Fort are 3 large islands. The nearest to the west point of Welligamme is the island of Amsterdam, formerly named Caradia, a desolate and wooded island between which and the coast of Welligamme is a channel of a short mile width. The island is greater in length than breadth, about 5 miles in circumference.

The islands west of Jaffanapatnam

Amsterdam

Right opposite the south is the island Leyden, formerly named Oeraturai, where are the villages Alepoeti (to the east), Velane, Oeraturai and the old Fort in the west. It is about 4 miles from the Jaffnapatnam Fort but only one mile from the island Amsterdam, between which islands is one of the oldest forts, Cays,[1] called by us now Hammenhiel, in the middle of this channel. Three miles west is the new fort Cangienturai which is in a position to prevent entry to all ships as it is very well provided with the necessary ordnance though in itself not very big. It has a fine view from outside and is held to be the gateway of Jaffanapatnam.

Leyden and its villages

The Fort Hammenhiel

Between the islands Leiden and Delft (which were formerly called Pongardiva[2]) are many small islands; to the west of the island Leiden[3] is a desolate island and to the northeast of Delft in the mid-waters is the island Middelburg,[4] near which lies the island Donna Clara[5] and the Brahmin's Island[6] and to the east of the desolate island and to the south of the Fort of Jaffnapatnam 7 or 8 miles off (though much closer to Palicoera on the east) are the islands Enkhuizen and Hoorn,[7] of which

The islands Delft, Middelburg, Hoorn, etc.

---

[1] Under the British, it was called Kayts, which name it still retains.
[2] Punguduthīvu. Valentijn is in error here. The island Nedunthīvu was renamed Delft by the Dutch.
[3] Ūrukāthurai.   [4] Punguduthīvu.
[5] Analathīvu. The island was owned, at the time of the Portuguese, by a lady Dona Clara and thus got its name. It was later renamed Rotterdam by the Dutch.
[6] Probably Naināthīvu which the Dutch later named Haarlem.
[7] Iranathīvu or Twin Islands.

the first is not over 1 mile from the eastern coast and the latter is about 5 miles away.

West of these islands which are all overgrown with trees and are uninhabited is a great reef that stretches south and northeast 6 miles distant and is 2 miles broad in the south, gradually getting smaller and finally disappearing.

It begins about 1 mile north of the island Delft or rather more to the west and stretches 1 mile beyond the island Amsterdam to the northeast. Three or four miles more to the northwest is a small shoal.

Apart from these islands there is another situated about 5 miles southwest of the island Delft named Chagodina.[1]

Here we move over from Jaffanapatnam (which lies 22 miles from Manaar Island which is 5 miles long and 2 miles at its broadest) to the eastern coast of this island, to proceed again with our description from Fort Calierauw southeastwards.

The land of the Bedas

A small mile southeastwards lies a large shoal, about 7 or 8 miles in circumference, attached to the coast, on which there are 2, 3, 4, 5, 6 and 8 fathoms of water.

Then follows the land of the Bedas[2] (or Weddas) that extends along the shore both to the south and west about 30 miles in circumference, in the west up to the District Hoerli and in the south to Trinkenemale or Trinquenemale (though correctly Tricoen-Male),[3] consisting only of very thick jungle.

Tricoen-Male gets its name from the Malabar deity Tricoen and Tricoen male means Tricoen's Hill as the word Tricol signifies the Tricoen temple.[4] To the north of Trinkenemale are 2 small rivers of which the first is 7 or 8 and the last or nearest only 3 miles away and is named Oetialle,[5] near which is also a small shoal close to the coast as there is also one 2 miles to the southeast, about 2 miles in circumference and

---

[1] Probably Cachathīvu.   [2] Veddas. The aboriginal inhabitants of Ceylon.
[3] Under the British and internationally it was and is known as Trincomalee. Valentijn is nearer to the old Tamil name which was Thirukōnāmalai.
[4] Valentijn's interpretation is partially correct. He is right in the view that the place derived its name from a famous temple on a rock or hill (*malai*—Tam.). But the name of the temple was Thirukōnesvaram. Thus the place was named Thirukōnāmalai.
[5] Probably Uppuvali.

right before the Fort of Tricoenmale, on which there are some small islands, one of which is called the great Trees Island.

Trinkenemale is a beautiful Fort where we have an *Opperhoofd*[1] with some officers and a good garrison, being well provided with everything and with 4 good bulwarks, though it mostly serves to keep others from there, being now and then abandoned by us. It lies on one of the most beautiful Bays of the whole of Ceylon, where the sea comes in in a northern and an eastern bight forming there two large bays, though the eastern is somewhat dry and the northern has 4 small islands. They are each 3 or 4 miles in circumference.[2]

The Fort of Tricoenmale

This Fort, like Baticalo, used to be a Commandement[3] in olden times but they have both been managed by subordinate chiefs for many years, whose names and terms of office I have not been able to learn.[4]

The actual Bay of Trinkenemale appears as one passes the Trees Island and yet another island that lies right before the Fort, being very wide in circumference. For between this bay and that of Cotjaar (that lies opposite in the southeast) is a width of 4 miles and it is about 5 or more miles deep.

The town of Cotjaar lies deep in the Bay of the same name to the southwest in the domain of the same name which is mountainous in the west and covered with jungle in the south-east. As one goes out of the Bay from the town of Cotjaar (where the land bulges to the north with a sharp angle and then curves and goes northeastwards), one sees, up to the city of Baticalo, nothing but a river, hardly 2 miles south of the angle of this Bay, and 5 miles further another somewhat larger. Also not far from Baticalo (this Commandery[5] begins with the river Palaveca,[6] 6 miles north of Tricoenmale) is the hill of Paligam (named after this district) about 2 miles from there

The town of Cotjaar

---

[1] An officer-in-charge.

[2] The praise of the Bay of Trincomalee has been sung by many European writers. See for example J. E. Tennent *Ceylon* (London 1866, Fifth Edition), Vol. 11, pp. 482–490.

[3] A separate command with a Commandant in charge, like Galle and Jaffna.

[4] A separate Commandement was set up for the east coast in 1671 with its seat in Batticaloa, extending to Trincomalee but after a few years it was abolished and this whole region brought under the Commandant of Jaffna.

[5] Another term for Commandement.   [6] Palambali Āru.

and near the River of Paligam or of Baticalo,[1] and also the village More[2] eastwards and Viado[3] and Occatoti situated a mile or two west of the river, to the west of which villages are again large forests.

Town and Fort of Baticalo

The town Baticalo lies in a district of the same name (also named Matecalo[4]) on a latitude of about 8 degrees. We have not drawn it as it had already been done by others. But the castle we portray in No. 13H and the city in perspective with the layout of the land in No. 13N.[5]

Representation of the City and Fort of Baticalo

The Fort lies on an island, 2 miles in circumference, being situated 2 miles within the lagoon and close by the river after which it is named. It has high, strong stone walls, 3 strong bulwarks on which are 11 metal and iron pieces, 5 metal falconets and some mortars; it is generally occupied by 100 men. Its border is the Gravet of Sangamcandi up to Panoa. We will speak in greater detail of this when describing the arrival of Joris van Spilbergen.[6]

Within the bay which is reasonably large there is the river of Baticalo to the south, another island and nearby on the shore the village Colahare[7] and somewhat southeastwards Patenoad,[8] where the land runs northwards to a sharp angle and for 3 miles is hardly a mile broad, gradually becoming sharper.

That Baticalo was also a Commandement has already been stated earlier, though that of Trinkenemale has always been more important. We describe Tricoenmale and Cotjaar later in more detail in a report of Mr. van Goens.[9]

To the east of this point is a shoal, stretching 3 miles south and north and about a mile broad on which there are 2, 4, 5, 8 and 9 fathoms of water.

---

[1] Difficult to identify this. There is no river of Batticaloa but several rivers and streams that fall into the Batticaloa lagoon. The name that approximates closest to Valentijn's Paligam is Pulukumawa river.

[2] Probably Mandūr.   [3] Unidentifiable.

[4] Maddakalappu. The Tamil name from which Batticaloa was derived.

[5] A double page picture of the city as seen from the harbour and a half page plan of the Fort. See Map 5.

[6] Dutch Admiral and commander of one of the early voyages to the east. He landed in Batticaloa in 1602. See below, pp. 279–94.

[7] Probably Kallār.   [8] Unidentifiable. Probably Paddiruppu.

[9] Valentijn V. 1, pp. 219–21.

A mile south of Patenoad is the town Aragoene[1] and the river Sengare,[2] south of which is a forest and to the west a steep hill, commonly named the Capel.[3] A mile to the south is the town Raddele[4] and nearer the village Coholawyle[5] and a half mile further the temple of Trincoli or Tricoil which is famous throughout the whole country.

A mile further is the village Coemene (where a reef is attached to the coast), another mile further the town Pamene and that of Mandagle on a river, named the Heddel Oye.[6] Somewhat further on is the town Pettin and 2 miles south of Pattene, the villages Ockande, Andenowe[7] and a mile further Memene after which are many hills and the Komboken Oye[8] which is reasonably large and springs from the western mountain Maimda Kinde.[9] It is the end of the jurisdiction of Gale and is a day's journey from Baticalo, 3 days from Mature and four from Gale. From the Komboken River to Walauwe[10] one had to travel 14 German miles.

South of this river are again some hills and 1 mile from Memene one comes across the village Mandegelle, one mile further amidst or near another mountain, the village Pattene and a mile further the village Jaleput on a river with another hill on the west, and in the east just outside the sea coast the rock Jale. Further south of the river, somewhat inland, is the town Catenagon and further south near the coast the town Leawawa.

A mile further (where the land gradually turns to the southwest) one sees some salt pans and a large mountain and then 2 miles from Leawawa the village Transalier,[11] a mile further Magame, after which one goes over the Cerinde River,[12] south of which close to the coast are some mountains and salt pans. But 1 mile inland is the village Coendeli[13] and further 1 mile west Kelligamme, Koekgalle, Anakanvelle, close to

[1] Unidentifiable. Could it be Irakamam?   [2] Sagamam.
[3] Unidentifiable. Probably Westminster Abbey. See below, p. 156 n. 2.
[4] Unidentifiable.
[5] Unidentifiable. There is a village called Kehelula about 50 miles inland.
[6] Heda Oya.   [7] Probably Andarakala.   [8] Kumbukkan Oya.
[9] Probably Namunukula range of mountains.   [10] Valavē Ganga.
[11] Māgama. The Portuguese named this place Transalier.
[12] Kirindē Oya.   [13] Probably Kurundana.

each other, near which there are several fresh inland tanks. But along the coast from the abovenamed river Cerinde to the great Walauwe River which springs from Adam's Peak, one sees nothing but high mountains and many salt pans.

Just southwest of the river is the town of Walauwe after which one sees a small hill and then a large plain up to the DolasDas Corle[1] and up to the Gerreweis.

From Walauwe to the town Tangale is 7 or 8 miles where this great plain appears at its most beautiful and it is customary to go on an elephant hunt. Off Walauwe, four miles into the sea, is a small shoal and 1 or 2 others like it between it and Tangale. From Tangale which lies on a small river to the village Ajalle[2] it is 2 miles and to Halpilame[3] another 3 miles where the Gerreways district is. At this last place the coast curves in somewhat, making a small bay and another larger one a half mile further on almost directly to the south.

The town Mature

A mile further from Halpilame one comes to Huwacare,[4] a little further Tannidar or Galiettis,[5] still about a mile further Dondore[6] and then the town of Mature on the beautiful River Melipu,[7] situated right in the south.

Here we have a Fort, an *Opperhoofd* and a garrison. Just west of this river is the temple of Tanaware[8] in the District of this name and 1 mile to the west the village Curaca.[9]

The village Billigam

Here the coast bends sharply inward to the north making a large bay (called the Red Bay or Bay of Billigam) which is 2 miles in depth and width, within which to the west side is the town Billigam in Billigam Corle.[10]

Four miles west of this Bay is the village Kaddogore[11] near a river, and a mile further the village Unawatte, and there the land turns further northwards making the Bay of Gale, where 2 small streams are seen. Thus we have roamed round this entire island.

[1] Dolosdas Kōralē.

[2] Unidentifiable. Sounds like Elalla but this village is 30 miles from Tangalle.

[3] Unidentifiable.   [4] Unidentifiable.

[5] The Portuguese used to call this place near the southernmost point of the island Galiettis.

[6] Devundara. In British times, the place was known as Dondrā.

[7] Nilvalā Ganga.   [8] Tenavarai, another name for Devinuvara or Devundara.

[9] Probably Akuressa, but this place is further inland.

[10] Weligam Kōralē.   [11] Probably Karagoda.

All these coastal places belong to the Company and also several interior lands all of which stand under the authority of the Governor of Ceylon.

Moreover there is on the coast of Madure, in the land of the Thevar[1] or the Naik of Tanjore,[2] opposite the west side of Ceylon, in a large bay, the city of Toetoecoryn on the north latitude of 8 degrees and 48 minutes, just south of Keypatnam and north of Cape Comoryn which are also under the Governor of Ceylon. Toetoecoryn

It is a large open town, without walls, gates or moats in which there are 3 beautiful churches which one observes even at sea. Most of the houses, which are many in number and stand on a number of wide blocks, are of stone.

We have had a residence here and an *Opperhooft* who is a *Koopman* and besides an *Onderkoopman* and some other officers to manage the affairs of the Company since the beginning of February 1658 when this place was conquered by us under the command of Mr. van der Meyden,[3] together with the island Rammanacojel,[4] Adam's Bridge, etc.

This city is also very famous through its pearl fishery which produces reasonably good pearls, but these or the Manaar pearls cannot match those of Ormus and Bahrein in beauty of lustre and purity. Also there are many *chanks*[5] or sacrificial horns fished here which are much desired in Bengal to make rings.

The Hon. Company derives its duty on the fishing of pearls and *chanks* from the Paravas[6] or divers and also trades greatly in cloth which is woven and painted here which gives us a handsome profit.

It is a city where there is an abundance of everything and especially of provisions which are very cheap. It is winter here in October, November and December, or the rain-monsoon, when on the other side of the Cape Comoryn or on

[1] The principality of Rāmnād.
[2] Nāyak of Tanjore. The ruler of the kingdom on the southern extremity of the Coromandel coast of India.
[3] Adriaan van der Meyden. Governor of Ceylon 1653–1662.
[4] Rāmēsvaram. This island was conquered by the Dutch later in 1690.
[5] From *sanku* (Tam.)—conch shell.
[6] *Paravar* (Tam.). A Tamil caste of fishermen and pearl divers.

Malabar it is summer, which change of season is caused only by the intervening mountains of Ballagate.[1]

The island Rammanakojel

On the island Rammanacojel is a very large and beautiful as also ancient temple, besides a fort of the Thevar or Lord of the Land. The island is in itself not large. It gets its name from the heathen deity Ramma[2] and the temple is much frequented by pilgrims.

We must here add a word of some more trifling information which will give the reader much light for a better understanding of the island.

Among the important passes or posts in the land here that of Alauw is in no way the least. It is the gateway to the Four Corles and the Seven Corles, lying 2 days journey from Anaragiepeore and from there to the northernmost Mangul Corle is a journey of 12 hours and from there again to Chilauw one daylight or 12 hours, as from Chilauw to Nigombo is 1 day and from Nigombo to Alauw 12 hours, from which it can be seen that a traveller on foot can go round the Seven Corles in 4 days in that part that belongs to us.

To cover the lands of Nigombo there is, six miles from there, on the Caymel River[3] near the village Dunaga, a striking watchhouse from which six miles on and higher is the famous station of Alauw just described.

From Alauw to Arandore is 3 hours and from there to Ruwanelle another hour and in six hours one can go from Alauw to Dunaga and from there it is 12 hours easily to Candi and again in 12 hours to Attenagale through the Hina Corle to Malvane from where in 2 hours' sailing in a boat one can come to Colombo. A great hour from Arandore lies Tontotte and from the first by land and from Tontotte by water in 2½ hours one can come to Ruwanelle (which lies on the Colombo River).[4]

From Arandore to Sitavaca is six hours and to Saffragam or to the headland of Adam's Peak 8 and to Colombo by land

[1] Pālgat. Valentijn is referring to that portion of the escarpment in peninsular India, called Western Ghats, which rises to a height of over 8000 feet in the Nilgiris and breaks to the south of the Nilgiri plateau to provide the Pālgat or Coimbatore gap.

[2] Rāma, the incarnation of Vishnu and hero figure of the Rāmāyanā.

[3] Deduru Oya.   [4] Kelani Ganga.

10 hours but by water only 6 hours. From Arandore via Ruwanelle to Suffragam is 11 hours and from Sitavaca 8 hours though others say 11 hours for this latter.

Four hours' travel from Saffragam lies another strong guard of lascarines which is named Denuaca. There is another fortress on the river of Calture[1] near the village Idangodde, 3 hours' travel below Saffragam off the river, and from here to Anguratotte 8 miles away is another watchpost. From Anguratotte to Calture is 5 miles, from Calture upwards to Saffragam 16 miles and from Saffragam to Colombo 18 miles via Sitavaca and the outposts but direct through Reygam Corle it is no more than 12 to 14 hours.

From Denuaca, an important boundary post in the Gale district, right through to Biblegamme is 4 hours but via Openake about 7 hours.

All the posts from Alauw to Biblegamme embrace only 15 miles but the posts lower down along the sea make 36 to 40 miles.

Now we shall consider this island once more from within and begin again with Gale and go up northwards.

Ceylon described from within

If we shall not say much of interior Ceylon this must not be surprising, as very few people come into this country[2] and those who obtain entry either as ambassadors or by other occasion are very closely guarded by the King at the place where they reside without being able to go elsewhere, though some may obtain a sound knowledge of the country, of which there is little chance because of the extensiveness of the forests, and most of all because he does not let any foreigner go out once they have come into the country but holds them prisoners all through their lives unless they find means to escape.[3]

Reason why not much can be said of the interior

I remember very well, when I was sailing from Batavia to Japara with some soldiers, in 1686, I met among them 2 Ensigns, N. Lamsweerd and Michiel Ram who, a year or two earlier as Sergeants, were sent in the name of the Hon. Company to Raja Singa[4] with the promise that when they

[1] Kalu Ganga.   [2] That is, the interior country or the Kandyan kingdom.
[3] This complaint of the inaccessibility of the interior was universal among European observers and was the result of deliberate policy of the kings of Kandy to whom isolation was security.
[4] King of Kandy 1629–1687.

returned they would be promoted Ensigns, as they were promoted shortly after.[1]

They went there courageously, were very well received by the King and lodged in a house covered with white linen, the highest honour which can be done to anyone. But they could not go out from there till the King permitted them to return, after some months' residence in that prison-house, which was pronounced a very unusual thing and almost without precedent in a great many years.[2]

I asked them about the conditions of the interior country but they could not tell me anything because of the above mentioned reasons, further that the fear of an eternal imprisonment had prevented them from going outside their house so that they might not give the King any reason for dissatisfaction. This appears to have had good effect but they could give no reason why they had been granted permission for the return journey and not our former ambassadors.[3] Later on in a report of the Elder Mr. van Goens delivered to Their Excellencies in A.D. 1675 we describe this interior land further for which reason we let it pass here.[4]

Now we shall speak first of all the lands from Gale onwards situated between this city and the Caliture River[5] in the north and between the Mature River[6] in the east and northwards up to Adam's Peak.

From Gale northwards

Between Gale Corle and Billigam Corle,[7] just west of the village Gannegamme is seen what we have conquered with our weapons (as we will see in detail later).

---

[1] Lamsweerd and Ram were sent as emissaries from the Batavian Government to Rāja Sinha, the king of Kandy, in early 1685, taking a letter containing proposals for peace from the Governor General Speelman.

[2] These facts are recorded in detail in their report on their return to Colombo. See Bericht van 't Gepasseerde op Ampe, door Lamswaarde en Ram, 21 March 1685. *Koloniale Archief* (The Hague) 1299, fos. 323–5. It is true that they were speedily sent back by Rāja Sinha, contrary to his usual practice, because he was then very old and wished to establish good relations with the Dutch before his death.

[3] Valentijn's report of a chance meeting with these two officers and his prying questions to them as well as the record of their answers he kept for use over 25 years later, shows what an inquisitive inquirer and methodical diarist he was.

[4] Valentijn V. 1, pp. 206–8.

[5] Kalu Ganga.

[6] Nilvalā Ganga.

[7] Weligam Kōralē.

This forest stretches up to the town Harcipote near the mountain of this name in Koekele Corle[1] to the north about 15 to 16 miles up to the Hoyberg in the northwest and to a great mountain to the northeast of the village Attenluwo[2] and thus about 25 miles in circumference.

There are no houses, or towns or villages there, except five miles north of Gale the town Mapulegam and somewhat westwards on the Gale River[3] the village Gedewellewitte, both west of it, and to the northeast of Billigam, 4 miles higher, the village Malimando (where the river makes a turn to the northwest) in its middle and 2 miles from the above named village Attenluwo. From there the river turns again to the east where 2 miles further, also on the river, lies the town Accuras, and directly to the north, 8 miles from Gale the town Harcipote[4] near the mountain of this name.

The town Mapulegam, etc.

North of Hoyberg is another large forest that stretches also above Harcipote and Koekele Corle and mostly extends outwards up to Naudum Corle (except that here and there a path runs between both) and to the east up to the Caliture River,[5] while in the east is a very steep hill about 5 to 6 miles in circumference.

The villages which are in the vicinity are these: 4 miles west of Hoyberg lies Peliwatte on the small Bentotte River[6] and 5 miles directly to the north, about 2 miles south of the Caliture River, the village Pelando. Four miles to the northeast of Pelando, less than a mile from the abovenamed river (which makes a two mile bend to the south), is Penegalelle situated 8 miles northwest of the town of Harcipote.

Six miles to the east lies the town Batugedra, near which two separate streams which make up the Caliture River and are 2 miles from each other, the one originating in the south and the other to the east of Adam's Peak, unite and flow into the sea with another stream near Caliture.

Two miles east of Batugedra is the town Dinavaca in between these 2 streams (of which the southernmost with a bend 3 to 4 miles from the other, which runs mostly south-west, flows from north to south and then northeastwards) in

---

[1] Kukulu Kōralē.   [2] Unidentifiable.   [3] Gin Ganga.
[4] Unidentifiable.   [5] Kalu Ganga.   [6] Bentota Ganga.

Adam's Peak

the principality of the same name,[1] also called Two Corles which is also an important place of the King of Kandy and where some kings held their court now and then.

Two miles south of Dinavaca is the town Jemature,[2] in the district Morrua Corle,[3] all of which districts belong to us. Five miles northeast of Dinavaca is the town Openake, a mile north of which is Adam's Peak which also lies 14 miles east of Colombo.

This is a remarkable mountain which is considered one of the highest in the Indies and certainly on this island from which most, and the largest, rivers of Ceylon take their origin.

It lies about 20 miles from the west coast and about the same distance from the south coast of Mature. It rises up into a sharp point, like a sugar loaf. It was named Pico de Adam by the Portuguese, Hamalelle[4] by the natives and Adam's Peak by us. The Cingalese believe that formerly Paradise was located here, that Adam was created here and that his footsteps are to be seen imprinted deeply, two feet long, in a certain stone (which lies alone) to which mountain the Cingalese make many pilgrimages to see the footsteps whose measure is protected by the Emperor of Kandy.[5]

This mountain is so difficult to climb that here and there heavy bolts and nails have had to be beaten in and iron chains hung from them to help in climbing as there is no other way to go up.

When we again go down from Adam's Peak and proceed 6 to 7 miles from the town Openake, we come to the village Dampale,[6] just west of the Mature River or the Melipu[7] and 2 miles southwestwards the town Barle which is situated 4 miles to the east and in the south 2 miles from the river.

Now we go over, after having dealt with this region, from

---

[1] Denavaka Kōralē. [2] Unidentifiable. [3] Morawak Kōralē.
[4] Samanola. An old name for the rock on which is the celebrated foot print. It is today called Sri Pāda.
[5] Valentijn is confusing the Arab and the Sinhalese traditions. The Sinhalese believe that the foot print on the rock was that of Buddha. Valentijn provides much information later on on Adam's Peak and its religious significance. V. 1, pp. 375–83.
[6] Unidentifiable. A few miles south of Opanake is a place called Mādampē.
[7] This seems to be an old alternative name for Nilvalā Ganga.

the Caliture River[1] to describe everything that lies between this river and that of Colombo[2] (which Corle is called Colona Corle[3]) in the north and in the east up to Adam's Peak.

Just north of the Caliture River, 5 miles from the coast in Reygam Corle is the town or the Fort Anguratotte where we have some forces for the protection of the cinnamon lands which belong to us. Somewhat more to the east there is Saffragam Corle,[4] where close to the river about 9 to 10 miles east of Anguratotte is the town Saffragam in the Cotta Kingdom. Somewhat north of the Saffragam town is the district of Correwitte Corle,[5] north of which there are first some hills and then opposite to Colombo River, Panavel Corle,[6] in the Principality of the Four Corles. The town Anguratotte and Saffragam

North of the Saffragam district, which lies 5 days journey from Colombo and 4 from Arandore, up to the Hevegam Corle and further up to the Malavane town, which is 2 miles from Colombo on this river and 12 miles north of Anguratotte, there are some mountains to the west and to the east, and further on is a large cinnamon forest that extends from the one to the other river about 10 to 12 miles distant, right to the north and also a good part to the east, all of which cinnamon land also belongs to us and they are very convenient, as between them from Caliture, from the Panature River[7] and from Colombo run many roads landwards to Adam's Peak to Mature and elsewhere. Malvane

Right north of the Saffragam town about 5 miles above the Caliture river lies the Corewitte Corle, to the south in that forest and to the east surrounded by a steep mountain, and a little northwards is the Corvite Fort with some soldiers for the protection of the cinnamon peelers. After this in the northeast is the District of Attelagam Corle, and in the north first a cinnamon wood and somewhat higher in the west the District Dehegample Corle,[8] directly to the north the Balane district and town of the same name, and to the east of it opposite the Colombo river which flows down north from Adam's Peak with a great bend is the district Kindigot Corle.[9] And Balane

---

[1] Kalu Ganga.   [2] Kelani Ganga.   [3] Kolonnē Kōralē.
[4] Sabaragamuwa Kōralē.   [5] Kuruviti Kōralē.   [6] Panāval Kōralē.
[7] Mahā Oya.   [8] Dehigampal Kōralē.   [9] Kinigoda Kōralē.

Sitavaca

When one goes 4 miles east along the river from Malivatte (where we have a palisaded entrenchment, with a moat, 8 pieces, and a garrison of 60 men under a lieutenant) one comes to the village Goerbevele and Hangwelle, both with guards and 4 miles east the city Sitavaca in the Kingdom of the same name, which is situated about 11 miles from Saffragam and 11 to 12 miles from Colombo inland on the same beautiful Colombo River or rather on a small stream that flows from it southeastwards. It is called Sitavaca after the Goddess Sita.

In this city where the kings also had their court formerly we used to have from olden times a Fort or field post with a garrison against the King of Kandy. Under it stand the 3 Corles or dominions, namely Koekele Corle,[1] that is cockcounty, and 2 others in which live many hundred farmers who possess large rice fields and orchards with fruit trees for which they must pay the appropriate tax to this Fort. Also this Fort protects the precious stones found here. The road from Colombo to here is very rocky, inconvenient and full of leeches.

The Fort and town Ruanelle

Four miles east of Sitavaca is the town and Fort Ruanelle, just north of the great Colombo river, a post built by us formerly and occupied with a force and later abandoned, where the King of Kandy now has his men.

From Ruanelle to Balane is 5 miles and apart from this I know of no other place between these two rivers, except lower on the same river Hangwelle and Gourbevele, as also Malvane, till on the mouth of the Colombo river Motuaal which is called Calane higher up. Therefore I shall continue my description in the east from Adam's Peak northwards up in the District Goddaponahoy or to the city Dietlicke and from the Colombo River up to the border of the Chilauw river.[2]

The City Manicramare

North of the Colombo river, 2 miles away, is the village Calane[3] and then the Nigombo river[4] 1 mile further, where to the east are forests. Just north of the latter river, 6 miles from Calane, in the district of Happittagam is the town Attengale and 4 miles eastwards, about 3 miles north of the Colombo river, the old city Manicramare, where the latter river has its

[1] Kukulu Kōralē.   [2] Deduru Oya.
[3] Probably Kolonnē.   [4] Mahā Oya.

source and south of which are also many high mountains which make a chain of mountains from there to Adam's Peak. One mile north of the Colombo river and 4 miles to the south-east of Manikramare is the strong fort Ganoor in the mountain of the same name which formerly belonged to us but is abandoned now and then.

The city of Manikramare, according to the evidence of the natives, is but an open town which is still reasonably large but has very poor bamboo houses, apart from which are seen here and there an old pagoda or temple and a large market.

The Fort Ganoor is a strong position if one wants to make oneself permanent there.

The Fort of Ganoor

North of the Nigombo river there is near the sea the District Hina Corle and somewhat northwards that of Pitigal Corle but to the east the District Happitagam Corle in the principality of the Seven Corles, in which 6 miles from Nigombo to the northeast is the village Alauw and 2 miles to the northwest from the city of Manikramare the village Maleriava.

Between Alauw and the District Three Corles, which lies about 5 miles away, there is, north of the Seven Corles, the Districts Billigal Corle in the west, and 4 to 5 miles eastwards Dehegample Corle[1] and Gabbade Corle[2] opposite the above named steep mountain where Manikramare lies and which run in a continuous chain from Adam's Peak first north by west till above the District Tuntonahoy or up to the mountain Bocaul and then further northeast and north till deep into the land of the Malabaars[3] and till very close to Jaffanapatnam.[4]

Between Billigal Corle, just north of a beautiful river, 5 miles from the village Alauw to the northeast there are near each other the towns Arandore and Alanha,[5] after which follows the District Tun Corle without any other place till the Chilauw river except the desert of Madampe and then the small river of Chilauw (which lies 5 miles from the river near Arandore) and 4 miles further lies the great Chilauw river which springs from

Various towns and villages

---

[1] Dehigampal Kōralē.　　　[2] Galboda Kōralē.　　　[3] Tamils.

[4] This is a gross error. The mountain chain ends long before the Tamil country.

[5] Unidentifiable. It could be Alauwa, about 10 miles from Arandora, but Valentijn identifies Alauwa correctly in the previous line.

the Bocaul mountain in the east and partly from the Alegol mountain in the southeast and is rather big.

East of Alanha is the large district Houteracorle[1] and still further east the district of Tun Ponahoy and the mountains Bocaul and Alegol, and between the two separate branches of the Chilauw river, of which the northernmost is called Dedero,[2] and which unite 4 to 5 miles from the City of Chilauw, is a very large forest of 7 to 8 miles circumference and in the east close by the mountain Bocaul and 2 miles south of the branch called Dedero lies the village Doldagom.[3] Thus having shown everything which is west of this stretch of mountains which runs north from Adam's Peak and lies between the Colombo river and the Chilauw River, we shall now see what is to be found from Adam's Peak to the District of Goddaponahoy, east of that steep mountain of Ganoor, Alegol and Bocaul.

Just north of Adam's Peak, 1 mile from there lies the village Collegemanach, 2 miles northeast of the town Callegom and 4 miles east as one goes across the Candi river[4] (which is the same as that of Bintene and Trinkenemale and which flows north to Candi) is the town Laggendenni, all of which places lie in the surrounding mountains and in the District of Deleswage.

Six miles north of Callegom one comes, after crossing a steep mountain not far from that of Ganoor, to the village Cormeol[5] in the district of Oedipollat, where the river of Candi splits itself into two streams and one runs right to the north of Candi and the other 4 miles east where this stream again divides into two, of which one runs direct to the village Combalauwla and the other northeast.

Thus now going west of the Candi River, we come to the village Bowagom, 1 mile north of Cormeol, in the District of Oedipollat, and 5 miles northwest to the village Diveli in the District Oerenoere and 5 miles directly north of the village Bowagom the town Elledat a large and ugly town near the Candi river. Four to five miles west of this city is the mountain Matapeti[6] and 3 to 4 miles to the northwest the town

The city Elledat

---

[1] Hatara Kōralē. [2] Deduru Oya. [3] Probably Dandagamuva.
[4] Mahāveli Ganga. [5] Unidentifiable. [6] Probably Malpitikanda.

Vittebatoe,[1] 1 mile northeast the town Jatti, a small mile further to the northeast the village Gamatani, a mile further northeast the town Ode in the District Jatti, another 1 mile northeast near the river the town Balane and finally just west of the river the city of Candi itself, of which we will speak as soon as we touch on the places situated to its west.

North of Balane is a forest and the steep mountain Bocaul situated about 4 miles from the Candi River and west of the District of Horsepot which district is just above the village Valgom, which lies 1 mile north of the Candi river, where it bends to the east and there is also a forest where we will stop at the mountain in the north from which the Chilauw river originates, up to the border of which we have brought our description.

Now to return to Adam's Peak and proceeding east of the Candi River 4 miles from Laggendenni into the Kingdom of Oeva one comes to the village Dinmullo, and directly north of Laggendenni is the District of Coetemale, 6 miles north a town of the same name just south of the stream and a very large forest both south and north of it. Five miles east of Coetemale is the town Poolepitte, to the east of which both south and north are some mountains.

Two miles east of Poolepitte, north of which is the village and Dietlicke Combalauwle, north of which are again some mountains and 5 to 6 miles north of the latter village the mountain Garlenda or Gauluda in the District of Goddaponahoy just west of which and about a mile from the Candi River is the royal city Dietlicke, in which Raja Singa has held his court since the rebellion of his subjects in A.D. 1664, as the strongest and most inaccessible in his Kingdom in spite of the fact that it is very rocky, stony and the most infertile part of the whole of Ceylon, looking more to his security than to his comfort as the mountain on which it lies is very high, besides there are 3 towns and rice-producing fields above it from which he receives his provisions in abundance, further that along its steep cliffs very few people can climb so that very few men are necessary to defend the city, being in itself only a nest of some

[1] Unidentifiable.

bamboo houses together, some small temples and beautiful shops but not provided with a market place.[1]

The palace of the Emperor is not very large in its circumference, but otherwise reasonably comfortably situated and provided with some beautiful galleries and other apartments with a view of some lakes. It has a strong garrison there but most of the time no one knows where the King is. Also there are some houses of nobles here but mostly incomplete as the King always gives them other work.

North of the town Coetemale is a large forest and four to five miles north of the town about a mile east of the Candi River the city of Nilobe.

Nilobe

This used to be the royal city of Raja Singa before the rebellion of 1664 but his people forced him to flee from there to Dietlicke, though it also lies very secure in the mountain and in the District of Hewahene.

It is now only a nest and had not been much better before. Just north of this mountain of Nilobe is another forest, and 4 to 5 miles northeast from there the village Potteagum and 4 miles to the northwest of this village the town Laleluja near the Candi River and just west of this town the famous city of Candi itself.

Candi

This is a city which is situated 30 miles from the city of Bintene and 21 miles from Baticaloa on the greatest river of the entire island called Mavilganga.[2] It is about 2 miles long and has many large streets and a great many stone, timber and bamboo houses. In the middle is the royal palace which is half a mile in circumference and is provided with 6 bulwarks as citadels and a very large gate on the south side. Inside there are also very many large stone buildings, being remains of Don Jan's time who later took the name Raja Singa.[3]

In the city there are many large blocks with houses, large

---

[1] After a rebellion against him in 1664, the king of Kandy, Rāja Sinha II, moved his capital from Nilambē to Diyatilaka.

[2] Mahāveli Ganga. The distances are erroneous. Kandy is much closer to Alutnuvara (Bintene) than to Batticaloa.

[3] This is an error. Don Jan took the name Vimala Dharma Sūrya and ruled Kandy from 1594 to 1601. Valentijn speaks of him in great detail. See below, Chap. 7, pp. 263–78.

squares and many shops in which lacquer, rice, salt, tobacco, spices and everything is on sale. Though there is no market, there are many heathen temples and many monasteries and other remains of the Portuguese.

This used to be the capital of Ceylonese Emperors in olden times but after they fell out with the Portuguese they retired first to Nilobe and then to Dietlicke.

Joris van Spilbergen has left behind a sketch on which, to speak the truth, one places as little reliance as on his description.[1] We shall speak in greater detail of it later on and proceed to talk of Candi and Bintene.

After the description of Candi, we now go from the Chilauw river which is the end of the cinnamon lands to the River Caula Weya[2] or to the District of Newecawala in the north and in the east from the District of Goddaponahoy where we stopped last, proceeding along the Trinkenemale River to the Bay of Cotjaar.

Just north of the Chilauw River begins the Kingdom of Candi which stretches south, north and east from there. One comes in the north first to a forest and 4 miles along the river to the town Corrinde Codwat, and 7 to 8 miles east, about 1 mile from the Chilauw River on the stream Dedero,[3] to the village Cornogale, and 5 miles eastward near the mountain chain in the east to the town Boender-Coos-wat. Two miles north of Boender-Coos-wat along that mountain which we will now follow up to the Caula Weya River[4] there is in the District of Hotcorle[5] a town Nickavar, 1 mile northwards the village Eredenne, another 1 mile northeastwards the village Dempitigal, after which northwards is the jungle waste of Parroah, and 2 miles to the northwest of Dempitigal is the town Parroah, east of which up to the mountains is another thick jungle.

Two miles north of Parroah lies the village Nicotticum and 2 miles further north the town Hondopoal which lies about 2 miles from the Caula River. Just north of which, right north of Hondopoal is the village Detelwaja,[6] and somewhat west

---

[1] *Reis van Joris van Spilbergen*, p. 46.   [2] Kalā Oya.
[3] Deduru Oya.   [4] Kalā Oya.
[5] Hat Kōralē.   [6] Probably Diwulveva.

the village Hotmittawajah[1] and a little north of it the town Ekpoelpol[2] in the district of Newecalawa.

In the west, north of Corinde Codwat, in the district of Palawi there is a large forest and then 6 miles to the northeast of Corinde Codwad the village Golgom, and 2 miles southeast the village Mendondunpe, between which and the Chilauw river 5 to 6 miles away to the south is a thick forest.

Five miles to the northeast of Golgom, east of the river Hembolonggom[3] which falls into the large, wide River Caula is the village Dollopottogum, five miles to the northeast of which lies the village Helballigal, where our limits on the west of our journey which we have fixed for ourselves are reached.

Various towns and villages Now we go forth from Candi east of this mountain along the river of Trinkenemale[4] up to the Bay of Cotjaar.

Just north of the River of Candi, which bends near this city from north exactly to the west for about 6 to 7 miles and is generally called the River Mawielle Ganga, there are three large Districts, in the west against the mountains: that of Horsepot, to the east, that of Dombera and further eastwards that of Porcipot. A mile north of the river lies the village Valgom on a small stream that falls there in the District of Horzepot. Four miles northeast in the District of Dombera is the town Verdre.[5]

North of Dombera and Porcipot are tall mountains and 3 to 4 miles to the northeast of Vendre the town Mondamanoere, and 4 miles to the northeast the village Singeles or Safalocki[6] on the River Maweleganga, which in front of the District Goddoponahoy and Porcipot turns again entirely to the north and at the place where it begins this turn and somewhat ahead, that is not far south of Singeles, some small streams fall into it.

North of Mondamanoere is the principality of Matule or Matalie where is the District of Roewat which is jungle-clad in the east and the north which goes on through the County of Bintene for 10 to 12 miles along the Cauragahing[7] mountain

---

[1] Unidentifiable. Could it be Halmillewa?
[2] Unidentifiable. Could it be Eppawala?
[3] Siyambalāgam Oya.
[4] Mahāveli Ganga.
[5] Unidentifiable.
[6] Probably Simbella. See p. 110 n. 12.
[7] Unidentifiable.

(which extends east and west of the river) without any village or town on this side of that mountain until the bay of Cotiari or to the land of the Bedas. But on the side of the River Mavilganga, 2 miles north of the village Singeles, lies the well-known city Bintene, also sometimes called Vintana and even Alloet.

This city lies not only on this beautiful and large river but the river even flows through its middle.

The city of Bintene

Here the old Emperors used to hold court as it is a beautiful city where there are many large streets, beautiful buildings and wonderful pagodas or heathen temples and among others there is one whose base is 130 paces round, extraordinarily beautiful, very tall, square on top and pointed like a pyramid, oval from below going up, painted white and heavily gilded, which makes it extremely wonderful from far.[1]

In it is also a beautiful and large palace of the Emperor full of beautiful buildings within. Here the best galleys and *sampans*[2] of the Emperors are made. Here are also many shops but no market, stone monasteries and a great many bamboo houses which stretch for a mile or two in distance along the river. This is one of the most beautiful cities of the entire island where everything that one thinks of can be obtained but it is not at all strong as it is almost in the middle of the country, though situated not more than 9 or 10 miles from the Bay of Cotiari and 1 or 2 miles further from Baticalo on the east coast.[3]

Proceeding from there to the Bay of Cotiari along this entire stretch of country is nothing but thick forest. But 2 or 3 miles south of the above named Bay are again some hills and then up to the Bay of Cotjaar and the land of the Weddas nothing but a large plain in which from the western hills some small streams flow and pour into the Bays of Cotjaar and Trinkenemale. We have now dealt with this part also.

When we again go to the west of the River Coula,[4] by the

[1] Valentijn is describing the famous Mahiyāngana Dāgaba of the 3rd century B.C.

[2] *Sampan* (Malay)—flat-bottomed boat.

[3] This is one of the rare contemporary descriptions of the ancient city of Alutnuvara. Valentijn has relied on Joris van Spilbergen's Journal (*Reis van Spilbergen*, pp. 44–6).   [4] Kalā Oya.

town Caddaumatris[1] northwards, we come into the District of Newecalawa, one mile north the village Ekpoepol,[2] the village Convava, four miles east the village Tonnowayawe, less than a mile north of Convava the village Polliwella,[3] still 4 miles northeast the village Maumine, eastwards the northeastern stream of the River Caula which divides into two near Detelwaja,[4] and further 2 miles northwards the town Anurajierpoere which is separated from Colliwilla by a great forest.

The town Anariegiepoer

Thereafter is a great plain of the same name and then again a large forest and east of it 5 miles from this town the village Hurcelg[5] opposite the mountain in the District of Hoerli which borders on the land of the Bedas to the east and in the north the land of the Malabars. In the east again is the con-

Many towns and villages

tinuing high mountains of Coeragahing[6] which run as a chain for 10 to 12 miles from the town Anaragiepoer to the salt River of Catehay[7] or up to the Poneri plain which lies just a mile south, and in the west is nothing but thick jungle which stretches right above the Aripu River[8] almost to the end of this country about 10 to 12 miles distant without any villages or towns in between.

In this great district there live no Cingalese but only Malabars who also have a prince of their own though he sometimes used to come under the Emperor of Ceylon.[9] With this we have completed the description of this country on this side so that nothing remains now except to describe the land east of the river of Mature[10] as well as east of Adam's Peak and east of the River Mawielleganga, to which we will first confine ourselves between the river of Mature and that of Walauwe.

Going east of the Mature River and then north one comes one mile west near the river to the town Baygams in the large principality of Mature and in the District of Dolasdas Corle where there is a very large cinnamon forest which belongs to us.

East of this river is a large plain used for the elephant hunt

---

[1] Probably Kaduruwēgama.   [2] Unidentifiable. See p. 152 n. 2.
[3] Unidentifiable.   [4] Probably Diwulveva.
[5] Unidentifiable.   [6] Unidentifiable.   [7] Kanagarayan Āru.
[8] Malvattu Oya.   [9] Valentijn is referring to the Vanni chieftains.
[10] Nilvalā Ganga.

and somewhat north about 6 miles from the coast a line of mountains which stretches up to the Walauwe River east to north and further north a mile higher from the town Katoene (which lies opposite the Mature river not far from an inland sea which is seen in the east) one comes to the town Oededibod, to the northeast of which about a mile further is the town Wallagodde which has some mountains near it to the east, just as to the north of this mountain is Curnagel Corle[1] similarly with a line of mountains up to the Walauwe river.

Four miles to the northwest of Wallagodde is the town Tammegamme east of which again is a large forest up to the mountain in the east and to the above-named river in Mende Corle.[2]

Two miles to the northwest of Tammegamme is the town Biblegamme, north of which is the Attulagam Corle,[3] in which 3 miles north from Biblegamme one comes to the town Kambevolle,[4] and a further 1 mile north the town Malpitte[5] which is situated about 2 miles from the Walauwe River and has some low mountains to the west that are connected to Adam's Peak.

The Walauwe River has its origins in Adam's Peak. It runs first 6 or 8 miles east then it turns southeastwards with a short bend and then on about 8 to 10 miles up to Walauwe and falls there into the sea.

With this we have completed this region and will proceed with the country east of Adam's Peak, north of the Walauwe River and north of the District of Goddaponahoy as well as to the east of the Mawielleganga River, beginning with the immediate north of Walauwe River and on to the Komboken River[6] and up to the Cadduwatte Corle,[7] or to the mountain Mainda Kinde in the Kingdom of Oeva going further towards the northwest.

Four miles to the northwest of this mountain which appears just north of the Walauwe River is the village Kolkgalle, 1 mile to the northwest Beddigamme[8] and 4 miles east by north Kelligame[9] and these are the only villages which

---

[1] Unidentifiable.   [2] Meda Kōralē.   [3] Atulugam Kōralē.
[4] Unidentifiable.   [5] Unidentifiable.   [6] Kumbukkan Oya.
[7] Kadawattu Kōralē.   [8] Unidentifiable.   [9] Unidentifiable.

appear in this entire region. For to the northwest of Beddigamme is a large forest that stretches 3 to 4 miles up to the Agras or a crystal mountain which runs round from south to north and east and touches the Cadduwatte Corle, after which one comes to the Cadduwatte Corle stretching in a great plain from south to north and up to the Maimda Kinde mountain, which last mountain runs from Mende Corle or rather from Adam's Peak first with an irregular bend east and then north about 18 to 20 miles like an inter-linked chain up to a great forest which separates the city of Vintana from this mountain.

The town of Jale When one goes north by east from Kelligamme one comes north of the River Kerinde[1] to the District of Jale where there is first a forest and then 6 miles north of Kelligamme one comes to the town of Jale, an ugly dog-hole, which has a large forest to the east and lies an equal distance from Leawawa on the coast.

To its northwest and to the northeast up to the Komboken River there is nothing but two large forests.

When we continue with our region north of the river Komboken up to Baticalo in the northeast and to the city of Bintene in the northwest we come first into the District of Panoa, in which are very large forests and right north in the middle up to the Heddel River a plain of 4 to 5 miles south and north and no less (or rather 6 miles) in breadth till near the sea and till near the village Ockande.

Directly to the north of this river up to the mountain called the Capel[2] is a forest 6 miles long, while in the east and in the west up to opposite the above named mountain is a large plain of equal size, though again in the east there is some jungle.

North of the Capel one comes to the County of Baticalo in the east and to the District of Vellas in the west, where to the north for a distance of 10 miles up to the Baticalo river which springs from the neighbouring district there is nothing but a

---

[1] Kirindē Oya.

[2] This hill, about 25 miles west of Thirukovil, was named Capel by the Portuguese. It was renamed Westminster Abbey by the British and appears so in modern maps. It is in a range of hills in the Wadinagala region.

thick forest and in the west, between that forest and the mountain in the District of Vellas, and also in the east to near Baticalo and to the place where this river falls into the sea, is a large plain of some miles in circumference.

Directly to the east of Bintene or Vintana, about 6 miles from there lies the city of Vellas or Nil Vaelle and 4 miles west of this city the village Vegamme and 1 mile to its east Neguriti.[1] But directly east of Neguriti, just east of that thick forest is also the village Viado[2] and 2 miles southeast the village Occatoti.

Vellas

Now we must return again a while to Adam's Peak to see what lies between the Mountain Maimda Kinde on the east side in the Kingdom of Oeva and between the District of Coetmale and Goddaponahoy to the north up to the city of Bintene along the River Mawielleganga.

East of the town Poole Pitte and the village Combalauwla about 3 miles from the latter is the village Parnegon[3] on a beautiful stream which springs from the mountain of Maimda Kinde and flows into the Mawielleganga after a course of 8 or 9 miles.

Six miles east of this village are the ruins of the town of Badule which lies in the middle of that mountain where it begins to bend and is very dense.

Four miles north of Combalauwle, somewhat northwesterly is the village Amboledo[4] and 4 miles east the village Bogedag[5] in the District of Jotta Kinde.[6]

Three miles to the northeast of Amboledo lies Joputtea,[7] just west of the abovementioned stream which falls directly north into the Mawielleganga.

Just north of this village is another thick jungle between this stream and the above named high mountain in the east and also between Joputtea and the village Mosponi (which lies 5 miles north in the District of Vallaponahoy also just to the west), as also north of this latter village up to Bintene extends another forest 6 miles long.

Having covered this region, we go over to see what is to be

---

[1] Unidentifiable. [2] Unidentifiable. [3] Probably Paranagama.
[4] Probably Abēcotta. [5] Unidentifiable. [6] Probably Yatakinda.
[7] Unidentifiable.

found along the Mawielleganga River north of the city of Bintene and north of Baticalo and the city of Vellas up to the Bay of Cotjaar.

From Bintene, Vellas and Baticalo up to Cotjaar, for a distance of 10 to 12 miles one sees nothing but large forests, except that 7 to 8 miles north of the city of Vellas in the District of Tambancarrewarre lies the village Bodelganne[1] on a small stream.

Also 3 to 4 miles northwest are some mountains from which various streams originate, which fall into the Bay of Cotjaar near the River Mawielleganga and further there is a large plain up to the above-named bay both in the east and in the north 10 to 12 miles in circumference.

We could have done this in another and more detailed way but we leave this till later because it will appear copiously in a report of the elder Mr. van Goens.[2] We also feared that we should enlarge too much, as we feel that this description we have made is detailed enough to give a rough idea of the spread of this island, for it is impossible to give a precise account of its interior condition.

[1] Unidentifiable.   [2] Valentijn, Vol. 1, pp. 204–46.

Third Chapter

[Society and nature]

Inhabitants of Ceylon. Of the Cingalese. Their nature. The hill people. Their dress. Dress of the Emperors, and of the chiefs. Their marriage. Economy. Furniture. Food. The slavishness of the women. Their cruelty with their newborn children. Their artisans. The elephant hunt, a picture. The beginning of their year, etc. Their addiction to sorcery. Become very old. Knowledge of sickness and healing. Their measures, yards, etc. Laws. Acrobats among them. Languages used here. Their scholarship. Their fear for the dead. Cremation or burial and mourning for the dead. Appearance of their nobles. And how those who die from the pox are dealt with. Of the Malabars. Bedas. Portuguese and other inhabitants. Of the produce of the land. Oxen ploughing and threshing here. The trees. The talipot tree. The kettule tree. The cinnamon tree. What cinnamon is. Where it is. Its three sorts. The orule tree. The doenekaja shrub. The capita shrub. The god-tree, etc. Many edible roots. Wonderful medicinal herbs. Different sorts of trees. The Pitsja tree and flower trees. Animals here. Elephants, etc. Birds. Bloodless animals. Fish. Mountain produce. Stones. Goods derived or found here. Coins. Measures and weights. Measure of cloth. Administration of this island by an Emperor. His bodyguard. Incomes. Where the taxes are given. The two chief officers of state. Incomes of the Governors. Their subordinate officers. Strength of the Emperors in war.

Having reviewed thus far the land of Ceylon, it is now time to begin to speak of its inhabitants.

The inhabitants are in part Cingalese, in part Bedas or Weddas, but besides these there are also Moors,[1] Malabars[2]

Inhabitants of Ceylon

---

[1] The Muslim community in Ceylon was generally referred to as the Moors by the Portuguese and the Dutch.   [2] Tamils.

(already referred to) and very many Portuguese, Dutch, and some English and French who are prisoners of the Emperor.

Of the Cingalese

As regards the Cingalese,[1] the native and oldest inhabitants of this land, they are not entirely black but brownish-yellow in colour, with long and wide ears, not large of stature, somewhat thin in the back, very weak of limbs, swift in body and very ingenious in mind, as they know how to make many beautiful things. They are very hardy by nature both in enduring many discomforts and in subsisting on poor food and little sleep.

Their nature

As regards their nature and character, they are very friendly, and very much attached to their language. But they are also very greatly conceited and very proud, to such an extent that they will eat no food prepared in a house of one of lower rank than they imagine themselves to be, nor will they ever marry with them. Lying is not a sin nor a shame among them but a natural thing and they will not blanch the slightest when caught at it.

They are very avaricious but not fighters or thugs, and not envious. On the contrary they are inclined to help all poor and serve all others. They detest robbery very much and are verbally very strongly for virtue. But they do not follow this closely in action. However they have a great esteem for upright and virtuous people.

As most Indians are superstitious, so also are the Cingalese in the utmost degree, and encountering the slightest thing as they go out is enough for them to return home or to abandon something that they have already begun. In the seriousness of their countenance, dealings and walk, they resemble very much the Portuguese.[2] They are very swift in judgment, quick in comprehension and very sharp-witted. But they are also cunning, crafty and very clever at discovering loopholes so that one should not believe them whatever promise they may make.

It is also true that the men are not at all jealous, having no

[1] Valentijn's generalisations on Sinhalese character are very similar to those of Knox. See Knox, Part III, Chap. 1, pp. 63–6.
[2] Cp. Knox 'In short, in Carriage and Behaviour they are very grave and stately, like unto the Portugals...', p. 65.

scruples about giving their daughter or even their wives to sleep for a time with their friends who are staying with them. But if a daughter comes to have dealings with someone below her rank, she may well put herself under the protection of her friends, as her father will certainly kill her, not because of a desire for virtue or out of an abhorrence of prostitution but only out of pride that she has fornicated with one less than he. Otherwise, there is no more common sin among them than whoredom to which they even lead their children. Also they will never insult each other as prostitutes, even in the utmost anger, except where a daughter has mixed with one of lower rank. Also a wife has not much to fear from her husband if she is inclined to adultery, if only she is not caught in the act; for then he has the right to put both to death.

The Cingalese who live on the coast are of a gentle and pleasant nature but the highlanders are of a brusque, cruel and hard nature and, though they are more pleasant and courteous in speech and manner than the inhabitants of the coast and lowlands, they are however of malicious and crookish nature so that one can trust them much less than the others.[1] *The highlanders*

The attire of the Cingalese, who generally have long, smooth hair and thick beard like the Swiss, consists of a piece of cloth made into a jacket with folds or a cotton *baju*[2] or a cloth that they wrap round their middle, pull through under the legs and let it hang down to the feet. On their heads they wear a red cap or cover it with something else. They decorate their ears with gold rings and jewels and they carry daggers[3] on the side which are decorated with gold, silver and ivory handles. *Their attire*

The women wear a poor white skirt which is stitched with blue or red flowers and hangs down to the knee or somewhat lower, according to their high or low status. There is great difference between them. They also wear many silver arm rings and also many silver rings on the fingers and toes, silver necklaces, chains with stones, and also silver and gold rings

---

[1] A common judgment, both among Portuguese and Dutch writers, caused partly by the political hostility of the Kandyans to Europeans.

[2] *Baju* (Malay)—a loose coat.

[3] The Dutch text uses the word *crissen*. *Keris* (Malay)—a dagger.

and other trinkets on their bored ears. They rub their hair with oil and bind it up in a hive or into a large bun, and carry a veil over the shoulder, girdles round the body and so on.

Dress of the Emperors

The King dresses himself as he likes. His cap is of silk and gold worked through each other and one yard high, being decorated in front with a beautiful carbuncle, all round with all sorts of precious stones and above with a bird of paradise. His shirt and waistcoat are of fine Indian cotton with gold threadwork or other buttons. He wears stockings and leather slippers instead of shoes. His coat and trousers are like the apparel of a Portuguese. Further he has under his right arm a large dagger or sword in a silver sheath and decorated with precious stones. On the left side, between the shirt and his cloth, he carries a long knife, inlaid with gold and precious stones, and also a stylus in a silver sheath for writing on leaves.

Of the chiefs

His courtiers may also clothe themselves with gold, silk and silver but not with precious stones unless they wish to risk their lives.

The Counts or Governors, whom he appoints to this and that Corla, may also do this, to whom he gives a staff with a silver head on which are the King's arms. They wear *Tsjeripoes*[1] or wooden clogs which they hold fast with their big toes by a small peg that stands up on them.

Those of the nobility follow them in rank and may go clothed like them. But they may not wear such an ornamental cap, though they may put something on their heads. Also they are followed generally by a slave carrying a *talipot*[2] leaf to use as a sunshade against the sun or against the rain.

After them follow in rank all clerks and then the peasants who cultivate the rice fields. They wear cotton clothing but no daggers, stockings, shoes or caps, but rather a knife and an iron pen. And the women of all these mixed people may also wear clothes which come down to the ground and may cover their bosoms, but these clothes may not cover the belly for a palm's breadth around the navel. This is permitted only to the wives of Courtiers, Governors, Counts and Noblemen.

After this follow the labourers who are of many types, the

[1] *Seruppu* (Tam.)—slippers.
[2] *Talapata* (Sinh.)—leaf of the *talagaha*, a variety of palm.

tappers, cinnamon peelers, fishers, soldiers, washers, tom-tom beaters, palanquin-carriers and others who are lower in rank, whose wives must go all naked in the upper part of their bodies on pain of being flogged, and some of them who are of the lowest rank always take a mat with them to sit on as they are not permitted to sit on the ground if they wish to rest. The nobles wear jackets or long coats and caps and sit on stools or logs, but never the lower orders who always go bare-footed.

As we have said, they will never marry with one of lesser rank, even though they could gain very much wealth by it. But as this is mostly observed for the daughter and, as a man does not worry about sleeping with one lower, he is never reproached for this if only he does not also eat and drink with her or marry her, nor is it considered a shame. For if he should marry someone lower he would be punished by the overlord with a fine or with imprisonment or both and is henceforth reckoned no higher in rank than his wife and cut off from his caste like a rotten limb. *Their marriage customs*

They let their daughters marry early at 10 to 11 years because they will be assured that their brides are still virgins, though others among them pay very little heed to it. The deciding of the marriage depends completely on the parents who give the daughters some property according to their ability. But as they separate now and then as easily as they come together, in such a case that property, being a bridal dowry, must first be returned. They also do not satisfy themselves with one wife but often take many if they have the ability to feed them. The bridegroom provides the bride's clothing and if he does not have enough he may borrow them.

In their housekeeping they are reasonably neat. And just as they never eat or drink with anyone of a lower status, they will also not do so with their own women. While drinking out of a goblet, they will never put it to their mouth but hold it high up and pour the water in. *Housekeeping*

Generally their houses are bad, small and low, but covered with straw or *atap*,[1] made of poles or sticks like huts and plastered with clay; but the walls are reasonably smooth and even. They may not build the houses high or cover them with

[1] *Atap* (Malay)—thatch for roofing.

tiles or whiten the walls with lime, though they have a sort of clay which is rather white.

They generally make these houses themselves and do not use nails or spikes but bind them very strongly to each other with *rotang*.[1] They do not know of chimneys for which reason the houses appear generally very smoky, as they make their fires here or there in a corner. This must be understood to relate to the ordinary people, for the chiefs have good, large and often double houses opposite each other.

Household effects

Their household effects are poor, consisting of some mats, 1 or 2 copper pots, some earth or porcelain ware, 2 or 3 wooden stools without arms (for arm chairs are royal), a rice mortar with an ebony pounder, a wooden mortar or curry-stone, a *parang*[2] or 2 to 3 axes, and some baskets to store one thing or another. They do not know of tables or table-cloths or of serviettes. The floor or a mat is their table and a banana leaf their table-cloth and serviette which they keep neat and clean at each meal.

Their food

Rice is their bread and they are satisfied if they have some salt, a little stewed vegetables with pepper and salt added and some lemon juice over it. To eat beef is a crime among them. There is not much of other flesh or fish and if they have some they will rather make money and sell it to foreigners than eat it themselves, but for the very important and the noblemen who have on their tables various curries[3] of fish or flesh steamed for a long time. For otherwise it is an honour among them to be sparing, miserly and stingy and those who know how to subsist very frugally are often praised. Their most important food consists of rice, bananas and in this and that other fruit which the land produces abundantly.

One sees few poultry or pigs, as the courtiers take them away mostly without payment wherever they find them, so that the common people are afraid to rear them. Also they could produce more cattle, birds, etc., but the civet cats and tigers do them great damage, besides the Emperor also desires that his subjects be poor.

---

[1] *Rōtan* (Malay)—cane.   [2] *Parāng* (Malay)—a chopper or cleaver.
[3] *Kari* (Hindi, Tam.)—spiced, dressed up dish eaten with rice. The word is now in vogue in the English language as curry.

No one except the Emperor or a foreigner may have goats and that is the reason why they must mostly restrict themselves to scanty *sayor*[1] or vegetables and a common curry.

The women have to serve the men while they eat and provide what is necessary. After the men have eaten the women eat what remains on their plates. Their rice and food is taken on porcelain plates or even leaves. The slavishness of women

Their drink is water or sometimes even some *suri*[2] or *towak*.[3] They are silent during mealtimes and speak little to each other. While the wife serves the rice from the pot, no one may speak but they may do so after this.

They wash their hands and mouth before and after eating. They always do this for themselves, never letting another do it for them (as happens in some cases among them), as they consider this a vile shame.

Also they are very clean in body and head as they are always accustomed to wash both very often.

The women must prepare the food, pound the rice, go to market, fetch firewood and carry it on their heads, doing nothing else other than eating arecanut the whole day and smoking tobacco or preparing this for their husbands. Moreover, no woman may sit on a stool in the presence of a man. Also they may not give any order to another in the King's name on pain of losing their tongue (this is only permitted to men). As against this is the privilege that women are free of all taxes in respect of their inherited goods which on death go to the King, as also all female animals which are also taxed.

If they go out they go well before daybreak and this gives them status, wearing jewels, and if they do not have these, they think it no shame to borrow them from another. They sleep on mats and the high status ones on quilts. But the children sleep generally without anything under the body.

Thus the men here are mostly lords and the women generally in the Indies mostly slaves of the men.

If they have children, they first consult with an astrologer whether it is born under a lucky or an unlucky star and if the Cruelty among them

[1] *Sayōr* (Malay)—vegetable. [2] *Sūri* (Hindi)—palm toddy.
[3] *Tuak* (Malay)—toddy.

Young children
born under
unlucky stars
Names of their
children

latter they kill it (though seldom the first born) or give it to other people who are inclined to rear it.

Also the children when they grow older never keep the name which they received in their childhood, but receive other lofty titles to which they are very much attached.

However noble anyone may be, it is no shame to work provided that he does not carry any weight, for this is the most shameful among them, and to work as a slave.

There are among them all kinds of artisans such as gold and silversmiths, ironworkers, carpenters, painters, potters, lime-burners, hunters and wild-game hunters, and barbers who rank close to each other and are next to the nobles. But the first will eat with none of the others, as again the next with none of the lesser ones.

After this are the toddy tappers, cinnamon peelers and the others who have already been described by us.

Artisans

There are among them those who are skilled in engraving beautifully in iron, steel, ivory, ebony and many other materials and in carving it artistically, as I have seen entire cabinets covered with ivory and very ingeniously carved.

One of their great businesses to which they are accustomed is the elephant hunt, of which variety of animal, the Ceylonese elephant, it is said, all other Indian elephants prostrate before it.[1] How this happens is described by the Rev. Baldaeus[2] as well as many others. But to get a proper idea of it here one could see the picture No. 14 with what is narrated in it where everything is seen much more detailed and more accurate than ever before in other accounts.[3]

In former times there were large elephant hunts but the Governor Simons has in his time begun the capture of elephants in small *kraals*[4] with much profit and ease for the native and for the Company, as appears from this short extract of the Dessave Bolscho.[5]

[1] This was a popular belief dating back to the classical writers on the east and repeated by many travellers up to the 18th century. Tennent, *Ceylon*, 11, 379–81.

[2] Baldaeus, Chap. 50, pp. 197–8.

[3] A double page drawing of an elephant hunt undertaken in 1717 in the village Horagala in the Alutkuru Kōralē.

[4] An enclosure into which elephants are driven and captured.

[5] Officer of the Company who served as Dissāva of Matara in the 1710's.

Extract from an Inspection Report of Mr. Bolscho on the Capture of Elephants.

In the Dissavany of Colombo there are 8 provinces, namely Hevegam, Hina, Happittigam, Billigal, Salpitti, Reigam, Pasdum, and Wallalawitti Corles.

The capture of elephants in small *coraals*[1] (first undertaken under the administration of Mr. Simons), has had good success and from August 1707 till the 31st October, in Midettere, Bondoepitte, Emoekelane and Eswatte, at 3 different times, 62 beasts were captured without significant expense and of these 40 fully-grown animals were kept for the Jaffanapatnam trade, namely:

	Height in Cubits					
5 tusked of	5	$3\frac{1}{2}$	$3\frac{1}{2}$	$3\frac{1}{2}$	and	$3\frac{1}{2}$
12 male	6	6	6	$5\frac{1}{4}$	$5\frac{1}{8}$	$5\frac{1}{2}$
elephants of	$5\frac{1}{2}$	4	$3\frac{3}{4}$	$3\frac{3}{8}$	$3\frac{3}{8}$	$5\frac{1}{8}$
23 female	$5\frac{1}{4}$	$5\frac{1}{2}$	$5\frac{1}{8}$	$5\frac{1}{4}$	$5\frac{1}{8}$	$5\frac{1}{4}$
elephants of	$5\frac{1}{4}$	5	5	$4\frac{3}{4}$	$4\frac{1}{2}$	$4\frac{1}{8}$
	$4\frac{3}{8}$	$4\frac{3}{8}$	$4\frac{3}{8}$	$4\frac{3}{8}$	$4\frac{3}{8}$	$4\frac{3}{8}$
	$4\frac{1}{4}$	4	$3\frac{3}{4}$	$3\frac{1}{4}$	and	$3\frac{1}{4}$

22 female elephants, all having defects, were therefore driven back into the jungle.[2]

The elephants have their own names such as Kindoelpittia, Widagamea, Waggecoatta, Henagaminea, Caprepittia, Parettea,[3] etc.

What alphabet and language the Cingalese use can be seen in the third part of Mr. Relands, Mengel-Dissertatien, Fol. 80 and Fol. 82.[4]

Their year begins on 28 March, has 265 days, 12 months which are divided into $4\frac{1}{2}$ weeks each (but each half week has only 3 days) and each week is divided into 7 days, but their

Beginning of their year

---

[1] Same as *kraal*—enclosure.　　　　[2] End of extract.

[3] Names given to elephants by their keepers, signifying some distinguishing characteristic.

[4] Adrian Reland, *Hadriani Relandi Dissertationum miscellanearum pars prima-tertia* (Trajecti ad Rhenum, 1706–08), pp. 80–85. On p. 80 he transcribes the Sinhalese alphabet.

days, of which the first day or Sunday is lucky and others very unlucky, have 30 divisions where we have 24 hours.[1] Nor have they heard of hour-glasses or timepieces and guess the time from the sun or according to their own estimate. But the King has a pitcher with a hole, which he fills with water, by which he estimates the correct time just as the Moors in Java and elsewhere fill a coconut shell with water.[2]

Their propensity for magic

They have great fear for magic and there are people among them who know how to charm this and that thing and again to exorcize it to whom they resort generally if something has been stolen—a matter to which all Indians are addicted and which is treated in detail elsewhere.[3]

Become very old

As they are a healthy people, they generally live to a very old age and are even then very strong and courageous.

Know how to heal their own sickness

Among them chicken pox and fever prevail strongly, from which each must protect and heal himself, as there are no doctors or surgeons here, so each one prescribes rough remedies for himself, generally having in the house very good ointments and wholesome oils which heal almost anything. Also they make some emetic and purging drinks for which they are able to choose certain leaves and barks of trees which are very useful and also a certain thorny tree and some oblong berries. There are few diseases for which they know no remedy, even to the extent of completely curing someone who is poisoned or is bitten by a poisonous creature, though this happens seldom without their being taken over by this or that magician.

They have berries in this land, of which they know how to make an ointment with which they can cure a broken leg and set it well again in a few hours.[4]

Measures, yards etc.

As there are all sorts of trade goods here, so there are exact measures, weights and yards for everything and a fixed price,

[1] Knox has more details on this. He says the Sinhalese year is of 365 days. Valentijn has obviously made a mistake in copying from Knox. Knox, pp. 110–11.

[2] Also taken from Knox (p. 111). Cp. also with Queyroz whose description of this pitcher-clock is similar to that of Knox. Queyroz, I, 106.

[3] More details of sorcery in Knox, pp. 112–13.

[4] Knox (pp. 113–15) gives more details of these medicines and the names of the plants that are used in their preparation.

which is clearly seen in Knox's third book, eighth chapter, together with the coins here current.[1]

There are among them certain permanent land laws or old customs, according to which most matters are directed, except where the Emperor makes any changes. Their laws

The immovable goods are inherited by the children but not just the oldest son alone, or, if this happens, he must maintain the mother and the children.

All debts are doubled every two years and he who has no means to pay enters into slavery with his wife and children.

None may marry the wife of another who has run away from him before that man is married to another.

The children of a freeman born by a slave fall into slavery, as on the contrary the children of a slave born to a free woman are free thereby so that the offspring here generally follow the status of the mother. A thief who cannot return the stolen goods sevenfold falls into slavery. Parents falling into debt, mortgage and sell their children. In disputed cases both the parties must swear in their temples before their gods, which will be treated in detail later.[2]

Those who break the laws are punished with a fine or with imprisonment and, if one does not pay up the fine promptly, he has his sword, knife, cap, and jacket taken away and must sit in captivity. If he does still not pay, he must carry a heavy stone on his back till he has paid it. Besides this they have others customs to force the debtors to payment, of which by no means the least is that creditors threaten the debtor that they would poison themselves, for which act he must be responsible.[3]

There are many acrobats and clowns among them who shine by their intelligence, swiftness and suppleness of limb as also their courage, doing various things which astonish one.

The languages customary in this island among the natives are either Cingalese or Malabar.[4] The first language is the real native language and is a language by itself having no relationship with the Malabar, as speakers of one cannot understand the other at all. It is very courteous or very pleasant and very Languages used here

[1] Knox, pp. 97–8.   [2] Valentijn V. 1, p. 408.
[3] Knox, pp. 101–5.   [4] Tamil.

rich in expressing different things distinctly, pleasantly and is particularly precise. Thus they can give 10 to 12 sorts of titles as honorifics to one and the same man or woman according to his state or rank, though they have more for the women than for the men.

Just as we address someone as 'Gij' [you] and 'U.E.' [your honour] or 'U. Ed.', they have 7 or 8 different words to express the different titles of 'you', each after his rank. But to the Emperor they give the title Dionanxi[1] which (as they say) is even higher than that of God, which Raja Singa allowed to be used before the uprising, but after this he has forbidden that anyone should give him this title.

When they speak to a prince or to a chief in the first person, they will never say 'I' but generally call themselves 'a piece of a dog' and also speak in a similar manner of their family.

Just as they have very many courteous expressions in their language, they also express themselves in many clever and forcible proverbs, full of meaning and attractive, by which they make their meaning very clear.[2] The Malabar language is also used here but we shall speak of it in greater detail under the subject of Malabar.[3]

Their science

There are no learned men among them as they have no opportunity or schools for this, learning nothing but reading and writing, which latter they do on a *talipot* leaf with an iron stilus and then roll it up.

This leaf is sometimes a foot or about 7 to 8 inches long and about 3 fingers broad, of which they make whole books, cut into one measure, thus using very little paper. They tie up such books with 2 cords and cover it with a plank on both sides which they then bind together. Also they have a still worse type of leaf on which they write ordinary things.[4]

The few books which they still have deal with their religion or medical science but are written in a superior language to the ordinary. That they are strongly attracted to

---

[1] *Deyianansē* (Sinh.)—Your Lordship.

[2] Knox provides a number of illustrations of Sinhalese speech and gives a large Sinhalese word list, pp. 104–10.

[3] Valentijn here commits a common contemporary error of equating Malabar and Tamil and assuming that Tamil was spoken in Malabar.

[4] Knox, pp. 109–10.

sorcery is sufficiently seen from what has been said before. Also there are among them those who practise astronomy though in a very defective manner. Thus they also make Almanacs, but these are of a month's duration, in which their good and bad days are noted. They presume to be able to foretell future happenings from the stars but generally they have no foundation and the astrologer can speak as he will. They use this advice however in sickness, marriage and other things, to know if they will die of such sickness and will be lucky or unlucky in such or such marriage. These astrologers must be informed of the correct time of birth of such a person.[1]

They fear nothing in the world more than the dead, to escape whom they summon the devil because they fear death even more and pray to be delivered from it.

Their fears of the dead

If they happen to die, against expectation, they are cremated, if of a high rank, but the lower classes are buried in the woods. For this they employ the necessary servants who wrap the body in a mat and carry it there. They mourn for their dead, the women with hair hanging loose make a dreadful braying, holding their hands like disconsolates above their heads, reciting at the same time the praise of the deceased even though he may have been a great rascal. They do this for 3 to 4 days together, morning and evening, while the men stand by and sigh. However it must be said that the women do this more out of custom and for the sake of propriety than from grief as they are generally bolder and more hard-hearted than the men. As soon as their husband is dead they look again for another, troubling themselves little over the deceased and much more over the new man whom they cannot do without.[2]

Burning, burying and mourning the dead

Those of the highest rank are laid in a hewn out tree after their entrails are removed, and the body is embalmed and strewn with pepper and it must remain there outside the house till the Emperor gives orders to cremate it, and this happens then generally under a sort of arch of honour which is covered with coconuts and other fruits with many beautiful leaves, though it takes place for lesser lords with less eulogy and with less honour. But if any one dies from chicken pox, even though he is a noble he is buried on thorns without any honour.[3]

How the bodies of nobles and those dead from pox are handled

[1] Knox, p. 110.   [2] Knox, p. 115.   [3] Knox, p. 116.

Of the Malabars   Besides the Cingalese, there are among the inhabitants also Malabars, not only spread here and there over the island, but also possessing and occupying a certain small part of the country near Jaffanapatnam in the north, situated between the Emperor's country and ours and separated from the Emperor's country by the Corunde Waye[1] river. They live here in freedom under a separate prince who is neither under us nor under the Emperor, though he gives us a small tribute of some elephants.[2] He has some friendship with the Emperor of Kandy also. His subjects are so slavishly subject to him that they would give him much more than the Cingalese to their King, though he treats them better than the Emperor of Kandy does his, paying his militia, while the Cingalese must serve the Emperor without payment.

Their territory has elephants, buffaloes, all kinds of wild game, wax, honey, butter, and milk, some rice, but no cotton. However they are able to get what they lack by exchanging cloth yearly for great herds of cattle, which they then bring to Newecalawe, loading their animals with cotton which they know how to weave into cloth better than the Cingalese and with rice which they take to their land. Likewise they are able to get their salt, salted fish, copper vessels and other necessaries from the Dutch in exchange, which they then exchange with the Cingalese, who may not trade with the Dutch, for other goods.

The Bedas   There are also Bedas there, also called Wedas,[3] or a kind of wild woodmen. They are the oldest inhabitants of this island. They are black in colour, with burning eyes, not large in stature but well set and nimble of limbs. They are found in numbers in the District of Vintana, Hoerli and in the District of the Bedas situated north of Trinkenemale. They remain generally in the thickest jungle. They speak Cingalese. They hunt wild game, heat it over the fire and sell it or exchange it with other Cingalese. They live on wild game, without eating rice or anything else. They have houses, villages and chiefs

---

[1] Kurundu Oya or Malvattu Oya.
[2] The Vanniyār chieftains. There were a few of them in the northern part of the country.
[3] Veddas.

(though they do not recognise any as King) and live generally under a tree, or under some lopped off branches near a stream or brook. They never cut their hair on their heads but bind it together into a large bunch and let it hang on their shoulders.

There are some among them who are very wild and whom one seldom sees, but there are others who are found to be tamer. They wear very short and narrow *bajus*[1] or cloth. Each has among them his own patrimony or his special boundary in which he must watch out for any harm from others or he will be shot dead with arrows not unexpectedly.

Their hunted wild game they preserve in holes in deeply hewn trees which they fill with honey. The bride price for their daughters, when they give them in marriage, consists of some hunting dogs, as they live on practising hunting. They appear to have been here long before the oldest Emperors of Ceylon and then to have been under a Queen who, like another Medea, was experienced in sorcery and of whom we speak elsewhere in a report of the older Mr. van Goens.[2]

Of the Portuguese, Dutch and other white people whom one finds in the country in numbers in the cities along the coast and also up in the Emperor's country, it is unnecessary to speak as I shall show hereafter in detail in dealing with them how they came here. _{Portuguese and other inhabitants}

After we have described the land's inhabitants we have to see next what are the products of the land, what trees are in the woods, as also what animals and birds, what fishes in the sea and what mountain produce, precious stones, etc. this large island produces.

Wheat is not known here but is brought from outside, from Surat or Bengal for the Dutch. The common grain of this land is rice as of the entire Indies, except Surat and Bengal which produce wheat also. There are here different sorts; one sort ripens in 6 to 7 months and the other in 5, 4, and 3 months, though all these sorts are of one and the same price. The tastiest is that which ripens first, but this variety grows in smallest quantity. Also they are able to arrange it so that they _{Of the products}

---

[1] *Baju.* See p. 161 n. 2.
[2] Valentijn's description of Vedda society is based partly on Knox (pp. 61–3) and partly on van Goens' report (Valentijn, V. 1, pp. 208–10).

Oxen ploughing and threshing

harvest all their rice at one and the same time, as they generally sow in July or August, after having ploughed their land with oxen, which later thresh the grain or trample it after the women have brought it in bundles and after they have first walked three times round the threshing floor with these bundles on their heads and after some sorcery is practised there, for which the women take as much rice as they can lay on the magic stone which they bring to the threshing floor.[1]

Besides rice there are also some other inferior grains and seeds used as food such as *coracan*,[2] *tanna*[3] etc., mustard seed, *mung*[4] (which is a sort of pea) and other seeds from which they make oil. Also there is another called *oemb*[5] which cooked with rice makes them drunk.[6]

The land or the earth produces many sorts of other products, of which we do not deem it necessary to say much because they are mostly similar to the products described under the heading of Amboina.[7]

The trees

So it is with the trees. For all sorts of fruit trees, which are in Amboina and elsewhere in the Indies, are found also in Ceylon and are described in detail in the Hortus Malabaricus of Mr. van Rheede.[8] However there are a few special trees which are found here and not elsewhere.

The Talipot tree

Among these is the *talipot*[9] tree which is particularly straight and as thick and tall as a large mast. It bears no fruit but only leaves which by their size and in other ways are of great use.

The leaf is so broad and so large in circumference that about 14 to 15 men can shelter under one leaf against rain without becoming wet. When dried it is very huge but also very manageable and pliable that it can be pleated together into a

---

[1] Based on Knox (pp. 7–11) who goes into greater detail on cultivation methods.

[2] *Kurakkan* (Tam. & Sinh.). *Eleusine coracana*.

[3] *Tana hāl* (Sinh.)—millet. *Setaria italica*.

[4] *Mung* (Sinh.)—green gram. *Phaseolus aureus*.

[5] *Amu* (Sinh.). *Paspalum scrobiculatum*.

[6] Knox, pp. 11–12.   [7] Valentijn III, pp. 153–260.

[8] Henrik Adriaan van Rhede tot Drakestein, *Horti Malabarici . . . ab* Almeloven 1673–1703. Van Rhede was an officer of the Company and served as Commander of Malabar in 1669–1677.

[9] *Talapata* (Sinh.). The name of the tree is *talagaha*.

fan and can without difficulty be carried very far on the person, since it is then hardly the thickness of a man's arm, besides being very light. It appears in shape as almost a circle but when it is cut in pieces it fits the shape of a triangle. If on a journey one puts it on one's head with the point in front it serves to clear the way of shrubs and thorns, besides it serves as a sunshade against the sun and a protection against the rain.

The leaves grow up to the top of the tree which never yields any fruit except on its last year and then at the top of the tree, extending itself in large branches which first produce beautiful yellow flowers that are very strong-smelling, even irritating, from which comes then a round hard fruit of a size like our largest morellos, though they serve as nothing but seed to reproduce the tree.

On this last year, however, it produces this fruit in such abundance that a tree gives enough fruit to plant an entire district. The kernel of this tree is also used to make a flour, when it is cut down for seed, and the native knows how to make delicious cakes which compare in taste to white bread. They use this before their rice is ripened or if they do not have rice in stock. How the leaf also may be written on with an iron stilus and makes a whole book, we have shown already.[1]

The *kitul*[2] tree also grows straight but is shorter than a coconut tree. It also has inside a kernel like the *talipot* tree and produces an unusually sweet sap that is desirable and pleasant to smell, very healthy, yet not denser than water. It can be extracted from the tree twice and sometimes thrice a day, so that an ordinary tree can produce about 16 cans daily,[3] from which juice, after boiling, they make brown sugar, and if they do their best they can even prepare very white sugar of a kind almost like the best.

The leaves of this tree are like those of the arecanut tree and also hang in one bunch which is hard and like a firm plank but full of nerves and threads which they use as yarn and from which they make ropes. So long as it is growing, its leaves fall off but when it has reached full growth they remain on the stem for many years and it does not get any new leaves.

Kitul tree

---

[1] See above p. 170.   [2] *Kitul* (Sinh.)—a palm. *Garyota urens*.
[3] Knox says '3 to 4 gallons' (p. 15).

When the bud at the top becomes ripe and withers, another appears again each year, continuously deeper and deeper, and gradually shorter till they come to the lowest of the branches. Then the tree has matured but still remains standing for 8 to 10 years and then dies.

Cinnamon tree The most important tree, the island's own, is the cinnamon tree. The Cingalese call it *corindo-gas*[1] and the cinnamon which makes the tree and this island so famous *curendo potto*.[2] These trees sometimes grow very tall and sometimes medium. Their leaves are comparable to a citron leaf or to a laurel leaf in thickness and colour but this has only one vein and the cinnamon leaf has three veins round which the green of the leaf extends. The young leaves on first coming out are as red as scarlet and when broken in pieces smell much more like cloves than cinnamon. The tree which is mostly medium in size is very rich in foliage and thick in branches and leaves, bears white flowers which have a very lovely and agreeable smell, from which comes later a fruit which is as big as an olive, somewhat yellowish and it ripens in June, almost like an acorn, though somewhat smaller and almost without smell or taste, in no way comparable to its bark, though some disagree, but if one boils it, it gives a beautiful and wholesome oil which when it cools bears a resemblance to candle wax and is of a lovely smell, from which a very salutary ointment is made for this or that pain or discomfort of the limbs, besides it is also burnt in lamps. But it is not used for candles, as the Emperor alone burns these. It is said that the fruit is almost like the nutmeg.[3]

This tree grows wild like other jungle trees and is not valued any higher by the natives.

It is mostly found west of the great Mawielleganga River and in great quantity, though in one place more abundant than in another.

About the This tree has a double bark, the outermost, which is not
cinnamon like cinnamon and which one first peels with a knife, and the innermost which is the real cinnamon and is peeled with the

---

[1] *Kurundu gas* (Sinh.)—cinnamon tree. *Cinnamomum zeylanicum.*
[2] *Kurundu patta* (Sinh.)—bark of the cinnamon tree.
[3] Very similar to Knox's description with slight variations, p. 16.

curved edge of a knife first in a circle and then lengthwise, and laid to dry in the sun where they roll into each other and are curled together as we generally see them.

After the tree is thus peeled, it does not grow any further but new trees grow from the fruits. The wood of this tree gives out no smell except when burnt, being white and soft, almost like fir wood, which the natives use in making houses and in the construction of fine cabinets and tables.

They do not grow everywhere on this island, for there is not one in the entire kingdom of Jaffanapatnam and on the island of Manaar. But it first occurs south of the Chilauw River[1] in the District of Nigumbo inland up to Gale. From the root of this tree the doctors derive a strong smelling camphor water and are able to extract the strongest camphor from it. *Where they occur*

There are three sorts of cinnamon here; first, the fine, which is peeled from the young and middle-aged trees; the second, the coarse, which comes from the thicker and older trees; and the third, the wood or wild cinnamon, which is also found in Malabar and in other quarters of which 1 *pikol*[2] can hardly fetch one-fifth the price of the real cinnamon. But the real cinnamon is found nowhere except on this island. However our Company is sole master of the wild and of the good cinnamon completely. A *bahar*[3] of the wild costs hardly 10 to 12 Rix Dollars, while a *bahar* of the other is 50 to 60 Rix Dollars.[4] *Three types of these*

We pass over the imagination of the ancients and the naive description of Herodotus that cinnamon, incense, myrrh, cassia, etc. grow nowhere except in Arabia and that large birds take the cinnamon to their nests and yet other fancies of which we have spoken in detail in our first part and which he and others narrate.[5]

---

[1] Deduru Oya.

[2] *Pikul* (Malay). A unit of weight used in the Malay world equivalent to about 133 pounds avoirdupois.

[3] A unit of weight used in India and Southeast Asia but varying from region to region and according to article weighed from 400 to 500 pounds.

[4] All the information on cinnamon after n. 3 (p. 176) is in addition to what is found in Knox and is based on Dutch knowledge of cinnamon in the lowlands.

[5] See above, Chapter 1, pp. 100–101.

Orula tree

Besides the cinnamon tree there are various other oil giving trees, which oil they use only in their lamps. There is also another kind which serves as a medicine or to purge the body, to dye their clothes black and to make rusted iron white. This they call the *orula* tree.[1]

Doenekaja shrub

The *doenekaja*[2] shrub is also rare. Its leaves are 2 fingers broad but 6 to 8 feet long and covered with thorns on both sides, besides having a row of thorns in the middle. They split these leaves to make mats out of them. This shrub has a tapering pointed bud, more than a span long, which is covered with some leaves that close round it like cabbage leaves. These buds smell very nice. They are golden yellow in colour, and each bud produces separate bunches of small white flowers which extend like a bundle of feathers. The roots of this shrub serve to make ropes and when it is split it can be made into thread.

The capita shrub

The *capita*[3] shrub which becomes as thick as a man's arm and of which the wood, bark and leaves have a medicinal smell, grows everywhere in Ceylon, except in the Kingdom of Oeva. It must be in some way of a poisonous odour, since all the cattle from the above-named kingdom, on coming only near it, immediately die. Other animals in the places where it grows are accustomed to it and do not die. But the leaf which is clear green, roundish, bushy and as big as an open hand is never eaten.

The God's tree, etc.

They have another rare tree which they call bo or God's tree,[4] asserting that their deity Boddum[5] when he was on earth sat under it often, as it gives a large shade and extends very widely with its branches and foliage. Also it always sways about somewhat. Because of their respect for this deity, they have a great respect for this tree and take more care for this tree than for any other tree. Also generally they lay many stones round it, keep it clean, set up lamps on it and put up their image of the

---

[1] *Veralu* (Sinh.). *Elaeocarpus serratus*. In the form it is given in Valentijn, it is an obvious borrowing from Knox (p. 17).

[2] *Dunukeyiya* (Sinh.). *Pandanas thwaitesii*.

[3] *Keppitiya* (Sinh.). *Croton laccifer*.

[4] *Bō gaha* (Sinh.). *Ficus religiosa*. Called God's tree by both Valentijn and Knox because it is holy to Buddhism (Knox p. 18).

[5] Buddha.

deity under it, also placing tables on which to put the offerings. They are seen everywhere on the roads, in the fields here and there, where the corpses are burnt, to the memory of the deceased and they believe that those who plant such a tree do not live long thereafter and also will go to heaven permanently. The first may in some ways be believed as not the young but always the old, mostly the very old, men plant these trees.

Throughout the whole year, except for the three rainy months, there are vines here. Moreover there are also mulberry trees to feed the worms from which yearly much silk is taken. There is also an abundance of ebony wood which is seen enough in the furniture that is found here.

Also among the natural products found here are ginger, cardamom, pepper and tobacco. Also many edible roots and other sorts of melons, water melons, asparagus, radish, and other Dutch natural products such as parsnip, cucumbers, pumpkins, rosemary, salad, fennel, mint, mustard and many others, as well as different sorts of delicious beans. *Many edible roots*

They have the most wonderful herbs that one can imagine for the curing of broken legs and wounds or for swelling of the throat, making ointments from them to smear over wounded limbs or preparing them into drinks for consumption which help the sick immediately or give relief and in a short time cure them. There are also very beautiful snakewood and very many medicinal herbs. *Wonderful medicinal herbs*

There are also many different flowers which grow in the field since they never plant them. There are white and red roses which do not differ from ours in smell and shape and we will not trouble ourselves to describe them further as they mostly compare with the sorts that we have described under Amboina. *Different flowers*

There is one called *pitsja*[1] which is white and is very similar to the jasmine. All who come across it on the way must give way and pass on the other side out of respect for the Emperor, for this flower is brought to the ruler every morning by certain persons after they have wrapped it in a white cloth, since it is beautiful and fragrant and wonderful to smell. They are also accustomed to planting it around rivers. *Pitsja flower*

[1] *Picca* (Sinh.)—jasmine. *Jasminum sambac.*

Flowering trees

There are also various flowering trees which compare with the sorts described under Amboina and we therefore do not repeat it.

Animals here

There are different animals, both wild and tame, on this island.

The wild are elephants, tigers, bears, wild deer, elks, buffaloes, civet cats, jackals, apes, snakes, squirrels, the Nigombo devil, sloth, mongoose and hares.[1] The tame are cows, oxen, tame buffaloes, sheep, pigs, goats and dogs. There are horses but these have been brought there from outside. Also there is on Cow Island a whole breeding ground of them from Portuguese times.[2]

Elephants, etc.

Elephants are so numerous here that it is impossible to travel without people and drums. Also there are many cases when they, on meeting this or that person, have done great harm and killed them.

The Ceylon elephant is the best and the biggest of the entire Indies and it is said that all others show respect to it which I simply do not believe.[3]

Here are also found those that are spotted and stained over their entire body which are generally brought to the Emperor as he esteems them very highly above all others.

How these elephants are captured can be seen in Baldaeus[4] and Knox[5] and also from our picture. It is necessary to carry out this hunt because they do great damage to the trees, the crops of the field and to the rice fields by eating them and treading on them.

They are also sought after for their beautiful tusks; besides the King generally uses an elephant as his executioner.

There are also tigers and even a kind which is black, but not very many and not as harmful as on other islands. Also now and then one sees a leopard but more bears are found, especially in the area of Matotte.

There are wild buffaloes in herds also in the land of Chilauw,

[1] This list has been taken from Knox. There are, of course, no wild tigers in Ceylon.
[2] Nedunthīvu or Delft as the Dutch renamed it where there was a horse stud farm.
[3] See above, p. 96.
[4] Baldaeus pp. 197–8. Valentijn has also referred to this. See above, p. 166.
[5] Knox, pp. 21–2.

and in Madampe hedgehogs or porcupines, though not very many. Elks are very numerous, somewhat more than ordinary deer. The deer are found in great numbers and of various sorts and sizes; some are not bigger than a hare. They call this small deer *meminna*.[1] It is grey in colour spotted with white patches and very delicious in taste. There are also snow-white deer, but very few and being a curiosity they are also brought to the Emperor.

Civet cats and ibexes are found in great numbers and the jackals here do much harm. There are also the Nigombo devils here which are one yard tall, three yards long, four-footed, with a very sharp and pointed mouth, sharp teeth and full of yellow shells which are round and like a harness on the body. The sloth is also found here. Of apes there are very many and many varieties. Also there are forest apes with the appearance of men. There are snakes of various sorts and sizes, many squirrels and, now and then, hares.

The tame, winged animals are in great abundance.   Bird

Among the birds are counted peacocks, also a sort of wild fowl, chicken thieves, night owls, geese, herons, wild and tame ducks, partridges, pigeons, turtle doves, parrots of all sorts, peewits, bats, large and small martins, carpenter birds, crows, wild pigeons, finches, snipes, swallows, sparrows, and a sort of bird which make their nests at the end of a branch to which they hang on very wonderfully and naturally like a cap with a long tip. Also there are many singing birds, such as nightingales, many skylarks, many seagulls and snipes and crows by the thousands.

In the interior are various other beautiful birds, some of which are snow-white with a tail a foot long, but the head pitch black, with a crest and a bunch of plumes on it. There are also more of this shape but of another colour, namely red or orangeish, but also with a black bunch of feathers on the head; possibly this is the female of the other.[2]

There is also in the country another bird, called *cardo*,[3] of

[1] *Miminna* (Sinh.)—mouse-deer.
[2] Probably the Paradise Flycatcher (*Tchitrea paradisi paradisi*).
[3] Knox has *carlo* (p. 28). The word sounds like either *diya kāva* (Sinh.)—black diver or *kurulla* (Sinh.)—woodpecker; but from the description it could be a Malabar Pied Hornbill.

the size of a wild swan which never comes below but always remains on the top of the highest mountains. It is black in colour, with short legs, long and round beak, having a white patch on both sides of the head and with a high outgrowth on his beak, like a cock's comb. Generally one sees them a few together hopping from one branch to the other and then making a great shout and scream that can be heard half a mile away and resembles the quacking of the ducks. They have an unusually fine taste.

There are also birds like our ducks but pitch black which can remain very long under water and then come up very far from there.

There are many other sorts of birds, much larger than a swan, which keep on the stagnant waters and bait fish, but know how to guard themselves especially against alligators.

Bloodless animals

There are here many locusts, fire-flies, bees, different kinds of bloodless insects, five or six types of ants, red, small black, very large black, which make exceptionally large nests on the branches of trees, yet another large black sort which lives in the earth and a fourth black sort which glitters very brightly and also hides itself under the earth and bites uncommonly fiercely, just like the red fire ants. The same sort has a red head and a white back, being a sort of white ant which eats up everything in a very short time. They call this *vaeos*[1] and the Cingalese are dreadfully plagued by it. There are also the bloodsuckers, fleas, mosquitoes, flies, all sorts of beautiful centipedes, scorpions, millipedes, toads, frogs, and very poisonous spiders. There are also rats and mice as also musk rats.

Fish

Among sea fish there are sea pigs, sharks, sword fish, Jacob Evertzen, jawfish, plaice, sole, kingfish, sailfish, pintails, Goanese cod, galleon fish, mullet, goldfish, sprat, sea lice, bat fish, crayfish, crabs, St. Pieters or the five fingers fish (which is two yards long and has five white spots as men have fingers), sole, oysters, mussels, shrimps, pampus fish, Corremans, Barbaras, Bonitos, Corcuados, turtles and many others of this sort.[2]

[1] *Veya*, pl. *veyo* (Sinh.)—ant. Knox, p. 24.

[2] Valentijn names many more varieties of fish than Knox, a knowledge which the Dutch secured from coastal areas. Some of the varieties cannot be identified in Sinhalese or Tamil. Valentijn has used his knowledge of sea products of Amboina in identifying and naming these species.

There are also many different varieties of sea shells and among these the most important are the *chanks* or sacrificial shells in entire shoals. They also have a king among themselves and if one finds one of these it can be sold for much money and some native kings give 700 to 800 Rix Dollars for each. There are also pearls found near Manaar and Toetecoryn in some pearlshells fished from there. Here there is in the sea also very good grey amber of which now and then good pieces have been found.

In the big river of Mawielleganga there is a sort of salmon and both in this river and in others many kinds of river fish. But most of the varieties are not native to this land or are to be found also in Batavia, Amboina and elsewhere.

There are many alligators here and, in the island of Manaar, very fat sea pigs with huge tusks whose flesh is very good to eat and whose females have large breasts full of milk. Now and then they come on land to eat greens.

Among minerals found here there are iron and crystal in great abundance—white, black, yellow, brown and red in colour. There is also saltpetre, sulphur, and antimony to be found. It is said that in the interior of the country there is also gold and silver but that the Emperor will not have them mined. *Minerals*

Here are formed also very beautiful and valuable stones such as rubies, white and blue sapphires, topazes, spinels, garnet, emerald, sky stones, cat's eyes and many other beautiful stones which are found in the mountains and in the rivers. *Precious stones*

The rubies are formed in a reddish, half stony and half sandy earth about one and a half fathoms deep, as if issuing out of the lode. If the swollen flood of a river moves such lodes, it carries the crumbled pieces downwards where the stones, as long as they are covered with water, preserve their appearance completely. But if they are exposed and lie in the sun for some days they become coal black as if burnt.

The sapphires form in a blue hard soil but the white in grey ground, hardly one fathom deep, also with loam and are carried downwards by the floods.

The goods which, from of old, are in demand here are these: *Goods brought here*

Various painted lacquers
Velvets of different colours
All sorts of drugs
Different kinds of silk stuffs
Plough oxen
Red caps
Porcelain
Opium
Spices
Steel
Radix China[1]
Tobacco
Camphor of Baros
Cotton
Musk
Sandalwood
Iron
Agilwood,[2] which the Javanese and Malays call Cajoo
    Garoe,[3] the Portuguese Pao d'Aquila and the Chinese
    and those of Cochinchina Calimbac; but Calimbac is a
    variety in itself and the choicest of Agilwood.
Saltpetre
Sulphur
Gilt looking-glass
Glass bottles
All kinds of sorted cloth and linens from the coast and
    from Surat.
In the Maldives is traded copper, opium, Rupees, cloth,
    rice, etc.

Those found here

Against these are the following most important goods found here:

Cinnamon
Pepper
Cardamom
Elephants and their tusks
Ebony wood

---

[1] A dried root used in medicines.
[2] *Ahil* (Tam.)—Aloe wood. *Aquilaria agallocha.*   [3] *Kaju garu* (Malay).

Caliatoer wood[1]
Black sugar
Antimony
Salt
Rice
Old Pinang,[2] also called Arecanut
Pearls
Chanks
Wax
Musk, but not much
Different types of stones such as:
   Rubies
   White and blue sapphires
   Emeralds
   Topazes
   Garnets
   Sky stones
   Cat's eyes
   Crystal of almost all sorts
Cauries[3] and Chanks brought from the Maldives

Besides the coins, measures, yards, and weights which can be seen in Cnox,[4] we think it useful to add the following:

The coins current here are Rixdollar[5] of 60 Stuivers   Coins
Rupees[6] of 24 or 30 Stuivers
Persian large Abbasis[7] at 1 Rixdollar for two and a half large and three and a half of small Abbasis
1 large Abbasi is 22 and a half Stuivers, 1 small Abbasi 18 Stuivers
Ducats[8] at 6 Guilders 12 Stuivers each
1 copper Casu[9] 1 Stuiver; 60 Casus in 1 Rixdollar
Provintie-Dollars at $1\frac{1}{10}$ Rixdollars each

[1] A type of sandalwood used for carving as well as to make dye.
[2] *Pinang* (Malay)—arecanut.
[3] *Kauri* (Hindi). A sea shell used as money in early times and later as ornament.
[4] Knox, pp. 97–8.   [5] The Dutch *Rijksdaalder*, a silver coin.
[6] The standard Moghul silver coin.
[7] A Persian gold coin.   [8] A European silver coin.
[9] *Kāsu* (Tam.). A copper coin of small denomination, anglicised into 'cash'.

1 Coer[1] Chankus[2] are 20 Stuivers
Pagodas[3] at 120 Stuivers or 6 Guilders each
1 Fanum[4] 5 Stuivers
1 Moor Ducat is 19 Fanum or $2\frac{1}{2}$ Rixdollars
1 Xerafim[5] is 1 Guilder

Measures and Weights

Measures and
Weights

1 Leaguer of wine, as in other comptoirs, 350 cans at
  10 mutsjes,[6] but for native drinks 396 cans at 11 mutsjes
  and proportionate to this.
1 Aam[7] at 90 cans
1 Parra[8] arecanut or old pinang has 3610 pieces, sometimes more and sometimes less
1 large Ammunam[9] pinang 27800 to 28800 pieces but in
  Jaffanapatnam 20000 pieces
1 small Ammunam pinang 23000 to 24000 pieces or 232
  pounds but from Pandi[10] 240 in Jaffanapatnam
1 Bois[11] is 30000 pieces in Tuticorin
1 Last[12] is 75 parra or 3000 pounds
1 Parra 40 pounds
1 Vat[13] saltflesh 400 pounds
1 Vat salt bacon 300 pounds
1 Vat butter 300 pounds
1 Verken[14] coconut oil is 120 cans
In paddy and rice there is a loss of 36%

---

[1] *Kūru* (Tam.). A quantity of 120 pieces, generally used in Madura to measure *chanks*.
[2] *Sanku* (Tam.)—conch shell.
[3] Gold coin current in southern India, also called *varaha* or *hun*.
[4] A gold coin of small denomination current in south India.
[5] A Portuguese gold coin.
[6] A Dutch liquid measure. Four mutsjes made a pint.
[7] A Dutch and German liquid measure varying from 37 to 41 gallons.
[8] *Parai* (Tam.). A measure of quantity to measure grain. Equivalent to about 45 to 50 pounds.
[9] *Amunam* (Tam.). A measure, generally of paddy and arecanuts varying widely.
[10] Another type of arecanut.   [11] Portuguese, probably a cartload.
[12] A weight varying with material weighed.   [13] A Dutch measure of capacity.
[14] Or Varken, a Dutch liquid measure, about 400 litres.

1 pot gingeli oil is 54 to 60 cans

1 Bahar[1] weighs 480 pounds ⎫

1 Bahar also weighs 744 pounds ⎪

1 Bahar is 12 Robbe[2] ⎬ of cinnamon

1 Robbe is 62 pounds ⎪

1 Markal[3] is 9 pounds ⎭

1 Catty[4] cauris 12000 pieces

1 Bahar in Tuticorin 510 pounds

1 Man[5] 25½ pounds in this place but in Jaffanapatnam 24 pounds

1 Ratel[6] is $1\frac{1}{16}$ pounds

1 Man is 24 Ratel

1 Medide[7] is 7 mutsjes

1 ounce weight is 1 Rixdollar

20 Mangeli[8] make 1 Calange[9]

1 Calange makes 11½ grain or 3¼ English

600 grains make 1 ounce

30 grains make 1 English

1 Carat[10] makes 4 grain

The measure of cloth is as follows: Measure of cloth

Tapi Sarassas,[11] new sort, 3½ yards long, half yd broad, 20 pieces a pack

Tapitsjindos,[12] length and breadth as above

Sarassa Gobars[13] and Sarassa New Chain work, 4 yds long, 3 yds broad, 10 pieces in one pack

[1] A unit of weight varying from region to region and according to article weighed from 400 to 500 pounds.

[2] A Sinhalese unit of weight also called *pingo*.   [3] *Marakkāl* (Tam.).

[4] *Katty*, of Chinese origin, widely used in Southeast Asia.

[5] An Indian unit of weight, now called *maund*. Varied from 25 to 50 pounds.

[6] From *rati* (Hindi), a seed used as goldsmith's weight in India.

[7] Probably from *midād* (Arabic), a dry measure of about 18 pounds.

[8] *Manjali* (Telugu), *manjadi* (Tam.). A seed used as a measure of weight generally to weigh gold and precious stones.

[9] A unit of weight to weigh pearls and precious stones.

[10] From *qīrāt* (Arabic), a bean seed used to weigh gold and diamonds.

[11] *Tapi-sarassa*. From *tapi* (Malay), a long unsewn skirt. A popular variety of cloth exported from India to the Malay Archipelago.

[12] *Tapi-chindai*. Another variety of cloth used for making *tapi* or skirt.

[13] A brightly coloured silk cloth, patterned with flowers and birds, exported from India. Very much in demand in the Malay Archipelago.

Painted committer,[1] all as before

Red Bethilis,[2] length 30 to 32 Hasta[3] breadth 1½ el[4]

Red Bethilis, length 40 Hasta, breadth 1½ el

Red Chavonis,[5] length 16 and breadth 2 cubits

Red Parcallen[6] length 15 to 16, breadth 1½ el

} Per pack[7]

Red Moeris,[8] length 18, breadth 1¼ el, per pack 100 pieces

Salempoeris,[9] length 30 to 32 Hasta, breadth 1½ el, per pack 80 pieces

The administration of this island by an Emperor

Now that we have presented the most important facts about this island, we can say in general (as we hereafter will speak in detail over these kingdoms) that in olden times this country used to be administered by various Kings whom some estimate at 7 and others at 9. But now it is ruled supremely from the interior by one supreme Emperor who has under himself several Kings, Princes, Counts and Lords of the territories, principalities, counties and feudatories, already mentioned by us earlier. It had its beginning with the reign of Don Jan or Fimala Darma Soria Ada[10] who died in 1604 and his successors (as we shall show hereafter in greater detail), and remains till now on the same footing.

His bodyguard

This King restricts himself now, for fear of his own subjects, to the mountain, in the city of Dietlicki where he has a strong

[1] Another variety of brightly painted cloth.

[2] *Bethile*. Muslin cloth dyed red or striped and embroidered. Exported to Europe from Golconda area.

[3] A north Indian measure, about 18 inches.   [4] *Ela* (Malay)—a yard.

[5] A light white cloth embroidered with coloured silk.

[6] A fine, high grade, white cambric cotton cloth of regular and durable weave, woven in Coromandel.

[7] A bundle of 20 or 22 pieces of cloth.

[8] *Mūri*. A staple cotton cloth woven in Coromandel and much in demand in Europe.

[9] *Salampūri*. A staple cotton cloth, often with red border, of varying quality. Woven in Coromandel and exported to Europe and Southeast Asia.

[10] Vimala Dharma Sūrya Adahassyn, the founder of a new dynasty in the kingdom of Kandy.

bodyguard, both of his principal officials and of a large number of soldiers under these chiefs. But he trusts most a special bodyguard of Moors who generally stand guard at the doors of his room. Besides these, he has many other young bodyguards, whom he chooses from the best castes and who are the bravest and most courageous youths in his land. They have long beautiful hair, generally go barefooted and are usually with him when he goes out or betakes himself anywhere.

The revenues of this ruler are very large.[1] Three times a year his subjects must bring him tribute. He collects the first in March, at their New Year, the second is the first fruits and the third a certain offering which is given in November in honour of their deity.

Incomes

Apart from these levies all are required to give the ruler everything that is needed in his palace; and the chiefs take it wherever it may be found, without giving anything for it, accordingly much robbery and other base corruption is committed by them in the Emperor's name.

All tribute and presents are wrapped in white cloth out of respect, and are brought first to the Emperor after he, on New Year's Day, has washed his head and cleaned himself in his bath, at which time he shows himself publicly to the entire military nobility expressly gathered there for this purpose and to all his chiefs, and the artillery is fired everywhere then.

Thereafter the chiefs and lesser folk come with all their presents of gold, silver, precious stones, rifles, silk material, and cloth, besides the taxes which they are obliged to pay him for the first instalment in money, palm wine, oil, rice, honey, wax, iron, elephant tusks, tobacco or other goods, and very often must remain at court for very long before those goods are accepted by the Emperor or his servants, which causes a great noise and bustle.

Where also the
taxes are paid

Apart from these revenues, which are fixed, he has many more which are uncertain and periodic.

When a man dies who has left behind animals, he takes, according to the laws of the land and his right, an ox, a cow, and a pair of buffaloes of both sexes, which are gathered by

[1] This description of taxes is a summary of Knox, pp. 47–9.

certain officers appointed thereto and very closely followed. Each year everyone must, at the time of harvest, give a certain amount of corn or rice according to the size of his land to the ruler which is sometimes bought off for all time with a sum of money; but this may happen no more.

The goods of the military men who have been killed in war are, however, free of these taxes, but otherwise not.

Also all lessees of the lands must pay a certain sum of money, above the fixed amount of corn. But as against that the lands that are given to priests or as charity do not pay anything. In olden times he also had the tolls of Cotjaar or Trinkenemale, Point Gale and Portaloon, but not now, as we collect these.

For all these taxes and presents which he receives in so many different ways, he has various treasure houses in his land here and there where these goods of all types are specially protected and stored, though there have been times when these kings on being attacked by their enemies, have thrown much of this treasure and jewels into the Mawielleganga River and elsewhere in the jungle so that the enemy might not get them.

The greatest state officials

Next to the ruler there are 2 Adigars or Chief Judges to whom all the lesser inhabitants can appeal if they have been denied justice by the lower judges, and if they think they have been wronged by them.[1]

Under them are very many officials who are very easily known by their shepherd-staff, for no one else may carry these, and one must respect their orders as if it was from the Adigar himself.

After them come the Dessaves or sheriffs and overseers of the district of which there is one in each county, though not all sheriffs[2] are Dessaves, for there are also those who are only overseers and have some soldiers under them.

Income of the Governor

These Governors must not only administer the districts well but also collect the Emperor's income. He chooses them generally from the nobility of the land, looking mostly to their birth. None of these chiefs has the power to kill anyone

[1] This account of the administration is a summary of Knox, pp. 50–54.
[2] Knox calls them Governors, p. 51.

without the Emperor's knowledge or to pass death sentences on anyone.

Each village now has, on the king's orders, a smith, a potter, a washer, and one of every type of artisan. Each of them knows what must be given to this Governor also for each piece of land, outside what is given to the Emperor, apart from which they, as petty kings, also receive very large presents from everyone who has dealings with them: for if they did not take from the lower people, how should they be in a position to bring as much yearly to the Emperor as they are forced to do (if they wish to remain in his favour). Their lower officials

The greatest difficulty for these Governors however, is that they must always be at the Emperor's court, therefore they must appoint under-Dessaves in their districts to manage their affairs. These they call Coerli Vidanis,[1] besides whom they have some other officers, called Congconnas[2] who again watch over everything that the Coerli Vidani does and give information of it to the Dessaves.

The Coerli Achila[3] is the executor of the orders of the Coerli Vidani and provider of all kinds of fruits for the Emperor's table, besides which he despatches all those who go to the court with any message.

There is also a Liannah[4] or chief writer of the district who reads and keeps all the letters, keeps records of everything that is sent to the court and writes all letters, so that one must consider him as the chief confidential secretary of the Emperor.

The Undia[5] collects the Emperor's money and brings it together in one lump, for which he is also called in Cingalese the Klomp.[6]

The Monnannah[7] is measurer of all corn that grows on the Emperor's lands.

---

[1] Knox has 'Courlividani' (p. 51). *Kōralē Vidanā* (Sinh.).   [2] Kankāni.
[3] Knox has 'Courli atchila' (p. 51). *Kōralē Ārachchi* (Sinh.).
[4] *Liyannā* (Sinh.).   [5] *Undiyā* (Sinh.).
[6] Here Valentijn has misunderstood Knox. Knox says: 'Next to him is Undia. A word that signifieth a lump. He is a person that gathers the King's Money: and is so styled because he gathereth the King's Moneys together into a lump'. Knox, p. 52.
[7] *Manannā* (Sinh.).

Not all towns and villages come under the Dessave: for all towns and villages which belong to the temples of the deities or of their priests are free of their jurisdiction, for they have been granted that right by the former kings and are considered holy. Also all villages and towns which the Emperor demarcates and gifts to his nobles and officials are free. Over these lands each man appoints his own servants.

These and many others are the highest officers of the kingdom; but those in this high position are the most miserable which one can imagine, since their lives depend on the whim of these Emperors and those who are raised to the highest rank and placed next to him are also generally nearest to their fall.

Strength of the Emperors in war

The greatest might of the Emperor, when he wants to go to war, consists in his maintaining himself in impenetrable jungle because this land is stronger through the abundant forests than it could be made with fortresses and therefore he has almost nowhere any fortress of importance. He has also here and there in the narrow passes of the mountains heavy thorn gates where there are thorns 3 to 4 inches long and many guards placed on all posts so that no enemy could approach him. No one may approach without a pass which consists of a piece of clay on which the Emperor's seal is impressed according to each one's rank and state.

He has also a great number of soldiers who watch by turns near his court and then go back to their piece of land which is given by the king as a heritage instead of pay and which also is inherited by the soldiers' children, since they are also soldiers, for generally all children of the Cingalese succeed their fathers, each in his occupation.

All these soldiers must pay their way and provide themselves with all necessities for this or that expedition so that the Emperor has no burden in the world from them.

The number of his soldiers is impossible to ascertain, but that this Emperor has taken the field with powerful armies will appear clear enough to us when we shall speak of their wars with the Portuguese later.

That some chiefs of their armies have performed many courageous deeds is not to be wondered at, as they, being

Fig. 6. An elephant hunt (Valentijn V. 1, facing p. 46, No. 14)

Fig. 7. Sinhalese man and wife
(Valentijn V. 1, facing p. 32)

Fig. 8. Lion carrying away the princess, Vijaya's grandmother
(Valentijn V. 1, p. 62)

Fig. 9. Adam's Peak
(Valentijn V. 1, p. 380, No. XIII, I)

Fig. 10. A Buddhist procession (Valentijn V. 1, p. 403)

given the order to accomplish a task, if they do not complete this, would have to expect nothing but a miserable death when they come to the Emperor.[1]

Here we think we have laid out in sufficient detail the most important facts that concern this island of Ceylon in general, both from outside and from within, so that it will now be time to speak specially of the matters that happened there from olden times to our own and at the same time to show how and when, first the Portuguese and thereafter we have come here and become masters of the coastal cities, towns and villages, and also of the best cinnamon lands.

[1] The account of the King's army and methods of warfare is a summary of Knox, pp. 54–7.

Fourth Chapter

[History (to 2nd century A.D.)]

Particular matters of Ceylon. Alexander the Great claimed as first discoverer of Ceylon. Information of the Cingalese on their first arrival. Vegea Raja, first discoverer of the island A.M. 1996. Further information on this. History of the old Kings of Ceylon. Vagoe Raja's marriage. The prophecy regarding his daughter. This princess, impregnated by a lion, produces a son and daughter, to which son she makes known his lineage. Further actions of this Prince. He is raised to King. Builds a royal city. Marries his sister and is crowned. This becomes a royal custom in Ceylon. Their children. Names of the two oldest sons who depart from the kingdom. And land on Ceylon. There they build a city. Vigea Bahu Comara first discoverer of Ceylon. He is married to the Princess of Madure and dies after a reign of 30 years. Tissanaon Ameti reigns 1 year. Simit Comara, Pandoe Vassajoe. Princes, fleeing here, build various cities. Pandoe Vassajoe becomes first Emperor. His children. Abeia Comara reigns 20 years. Sagoeganatissa. Digagamoenoe. Pandoe Cabaja. Builds the city Anoereajapoere. Moeta Singa Raja. Deveni Petisse Maharaja. Soeratissanam. Two Malabar Princes. Assalanam Raja. Etalunam. Gelinitissa Raja. Goloeumbera. Ganatissa Rajoe. Of the noble administration in his name. Doetoe Geinoene. Maha Raja. Sedetissa Raja. Tullenam Raja. Lemenetissa Caloeman Raja. Walagam Bahu Raja. Five Malabar Kings rule thereafter. Vallagamboe Raja. Chonanga Raja. Bemminitissa. Mahadeliatissa. Chorawa. Coeda Tissa Rajoe. Anularan Bisava Coelavaon. Tomo. Maloelantissa. Batia Raja. Madilimanna Raja. Adague Muwene Raja. Cada Ambera Raja. Nalabissava. Elunna Raja. Sandamoehoenoe Raja. Asnapa Raja. Vacnelisinam Raja. Bapa Raja.

If we would first begin with the oldest times, when this island was first discovered, according to the view of some of the ancient scholars, Alexander the Great was the first to have given the inducement to the discovery of the island, seeing that he was anxious to know if there was not yet another world which he could conquer, Nearchus, one of his admirals, observing this, offered himself voluntarily to investigate it.[1]

He took Onesicritus with him, with the command of Alexander that each of them should keep a separate diary of their discoveries, which they would certainly have done. But these diaries we have never come to see.[2]

But Diodoor the Sicilian[3] is one of the oldest historical writers who appears to have preserved something of the description of this island in his work, in respect of its extent, giving a circumference measure of 200 miles. To speak the truth, this evidence of the discovery of this island which we find in Diodoor is a proof of his accurate annotation, but is of little importance in itself as are also the lofty claims of the ancients for this expedition of Nearchus and Onesicritus, on which there is much uncertainty in the records some being of the opinion that Nearchus went only along the shore up to the Arabian coast, though others add that Onesicritus would have proceeded up to the island of Sumatra. For myself, I believe the one as much as the other, that is that all are without any foundation as the times were entirely not suited for making such voyages and certainly for going so far away from the coast and across the sea to Sumatra. And if they had been there they would have spoken of it in such a way that one could sense that they had been there.

If we consult the Cingalese on the first discovery and the early origins of Ceylon, we cannot find such an accurate account that one could be fully satisfied in this matter. The

Special matters of Ceylon

Alexander the Great as first discoverer of Ceylon

Information of the Cingalese on their first arrival

[1] Whether Nearchus, Alexander's admiral, sailed down the coast of India is doubtful. It seems unlikely, considering that the insular character of Ceylon was in doubt in the classical works till later.

[2] Onesicritus' diary did not survive in its original form but fragments were used by later writers such as Strabo and Pliny and contained many fanciful statements.

[3] Diodorus Siculus. Greek historian who lived in second half of first century B.C. Author of *Bibliotheca Historica*. See Majumdar, *Classical Accounts* ..., pp. 162 ff.

safest course appears then to be to inform ourselves in some way of the narrative of the oldest and most intelligent people of this land such as they have handed down from time to time and from father to son by oral transmission.[1]

The Cingalese, to give their Kings a noble descent, relate this fable:

All people from beyond the Ganges and outwards in the Kingdoms of Pegu, Tanassery, Siam, Cambodia[2] and beyond in that region, living without a king, law, order or any administration which could distinguish them from wild animals, lived in the hollows of the mountains and caves, ate grass and herbs without having any knowledge of agriculture.

The natives of Tanasserim or Tanassery,[3] one morning as the sun rose, observing its beauty and first rays, saw that it opened itself unexpectedly and that from its innermost parts came to view a very beautiful and stately person, worthy of great respect for his appearance and manner and in his form entirely different from other men. All who saw him rushed after him, amazed to the utmost at this miracle, and asked him with much humility and respect what man he was and what he wanted, whereupon he replied in a Tanassery language that he was a son of the sun and was sent from God to rule this kingdom. Thereupon they all threw themselves on the ground to worship him and said they were ready to receive him as their ruler and to obey him.

He was then taken by them, placed on a high place and began to rule over them. The first thing he did was to take them out of the woods and to bring them to a settled and civil environment, ordering them to build houses and villages, after which he instituted very good laws among them.[4]

This King, having ruled many years among them, left behind many sons, among whom he divided his kingdom,

[1] Valentijn is referring to the oral tradition that had been committed to writing from the 1st century B.C.

[2] These are all Southeast Asian countries and it is significant that Valentijn's version of the legend of the origin of the Sinhalese places the action in Southeast Asia rather than India. See Introduction, p. 36.

[3] Tenasserim, in Lower Burma. Couto and Queyroz also have Tenasserim as the place where prince Vijaya's grandfather lived.

[4] Hindu and Buddhist myths of the origin of kingship have all this drift of events. Couto relates a similar legend (Couto, p. 101).

whose descendants (who remained in being for more than 2000 years) and all their heirs named themselves Soeriavas[1] or descendants of the sun race. From this King was descended in direct line Vigea Raja,[2] of whom we will speak further in the following as the founder of the Cingalese Emperors.

Based on this belief (of which traces are also found among the first Incas of the Peruans and which idea appears to have been brought over there from China and was first brought to America as Inca Manco[3] and his wife Coja Mama,[4] also from there, as appears in *Hoornbeek de Convers. Indorum*[5] and in Hornius in *Orig. Americ.* Book XV, Chap X,[6]) is the common saying of the Cingalese that their first and oldest origin on this island which they are able to assert is in A.M. 1996[7] (as we according to our reckoning of years of rule of their kings calculate backwards) and that the first King would have been a certain Vigea Raja who would have first set foot on the coast with 700 men at the River Walauwe[8] at the southeastern end of this island (though others speak of the island Manaar, and of Matotte or Calpentyn and others of Tricoenmale which is the most probable[9]) and from there had gone inland to build a city or town.

Viga Raja first discoverer of the island A.M. 1996

It is also said that then some wise men from Persia had come there with very beautiful women and had engaged in war with their neighbours over them.[10]

---

[1] *Sūriya vangsa* (Sinh.)—the sun dynasty.   [2] Vijaya Rāja.

[3] The origin myth of the Incas, a Peruvian tribe, traces their ancestry to four brothers, the chief of whom was Manco. He was the high priest of the tribal God, the sun.

[4] Mama was the title of the wives of the four brothers.

[5] Johannes Hoornbeek (1617–1666), Professor at the University of Leiden. Author of *De Conversione Indorum et gentilium* libri duo (Amsterdam, 1669).

[6] Georg Horn or Georgius Hornius (1620–1670), Professor of History at Leiden University. Author of *De Originibus Americani*. Libri quatuor, Societas illaesa Hagae Comitis Lugduni (Batavorum, 1652).

[7] A.M. is presumably Anno Mundi—in the year of the world used in reckoning dates from the supposed period of creation. This date here appears to be 1996 years before the present which is a date that tallies with Buddhist chronological tradition in a source written in the 15th century A.D.

[8] Valavē Ganga.

[9] Valentijn is here referring to differing traditions on where Prince Vijaya and his followers disembarked in Ceylon.

[10] Valentijn antedates a much later tradition of a Persian settlement in Ceylon in the 6th century A.D.

This Vigea Raja, say the most learned among the Cingalese, originated from the Kingdom of Tillingo,[1] bordering on Tanassary,[2] formerly named Ajota[3] and politically under Siam, of whose King he was a son and of whom the priests had prophesied to his father that he would be the cause of much unrest, even of the decline of his kingdom if he remained there. His father, then, after mature consultation with the priests was persuaded to order his son to leave the kingdom and betake himself to another land, as shortly thereafter was done by him.

As soon as he came to the land of Ceylon, he asserted that he was not only a King's son but a child of the sun and the son of a lion, or sprung from both by blood, at which the oldest inhabitants of this island, honouring the sun as their highest God, together with the Malabars, with the name Eswara,[4] accorded such high esteem to this foreign prince at once that they immediately accepted him as their King. A narrative of the native that, we at once must remark, is like a narrative of the Greeks and of the Romans of matters occurring in their *Aetas Fabulosa* by which they, not in a position to go back to the times of their ancestors, produce for their successors a fabulous tale (to show that they were at the end of their reckoning) as those mentioned and many other people are accustomed.

It is for this reason that the Emperors of Ceylon still call themselves Suriya Wangsa[5] (in Cingalese, the race of the sun) and lords of the golden sun. And in former times one comes across those among them who bore the name Comara Singa[6] which means the son of a lion. And one dreads even the name Cingalese, it is said, as Singa-le[7] means the blood of a lion in their language, as also in Malay and Sanskrit (the mother of all the eastern languages). All of this very clearly has its relevance here. There are also those who will have it that the name

---

[1] Probably Kalinga, but Valentijn places it wrongly.

[2] Tenasserim in lower Burma.

[3] Ayothya, a kingdom in Thailand. Valentijn here confuses a number of traditions and widely separated place names: Kalinga in northeastern India, Tenasserim in Lower Burma, Ayothya in Thailand.

[4] *Isvara* (Skt.)—God, lord.   [5] *Sūriya Vangsa* (Sinh.).

[6] Kumāra Sinha.   [7] *Sinha* (Sinh.)—lion, *lē* (Sinh.)—blood.

Cingalese is adopted not from the island of Ceylon but from the word Singa, a lion, and they were called thereafter Cingalese (or descendants of the lion).

Other Cingalese agree with this whole narrative, but differ only in this that they call the first King of Ceylon Vimala Dharma Soeriya Adasseyn,[1] that is the well-beloved son of the sun which is never still, adding further that it appears from their old books, of which some appear still to be preserved, that this ruler was of Chinese descent, and without any design, very much by chance landed there in a junk, claiming himself to be a son of the sun, for fear of being killed otherwise, whereupon the Cingalese accepted him voluntarily as their King and overlord, as they honoured the sun as their overlord.[2] But to narrate this more accurately and in detail we will set down here a detailed list of Ceylonese kings, never before brought to light by anyone, to our knowledge, with an exact account of their origin, as we have uncovered from the oldest writings and accounts of the natives.

History of the First Emperors and Kings of Ceylon

To the south side there was a King named Vagoe Raja,[3] who was married to the daughter of Calinga Raja, who being impregnated by him, brought forth an exceptionally beautiful daughter, of whom the astrologers prophesied at that time that she would be carried away by a lion at the age of 16 to be his wife.[4]

There were those among the courtiers who, on hearing this, joked about it, since a woman could be no match for such a wild animal as a lion and it was not conceivable that such an

A.C. 105
History of the Kings of Ceylon

Vagoe Raja's marriage

Strange prophesy about his daughter

[1] Vimala Dharma Sūrya Adahassyn. Valentijn is here confusing the founder of the Kandyan Kingdom and the founder of the Sinhalese dynasty.

[2] A garbled version of Chinese involvement in the politics of the Sinhalese kingdom in the 14th century. Myths on the Chinese origin of the Sinhalese were prevalent when the Portuguese came to the island.

[3] Neither the *Mahāvamsa* (*Mv*) nor the *Rājāvāliya* (*Rv*) gives the name of this king, the father of Sinhabāhu. Either Valentijn's source provides this name or he confuses the suffix Bāhu in Sinhabāhu for the name of this king's father.

[4] The story that follows is much more elaborate than in the *Mv* or *Rv*. An abridged version appears in van Goens' Report, Valentijn V, 1, pp. 210–11.

unfortunate kidnapping should happen to the King's daughter. The King however was concerned for his daughter, and, believing this prophecy, according to the general super- stitions of the easterners, deemed it best, in order to prevent such a great misfortune, first to have a royal residence built which rested only on one pillar and to which entry would be denied to all others. He provided it for 16 years with all necessary provisions, put his daughter with some of her friends and other women in it, had the door well locked and placed some guards of soldiers with their head officers on whose faith he could have confidence.

After the stipulated 16 years had passed, the King let the doors open again and inquired from the nurses if his daughter was still alive. As he was going away, there followed also other servants, maids and finally the Princess, as she should otherwise have remained there alone; and the guards, not knowing her, let her also go away. She arrived in the company of some other people, first in the middle of the city and, shortly after, outside it and, being led astray by a company of carts and camels, came with the merchants who were there and were returning home after the completion of their trade through the middle of a very large forest, called Cadda Desa,[1] where they rested for a while, as the road ran through the middle of the forest and they were rather tired, which gave one of their merchants the opportunity to cast his eye some- what closer on her, and finding her so very satisfying in her lovely appearance, he determined to take all steps to obtain her as his wife.

While he was making this plan, a huge lion came springing suddenly out of the forest, which drove the entire company immediately to flight and by its roaring the Princess was driven to such a fright that she was not in a position to flee and, having become stiff through fear, was carried away by him and was dragged to his cave.

While this happened in the forest, the King came with a large following of nobles and courtiers to the house, but not finding the Princess there and, however much he inquired from the guards, learning nothing from them or of anyone

[1] *Mv* has Lala Desa, *Rv* has Lada Desa.

there or from the people in the city, was very sad and even more so when he heard later from some travellers that a certain unknown maiden (who he was sure was his daughter) was carried by a huge lion deep into the forest, without anyone daring to help her or to follow the lion.

The Princess, having been ravished by this lion, later bore twins, namely a son and a daughter, of which the son was named Singa Bahoe Comara,[1] and the daughter Singa Valli Comari,[2] that is human children born of a lion. The Prince, Singa Bahu Comara became 15 years of age and was very strong in body and mind, ate no other food than what the lion brought him from time to time.

The Princess is impregnated by the lion and brings forth a son and a daughter

At a certain time he asked his mother how it came about that they did not resemble their father. His mother told him that there was a great reason for this which she would tell him when he was somewhat older.

Thereafter she let him know that she was the daughter of Calinga Raja and how he and his sister were born.

To which son she makes known his descent

As soon as the Prince heard it, he developed a great hatred for the savage life with this lion and tried with his whole heart to return to his rightful authority and to the court of his grandfather.

When the lion was out hunting, he lifted a huge stone on his shoulder to prove his strength, carried it 70 miles away and returned before the lion had come back.

On another day, after the lion had again gone on a hunt, he rolled away the stone with which the lion had closed the cave, carried his mother and sister, who were clothed in animal skins like him, away from there, resting them on his shoulders and brought them to the land of the King his grandfather. The lion returned and, not finding his wife and children in the cave, roared fearfully, followed their footsteps and devastated everything in the area so that he could not be comforted in his fury either by the King or by the soldiers that he sent there.

The King, fearing greater harm, opened his treasury, took some precious stones and pearls from there, let it be carried round the entire city by someone on an elephant and promised

[1] Sinhabāhu Kumāra.   [2] Sinhavalli Kumāri.

to present them to those who were able to put to death this lion. The Prince, Singa Bahu, hearing this, proposed to his mother and sister to undertake this bold task but they, knowing that it was their father, dissuaded him from it as a very shameful thing that a son should kill his own father and should besmirch himself with such a scandalous act. He went away, however, and offered himself to the King who promised him in addition that, if he accomplished it, he would become the second in the kingdom and next to him. Thereupon he set out, took bow and arrow with him and shot twice at the lion after he had first informed the lion that he was his son, though the lion knew this already by the smell and therefore he took the shooting by his son as in jest. But he shot him thrice severely in the head so that the lion observed too late that it was serious and no game, so that he finally fell down dead.

The Prince now, thinking of the words of his mother and sister, and considering what a cruel deed he had done, began lamenting and weeping and revealed his whole life to the King's servants, from which they understood that he was the son of their lost Princess.

He thought long over whether he should cut off the head of the lion and agreed finally because he was sure that otherwise someone else would do it and deprive him of the great treasure and even greater privileges.

He cut off the head, took it away and brought it in one day over a road of 7 days' journey, till he finally came to the King to whom he revealed his descent and the misfortune of his mother, who thereupon was immediately fetched along with his sister and brought to the court.

The Princess having come there with her daughter and they having the lion's head in their sight, began to lament bitterly, the one the fate of her husband and the other that of her father. But the King was very happy in that he had seen his daughter again for himself. He had her and her daughter and son clothed in royal manner and the body of the lion cremated with great honour, in the custom of the country, because of the singular relation of his daughter to it.

A royal city is built

In the meantime he made the Prince Singa Bahu Comara

King of Nalunaratta,[1] and the royal city which he built there shortly after was named Singa Bahu Nuwara.[2]

Thereafter he took his sister Singa Valli Comari as his wife because there was no other princess who resembled him and was thereafter crowned according to the custom of the land as the laws for kings did not permit his being crowned before he was married. It is for this reason that the Emperors of Ceylon have always married their sisters since.[3]

Married his sister and was crowned

He had by his wife 32 sons in the six times that she bore children; the first born was named Vigea Comara[4] and his next brother Simit Comara,[5] which Princes were cared for by 700 companions.

Their children

These two Princes, having become big, made it so unbearable to the inhabitants everywhere, that they complained to the King over it, with the request to move elsewhere either them or the Princes. The King, who was righteous and took more notice of his obedient subjects than of the two lawless Princes with their playful companions, ordered some vessels to be made ready immediately, in which he made his two sons with their 700 companions leave voluntarily to go to seek their fortune on sea or in another land.

Names of 2 oldest sons

They depart from the kingdom

Having departed, they were cast away not long after on the island of Ceylon where they came to land in a bay named Tammennatotte,[6] now named Tambuligamme,[7] situated near Cojaar.[8]

And land in Ceylon

They found this land then still a wilderness and without inhabitants, where they built a city immediately which they called Tammena Nuwara.[9] From this time the reign of the Kings of Ceylon for 2007 years makes a beginning, this island having been first discovered by the Prince Vigea Comara,

There they build a city

Vigea Bahu Comara, first discoverer of Ceylon

---

[1] Neither *Rv* nor *Mv* mentions this place. They say that he ruled in Lala Desa or Lada Desa.

[2] Sinhabāhu Nuvara. *Nuvara* (Sinh.)—city.

[3] This is a gross untruth. The story of the brother-sister union was intended to illustrate the purity of descent of the Vijaya dynasty.

[4] Vijaya Kumara.   [5] Sumita Kumara.

[6] Tamannatota, on the west-central coast.

[7] Valentijn is here confusing Tambapanni which was another name for Tamannatota and Thambalakamam on the east coast.

[8] Kottiyār on the east coast.   [9] Tamana Nuvara.

who was later named Vigea Bahu Raja and installed as King for the above mentioned grounds.[1]

He was now here as the first King but had no wife. Therefore he sent ambassadors with letters and presents to the King of Madure, named Pandei Maharadja,[2] and sought his daughter in marriage. He sent her to him with 700 maids-in-attendance and 18 pairs of various high and low castes and 5 pairs of artisans, namely, goldsmiths, blacksmiths, carpenters, stone cutters, and brass founders.[3]

He is married to a princess of Madure

The Princess having left for Ceylon (then called Langcauwn[4]) with her retinue, came to land in the bay of Mahatotte,[5] near the district of Cotjaar[6] and was received by King Vigea Bahu Raja with much affection and with great honour and joy, and he married her shortly thereafter and was crowned after the custom of the land.

After this time he built another city called Utapisse,[7] ruled for a total of 30 years very righteously and died, leaving the kingdom to his brother.

Tissanaon Ameti reigned 1 year

After his death one of the chiefs called Tissanaon Ameti[8] would not obey his brother Simit Comara, but seized the city of Utapisse[9] and ruled for 1 year there.

Afterwards the Prince Simit Comara took his brother's widow as wife and was crowned as King of Langcawn, had three sons by her and reigned for 22 years.[10]

Simit Comara

His youngest son Pandoe Vassaja,[11] having gone to the land of his grandfather, returned from there with 32 companions,

[1] Valentijn does not mention the Kuvēni episode which is found in both *Rv* and *Mv*. Nor does he note the coincidence recorded in all Sinhalese traditions of the landing of Vijaya in Ceylon with the date of the *parinibbāna* (enlightenment) of the Buddha.

[2] Pāndya Mahārāja. King of the Pandyan dynasty ruling at Madurai in south India.

[3] Compare with *Mv* account of the craftsmen of 18 guilds who accompanied the Pandyan bride. *Mv*, p. 59.

[4] Lankāva.   [5] Mahātota or Māntota, near Mannār.

[6] Again Valentijn is confusing the east coast and the west coast. Mahātota is on the west coast, while Kottiyār is on the east coast.

[7] Upatissagama, up the Malvattu Oya.

[8] This ruler is not recorded in the *Mv* or the *Rv* but they both refer to an interregnum between Vijaya and the next king, which gives plausibility to Valentijn's record.

[9] Upatissagama.

[10] According to the *Mv*, Vijaya's brother Sumita did not rule in Ceylon.

[11] Pānduvasudēva.

seized Utapisse very suddenly and treacherously and made himself King through his great following.[1]

Some time thereafter came a certain Princess named Badacassaje,[2] a daughter of a Sacca Rajoe[3] of old, having fled to Ceylon with some vessels and many companions who were very well received by Pandoe Vassaja, treated in a royal manner, taken as his wife after which he was crowned as King. *Pandoe Vassaja*

Shortly thereafter there came here 6 more Princes, brothers of the new Queen, who were also received very well by the King, ordering for each of them a city to be built here after their choice and comfort and to live there as free Princes under his overlordship.

One of the Princes, Ramanaon Sasse Comara,[4] built a city which he called Ramagonan Nuwara.[5] The second Prince, Nauvelanam Sassa Comara,[6] built another city to which he gave the name of Mahavelligam Nuwara.[7] The third Prince, Vigitenam Sacca Comara,[8] built the city Vigitapoera Nuwara.[9] The fourth Anuraadanam Soccea Comara[10] built a city which he called Anuraadpoera Nuwara.[11] But what cities the other two Princes built or what they were named is not mentioned in the old history of Ceylonese Kings.[12] *Princes having fled here, build many cities*

In the meanwhile Pandoe Vassaja had obtained so many Kings and lesser Princes under himself and his might had extended so far in the island that he decided to give himself the title of Emperor and was the first who took this title here. *And became first Emperor*

He had 6 sons and 1 daughter of whom his first born son was named Maja Comara, the second Sagoeganatissa Comara and the Princess (the third in rank) Matsit Comari.[13]

---

[1] Pāṇḍuvasudēva was a great hero in the *Mv* tradition, but apparently not in Valentijn's sources.

[2] Bhaddakaccana.   [3] *Mv* has Sakka Pāṇḍu.

[4] *Mv* has Rama, *Rv* has Ramagot. Sakka Kumara is common to the names of all the princes.

[5] Ramagona (*Mv*), Ramagotpura Nuvara (*Rv*).

[6] Uruvela (*Mv*), Uruvel (*Rv*).   [7] Uravela (*Mv*), Vilba Nuvara (*Rv*).

[8] Vijita (*Mv* and *Rv*).   [9] Vijitagama (*Mv*), Vijitapura (*Rv*).

[10] Anuradha (*Mv* and *Rv*).   [11] Anuradhagama (*Mv*), Anuradhapura (*Rv*).

[12] Suddhodana built Gampala Nuvara and a sixth prince (unnamed) built Māgama Nuvara (*Rv*).

[13] The various traditions are in conflict over the number and names of children Pāṇḍuvasudēva had. *Mv* says he had 10 sons and one daughter whose name was Citta and *Rv* that he had one son Abhaya and one daughter Umatusita.

She was maintained in a house which was built on one pillar and married one of her cousins called Digagamenoe Comara,[1] about which time the Emperor Pandoe Vassaja died after he had reigned for 13 years, leaving behind a great and memorable name.[2]

Abeia Comara rules 20 years

His eldest son, having taken the name of Abeia Comara,[3] was his successor in the Empire and ruled for 20 years with no less praise than his father.[4]

After him followed the second son of Pandoe Vassaja, named Sagoeganatissa who ruled for 17 years.[5] His brother-in-law, Digagamonoe,[6] followed him on the throne and administered the Empire very well for 37 years.

He was succeeded by his son Pandoe Cabaja[7] who killed nine of his uncles and married the Princess Ranapalla[8] (a gold jewel) who was a daughter of King Mailkari Coedanan Rajoe.[9]

Built the city Anoerajapoere

His reign began after he was 37 years old and he ruled for 33 years,[10] in which time he built anew the city of Anoerajapoere[11] very beautifully.[12] He also made paddy lands to which water could be led in and out at need, which piece of land was called Raja Veva.[13] He showed his subjects also many places in his kingdom which were suitable for the building of strongholds and fortifications. He administered his people very intelligently and righteously, died very piously and left behind for his successors and neighbours a glorious name.

Moeta Singa Raja

His son Moeta Singa Raja[14] followed him in the kingdom, planned a large coconut grove in the wilderness, which

[1] Dighagāmani, son of Prince Dighaya.

[2] Mv assigns him a reign of 30 years, Rv of 32 years. He is a great hero in both these accounts.

[3] Abhaya Kumara.

[4] King Abhaya to whom both Mv and Rv assign a reign of 20 years.

[5] Ganatissa in Rv who is however placed after Pandukabhaya who succeeded Abhaya.

[6] Dighagāmani, whom Valentijn mentions as having reigned at this point, is not mentioned either in the Mv or in the Rv.

[7] Pandukabhaya, a great hero in the Mv.

[8] Suvannapalli in Mv, Pallavati in Rv.

[9] Girikandasiva in Mv, Harikanda Raja in Rv.

[10] Both Mv and Rv ascribe him a reign of 70 years.

[11] Anurādhapura.   [12] Confirmed by Mv and Rv.

[13] Could be either Abhaya Veva or Tissa Veva. Valentijn is referring to an irrigation tank—$Veva$—tank.

[14] Mutasiva in Mv, Mutatissa in Rv.

plantation he named Mahamoena.[1] He ruled for very long and died after he had governed his people for 60 years as a father his children.[2]

Deveni Petisse Maharaja,[3] his son, succeeded him. This King was not only generous but was also a God-fearing ruler. He was a student of Mihinda Mahatea,[4] who was one of his priests, and offered to build in his honour a pagoda in the middle of the forest, to which he later added many others here and there in the island. Also he gave very much alms to the poor.

In his time there came here 8 brothers and sisters, Princes and Princesses from the south side, out of a land called Madanpadipe.[5] They came in the company of those who brought the tree of their Budum,[6] Siermahabodi,[7] which tree is now to be seen in the great pagoda of the Seven Corles.[8]

The names of these Princes were the following: Mahapopot Comara, Deugot Comara, Dangot Comara, Hierugot Comara, Sisigot Comara, Jurindra Comara. The names of the two princesses are not mentioned here.[9]

The Emperor Deveni Petisse Maharaja[10] favoured these Princes very much, built many cities both for them and for their subordinates, lived very religiously and died in ripe old age after he had ruled for about 40 years.

One of his brothers named Soeratissanam[11] followed him but only ruled for 10 years.

After him two Malabar ambassadors who brought horses to Ceylon usurped the government by great treachery, against

Devenipetisse Maharaja

Soeratissanam

Two Malabar Ambassadors

---

[1] Mahāmevana or Mahāmēghavana.　　[2] Confirmed by both *Mv* and *Rv*.

[3] Devenepetissa or Devānampiyatissa.

[4] Mahinda Mahāthēra, the Buddhist missionary who, tradition has it, was sent by Emperor Asoka to Ceylon and converted King Devānampiyatissa to Buddhism.

[5] Unidentifiable. *Rv* has Dambadiva as the place from which Mahinda left for Ceylon.

[6] Buddha.

[7] Sirimahābōdhi. The sacred bo tree under which Buddha achieved enlightenment.

[8] It is actually in the Mahāvihāra in Anurādhapura.

[9] This tradition concerning the princes who accompanied the sacred bo tree is not to be found in the *Mv* or *Rv*. The names are unidentifiable.

[10] Devenepetissa.

[11] Suratissa. *Mv* has two kings in between: Uttiya and Mahāsiva.

all expectation, and by their good management and unity administered the kingdom for 22 years.[1]

Assalanam Raja

After the lapse of some time, a younger brother of Deveni Petisse Maharaja called Assalanam Raja[2] killed the two Malabars who were brothers, and again seized the land and held the throne for 14 years, after which time he came to die a violent death.[3]

Etalunam

In this same period a King from the Malabar coast came there, named Etalunam Raja,[4] seized the city of Anoeraja Poere,[5] killing the King Assalanam Raja and many others very cruelly. He set himself up as Emperor and ruled for 44 years.

Gilinitissa Raja

About this time came the King Jattalatissa, or Gilinitissa Rajoe[6] from Roene,[7] set himself up as Emperor and was able to keep himself on the throne for 20 years.

Goloeumbara

One of his cousins named Goloeumbera Raja,[8] followed him on the throne, held his court in the territory of Roene which was afterwards devastated, and ruled for 10 years.

Ganatissa Raja

His son Ganatissa Rajoe[9] married a daughter of Gilinitissa Rajoe named Assellanam Bisa.[10] He became Emperor in his place and had 2 sons, of whom the eldest was called Doetoegeinoenoe Maha Raja[11] and the other Sedetissa Comara.[12]

The chiefs rule in his name

This Prince ruled the Kingdom of Roene (for it was then so called by the Cingalese) very righteously for four years. But it was administered for another 30 years in his name by the chiefs as they were able to keep secret his death. But his oldest son Doetoegeinoenoe Maha Raja having come thereafter, took these chiefs prisoners, placed himself on his father's throne, punished them just at the time when the whole of Ceylon was conquered by the Malabars and their entire religion had expanded everywhere on the island.[13] But he was able, shortly after, to collect together between 11 and 12

---

[1] Sēna and Guttika. Tradition confirmed by *Mv* and *Rv*.   [2] Asēla.
[3] Both *Mv* and *Rv* assign him 10 years.   [4] *Mv* and *Rv* call him Elāla.
[5] Anurādhapura.   [6] Jatalatissa or Kelantissa.
[7] Rūhuna on the south-eastern coast.   [8] Probably Gōtābhaya.
[9] Kākavannatissa.   [10] *Mv* gives her name as Vihāradēvi.
[11] Duttugemunu, one of the greatest heroes of early Sinhalese tradition.
[12] Sadātissa in *Rv*, Saddhatissa in *Mv*.
[13] Refers to the spread of Hinduism, the religion of the Tamil ruler Elāla.

thousand men, climbed on an elephant called Caddolhotoe,[1] left for the land of Roena from which he had fled, fought the Malabars in their 32 strongholds which they had made there and elsewhere in Ceylon, killed, in the first attack, 129000 men of the enemy, seized the city of Anoeraja Poere, killed even Ellala,[2] the King of Malabar, and cleared the entire island of all the Malabars whom he found. Thereafter he had himself crowned as Emperor and reigned for 24 years very peacefully.

His brother, Sedetissa Raja,[3] followed him. This King was very gentle and God-fearing. He built the pagoda Goenoeditehera[4] and made 10 beautiful paddy or rice fields where the water could be let in and shut out. His government lasted 18 years and was without any commotion or invasion from outside or from within. Sedetissa Raja

His son, Tullenam Raja,[5] followed him, also built a pagoda in a village called Chamanda Landaroe,[6] ruled 1 year, 9 months and 10 days and was thereafter killed by Lemenetissa Raja[7] who installed himself as King. Tullenam Raja

This Lemenetissa Raja ruled for 39 years and $8\frac{1}{2}$ months and was succeeded by his brother Caloeman Raja[8] who ruled this great kingdom for 16 years. Lemenetissa Raja
Caloeman Raja

Thereafter came his other brother, Walagam Bahu Raja,[9] in his place, but after 8 months of his rule came 7 Malabar brothers with 7 separate armies from the opposite coast of Malabar, disembarked their people in 7 separate bays of Ceylon, fought against this Emperor and put him to flight without anyone knowing what became of him. Walagam Bahu

Five of these brothers, being Kings, remained to rule on this island, but the 2 others returned to their land with the Five Malabar kings rule thereafter

---

[1] Kandula.

[2] Valentijn who has previously called him Etalunam Raja (se p. 208 n. 4), now calls him Ellala which agrees with the *Mv* and *Rv*.

[3] Sadātissa.

[4] Sadātissa built a number of temples. This one is unidentifiable.

[5] Thulathana in *Mv*, Tulna in *Rv*.

[6] Unidentifiable. *Rv* does not give the name of the vihāra he built, *Mv* gives it as Kandara.

[7] Leminitissa in *Rv*, Lanjatissa in *Mv*.

[8] Not mentioned in *Rv*, but *Mv* has him as Khallalanaga.

[9] Valagambāhu or Vattagāmani.

relics or the bones of their idol Budum,[1] and their brothers ruled for 36 years and 7 months.[2]

Vallagamboe Raja

In the meanwhile the King Vallagamboe Raja came from the kingdom of Majaduma[3] with a large army, killed the five kings, seized the kingdom again and ruled for 12 years and 5 months.

Chonanga Raja

His son Chonanga Raja[4] succeeded him and ruled this kingdom for 26 years.[5]

Bemminitissa

After him followed one of his chiefs called Bemminitissa[6] who intruded forcefully, made himself very powerful and ruled for 12 years.

Maha Deliatissa

Thereafter the son of Caloena Raja called Maha Deliatissa[7] succeeded him and ruled for 14 years.

Chorawa

In his place followed the youngest son of Valagam Bahu Raja, called Chorawa.[8] He was a godless King, as he destroyed many pagodas. However he ruled his people for 12 years very righteously, but he plagued his chiefs and courtiers very much because they oppressed the people too much according to their will. They therefore rose up against him altogether and put him to death, claiming that his soul had gone to Hell (which they called Lovamahanara Caddia).[9]

Coedatissa Rajoe

The son of Mahadeliatissa whose name was Coeda Tissa Rajoe[10] succeeded him. He ruled for 3 years and was put to death by his wife Anularam Bisava[11] who ruled for one year after him.

Anularam Bisava

Coelavaon

As treacherously as she had killed her husband, so murderously was she put to death by a Malabar, her consort's confidential secretary named Coelavaon,[12] who imposed

---

[1] The relics of the Buddha which were enshrined in some of the Vihāras of Ceylon.

[2] Both *Mv* and *Rv* assign them 14 years.

[3] Unidentifiable. According to *Mv* and *Rv*, Valagambāhu took refuge in the hill country called Malaya.

[4] Choranāga in *Rv* and *Mv*.   [5] *Rv* and *Mv* assign him 12 years.

[6] This king is mentioned neither by *Rv* nor *Mv*.

[7] Mahādēliyatissa is mentioned by *Rv* but not as a king. *Mv* does not refer to him at all.

[8] Probably Choranaga, the same as n. 4.

[9] *Lokantarika* (Sinh.)—the nether world.   [10] Kudatissa.   [11] Anula.

[12] *Rv* does not give the name of this Tamil secretary whom Anula put on the throne. *Mv* gives the name of a Brahmin whom she put on the throne as Niliya.

himself on the throne after her death, very craftily. But he held it only for a short time as he, after a reign of 13 months, was killed by another, named Tomo,[1] who also ruled only 4 months.

Tomo

At this time there was a prince of royal blood, a son of the above mentioned murdered Coeda Tissa Rajoe, named Maloelantissa,[2] who established himself on the throne of his father and adorned it for 26 years with much fame.[3]

Maloelantissa

He made himself very much liked by his subjects through his gentle government and very much feared by his neighbours, because he paid attention to everything, and there was such good order everywhere in his lands and especially in his ports and bays, that it was impossible to come in even in a small vessel without his knowledge and without his permission, for which reason no one dared to approach his land.[4]

His son, Batia Raja,[5] who followed in his place was very God-fearing, had a large pagoda built, offered very much to his Gods and ruled for 28 years very peacefully, as he followed the footsteps of his father.

Batia Raja

He was succeeded by his brother Madilimanna Rajoe[6] who also had built a beautiful pagoda in a village called Amboeloe Vagala.[7] He installed his Gods and the bones of his saints there, took no taxes from his people but gave himself over entirely to religion, ordering his people to pray to his Gods also. He had a courtyard full of flowers built round the pagoda and beautified it further with everything that in any way could give any lustre to it.[8]

Madilimanna Rajoe

His son, Adague Muwene Raja,[9] came in his place to the throne, had two large rice fields cultivated, ruled his people gently and ordered his people to do nothing other than serve his Gods. During his reign he did not have one man put to death and died after a rule of 9 years and 8 months.

Adague Muwene Raja

---

[1] Does not correspond with any of the names in *Mv* or *Rv*.
[2] Maklantissa in *Rv*, not mentioned in *Mv*.
[3] *Rv* assigns him 22 years.
[4] This is new information, not to be found in *Rv* or *Mv*.
[5] Bhatiya in *Rv*, probably Bhatikabhaya in *Mv*.
[6] Mahādēliya in *Rv*, Mahādathikamahānāga in *Mv*.   [7] Ambulu Dāgaba.
[8] His religious activities are confirmed by *Rv* and *Mv*.
[9] Adagemunu in *Rv*, Amandagamani Abhaya in *Mv*.

Cada Ambera
Raja

His successor was his son, Cada Ambera Raja,[1] who remained on the throne only 6 years and then died.

Nalabissava
Raja

His sister, the Princess Nalabissava,[2] succeeded him and ruled just as long as her brother. After this she married her

Elunna Raja

mother's sister's son Elunna Raja[3] who also wielded the sceptre for 6 years, after which time his younger brother

Sanda-
moehoenoe
Raja

Sandamoehoenoe Raja[4] who also reigned for exactly 6 years was killed, which fate also befell this King.

Asnapa Raja

He was killed by the Prince Asnapa Raja[5] who laid out 16 rice fields, made very good water channels, had many pagodas built and ruled for 41 years with much glory, as he improved his land uncommonly and brought many benefits to his subjects.

Vacnelisinam
Raja

His son, Vacnelisinam Raja,[6] succeeded him but ruled only 3 years.

Bapa Raja

He was followed by his son, Bapa Raja,[7] who had as his son Gaja Bahu Comara,[8] on whose birthday was also born the son of a washerman, Milo,[9] who grew up with this prince. They both were as strong as giants.

The Emperor, his father, had an iron cane made for him which required 60 strong men to carry it, having the thickness of 22 closed fists and the length of 35 spans. Its handle was overlaid with gold and on its head was a large and priceless ruby. This stick he carried playfully in his hand and his servants often carried one also after their lord.

Under the rule of this Bapa Raja a great army came from the Malabar coast, attacked Ceylon and took 12000 prisoners while this Prince was still a youth. Apart from this event, he ruled peacefully for 12 years.

---

[1] Probably Kuda Aba in *Rv*, Culabhaya in *Mv*.

[2] Sivalli in *Rv*, Sivali in *Mv*.   [3] Elana Sandamuhunu in *Rv*.

[4] See fn. 3. Valentijn's sources give these two names as two kings; *Rv* combines the two names and makes them one king. *Mv* mentions Sandamukhasiva as a king and notes that Ilanaga preceded him, thus seeming to agree with Valentijn's version.

[5] No parallels in the *Mv* or *Rv* list. *Rv* mentions a Vehep who constructed many tanks and ruled for 44 years.

[6] Vannesinambāpa in *Rv*.

[7] According to *Rv*, Bāpa was another name for the previous king Vannesinambāpa.

[8] Gaja Bāhu.   [9] *Rv* has Nila.

Fifth Chapter

[History (2nd to 15th century A.D.)]

Gaja Bahu. His courageous deed in Malabar. Mana Raja. Hamatissa Raja. Coeda Raja. Venetissa Raja. Ambaheraman Raja. Sirina Raja. Vierdoe Raja. Sangatissa Raja. Sirisanga Rodi Raja. His agreement with the devil. Lemini Goloe. Amba Raja. Courageous action of Sirisanga Bodi Raja. His decapitated head speaks. Guwelaguwem Dettatissa. Malasen Raja. Guitsirimenaon Raja. Deva Tissa Raja. Rajas Raja. Upatissa Manam Raja. Senam Raja. Leminitissa Raja. Visenan Caralsoo Raja. Seven Malabar Princes. Dacem Goelia Raja. Comara Dahai Raja. Lemini Patissa Raja. Amlam Heranam Raja. Dajoelsen Raja. Dalam Ajali Raja. Cadda Ginitsirmenam Raja. Senneni Raja. Melisinganam Salandana Roo. Acbora Raja. Acboraja. Dos Raja. Ariacsa Chaccaravarti Raja tries for the crown. Though only King of Jaffanapatnam. Boewanaca Bahu Raja, King in Degampola. Flight to Reygam. The King of Jaffanapatnam put to rout. But the Cingalese will not recognise Boewanaca any more. Ruccule Pracaram Bahu Raja. Defeats the army of the King of Canara. A Prince in the highlands deserts the Emperor. But is defeated. Emperor's power increases. The King of Jaffanapatnam defeated and another put in his place. Laurens D'Almeida lands in Ceylon A.D. 1505.

After Bapa Raja, his son Gaja Bahu followed on the throne, Gaja Bahu who when he became somewhat older, hearing how the Malabars had carried away 12000 men of his father's subjects, began to tremble with anger, swearing to avenge this insult.

He went alone, accompanied by his friend Mila Jojada,[1]

---

[1] *Rv* has Nila.

with his walking stick in his hand, out of the land of Roena[1] and the city of Guliapoera Nuwara,[2] taking the route from the island of Manaar to the coast of Madure without using a vessel but swimming across, came to the land of the King of Malabar, chased away the guard whom he found there, who immediately made this known to their King, who having heard that he had come to his capital city, ordered the closing of the gates. But the Emperor Gaja Bahu, coming there, broke it with his stick in pieces, went into the court of the King of Malabar, set all the doors on fire, as he could not find the King, and found him finally in a small room and went near him where he lay on his bed without speaking to him.

Shortly thereafter he laid his stick on the body of the King who, because of its great weight and his fear, was not in a position to utter a word.

In the meanwhile his companion devastated the entire city, not only smashed up all the men who came in his way but threw one horse against the other and at one blow with his staff struck an elephant dead.

The King, in the meanwhile, recovering his breath a little by the uplifting of the stick and seized with a deadly fear, asked the Emperor where his army was and how strong it was; he received the reply that he and his comapnion had come over alone.

He further asked for what purpose he had come there, and the Emperor then replied: I came here only to release the 12000 imprisoned subjects of my father's kingdom which has now become mine.

The King, still in mortal fear, gave him all these prisoners, so far as they were still alive and delivered others in place of those dead. But the Emperor was not to be pacified by this. He wanted to have 24000 men from him or threatened to lay waste his entire land immediately. To be freed of all these difficulties, he satisfied the Emperor's demand, giving him vessels and the necessary provisions to depart immediately as he no longer wanted this awesome guest.

With this Gaja Bahu returned to Ceylon, settled the 12000 men in the district of Gale, now called Dolas das Corla (which

[1] Rūhuna.   [2] Unidentifiable. Not mentioned in *Rv*.

means 13000),[1] and the others in various parts of the island, of whom some spread into Aboe Coeroewa,[2] a part of the Seven Corles, and some in other parts there.

After this time he ruled with much honour and for 22 years this kingdom was governed with such fear from its neighbours that they shuddered if they only heard the name of Gaja Bahu.[3]

He was succeeded by the oldest son of his mother's sister, whose name was Mana Raja[4] and he ruled for 16 years, but very little happened in this time. Mana Raja

His son, Hamatissa Raja,[5] followed after him who ruled 26 years without anything of his deeds being mentioned except that he built a pagoda for the holy relics. Hamatissa Raja

His mother's sister's son, Coeda Raja,[6] stepped into his place and ruled for 31 years. Coeda Raja

He was succeeded by his son, Venitissa Raja,[7] who ruled for 22 years. Venitissa Raja

He was again followed by his son Ambaheraman Raja[8] who ruled for only 6 years. Ambaheraman Raja

After his death the kingdom fell to his brother Sirina Raja,[9] who ruled the kingdom for 2 years. Sirina Raja

In his place followed his son Vierdoe Raja[10] who ruled 6 years. Vierdoe Raja

He was succeeded by the Prince Sangatissa Raja[11] who ruled for 11 years. Sangatissa Raja

After him Sirisanga or Sirisanga Bodi Raja[12] was Emperor. In his time there was a great pestilence caused partly by a devil or evil spirit, Ratenam Racsea[13] (which means a devil with red eyes). He asked the devil for the reason for this and why he plagued the land thus. The devil replied that he must have a Sirisanga Bodi

---

[1] Error for 12000, *Dolosdaha* (Sinh.)—twelve thousand.   [2] Alutkuruva.
[3] This tradition of Gaja Bahu's expedition to south India is found in *Rv* but not in *Mv* (*Rv* pp. 40–2.).
[4] Mahalu Mana in *Rv*, Mahallanāga in *Mv*.
[5] Bhatiya Tissa in *Rv*, Bhatikatissa in *Mv*.
[6] Kudana in *Rv*, Khujjanāga in *Mv*.
[7] Veratissa in *Rv*, no king corresponding to this name in *Mv*.
[8] Aba Sen in *Rv*.   [9] Siri Na in *Rv*, Sirināga in *Mv*.   [10] Vijayindu in *Rv*.
[11] Sanghatissa in *Rv*, Samghatissa in *Mv*, but not in this sequence.
[12] Siri Sangabo in *Rv*, Sirisamghabodhi in *Mv*.
[13] Rataki Rakshasa—the red-eyed devil.

certain number of people to his service and if he had this then the pest would cease. The King said that he had no power to give his people away to be killed, but if he could give himself over to him instead of his people, he was ready to do so.

The devil replied thereon that not a hundred devils would have the power to kill such a noble and matchless God-fearing Emperor.

His agreement
with the devil

Then the devil made an agreement with the Emperor, that he would not kill anyone any more, but that if anyone was sick, some images of the devil were to be made and gifts brought for him, which the Emperor undertook to see that his people should maintain.[1]

Lemeni Goloe
Amba Raja

During the life-time of this Emperor there also came a king, called Lemeni Golooe Amba Raja,[2] with a great army to this land, attacked and drove him out to become master of the kingdom. Not satisfied with this, he placed a great price on the Emperor's head, besides killing many people for this purpose.

A foreigner, hearing that the Emperor was in the Pagoda of Attengale,[3] found him there and told him that many heads of the chiefs had been cut off because they had not delivered his head to the usurper, and that even he feared that therefore he will lose his head too, if it was known that he had seen and spoken to the King and had not delivered his head to the tyrant according to his order.

Courageous deed
of Srisanga Bodi
Raja

The Emperor, hearing this, and being attached less to his own than to his subjects' welfare, gave himself over immediately and ordered the foreigner willingly to sacrifice his life as it was better that he died for the welfare of his people and his land than that so many innocent persons should die.

The foreigner, praising to himself the Emperor's courage, but on the other hand seeing his own danger and the great reward which was set on his head, took his sword, cut off the Emperor's head, and bringing it into the city of Roena, offered it to the new Emperor Goeloe Amba Raja.

His decapitated
head speaks

This ruler, doubting if it was the right head, as it looked

[1] Both *Rv* and *Mv* relate a similar tradition (*Rv* pp. 42–3, *Mv* p. 262).
[2] Golu Aba of the Lemini family in *Rv*, Gothakābhaya in *Mv*.
[3] Attanagala Vihāra.

very swollen, ordered the bringer to be killed as a cheat. But he, lifting up the head, threw it away and swore by all his Gods as proof that this was the head of Sirisanga Bodi Raja, whereupon it immediately raised itself in the air, while a great fire and smoke trailed above, when the head, speaking of itself, told the new Emperor: I am the head of Sirisanga Bodi Raja who attests by God's might that I have been cut off by this bringer from my body.

This unexpected speech of this head frightened Lemini Goloe Amba Raja and all who were with him, so that they did not know where they should hide themselves in fear.

He ordered that this foreigner be given immediately the price placed on this head, fearing otherwise to be followed by the murdered Emperor's ghost.

He buried this head with great honour, built above it a wonderful pagoda, let his body also be brought to that grave and held it as one of the best and most valuable relics, honouring the Emperor, whom he had so bitterly pursued, as one of his greatest deities.[1]

He lived after that very piously, built another pagoda in Anoeraja Poere,[2] gave much alms and ruled the people for 22 years very gently and righteously.

In his place came, through his appointment, the son of the former Emperor, Guwelaguwem Dettatissa,[3] on to the throne.

Guwelaguwem Detatissa

He ordered 8 of the most important chiefs and subjects of the former Emperor that they should always spit, because they had advised this ruler to kill his father.[4] He re-established everything in his kingdom as it had been at the time of his father, built many pagodas and ruled for 10 years.

After him followed his brother Malasen Raja.[5] He gave himself over entirely to the service of the devil. He had himself instructed in it by the priests who taught him all their arts, by which he had had prepared ten hundred and seven thousand rice fields. This was the most important thing

Malasen Raja

---

[1] Both *Rv* and *Mv* relate a similar tradition (*Rv* pp. 43–4, *Mv* p. 263).
[2] Anurādhapura.   [3] Kālakandetu Tissa in *Rv*, Jetthatissa in *Mv*.
[4] This singular tradition is not to be found in *Rv* or *Mv*.
[5] Mahasen in *Rv*, Mahāsena in *Mv*.

that this ruler did in 24 years of government, keeping himself busy single-mindedly with agriculture.[1]

At this time 846 years, 9 months and 20 days had passed since the death of the Buddha.[2]

Guitsirimenoan Raja

Then came the Emperor Guitsirimenaon Raja[3] on the throne.

In his time appeared a Prince and a Princess, being the brother's and sister's child of Mahasira Raja,[4] from the land of Calinga[5] and from the city of Dantapoere[6] there.

The Prince was named Danta Coemara[7] and the Princess Raon Valli.[8]

They both changed their dress as *yogis* and Brahmins and departed from their land with many attendants and fled with them to Ceylon where they were received in a friendly manner by the Emperor and overloaded with many gifts.[9]

After this he built many pagodas and ruled 28 years very piously.

Deva Tissa Raja

After him followed his brother Deva Tissa Raja,[10] who changed with his own hands many images of deities and representations of Buddha, making them of ivory and sandalwood so beautiful and charming that they could not be bettered.

He spent his time in the service of his Gods with happiness and prosperity in the 9 years of his government.

Rajas Raja

His son Rajas Raja[11] succeeded him in that government. He summoned many priests, astrologers, medicine men and others whom he ordered to bring some profit to their land. He maintained in his time 500 priests to whom he gave much alms and ruled very piously for 31 years.

Upatissa Manam Raja

After him followed his son Upatissa Manam Raja,[12] in whose

---

[1] Valentijn confirms all the traditions on this king with respect to his heterodoxy in religious matters and his great reputation as a builder of innumerable irrigation works.

[2] *Rv* has 844 years, 9 months and 25 days. Unlike the *Rv* and the *Mv*, Valentijn does not record a break in the dynasty at this point.

[3] Kitsirimēvan in *Rv*, Sirimēghavanna in *Mv*.   [4] *Rv* has Guhasiva.

[5] Kalinga, in east-central India.   [6] Dantapura.

[7] Danta Kumara.   [8] Ranmali.

[9] Tradition similar to that narrated by *Rv* (*Rv* pp. 45–6).

[10] Detutis in *Rv*, Jethatissa in *Mv*.

[11] Bujas in *Rv*, probably the same as Buddhadāsa in *Mv*.

[12] Upatissa in *Rv* and *Mv*.

time a very great teacher named Vatturas Terunnanse[1] came here from the Choromandel coast, who distributed 2000250 copies of his teachings in Sanskrit among the people. They were transcribed by 361000 students and contained a new religion which they now call Attua Cattava.[2] They were an explanation of his new dogma which in itself was not different from what we have described under the treatment of the heathen religion on Choromandel and which doctrine is contained in the Vedam.[3] The Emperor had great esteem for this teacher and his religion and exerted all strength, in the period of his rule which lasted 26 years, to bring his people to the point that they might give themselves over to that faith, which however had to have its time.

His son Senam Raja[4] succeeded him, ruling 6 years.

Senam Raja

After him followed his brother (or uncle of Senam Raja) named Leminitissa Raja[5] who also ruled this kingdom for 6 years.

Leminitissa Raja

Vissenan Caralsoo Raja[6] succeeded him on the throne, and was put to death after a rule of 6 years.

Vissenan Caralsoo Raja

Seven Princes of Malabar attacked him with a great army, killed him, divided the kingdom among themselves and ruled together for 27 years.

Seven Malabar princes

At this time there was a Prince among the Cingalese named Dacem Goelia Raja[7] who was accustomed to living in the wilderness as a *yogi*, who hearing that the Malabar Princes had seized the whole of Ceylon, assembled a large army, slew

Dacem Goelia Raja

[1] This is probably Buddhaghōsha, the great fifth century Indian Buddhist scholar who came to Ceylon and committed to writing the Thēravāda Canon in Pali. Valentijn's sources probably record another name by which he was known in Ceylon. Both *Rv* and *Mv* assign his arrival in Ceylon to the reign of Mahānāma, the king who succeeded Upatissa.

[2] Probably Atthakathā. Valentijn appears to have misunderstood his sources. It was not a new religion but a number of commentaries on the old scriptures. These were the first Sinhalese commentaries.

[3] Valentijn V. 1, *Beschrijvinge van Choromandel*, pp. 71–125.

[4] In both *Rv* and *Mv* the king who ruled at this time was Mahānāma. His reign lasted 20 (*Rv*) or 22 (*Mv*) years. This is one of the rare instances when Valentijn differs from both these sources in matters of importance. Valentijn's Sēnam Rāja was probably Sengot in *Rv* and Sothisēna in *Mv* who succeeded Mahānāma. It is also likely that Valentijn combines Upatissa and Mahanama and makes Upatissa Manam Raja.

[5] Not mentioned in either *Rv* or *Mv*.

[6] Mitsen Karalsora in *Rv*, not mentioned in *Mv*.   [7] Dacenkeliya in *Rv*.

them all and seized back the kingdom, setting himself on the throne.

This ruler ruled the people righteously, lived very piously, made many rice fields with the necessary irrigation works, had 18 pagodas built, held as many feasts, namely one in each year of his reign, and ruled 18 years.

Comara Dahai Raja

After him followed his son Comara Dahai Raja[1] who ruled his kingdom for 29 years.

A certain prostitute at this time killed a great poet, which the Emperor took very seriously, as he was distinguished above all others in his art, and because the ruler also was a lover of poetry. He ordered not only the immediate death of this prostitute but, out of love for this poet and out of an irresistible grief, when he was to be burnt, had his own body consumed in the fire, choosing rather to be burnt with his friend Calidassa,[2] than to remain living without him in continuous sorrow.[3]

Lemini Patissa Raja

After his death Lemini Patissa Raja[4] came to the throne but ruled only 1 year and 10 months as he was then murdered.

Amlam Heranam Raja

In his place came Amlam Heranam Raja[5] who ruled the kingdom for 13 years.

Dajoelsen Raja

His son Dajoelsen Raja[6] ruled only 6 months and was treacherously murdered by his mother's sister's son.

Dalam Ajali Raja

His name was Dalam Ajali Raja[7] and he ruled the kingdom for 2 years very peacefully.

Cadda Ginitsirmenam Raja

His son, Cadda Ginitsirmenam Raja,[8] ascended his father's throne and was murdered after he had reigned very well for 31 years.

Senneni Raja

His successor Senneni Raja[9] suffered the same fate after 3 years' rule, as he also was murdered by one of his court servants named Melisinganam Salandana Roo.[10]

Melisinganam Salandana Roo

He usurped the throne with much cunning but ruled only

[1] Kumaradasen in *Rv*, but there are two other kings in between; Kumaradhātusēna in *Mv*.

[2] Kālidāsa. [3] *Rv* relates this tradition in an abbreviated form (*Rv* p. 47).

[4] Lemini Upatissa in *Rv*, but after two other kings, Upatissa in *Mv*.

[5] One of few names in Valentijn's list not traceable in *Rv* or *Mv*.

[6] Dupulusen in *Rv*.   [7] Probably Dalamugalan in *Rv*, Mogallana in *Mv*.

[8] Kuda Kitsirimēvan in *Rv*, Kittisirimēgha in *Mv*.   [9] Senevi Mana in *Rv*.

[10] Lemani Sinha, also called Saladala Bona in *Rv*. Valentijn's name seems to be a combination of these two names.

9 years and was murdered by his mother's sister's son Acbora Raja.[1]

He also succeeded him on the throne, made a rice field named Corondoe Veva,[2] and ruled 6 years.   Acbora Raja

After his death he was succeeded by his son Acboraja[3] who sat very peacefully on the throne for the period of 51 years.[4]   Acboraja

After his death Dos Raja[5] succeeded him and was captured in the sixth year of his reign by a great Malabar host and taken to that land.   Dos Raja

At this time the King Ariacsi Chaccaravarti Raja,[6] a King of great power, ruled in Jaffanapatnam and had a much greater army and more money than the Emperor of Candi. He, seeing that there was no Emperor in the lowlands, proposed to seize the kingdom of Ceylon. He marched into the land of the Cingalese, pretending, to cover up his intention, that he only came to visit the country and seized it in this way.[7]   Ariacsi Chaccaravarti Raja attempts to get the crown

At this time there was a great noble to whom the Cingalese showed very great honour (his name was Alagues Vira Mandrim.[8] This last word means a Count). He, having noted the aim of this King, proceeded to the village of Reygamme[9] with some people and lay in ambush there to do battle against him.   Though only King of Jaffanapatnam

The King of Jaffanapatnam in the meanwhile collected everywhere the taxes of all the inhabitants as there was no other authority in Ceylon at this time except those of the 7 sea ports.

In the meanwhile the above named Count, Alagues Vira,

---

[1] Akbo in *Rv*, Aggabōdhi in *Mv*.   [2] Kurunduvēva.   [3] Kuda Akbo in *Rv*.

[4] *Rv* assigns him only 10 years. At this point there is a wide gap of about 725 years in Valentijn's list. Kuda Akbo or Aggabodhi 11 ruled till A.D. 618.

[5] Dos Raja is referred to in the *Rv* as the king of Great China, who landed in Lanka with an immense army during the reign of King Vijaya Bāhu and carried him captive to China (*Rv* p. 57). This presumably refers to the expeditions of the Chinese Admiral Cheng Ho, the second of which (1411) took the Sinhalese king captive. Valentijn, besides skipping over a number of Sinhalese kings, gives a version of events very different from what is known from other Sinhalese traditions. The trustworthiness of his sources seems to break down at this point, but they again resume their effectiveness in his subsequent narrative.

[6] Āriya Chakkaravarti who founded a dynasty of kings of Jaffna and ruled in the first half of the 14th century.

[7] This expedition of Āriya Chakkaravarti to south Ceylon was in the 1350's.

[8] Alakēsvara Mantri.   [9] Rayigama.

had a walled city built in Reygamme which he provided abundantly with people and provisions and yet another between the 5 villages, named Cotta,[1] and built a moat and wall round it which he also supplied with the necessary people and provisions of war, returning thereafter again to Reygamme.

After Ariacsi Chaccaravarti Raja had seen all this, he got ready to resist, obtained the help of 100,000 men from Malabar,[2] whom he sent against the enemy by sea and by land. Those who went by land made their armed camp in the land of Matole[3] to fight against the Emperor of Candi.

Those who went by sea disembarked in the Bay of Colombo and some in the Bay of Panture[4] and made their encampment in Gorkane.[5]

Boewanaca Bahu Raja, King in Gampala

At this time in the highlands of Candi ruled King Boewanaca Bahu Raja,[6] who was actually king in Degampala.[7] It was richly populated but did not have the power to resist the King of Jaffanapatnam and so he fled with some of his people to the city of Reygam to Alagus Vira Mandrim.

Flight to Reygam

The Cingalese in this district, seeing themselves now entirely defenceless and without a King (for there was no Emperor then in the kingdom of Cotta), and fearing that they would become slaves of the King of Jaffanapatnam, decided, after a meeting of the 5 districts, to prepare themselves and attack the enemy, since by the cowardliness of the King they had been left as everyone's prey.

King of Jaffanapatnam is beaten

They did this in the morning at cock's crow, fell like savage lions on the enemy in the land of Matule and beat the King of Jaffanapatnam so decisively that most of his people remained dead on the spot.

The Count Alagus Vira Mandrim, hearing this, mounted his elephant, fell on the people that were still in Matagode,[8] defeated them severely, slew them by the thousands, broke up their vessels in the Bay of Colombo, returned then to Panture and Gorkane and carried on the attack there also against all their vessels and defeated many more of the remain-

---

[1] Kōttē. [2] The Pandyan king of south India with whom he was allied.
[3] Mātalē. [4] Pānadura. [5] Gorakane, near Colombo.
[6] Bhuvanēka Bāhu V. [7] Gampola. [8] Madagoda.

ing, so that he returned to Reygam with a complete victory.[1]

The King Boewanaca Bahu Raja, seeing that his lands were now fully free of all enemies, returned with a peaceful heart to his kingdom of Degampala. But the Cingalese swore that they would never recognise such a coward as their King. There was then a Prince educated in the Pagoda Vida Gamma,[2] who by his distinguished descent could be compared to the sun, for he had royal blood and was of the unblemished race of the King Sacca Raja[3] and of the race of Ittahasammata Raja[4] and of Simit Raja,[5] a nephew of the King Praccaram Viga Raja[6] and son of the King Savluviga Bahu Raja[7] and of the Queen Simittra Dewa.[8]

The Cingalese will not recognise Boewanaca

This Prince was installed on the throne of the Emperors of Cotta by the Gane or Priest Atahasuwamie,[9] also of royal family, living in a Pagoda, on the 8th day (new moon) of the month May, on a Thursday, with the name Ruccule Praccaram Bahu Raja.[10]

Ruccule Praccaram Bahu Raja

He married a princess of the royal house from the village Quirivella[11] who was of the family of Ontnurudda Comara.[12]

Having then been crowned (which time is said to be 1958 years after the death of Buddha or 1415 years after the birth of Christ) he remained for 3 years in Reygamme, departed then to Cotta, built there a remarkable city, entirely of blue stone, and a beautiful palace for himself of the same stone, but with a sort of newly discovered gilding, and with some new temples

---

[1] The outlines of this victory are given in the *Rv* (pp. 57–8). Valentijn here provides a more detailed account.

[2] Visidāgama.

[3] Sakya Pāndu, by tradition the first cousin of Buddha whose daughter married Panduvasa, the third Sinhalese king of Ceylon. This was to establish that he was in direct line of succession to the throne.

[4] Idahasammatā. Mythical ancestor of Buddhist kings. Synonymous with Mahāsammatā and meaning Truly Honoured One.

[5] Probably Sumitra, a prince held to be related to Emperor Asoka who had accompanied the Mahābodhi tree to Ceylon.

[6] Probably Parākrama Bāhu V.   [7] Savulu Vijayabāhu.

[8] Sunētrādevi. Valentijn's sources here make an attempt to provide legitimacy and a good pedigree to king Parākrama Bāhu VI. On this king's ancestry, see *University of Ceylon History of Ceylon*, I, 11 (Colombo, 1960), 660–66.

[9] Unidentifiable. *Rv* says it was the venerable monk Visidāgama who had him crowned (*Rv* p. 58).

[10] Parākrama Bāhu VI, also called Rukulē Parākrama Bāhu.

[11] Kirawella.   [12] Anuruddha Kumara.

for demons and for deities which he worshipped. Here he lived in the company of a priest whom he esteemed very highly, protected the relics of Buddha and built a special house or cloister for his priests. Also he took as his wards two Princes of royal blood, Sappoe Comara[1] and Coeda Comara[2] to whom he showed very great favour.

Some time later the Empress brought forth a daughter, to whom was given the name Ulacoedajanam Dewa,[3] which word Dewa[4] in their language means a Goddess.

Defeat of the army of the King of Comara[5]

Shortly thereafter the Emperor was very unexpectedly attacked by a great army that was sent to Ceylon by the King of Canara[6] with a large fleet. But the King, having speedily assembled together some people, defeated this powerful army, which gave him a very respectable name through the entire east and made him much loved by his people.[7]

Shortly thereafter he sent a vessel with cinnamon to the opposite coast of Malabar, which landed in the Bay of Driampatam.[8] It was attacked with hostility by the Governor there, Rajam Malavaragam,[9] and everything was stolen from it and all the people there taken captive.

The Emperor, hearing this, caused the land of this Governor immediately to be laid waste with fire and with sword by his people. From there they went to another district named Soliratta,[10] seized the city of Mahacoelan Cottaja,[11] devastated another 7 of the subordinate villages, after which victories they returned with joy.[12]

A prince in the highlands attacks the Emperor

While everything was now in peace in the Emperor's lands in Ceylon, there was a Prince in the highlands named Jottia Sitti or Jothia Stoenau Raja,[13] who used to pay the Emperor

---

[1] Sapumal Kumāraya. [2] Kudā Kumāraya.
[3] Ulakudaya Dēvi. [4] Error for Devi or Dewi.
[5] Error for Canara, which he spells correctly in the text.
[6] The Vijayanagar Emperor Devaraya II.
[7] This record by Valentijn appears to be the only extant source that mentions this expedition.
[8] Adirampatnam on the Madura coast of south India.
[9] Malavarāya, probably one of the Vijayanagar governors of the Ramnad area.
[10] Solaratta. Sinhalese term for Chola country, probably around Tanjore.
[11] Makudankōttai.
[12] This expedition is referred to briefly in *Rv* (p. 59). [13] Jotiya Sittu.

annually a tribute and now let him know that henceforth he was not inclined to do that. He called together his people from the 5 districts over which he ruled and decided to make himself free of the Emperor and set himself up as a ruler and, in order to make himself stronger, he distributed many villages and lands to this and that chief and gave them high honorific titles (to which the Cingalese are strongly attached).

The Emperor, having perceived this, sent a huge army against him, slew many thousands of his people, took many of the nearest blood relations of this defeated Prince prisoner and placed one of his wards, Ampoeloewagala Comara,[1] a vassal who paid him an annual tribute, as King of Candi (as he had driven the Prince out of Candi).

But is defeated

Some years later, from the Wannia[2] another 18 village heads subjected themselves to the Emperor, by which his kingdom increased markedly.

The Emperor's power increases more

The King of Jaffanapatnam, fearing that the Emperor would seek revenge on him at one time or another, took the necessary care everywhere against it, but let himself in the meanwhile be called Emperor of Ceylon, which as soon as the Emperor of Cotta heard, he decided immediately to make himself master of Jaffanapatnam and sent away an army under Sappoe Comara[3] and informed the King through his field commander that, as it was unbecoming for Ceylon to have two Emperors, he had sent this commander to deprive him of the new title and, if he could not drop it or be satisfied with what was his, to give him more rest.

The King of Jaffanapatnam defeated

At first the commander seized many of this King's lands, but as he heard that he had begun to approach the city of Jaffanapatnam, he sent one of his courtiers, Conta Cara Demalis, and yet a second and a third named Panigevorum and Valumunivorum to stop him.[4] But all these were defeated in a short time by Sapoe Comara who made ready to assault the city with his blue horse with green mane.

The besieged King, seeing him come, sent Varacara, a brave

---

[1] Ambulugala Kumāraya.   [2] Vanni, in north-central Ceylon.
[3] Sapumal Kumāraya.
[4] The names of the commanders of the Jaffna army are not given in any other extant source. Valentijn's names are, however, mutilated beyond recognition.

horseman who had promised to cut him in pieces, to meet him, but he was speared by the commander's people even before he came near him. In the meanwhile the Prince Sappoe Comara entered the city, conquered it with all the King's riches, took many of his chiefs captive and brought them together before the Emperor, as the King had fled,[1] who appointed one of his nephews with the name of Ariatetoe Addum Prauwmal,[2] as King of Jaffanapatnam.

After this time the Emperor ruled with much peace for a period of 55 years, spending his last years mostly in the service of the Gods.[3]

Laurens D'Almeida lands on Ceylon, 1505

In the 52nd year of his reign, Laurens D'Almeida, son of the Viceroy of Goa, arrived on the island of Ceylon in 1505, being the first Portuguese to come here.[4]

[1] This contradicts the *Rv* account which says he slew the king (*Rv* p. 59) and is the more accurate version. The deposed king, Kanagasūriya Singai Āriyan, returned after 17 years to recapture the kingdom.

[2] Āriya Vellayarum Perumāl.

[3] Valentijn's account of this ruler confirms and supplements significantly other extant evidence on this king and has been used by a number of modern historians to reconstruct the history of that period. See H. W. Codrington, *Short History of Ceylon* (Colombo, 1939), pp. 90–92. *University of Ceylon History of Ceylon*, 1, 11, pp. 660–70. C. W. Nicholas and S. Paranavitana, *A Concise History of Ceylon* (Colombo, 1961), pp. 306–12.

[4] Valentijn is having difficulty with his chronology here. Parākrama Bāhu VI abdicated in 1467. D'Almeida arrived in Ceylon during the time of Parākrama Bāhu VIII or Vīra Parākrama Bāhu.

Sixth Chapter

[15th and 16th centuries A.D.]

*Jaja Wira Praccaram Bahu. Defeats the Count of Pasdum
Corla. Maha Pandita Praccaram Bahu Raja. Is defeated by the
King Ambulvagala. He becomes Emperor in his place. Derma
Praccaram Bahu. His four brothers. A Moor of Calpentyn,
with a large army, is defeated by two of his brothers. The King of
Candi names himself Emperor of Ceylon. But is defeated.
Children of his daughter. He again fights with the Emperor. A
ship from Portugal anchors in the Bay of Colombo. With whose
chiefs the Emperor makes a treaty. Thereafter he dies. Viga
Bahu. The third Portuguese ship comes here. With whose chiefs
the Emperor makes an eternal treaty. The Emperor's sons by a
Princess whom he and his brothers had together. Is killed by his
sons. Bowaneca Bahu Maha Raja. Happenings in his reign.
The King of Candi defeated. The Emperor attacked by his
brothers. Obtains relief from the King of Portugal. The death of
the King of Raygam. The Emperor kills his older brother. Is
shot dead. Darma Palla Maha Raja. The King of Majadune
defeated. The Viceroy of Goa comes to help the Emperor.
Defeats the King of Majadune. And returns to Goa. Vidia
Rajoe, the Emperor's father, fights the Portuguese. Marriages
and children of the King of Candi. Is defeated by his son, and
flees to the King of Majadune. He grants him refuge in his land.
The King of Irigal Rajoe described. Captured Councillor returns
from Goa back to Ceylon. A Franciscan Monk baptizes the
Emperor. Further actions of Videa Rajoe. King of Majadune
makes peace with the Emperor. Further actions of Vidia Rajoe.
The Prince Tiquiri Rajoeroe Bandara is named Raja Singa
Rajoe. Vidia Rajoe kills the King of Seven Corles, and becomes
its King. Is put to flight. Raja Singa seizes Seven Corlas. The*

*Emperor Dharmapalla Raja conquers the country of Mature,
but loses it again. Raja Singa defeats the Portuguese. Expels
Dermapalla and becomes Emperor of all Ceylon. His further
actions. Indications of the defects of this history of the Ceylonese
Emperors. List of Ceylonese Emperors. Narrative of others on
these Emperors. Don Jan marries Donna Catharina, daughter
of Mahadasseyn. He puts Raja Singa to flight, and makes
himself Emperor. Is defeated by Don Jan. Wounds himself in
grief and dies. Old hatred between him and Don Jan. His father
is taken captive by Raja Singa and shot to death with wooden
pellets. Successors of Don Jan and his half-brother Cenuwieraat.
And their further actions.*

Jaja Wira
Praccaram Bahu

After him followed his grandson, son of his daughter
Ulacoedajanam Dewa[1] who named himself Jaja Wira
Praccaram Bahu.[2]

At this time there was a Count of Pasdum Corla from the
village Caculandola,[3] also of royal blood, named Srivardanam
Pati Raja[4] who, with all the inhabitants who lived above and
below the river of Caliture,[5] keeping himself on the other side
of the River of Waluwe, rose up against the Emperor of Cotta,
whereupon this ruler sent his mother's sister's youngest son,
Ambulvagala,[6] against him with a powerful army, who took
Pati Raja prisoner and brought him to the Emperor of Cotta,

Defeats the
Count of
Pasdum Corla

who appointed the Prince Ambulvagala as Count in Pati
Raja's place and put him in prison.

After the course of some years the Emperor let this Pati
Raja come out of prison before him, and not only gave him
freedom but also gave him many presents, and had such great
faith in him that he handed over to him one of the Princes
he had brought up, ordering him to install this Prince after
his death as his successor on the throne as he, being attacked
by a heavy sickness, believed he would soon be a corpse.

He died shortly thereafter, having ruled for 7 years.[7]

---

[1] Ulakudaya Dēvi.   [2] Jayavīra Parākrama Bāhu.   [3] Kalanidola.
[4] Sirivardhana Patirāja.   [5] Kalu Ganga.   [6] Ambulugala.
[7] Valentijn and *Rv* are at variance here. According to *Rv* these events took
place under the reign of Bhuvanēka Bāhu (*Rv* pp. 60–61). Valentijn does not
mention the enthronement of Sapumal Kumāraya as Bhuvanēka Bāhu.

This abovenamed Prince followed after him as Emperor of Cotta but he took the title of Mahapandita Praccaram Bahu Raja,[1] by which Pati Raja faithfully fulfilled his promise given to the dead Emperor.

Maha Pandita Praccaram Bahu Raja

In this time the King of Ambulvagala had 5 sons and a daughter, and he hearing that a ward of the former Emperor had become Emperor in his place, though he had much more right to the throne, ventured to fight the Emperor of Cotta with the people of the county of Four Corlas.

The Emperor, having obtained information of his intention, appointed the Count Pati Raja as Commander and one Inuwa Aram[2] as deputy over his army which encamped in the village Calane.

The next day they met the army of Ambulvagala in a certain field, called Hinker Devela,[3] where the armies engaged each other. But the Emperor's army was pitifully defeated along with that of the Count and another noble, whereupon Ambulvagala following up his success, marched to the city of Cotta which he besieged and seized in one day by treachery.

Is defeated by the King Ambulvagala

The Emperor, hearing this, killed his Queen and all her noble attendants, so that they might not be insulted by the enemy. He would even have taken his own life, if he had not been prevented. They fled with him to a certain house, of which the King Ambulvagala was informed, who, making him a prisoner, after a year took away his life and became Emperor in his place, with the title of Wira Praccaram Bahu.[4]

He becomes Emperor in his place

He ruled for 20 years very peacefully and prosperously and after his death the oldest of his 5 sons stepped on the throne with the name of Derma Praccaram Bahu.[5]

His second son, Taniam Vallaba[6] became King of Candoepiti Madampe.[7]

Derma Praccaram Bahu

The third became King of Manicaravare,[8] with the title of Siri Raja Singa,[9] the fourth King of Reygamme and the fifth

His 4 brothers

---

[1] Mahāpanditha Parākrama Bāhu.

[2] Unidentifiable. Not mentioned in *Rv.*   [3] Inkenda.

[4] Vīra Parākrama Bāhu. *Rv* relates substantially a similar version of these events (*Rv* p. 61).

[5] Dharma Parākrama Bāhu.   [6] Taniyan Vallaba.   [7] Mādampē.

[8] Menikkadavara.   [9] Sri Rāja Sinha.

was made King of Oedoegampala[1] with the title of Saccalacala Valaba Raja.[2]

A Moor of Calpentyn with a big army attacked by 2 of the brothers

At this time came Adiracarajan,[3] a Moor from Calpentyn,[4] with a powerful army of Moors and a big fleet and disembarked in the Bay of Chilauw to go on an elephant hunt and to fish for pearls around Chilauw or Manaar.

The King of Oeddoegampala, having heard this, went on the order of the Emperor, his brother, with his entire force to the kingdom of Candoepiti Madampe and consulted with his brother Taniam Vallaba[5] what they should do against this Moor.

Finally they decided to attack him, surrounded his army and defeated it in a short time.

Saccalacala killed the Modeliar, or one of the first colonels of the Moors, Adirakarajam, with an *assagai*.[6] Thereafter he destroyed all their vessels and obtained a complete victory, came with great joy to his brother the Emperor and returned again like his brother, each to his land.[7]

The King of Candi calls himself Emperor of Ceylon

About this time there was also a King in Candi who made bold to take the name of Emperor of Ceylon and even to mint a new coin, while earlier he had paid tribute to the Emperor of Cotta.

The ruler, hearing all of this, immediately sent his brother Siri Raja Singa, King of Manicavare,[8] to him, who pressed this conceited King so hard that he sent 3 million fanums,[9] 3 elephants with tusks and the Princess his daughter to the Emperor as bride, whereupon he was accepted in favour, under a firm promise of improvement.[10]

The Emperor gave this Princess to the King Dequiravella[11] as consort, who had 6 sons by her whose names are seen in the old histories as Vellicolla Ralahami,[12] Gungemmeva Ralahami,[13]

[1] Udugampola.   [2] Sakalakalā Vallaba.   [3] Adirāsa Rāyan.
[4] Kalpitiya. He was really from Kayalpatnam on the south Indian coast.
[5] Taniyan Vallaba, king of Mādampē.
[6] A spear of hard wood. From *azzaghayah* (Arabic).
[7] This incident is confirmed by *Rv* (p. 62).   [8] Menikkadavara.
[9] From *panam* (Tam.)—a gold coin current in south India worth about a quarter florin or 6d.
[10] The event is confirmed by *Rv* which says three lakhs *panam* (i.e. 300,000) and two elephants were sent (p. 62).
[11] Kirāvella.   [12] Velikola Rālahamy.   [13] Gumgamuwa Rālahamy.

Velagi Ralahami,[1] Oenarawe Ralahami,[2] Tissamawa Ralahami[3] and Quiravele Ralahami[4] and a Princess who married
the King Jaja Vira Bandara[5] but her name is not mentioned.

Some years later the King of Candi began again to fight | He fights the
against the Emperor of Cotta, who therefore sent his brother | Emperor again
Saccalacala Valada,[6] with an army against him, who humbled
him again in such a way that he had to fall down before the
feet of Saccalacala Valada without parasol and without white
shield after he was accepted in favour but with much harder
conditions.[7]

About this time, during the lifetime of this Emperor of
Cotta, a ship that left from Portugal landed for safety in the
Bay of Colombo and this was the second that came here around
1530.[8]

As soon as the Emperor Darma Praccaram Bahu heard this,
he called the 4 kings his brothers together (as this history
says), consulted with them whether these foreigners should be | A ship from
granted admission into this land, whereupon the king of | Portugal comes
Oedoegampala[9] said that he would first go to see those | Bay of Colombo
people. He did this, found them very good, and advised the
Emperor to enter into a treaty with them. Thereupon the
Portuguese went with presents to Cotta, where they were | With whose
very well received by this ruler, who made a treaty with them | heads the king
to their complete satisfaction, after which they again departed | makes a treaty
from there.[10] The Cingalese narrate this account of this Emperor
but it happened in the time of the former Emperor, as we will
mention subsequently under the subject of the arrival of the
Portuguese.[11]

---

[1] Valageyi Rālahamy.   [2] Ennoruva Rālahamy.

[3] In place of this name, Rv has Obberiya Rālahamy.

[4] Kirāvella Rālahamy.   [5] Jayavīra Bandāra.   [6] Sakalakalā Vallaba.

[7] Confirmed by Rv (p. 62).

[8] Rv gives the date as 1522 (p. 63). Valentijn is here repeating what his Sinhalese source says which he realises is in error about the date of this event and
which contradicts what he himself says in Chapter VII about early Portuguese
contacts with Ceylon. See the next paragraph and below pp. 257–60.

[9] Udugampola.

[10] Rv p. 63, where the name of the prince who went to see the Portuguese is
given as Chakrayuddha.

[11] See below p. 258. Valentijn is correct here. The first contact with the Portuguese took place under king Parākrama Bāhu VIII or Vira Parakrama Bāhu
(1484–1513) and the second under King Vijaya Bāhu VII (1509–1521).

He dies

Some time later this Emperor came to die after he had given much alms to the poor, gifted away many elephants, indeed as many as a thousand of these, and had ruled for 25 years.

Viga Bahu

In his place, according to choice, king Saccalaccala Valaba should have succeeded, as the wisest of the four brothers, but as he refused it, it fell on the king of Reygam, with the title of Viga Bahu.[1]

The third Portuguese ship comes here

At this time again a Portuguese ship came to anchor here in the Bay of Colombo with many presents. But they were prevented by the Emperor's guard in their wish to unload their goods and were attacked in a hostile manner, but these were driven to flight by the guns of the Portuguese.

With whose head the Emperor makes an eternal treaty

The Emperor took this action of his guard with much displeasure as they had no such orders. He sent some of his courtiers to the Portuguese to show them that this was a mistake of his people without his knowledge and allowed 2 or 3 Portuguese to be taken above ceremoniously, where he received them very pleasantly, entertained them very royally and made an eternal treaty with them.[2]

After this time the Portuguese began to settle and establish themselves in Colombo as the Emperor allowed them to build a fortress there.

The Emperor Viga Bahu and his brother Siri Raja Singa of Manicavare, being still youths, had only one wife in common, a princess of the family of Quiravelle, who was called Quiravelle Mahabisso Adassyn.[3]

The Emperor's sons from a Princess whom he and his brother had together

She had 4 sons by these two brothers of whom the first, Maha Reygam,[4] died at the age of ten, and then the princess also died, but the 3 other sons survived.

The second was called Bowanaca Bahu Maha Raja,[5] the

[1] Vijaya Bāhu.

[2] This appears to have been Lopo Soarez's expedition of 1518 which resulted in a treaty between the Sinhalese and the Portuguese. Valentijn's chronology and succession of Sinhalese kings is confused. Some of the confusion is caused by the fact that Dharma Parakrama Bāhu and Vijaya Bāhu VII appear to have ruled together for about six years before Vijaya Bāhu became sole king. For details of this expedition, see Barros pp. 38–46.

[3] Kirāvella Mahābiso Adassyn.

[4] Mahā Rayigam.

[5] Bhuvanēka Bāhu.

third Para Raja Singa Raja[1] and the fourth Majadunne Raja.[2] After the death of this princess the Emperor married another wife of the family of Quiravelle who was named Dewa Raja Singa Comari[3] after her marriage.

The Emperor took great care of the 3 abovenamed Princes. But his wife, seeing that he loved them so much, sought means to get rid of them, helped by 2 of the most important courtiers, Candura Bandara[4] and Canaca Modeliaar.[5]

The Princes obtained timely knowledge of this through their good friends, fled to a Pagoda and were hidden stealthily by 2 priests where the 2 eldest remained a long time, but the youngest went to Candi to the king Jaja Vira Raja,[6] who was married to a cousin of this Prince, Ceravella,[7] where he was provided with a large army. Thereupon he called his brothers together and they fought jointly against the Emperor, their father, whom they brought to a critical position, forcing him to surrender the two above-mentioned courtiers to them.

Is killed by his sons

Being not satisfied with this, they marched to the city of Cotta, seized it and the palace, stole all the treasure of the Emperor and ordered their father, who had been against them along with his wife, to be put to death. None of the subjects was inclined to slay the Emperor with his own hand, but finally there appeared a foreigner named Seelam,[8] who performed the scandalous deed.[9]

This was the end of this Emperor after he had ruled 8 years.

The next morning the eldest brother was crowned as Emperor with the title of Bowaneca Bahu Maha Raja.[10]

Bowaneca Bahu Maha Raja rules as Emperor

A certain sister's son of the Emperor Viga Bahu called Viria Soeria Pitlesse Vidia Bandara[11] and entitled Prince of Pitlesse,[12] together with one Manaperi Asala Araatie,[13] led a rebellion against the ruler but they were defeated and their

---

[1] Pararāja Sinha. *Rv* has his name as Mahā Rayigam Bandāra who Valentijn says was the eldest and died at the age of 10.

[2] Māyādunnē.   [3] Dēvarājasinha Kumāri. Not mentioned in *Rv*.

[4] Kandura Bandāra.   [5] Ekanāyaka Mudaliyār.   [6] Jayavīra.

[7] Kirāvella.   [8] Probably Selamba; *Rv* has Salma (p. 66).

[9] These events are confirmed by *Rv* pp. 64–6.

[10] Bhuvanēka Bāhu VII. This took place in 1521.

[11] Wīrasūriya Pilassē Vidiya Bandāra.

[12] Prince of Pilassē.   [13] Manampēri Asvela Ārachchi.

lands were given to the Panneas,[1] a caste that used to cut grass for the horses and elephants, as prize.[2]

After this the Emperor gave a great feast to celebrate this occasion, raised Raja Singa as king of Reygamme and one of his wards, Araja Dara,[3] as his highest councillor, making also a permanent treaty with both his brothers, the kings of Reygamme and Majadunne. He had a daughter who was called Samoedra Dewa,[4] that is sea-goddess.

Happenings in his rule

At this time there was a Malabar king from the lands of Jaffanapatnam, married to a daughter of the king of Madampe, Tanian Vallaba, by which wife this Malabar ruler had a son named Vidia Bandara Raja,[5] who married the royal princess Samoedra Dewa, by whom he had two sons, the oldest called Darma Palla,[6] and the youngest Jaja Palla Astana.[7]

The oldest was brought up by the Emperor Bowaneca Bahu, his grandfather, and besides this the queen brought up another Prince of her kin, named Singa Bandara, who was very wise, but the Emperor desired that Darma Palla should follow him on the throne and arranged to get rid of Singa Bandara, to forestall all difficulties, though the queen did not know more than that he died by himself through a strange and unexpected accident.

The king of Majadune,[8] the Emperor's younger brother, had 4 sons and 2 daughters of whom the oldest son, 20 years old and called Maha Rajoere,[9] died. The second took the name of Timbiri Palla Bandara.[10] The third that of Santana Bandana[11] and the fourth Tiquiri Rajoeroe Bandara,[12] of whom the astrologers predicted that he would eventually become the overlord of the entire island.

---

[1] Pannayō. A Sinhalese low caste of grass-cutters.

[2] Confirmed in *Rv* p. 66.

[3] *Rv* does not mention him but names one Arya who was minister to Māyā-dunnē.

[4] Samudrādēvi.

[5] Vidiyē Bandāra. *Rv* says his father was a Soli (Chola) prince and his mother the daughter of Taniyan Vallaba (pp. 67–8).

[6] Dharmapāla. [7] Wijayapāla Asthāna.

[8] Māyādunnē was his name. Valentijn repeatedly refers to him as King of Majadune.

[9] Mahā Rajjuru Bandāra. [10] Timbiripola Bandāra.

[11] Santana Bandāra. [12] Tikiri Rajjuru Bandāra.

About this time the king of Candi again opposed the Emperor and sent a large army to destroy the lands of the Four Corlas.

The King of Candi defeated

The King of Majadune, hearing this, since these were his lands, sent a powerful army against him, defeated his men and forced Jaja Vira Raja to give him 24 million Fanums[1] and then make peace with him, with a promise to conduct himself more obediently henceforth.

In the meanwhile the kings of Majadune and Reygamme proposed to fight the Emperor, their brother, because he had appointed his grandson Darma Palla as heir of the kingdom.

The Emperor immediately wrote to the king of Portugal and said that he delivered his grandson Darma Palla into his hands, with the request that he offer his helping hand in his inheritance after his death as his successor against those who would dispute this right. He sent him along with his grandson[2] much gold, silver and ivory images made most artistically and worth a great treasure, in addition to his trusted servant, Salapuwe Araatie,[3] as ambassador to Portugal, who gave the king an accurate account of the Emperor's affairs, whereupon this ruler immediately supported the Emperor with a large fleet and many people.

Obtains assistance from the King of Portugal

About this time the king of Reygamme went on a certain day to the village Mahoe Pitigam,[4] which is a dependency of Malvane, became sick there and died.

Death of the King of Reygam

After the king of Majadune had witnessed the death of his brother and also the departure of this ambassador to Portugal, he asked help from the Moors of the opposite coast, who immediately welcomed the request and besieged the city of Cotta with him.[5] But all their plans were rendered futile by the Portuguese and thereupon he sought a peace which he obtained on the condition that he should hand over the two generals of

The Emperor defeats his other brother

[1] See p. 230 n. 10.
[2] Valentijn's meaning is unclear here. What was sent to Lisbon was an image of the prince in gold, along with an ambassador.
[3] Salapuri Ārachchi. This embassy was sent in 1540.
[4] Māpitigama.
[5] The reference here is to Māyādunnē's seeking the assistance of the Zamorin of Calicut who sent a fleet under Paichi Marikkār, Kunjali Marikkār and Ali Ibrahim to help him. This fleet was intercepted and driven back by the Portuguese in 1537–38. See Couto, pp. 90–94.

that Moorish army, which he being not inclined to do, the Emperor attacked him again more forcefully.[1] The Portuguese also carried out a strong attack on his people, destroyed them, advanced to Sita-Vaca,[2] the capital of the Majadune kingdom, put the king to flight to Saffragam and threw away all his royal insignia.[3]

He remained for some time in the village Batoe Gedra,[4] hiding from the Emperor, but came after the Emperor's departure with the army again into Sita-Vaca with the intention of renewing the war.

Was shot dead

After this information came to the ears of the Emperor, he left with the Portuguese with a large army to Calane,[5] where there was a magnificent large house of the King of Majadune, remained there for some time and on a certain day was shot through the head with a bullet by a Portuguese (as some say, purposely, but as others say, by mistake[6]) after he had ruled 11 years.

Darma Palla Maha Raja

Darma Palla Maha Raja followed in his place and was installed on the throne by the strong hand of the Portuguese, which as soon as the king of Mahadune[7] saw, he marched again with a large army to Cotta and attacked him and the Portuguese courageously, but was again beaten by the Emperor's people.

The King of Majadune defeated

In the meanwhile, Darma Palla gave accurate information of everything to the king of Portugal and to the Viceroy at Goa who sent him on his request fresh troop reinforcements.

The Viceroy of Goa comes to help the king

Shortly thereafter came the Viceroy of Goa, Don Louis de Taydo[8] himself, and his sister's son, Don Joan,[9] with a large fleet and an extensive war-machine, with much money to

---

[1] Events described in detail in Couto, pp. 104–7.

[2] Sitāvaca.

[3] The *Rv* is silent on these events which Couto describes in detail.

[4] Batugedara.

[5] Kelaniya.

[6] This doubt about the circumstances surrounding the death of king Bhuva-nēka Bāhu is also voiced by *Rv* which says: 'God alone knoweth which is true' (p. 68). See Illustration 11.

[7] Māyādunnē.

[8] Error for Dom Alfonso de Noronha. Don Louis de Ataide was a later Viceroy.

[9] Dom João Henriques who was made Captain-Major by the Viceroy.

Fig. 11. Death of King Bhuvaneka Bahu VII (Valentijn V. I, p. 77)

Fig. 12. Raja Sinha fleeing from capital during the rebellion of 1664 (Valentijn V. 1, p. 199)

Ceylon, anchored in the Bay of Colombo and proceeded immediately to Cotta where they were received pleasantly.[1]

After everything had been maturely considered, the Viceroy left the next day for Sita-Vaca, drove the king of Majadune to flight, forcing him to abandon his capital city shamefully and to leave this to the enemy as booty.

He first took his flight to the village of Dreniagala,[2] but departed immediately from there to the village of Balatga Palla.[3]

Defeat of the king of Majadune

In the meanwhile the Viceroy De Taydo[4] set the city of Sita-Vaca on fire,[5] returned to Cotta, left his sister's son, Don Joan Henriques, there to help the Emperor and departed again for Goa.

Shortly thereafter, Don Joan Henriques became sick, handed over his office to Captain Diego de Melo,[6] left behind an instruction in which he ordered that the Emperor's father Videa Rajoe[7] and the Councillor Tammittee Bala Soeria Sena Dipati[8] be taken captive and sent to Goa, without giving any reason for this.[9] Shortly after Don Joan[10] died, leaving the Commander-in-Chief Diego de Melo as Captain General, who shortly thereafter took these two above-mentioned gentlemen prisoner and sent them to Colombo. But the two wives of Vidia Rajoe knew how to devise means for his liberation, sending over some slaves who secretly burrowed under the jail and gave him the opportunity to escape.[11] The Captain Melo put the abovenamed Councillor on board ship and sent him to Goa that he might not also escape.

And return again to Goa

Vidia Rajoe, having escaped, went to Reygam Corle, to the village Attulagamme,[12] pursued his way to Pasdum Corla,

Vidia Rajoe fights the Portuguese from there

[1] This expedition is referred to by *Rv* (p. 68) and took place in 1552.
[2] Deraniyagala. [3] Bulatgahapola.
[4] Again error for de Noronha. [5] Confirmed by *Rv* (p. 69).
[6] Diego de Melo Coutinho. [7] Vidiyē Bandāra.
[8] Senāthipathi (Commander-in-Chief) Tammita Bālasūriya in *Rv*. He was the younger brother of Vidiyē Bandāra.
[9] *Rv* gives the reason that Vidiyē Bandāra married Māyādunnē's daughter (*Rv* p. 69). But this appears to have taken place later.
[10] Dom João Henriques.
[11] Confirmed in a slightly different version by *Rv* (pp. 69–70) and Couto (pp. 160–61).
[12] Atulugama.

made a house and fortress for his people in the village Pellenda[1] and began to fight the Portuguese from there.

Marriages and 2 children of the King of Candi

While the king of Majadune remained at Dereniagala, Jaja Vira Raja ruled still in the highlands of Candi, being married to a cousin of this king, by whom he had a son Coralliadda Bandara[2] and a daughter, but the queen having died shortly after the bearing of these children, the king of Candi was married not long afterwards again to the princess of Ganga Palla,[3] who was of the same family as his former wife.

He had some children by her also whom he loved much more than the children of the first marriage, a love which went so far as to stop short only of killing the latter children.

The Prince Coralliadda Bandara, becoming aware of this hatred of his father against him and his sister, immediately took flight to a district of Candi called Parcia Pattoe[4] and, consulting with his friends there, decided with the agreement of the king of Majadune, his uncle, to fight against the king, his father.[5]

Is defeated by his son and flees to the King of Majadune

He put this into action shortly after, seized his capital of Candi, and made himself master of the entire kingdom of this name, as he was much loved by all the subjects.

The king Jaja Vira, not knowing where to turn, went with his consort, his other children and a large following and with the royal elephant called Aira Vatta,[6] to the place where the king of Majadune was, took the crown from his head, laid it at the king's feet and told him all his mistakes, but could not move him to help him against his son in his undisputed right to the crown, which Jaja Vira had unlawfully tried to steal from him in favour of his second consort and of her children.

Gives him a hiding place

However, in order not to rebuff him entirely, he gave him some villages for his maintenance, showed him much favour and ordered him to remain in his lands and keep quiet, with the assurance that then he need not expect any secret dealings.[7]

At this time there was a king on the side of the Seven

---

[1] Pelenda.   [2] Karaliyaddē Bandāra.
[3] Sampala Dēvi.   [4] Pansia Pattu.
[5] Confirmed by *Rv* (p. 70), but it does not mention any agreement with Māyādunnē.
[6] Airāvatta.   [7] Confirmed by *Rv* (p. 70).

Corlas in the principality of Dewa Godea,[1] in the village Monda Conda Palla,[2] where he had built a city.

He was king of Irugal Rajoe, bore the name of Hedrimano Soeria Rajoe,[3] was of higher caste than any other king in the whole of Ceylon and lived with all his neighbouring rulers in a good peace.

The King of Irugal described

In the meanwhile the councillor sent to Goa, Tammutta Bala Soeriya Sena Dipati,[4] found occasion to make himself so esteemed by the Viceroy of Goa that he returned to Ceylon with gifts.

The imprisoned Councillor returns from Goa to Ceylon

At the same time a Franciscan priest, Fra Joan Villa da Conde,[5] and a captain Alfonso Pereira[6] departed with him to Ceylon, coming first to Colombo and then to Cotta to the Emperor Darmapalla while he was preparing for a serious battle, in which the Portuguese also helped.

A Franciscan Monk baptises the king

After the priest had been here for some time, he influenced the Emperor so much that he was baptized in the presence of the Captain General, together with many of his chiefs and a great part of his people.[7]

About this time, the Emperor's mother or the wife of Videa Rajoe died, who, having heard of her death when he was still in Pellenda, made peace with the King of Majadune and then married his daughter Maha Tiquiri Bandara,[8] besides giving his son Jaja Palla Astana,[9] lawful brother of the Emperor, in marriage to a cousin of the king, Coeda Tiquiri Bandara,[10] to seal that much more firmly the bond of friendship.

After the conclusion of this marriage, he paid no attention to the king of Majadune nor to the Portuguese, but began on the contrary to do them damage and claimed that he was the rightful heir to the kingdom.

The youngest son of the king at Majadune, named Tiquiri

King of Majadune makes peace with the Emperor

---

[1] Dewameda Kōralē.   [2] Mudukondapola Nuvara.
[3] Edirimana Surya. *Rv* says he was of the Irugal race (p. 72).
[4] Tammita Bālasuriya Senāthipathi.   [5] Friar João de Villa de Conde.
[6] Afonço Pereira de Laçerda, Captain of Colombo in 1553.
[7] The conversion of Dharmapāla by Fra João de Villa de Conde is also mentioned in *Rv* (p. 68), though the name of the friar in that account is wrong.
[8] Mahā Tikiri Bandāra.   [9] Wijayapāla.
[10] Kudā Tikiri Bandāra.

Rajoere Bandara,[1] then 12 years old and still sucking his nurse, was sent with a large army under the command of Wickrama Singa,[2] one of the chiefs of his kingdom and Modeliaar and noblemen of the king's house, speedily to fight against king Vidia Rajoe. He defeated him very luckily, obtained the head of the Modeliaar Samaracon[3] and obliged the others to flee into the deepest jungle.[4]

After this time the king of Majadune made peace with the Emperor Darmapalla Raja and with the Portuguese and again fought against Vidia Rajoe through both his sons, Maha Rajoe Bandara[5] and Tiquiri Rajoeroe Bandara, as also through his Modeliaar Wickrama Raja.[6]

Further acts of Vidia Rajoe

Their army marched up from Pasdum Corla, attacked a fortress in the village of Malcava[7] and marched hastily across the Pellenda[8] river. Then Vidia Rajoe sent his wife and his son's wife, daughter of the king of Majadune, with all their female slaves and attendants, along with the royal ensign, to the city of Pellenda, he fleeing only with some of his trusted friends, Araaties[9] and with some Modeliaars (or Colonels) to the Walauwe[10] side where he hid himself.

The Princes, seeing the city of Pellenda abandoned, went in, found their sister and cousin with their retinue whom they immediately sent to Sitavaca.[11]

In the meanwhile Vidia Rajoe went to Candi and consulted with the king (son of Jaja Vira)[12] what he was to do next.

He again assembled an army, and positioned himself in the lower Galbade Corla,[13] against which the king of Majadune sent his son, Tiquiri Rajoeroe Bandara, and Wicrama Singa, his Modeliaar, with a large army that was encamped in the village Cottoega Hawatte.[14]

As soon as the armies came within sight of each other, the

[1] Tikiri Rajjuru Bandāra, the future Rāja Sinha I.
[2] Wickramasinha Mudali.   [3] Samarakōne Mudali.
[4] Confirmed by *Rv* (p. 71).
[5] Mahā Rajjuru Bandāra. He was Māyādunnē's eldest son but *Rv* says he died at the age of 20 and that it was the second son, Timbiripola, who accompanied Tikiri Bandāra on the campaign against Vidiyē Bandāra (pp. 70–1).
[6] Wickramasinha Mudali.   [7] Unidentifiable.   [8] Pelenda.
[9] Ārachchies.   [10] Probably the Valavē Ganga in the far south.
[11] Confirmed by *Rv* (p. 71).   [12] Karaliyaddē Bandāra, son of Jayavīra.
[13] Galboda Kōralē.   [14] Katugahawala.

battle raged very fiercely. But Vidia Rajoe was again beaten so that he fled to the mountain of Elpitti Conda[1] and from there retired to Candi. He renewed the fight, coming down again with a very large army. But the people of the four districts who stood under him deserted him treacherously and submitted to the Prince Tiquiri Rajoeroe Bandara, whereupon Vidia Rajoe again quietly but hastily escaped to Candi with one slave, while most of his army was driven to flight. He then lost an innumerable number of people, as thousands were hacked to death while fleeing, moreover a great many were captured.[2]

After this great victory, when the Prince Tiquiri Rajoeroe returned to his father, the king of Majadune, the King assembled all his horsemen, courtiers and the greatest men of his kingdom, ordering them that they should henceforth give this Prince the title of Raja Singa Rajoe.[3]

The Prince Tiquiri Rajoeroe Bandara is named Raja Singa Rajoe

Then this Prince went to the Four Corlas, re-established everything there, gave new laws and directed everything according to the order which he had obtained from the King his father.

After everything had returned to peace, the king of Majadune sent his uncle, Jurugal Ralahami of Obbera, Lord of Quirivella,[4] to Candi as ambassador and requested the king that he should not allow Vidia Rajoe to re-establish himself in his lands, but that he should get him to leave his land immediately or that otherwise he would force him to do this.

This ruler, very much embarrassed by this and not inclined to wait for Vidia Rajoe's arrival, ordered him to leave his land immediately, who then took flight to the king of the Seven Korlas. This king called Edirimanna Soeria[5] was very closely related to the king of Iroegal,[6] and so Vidia Rajoe requested of him in the city of Mudda Conda Palla[7] that he maintain him and favour him with a residence in his lands, whereupon he gave him and his people the village Bogade.[8]

---

[1] Elpitikanda.   [2] These events are confirmed by *Rv* (pp. 71–2).
[3] Rāja Sinha Rāju.
[4] Kurugala (?) Rālahami of Obbēriya, Lord of Kirāvella.
[5] Edirimana Sūrya.
[6] Irugal.   [7] Mudukondapola Nuvara.   [8] Bōgoda.

Vidia Rajoe has
the King of
Seven Korles
murdered

Vidia Rajoe settled down there but, as an ungrateful trouble-maker, could not rest peacefully but conspired with an Arratje (or Captain) named Vella Joeda[1] to put to death the King of the Seven Corlas, who had shown him so much favour and had received him as a friend.

To carry out this villainy, it was decided that he would go to visit the king and that his people would start a fight, while he spoke within with the King. Then he was sure the King would come out and try to prevent this fight, at which time the Arratje would take the opportunity to kill the King.

On a certain day he went with much humility to the King's palace, fell down many times before the throne, thanking him for the great favours which he enjoyed in his land, but the king ordered him once or twice to stand up and come to sit next to him.

And became
King

In the meanwhile Vidia Raja's people began to make a great din from outside, and to engage in a fight among each other so strongly that the King began to be annoyed, so that he went outside with much disgust to prevent it. But half way up, the Araatie, Vella Joeda, made sure that he was immediately despatched. Then the inhabitants of the Seven Corlas chose Vidia Rajoe as King, who first feigned that he would not accept finally allowed himself to be persuaded.[2]

After Vidia Rajoe had established himself by his cunning and continuous manoeuvring he requested his son, the Emperor Darma Palla Raja, for help with a large army to attack those of the Four Corlas. He got this from him and from the Portuguese and departed for the Four Corlas but the king of Majadune sent his second son, Maha Rajoera Bandara,[3] and his Moedeliaar Wicrama[4] with a large army to oppose him, the latter of whom alone defeated him decisively near a pass of the River Poena Cattale Totta,[5] with all his Portuguese, and obliged him to flee helter-skelter to the city of Monda Conda Palla.[6]

He had such a stubborn head and the spirit not to give up for lost, that he renewed the fight against the youngest son of

[1] Vēlāyudha Ārachchi.
[2] These events are referred to very briefly in *Rv* (p. 72).
[3] See p. 240 n. 5. *Rv* has Timbiripola.   [4] Wickremasinha Mudali.
[5] Puwakella Totta.   [6] Mudukondapola Nuvara.

the king of Majadune, Tiquiri Rajoeroe Bandara, but now named Raja Singa Rajoe, who seized all his strongholds and fortresses and even besieged the city of Conda Palla Nuwara[1] from which Vidia Rajoe fled.

From there he went by ship across the Bay of Portaloon or Puteleon,[2] left for Jaffanapatnam and took refuge in a port or bay which has since been called Anaxaddie or Anacse Heriatotte,[3] that is, the pass of the King's transit.[4]

Raja Singa Rajoe, having landed there, seized the city of Monda Conda Palla, pursued Vidia Rajoe everywhere, took his Araatie,[5] who was the treacherous murderer of Edirimanna Soeriya, King of the Seven Corlas, prisoner and had him immediately impaled on an iron pike.[6]

Raja Singa Rajoe seizes the Seven Corlas

Thereafter he subjugated the entire Seven Corlas, re-established the laws of the land, put everything in good order and retired hastily again to Sita-Vaca.

Vigea Rajoe[7] with his son Jaja Palla Astana[8] and their retinue went to the village Tammaraccoelam[9] but there he was robbed of everything by the Malabars after an unexpectedly short battle.

About this time the Emperor Darma Palla Raja brought the land of Mature[10] and many forts under his sway with the help of the Portuguese, making that entire district pay taxes, and made them tributaries while formerly they had been subject to the king of Majadune. He accomplished this very easily through a new Mudeliaar, Mamampeia,[11] but shortly thereafter this Modeliaar was put to flight by the people of the king of Majadune and forced to leave Mature, when he was so hotly pursued by the enemy who obtained new reinforcements, that he and many Portuguese had the misfortune to be taken captive to Sita-Vaca, by which the Emperor again lost the whole of

The king Darmapalla Raja conquers the land of Mature but loses it again

---

[1] Mudukondapola Nuvara.   [2] Puttalam.

[3] Arasadi Totta or Arasuēriya Totta. Old names for Kalpitiya.

[4] Valentijn's translation of the place names is correct. It can also mean: pass near the banyan tree [*Arasamaram* (Tam.)—banyan tree].

[5] Vēlāyutha Ārachchi.   [6] Confirmed by *Rv* (p. 73).

[7] Vidiyē Bandāra.   [8] Wijayapāla Asthāna.

[9] Thamaraikulama. *Rv* says Tarakulama (p. 73) but Valentijn's version is more correct. It is a village in the Jaffna peninsula on the outskirts of the city of Jaffna.

[10] Mātara.   [11] Manampēri Mudaliyār.

Mature and the people of the king of Majadune conquered that territory.[1]

The Portuguese thereupon dispatched a renowned commander, who encamped at the small Naclagam pass,[2] and from there gradually penetrated higher, seizing everything that he passed.[3]

Raja Singa Rajoe

This happened at a time when the king of Majadune had become very old, handed over the kingdom of Sita-Vaca to his son Raja Singa and had placed him on the throne of Majadune.[4]

Defeats the Portuguese

Hearing that the Portuguese were approaching to make themselves masters of his land, he assembled a powerful army, took the Modeliaar Wickrama Singa and many experienced commanders and left for the village Moleriava,[5] where he awaited them.

He saw them finally coming proudly, and was attacked by them very fiercely, as a result of which his people suffered considerably at first. But when he fell on them with the bulk of his army very furiously, he defeated the entire army and gained a complete victory.

Some days later the Portuguese renewed the battle, but were driven to flight helter-skelter, so that they were so embittered against this ruler that they began to devastate all the lands around Colombo and Cotta and to seize all the ports and villages belonging to Ceitavaca[6] and to depopulate the coastal villages.

Drives out Darma-Palla and becomes Emperor of all Ceylon

The Kingdom of Cotta lasted only for 10 years since the Emperor was driven away from there by Raja Singa and he was obliged to flee from there with the Portuguese and abandon everything.

It is said that this is found there in a certain old manuscript and it is written there that this happened in A.D. 1514 on 15th March (though later).[7]

---

[1] Events confirmed by *Rv* (p. 74).

[2] Nakolagama, now called Nagalagam, on the Kelani Ganga.

[3] This Portuguese was Captain Affonço Pereira.

[4] In 1581; the throne of Sitāvaca is meant.   [5] Mullēriyāva.   [6] Sitāvaca.

[7] Kōttē was abandoned by Dharmapāla in 1565 long before the death of Māyādunnē. Valentijn is unable to control the dates of events from his Sinhalese sources. The Saka year 1514 is mentioned in the *Rv* as the date of the death of Rāja Sinha (p. 81) and it is this date in the Saka era that Valentijn has taken from his sources. The Saka era begins in A.D. 78.

The Emperor Raja Singa brought the whole of Ceylon, except Colombo and Gale, in a very short time under his authority and made himself much feared everywhere. He died about A.D. 1593[1] as we shall see more clearly hereafter.[2]

From another manuscript, it appears that Raja Singa had a daughter, from the lineage of the king of Oedampel,[3] named Menniok Biso Bandara[4] who was married to a king of the Malabar coast, Araatie Sowara,[5] by whom she had 2 sons who, hearing that their grandfather was dead, came to Sita-Vaca and were received by all the courtiers with much affection and found the country everywhere in peace.

Also during the lifetime of Raja Singa, a very learned author, named Vidumal,[6] came from the Malabar coast solely to serve Raja Singa. He elevated this man to a specially high position, gave him a new title of Manaperoema Mucaveti,[7] that is Prince of Poets, and also made him a Dessave or Governor. He sent him to Andupanduna,[8] which lies in Gabbada Corla[9] in the village Cadnugarrupa, where he settled with his people.

From the above-mentioned marriage of Raja Singa's daughter with this Malabar king Araatie Sowara[10] (called by the Cingalese Tiragam Bandara,[11] that is, a foreign king) sprang a Princess and a Prince, who after the death of their parents were brought up by the Queen, their grandmother.

They named the Princess after her mother Meninik Bisso Bandara,[12] which Princess left for Degigampala Corla[13] and settled in the village Matamogore.[14]

The two Princes, grandsons of Raja Singa, on seeing that the court chiefs did not show them as much respect as on their first arrival, the oldest went to Manicravare[15] and remained there but the youngest went to his aunt, the Princess of

---

[1] This date is correct.
[2] Valentijn deals later in detail with events surrounding Rāja Sinha's death. See below pp. 265–7.
[3] Udapola family.   [4] Menika Biso Bandāra.
[5] A Pandyan prince called Harinēsvara Kumāraya.
[6] *Rv* refers to him as Aritta Kivendu Peruma (p. 80).
[7] Manampēruma Mukavetti.   [8] Handapanduna.   [9] Galboda Kōralē.
[10] Harinēsvara.   [11] Kirāgama Bandāra.
[12] Menika Biso Bandāra.   [13] Dehigampal Kōralē.
[14] Maddamagoda.   [15] Menikkadavara.

Matamagore,[1] who decided to make her nephew the Emperor of Cita-Vaca. She spoke to the chiefs about this and they agreed with it. But they acted treacherously and warned Manapenoema Mucaveti[2] that the prince Jaja Vira Comarea[3] had this intention, whereupon they seized the pass of Tintotta,[4] where the prince was, and thereby prevented the entire plan.

The Prince, repulsed by this in his plan, fled to Sita-Vaca. But then the other came there shortly after and put the prince to death, abducted the princess and placed himself with force on the throne, but as Manampenoema Mucaveti was in agreement with the chiefs of the land in this, they willingly handed over the kingdom to him.

The eldest Prince Jaja Soeria Comarea,[5] brother of the murdered Prince, hearing this and fearing a similar fate, fled to Colombo to the Emperor Darmapalla who received him very amicably.[6]

The account of the Affairs of the Emperors of Ceylon brings us thus far. And this is all the information that is to be found with the oldest and most experienced Cingalese in the affairs of their land. It is to be regretted that the times and incidents are not distinguished better, for then we could better calculate backwards to our system and easily bring them to agree with the years of the world, which cannot be done now, especially as it will clearly be discovered from the following list of Emperors, that many years are missing to make up the 2007 years which they ascribe to their Emperors.[7]

List of the Ceylonese Emperors

Vagoe Raja, King of the south, marries the daughter of Calinga Raja and produces a daughter by her, who is carried

---

[1] Maddamagoda.   [2] Manampēruma Mukavetti.

[3] Jayavīra.   [4] Tuntota.   [5] Jayasūriya.

[6] *Rv* gives a different account of the fate of these two princes. It says that they were killed by Manampēruma Mukavetti (p. 81).

[7] Valentijn has had difficulty in translating the chronology in his Sinhalese sources into the Christian calendar, a difficulty that is enhanced by the fact that his king-list is incomplete.

away by a lion and is impregnated, of which union is produced:

From the marriage of this Prince with this Princess 32 sons are born, of whom the 2 oldest were obliged to leave the country, namely Vigea Comara and Simit Comara, who arrive in Ceylon to become the first Kings of Ceylon.[1]

The Prince, Singa Bahu Comara ⎫
and ⎬
The Princess Singa Valli Comara ⎭

		From A.D.	To A.D.
1. Vigea Comara (by others named Vigea Comaroe or Vigea Bahoe Raja) ruled	30 years	106	136
2. Tissanaon Ameti, one of the chiefs	1 year	136	137
3. Simit Comara	22 years	137	159
4. Pandoe Vassaja, the first Emperor, under whose reign a Princess and 6 Princes came to this island and built various cities	13 years	159	172
Other ascribe him 30 years			
5. Abeia Comara	20 years	172	192
6. Sagoeganatissa	17 years	192	209
7. Diagagamoenoe	37 years	209	246
8. Pandoe Cabaja	33 years	246	279
He rebuilt Anoeragia Poere			
9. Moetta or Motta Singa Raja	60 years	279	339
10. Deveni Petissa Maha Raja	40 years	339	379
He built Pagodas and received the doctrine of Buddhism and 8 foreign Princes			
11. Soeratissanam	11 years	379	389

---

[1] Valentijn's first king Vijaya begins his reign in A.D. 106. In the Sinhalese tradition the beginning of Vijaya's reign coincides with the date of Buddha's enlightenment, i.e. 544 B.C. There is thus a 650 year gap which makes up for the absence of a large number of kings in Valentijn's list from Acboraja to Rucculē Parākrama Bāhu.

		From	To
		A.D.	A.D.
12. Two Malabar impostor ambassadors; according to others ruled only 20 years	22 years	389	411
13. Assalanam Raja	14 years	411	425
14. Etalunam or Etalanam Rajoe	44 years	425	469
15. Jattalatisse Guelinitissa Rajoe He built the Calane pagoda	20 years	469	489
16. Goloeumbera or Ambera Raja Held court in Roene	10 years	489	499
17. Ganatissa Rajoe	4 years	499	503
18. In his name the kingdom was still ruled	30 years	503	533
19. Doetoegenoenoe Maha Raja Expelled the Malabars and their religion	24 years	533	557
20. Sedetissa Raja He built Goenolaittahena and 10 paddy fields	18 years	557	575
21. Tullenam Raja	1 year 9 mth. 10 d.	575	577
22. Lemenetissa Raja	39 yr. 8½ m.	577	617
23. Caloeman Raja	oo[1]	617	633
24. Walagam Bahu Raja Was driven out by 7 Malabar brothers	8 months	633	634
25. Five Malabar Princes They and two others sent away the relics of Buddha	36 years	634	670
26. Valla Gamboe or Vallagam Bahoe Raja Defeated the 5 brothers	12 yr. 5 m.	670	683
27. Choranga Rajoe	26 years	683	709
28. Bemminitissa	12 years	709	721
29. Maha Delia Deliatissa Son of Caloenam Rajoe	14 years	721	735
30. Chorawa Rajoe Son of Valagam	12 years	735	747

[1] This is an error for 16. Both the regnal dates and the account in the text agree on 16 years.

			From	To
			A.D.	A.D.
31.	Coedda Tissa Rajoe Son of Naha Deliattissa	3 years	747	750
32.	Anularan Bissava His queen	1 year	750	751
33.	Coelavaon Secretary of the Queen	1 yr. 1 m.	751	753
34.	Tomo A commoner	4 mths	753	753
35.	Maloelan Tissa	26 years	753	779
36.	Batian or Batta Raja	28 years	779	807
37.	Madilimanna Raja His brother	12 years	807	819
38.	Adague Muwene or Moenoe Raja	9 yr. 8 m.	819	829
39.	Cada Ambera Rajoe	6 years	829	835
40.	Nalabissava, Queen His sister	6 years	835	841
41.	Elunna or Clunna Raja Her husband and sister's son	6 years	841	847
42.	Sanda Moehoenoe or Sandamoe Hoenoe Raja	6 years	847	853
43.	Asnapa Raja Killed the former	41 years	853	894
44.	Vacnelisinam Raja	3 years	894	897
45.	Bapa Raja	12 years	897	909
46.	Gaja Bahu	22 years	909	931
47.	Mana or Maria Raja	16 years	931	947
48.	Hama Tissa Raja	26 years	947	973
49.	Coeda Raja	31 years	973	1004
50.	Veni Tissa Raja	22 years	1004	1026
51.	Ambaheraman Raja	6 years	1026	1032
52.	Sirina or Suina Raja	2 years	1032	1034
53.	Vierdoe or Vijemdoe Raja	6 years	1034	1040
54.	Sanga Tissa Raja	11 years	1040	1051
55.	Siri or Suisanga Bodi Raja	22 years	1051	1073
56.	Leminie Goloe Amba Raja	13 years	1073	1086
57.	Guwelaguwem or Quelaguwem Dettatissa	10 years	1086	1096

		From	To
		A.D.	A.D.
58. Malasen or Mahason Raja	24 years	1096	1120
59. Quitisiriamenaon Raja	28 years	1120	1148
60. Deva Tissa Raja	9 years	1148	1157
61. Rajas Raja	31 years	1157	1188
62. Upatissa Maram Raja	26 years	1188	1220[1]
63. Senam Raja	6 yr. 1 m.	1220	1227
64. Lemini Tissa Raja	6 years	1227	1233
65. Visenam Caralsoo Raja	6 years	1233	1239
66. Seven Malabar Princes	27 years	1239	1266
67. Dacem Goelia Raja	18 years	1266	1284
68. Comara Dahai Raja	29 years	1284	1313
69. Lemini Patissa Raja	1 year	1313	1314
70. Amlam Heranam Raja	13 years	1314	1327
71. Dajoelsen Raja	6 mths.	1327	1327
72. Dalam Ajali Raja	20 years	1327	1347
73. Cadda Ginitsirmenam Raja	31 years	1347	1378
74. Semini Raja	3 years	1378	1381
75. Melisinganam Salandana Roo	9 years	1381	1390
76. Acbora Raja	6 years	1390	1396
77. Acboraja	51 years	1396	1447
78. Dos Raja	6 years	1447	1453
79. Rucculei Praccaram Bahu Raja	55 years	1453	1508
Under him Don Laurens d'Almeyda landed in Ceylon in A.D. 1505			
80. Jaja Vira Praccaram Bahu	7 years	1508	1515
81. Maha Pandita Praccaram Bahu Raja	1 year	1515	1516
82. Vira Praccaram Bahu	20 years	1516	1536
Lopez Suaar Alvarenga made a treaty with this Emperor in A.D. 1518 and in his time 2 ships from Portugal appeared here in A.D. 1530			
83. Darma Praccaram Bahu	25 years	1536	1561
84. Viga Bahu	8 years	1561	1569
85. Bonacca Bahu Maha Raja	11 years	1569	1580
86. Darma Palla Raja	10 years	1580	1590

[1] The calculation of dates is wrong here. It should be 1188 to 1214.

		From	To
		A.D.	A.D.
87.	Don Philippo	very short time	1520[1]
88.	Raja Singa Rajoe	3 years 1590	1593

1465 yrs. 2½ mths 10 days

Thus the years of reign of the 88 Emperors of Ceylon total 1465 years 2 months and 25 days instead of 2007 years (as they claim).[2]

		From	To
		A.D.	A.D.

Now we shall add here the Emperors of whom we shall speak in the following.[3]

		From	To
89.	Fimala Darma Soeria	11 years 1593	1604
	Also called Don Jan		
90.	Cenuwieraat	28 years 1604	1632
91.	Raja Singa Raja	1632	1687
	He ruled very long		
92.	Fimala Darma Soeria Maha Raja	20 years 1687	1707
			4 June
93.	Wira Praccaram Narendra Singa	— 1707	—
	By others called Wira Praccaraman		
	Reendre Singa		

1554 yrs 2½ mths 10 days

Others who claim to have a more exact knowledge of the affairs of these Emperors say that the eighth Emperor before Fimala Darma Soeria,[4] or rather the 80th in rank, was also called Fimala Darma Soeria Adassyn,[5] that is, the well loved

Account of others of the Emperors

---

[1] Error for 1590.

[2] The figure of 2007 years shows that Valentijn was aware from some of his documents of the Sinhalese tradition that dates the beginning of their kings in 544 B.C.

[3] The accuracy of the chronology improves considerably now as Valentijn draws not only from traditional sources but also from European records.

[4] Vimala Dharma Sūrya.

[5] Vimala Dharma Sūrya Adahasyn. Adahasyn was a royal title of honour.

son of the Sun, though again others have applied this title to the first discoverer of Ceylon.[1]

His son was Langcau Pati Mahadassyn,[2] that is the well loved great lord of the land.

His son followed him on the throne and was named Langcau Singa Mahadassyn,[3] that is well loved lion of the island.

He left behind a son, Mara Singa Mahadassyn,[4] that is well beloved lion killer.

He left behind two sons, Langcau Pati Mahestana,[5] that is, the apple of the eye of the whole country and Radjora Adassyn,[6] that is, well beloved king.

From these two Princes sprang many sons and daughters.

The elder lived for only 17 years but the younger for 78 years, fighting great battles in this short time against each other.

The elder left behind an oldest son with the name Marandona Radjora,[7] that is, you shall kill the king, and the younger, one Marandona Mahestana,[8] that is, you shall kill the apple of the eye.

The first fought for six years after his father's death against his uncle, and after his death another 4 years with his uncle's subjects, till finally a marriage was concluded between the daughter of Marandona Radjora and the son of Marandona Mahestane, Manabande Bandinge,[9] that is the first selected queen, and Issere Balande Radjora,[10] that is the first selected King.

These two having married each other, everything was at peace, and they had many daughters and at last a son with the name Fimala Darma Soeria Adassyn, that is the well beloved son of the Sun who is never still.[11]

---

[1] Valentijn has referred early to this tradition of a previous Vimala Dharma Sūrya from whom the later kings descended (see above p. 199). This was probably an attempt by traditional hagiologists to bulid a mythical ancestry to legitimise Konnappu Bandāra who assumed power as Vimala Dharma Sūrya in 1592.

[2] Lankāpati Mahādasyn.　　　　[3] Lankāsinha Mahādasyn.
[4] Mārasinha Mahādasyn.　　　　[5] Lankāpati Mahāstana.
[6] Rajjuru Adahasyn.　　　　　　[7] Marandana Rajjuru.
[8] Marandana Mahāstana.　　　　[9] Mānabanda Bendigē.
[10] Issara Balanda Rajjuru.
[11] This account of the ancestry of Vimala Dharma Sūrya appears to be a

He, who was otherwise known by the name of Don Jan,[1]
made himself master of the whole of Ceylon in A.D. 1593, and
those who would not voluntarily obey him he brought under
his might with the force of weapons. He took his cousin
Raketto Bandige,[2] that is the beautiful Queen, captive, also
known by the name of Donna Catharina, and daughter of
Mahadassyn, that is the great and very well loved, and
married her.[3]

This Mahadassyn, otherwise named Darmapalla Raja, was
at this time, or somewhat earlier, Emperor of Candi, though
he was the lawful heir of the entire kingdom of Ceylon. But
Raja Singa Adassyn, king of Sita-Vaca and his daughter's son,
fought and pursued him so closely that he drove him out of the
kingdom.

Then Raja Singa seized the entire kingdom up to Colombo
and Gale. He was the son of a king and cousin of the Emperor
of Cotta.[4]

The Portuguese say that he was a barber but this is a
mistake and in Spilbergen's Journey (when he came to Ceylon
as we shall see at the proper time),[5] he appears as the son of
Ragu, born by a dancing girl, and as one who put to death his
three legitimate brothers (for he was a bastard) and his father.[6]

Having driven Mahadassyn to flight (who fled into the
jungle, abandoning all his treasure which he scattered here and

*Don Jan
marries Donna
Catharina*

*Daughter of
Mahadassyn
whom Raja
Singa put to
flight*

*And makes
himself
Emperor*

*Was attacked by
Don Jan*

---

tradition independent of the *Rv*. It is an attempt to construct a lineage for this
king. *Rv* has no reference to this. Baldaeus relates a similar version, but with
less detail and both he and Valentijn seem to have had access to a common
source (Baldaeus p. 2).

[1] Dom João, a baptismal name he took when he became a Christian. He was
the son of Vīrasundara Bandāra, a Kandyan nobleman who was killed by Rāja
Sinha.

[2] Rakētu Bendigē.

[3] She was the daughter of Karaliyaddē Bandāra, ruler of Kandy, who had
been dethroned by Rāja Sinha and had taken refuge with the Portuguese. She
was baptized as Dona Catharina.

[4] Valentijn is referring to Karaliyaddē Bandāra, who was related to the King
of Kōttē, Dharmapāla, by marriage.

[5] Joris van Spilbergen's journey to the Court of Kandy described below
Chapter VIII, pp. 279–94.

[6] *Reis van Joris van Spilbergen . . .* , pp. 54–61. The account reflects the
mythology that had been built around the fascinating personality of Dom João
who became king as Vimala Dharma Sūrya.

there), he was then attacked by Don Jan who later married Mahadassyn's daughter.[1]

Wounds
himself out of
spite and dies

He attacked him very furiously and put him to flight and brought Raja Singa to such despair and rage that when he saw that things had gone against him, out of spite and anger, he trod on a thorn from which wound he died, as he would not let it be dressed, and shortly after the fever entered him.[2]

Old hatred
between him
and Don Jan

Between him and Don Jan there was an old and unquenchable hate, over the action of Don Jan's father. He, who was called Fimala Mantra or Fimala Lamantia,[3] was Governor of Raja Singa and looked after all the Emperor's affairs in Candi. But he set himself finally against this ruler and set himself up as Emperor, on the advice of those of Candi, fighting against him for some time without being brought to subjection or repentance by him.

Raja Singa, seeing that this could not be won by a lion's hide, put on a fox's skin for some time.

He made a treaty with him, promised to present him with all jewels, precious stones and gold trinkets which he had conquered in the war against Mahadassyn,[4] provided that he would henceforth come under him.

He makes his
father prisoner.
And shoots him
to death with
wooden balls

Fimala Lamantia, believing him, came to the court at Sita-Vaca, against the advice of those of Candi. But as soon as he was there, he was taken captive and then buried alive under the earth, so that only his head was seen, after which, on the King's orders, he was shot at with wooden balls till he was dead.[5]

Then Raja Singa Adassyn left for Candi, seized that kingdom, made all the inhabitants slaves and committed massive cruelties on them.

To avenge this insult to his father, Don Jan attacked Raja Singa, but he died by a foolish rage against himself, outside the

[1] These events are described in greater detail later by Valentijn. See below Chapter VII, pp. 274–5.

[2] This tradition of the death of Rāja Sinha by a festering wound from the prick of a thorn is found in *Rv* also (p. 80).

[3] Vimala Dharma, but this was not his real name. He was Vīrasundara Bandāra.

[4] Dharmapāla, King of Kotte.

[5] *Rv* gives a slightly different version. It says he was trapped in a pit where stakes were fixed and he died there (p. 77).

battle (as we have already seen), leaving Don Jan master of his kingdom, though before things came so far, still various other things happened during the lifetime of Raja Singa, of which we cannot speak before we have begun to show how and when the Portuguese came to Ceylon. But before this we must refer to some further matters, touching on the caste of Don Jan, which will shed great light in the following matters.

After Don Jan was married to Donna Catharina, daughter of Mahadassyn (or Darmapalla)[1] (which happened in A.D. 1590), he had by her a daughter named Soeria Mahadasseyn,[2] a son Mahestana[3] and a daughter Hantana Adasseyn.[4]

Successors of Don Jan and his half brother Cenuwieraat

Then Don Jan happened to die in January 1604 and Donna Catharina married his half brother Cenuwieraat (or Senerat Adassyn).[5]

From this marriage were born Comara Singa Hastana,[6] Vidia Palla[7] and Mahestana, later named Raja Singa Rajoe.

And their further actions

Then Donna Catharina died in A.D. 1613 and Cenuwieraat remarried with Soeria Mahadasseyn, Don Jan's and Donna Catharina's oldest daughter, by whom he had a daughter named Lamia Adasseyn,[8] and who died in childbirth in 1617, and this daughter in 1636 married the youngest son of Cenuwieraat and Donna Catharina named Mahestane or Raja Singa Rajoe.

The Prince Mahestane, son of Don Jan, died on 22nd August 1612[9] and Comara Singa Hastane, Prince of Oeva, in 1636 and his brother Prince Vidia Palla who was Prince of Matule,[10] later fled to the Portuguese.

---

[1] Again Valentijn makes a mistake in referring to Dona Catharina as Dharmapāla's daughter. She was the daughter of Karaliyaddē Bandāra, ruler of Kandy. See p. 253 n. 3.

[2] Sūrya Mahādasyn.　　[3] Mahāstana.　　　　　[4] Hantāna Adasyn.

[5] Senerat.　　　　　　[6] Kumārasinha Asthāna.　[7] Wijayapāla.

[8] Lamaya Adasyn.　　[9] *Rv* says he was 'caused to be drowned' (p. 86).

[10] Wijayapāla, Prince of Mātalē.

Seventh Chapter

[Portuguese in the 16th century]

First arrival of the Portuguese in Ceylon. Laurens D'Almeida enters the Bay of Gale 1505, and enters into a treaty with the Emperor. 1518, Alvarenga forces the Emperor to build a fort. Joan Silveira first Caretaker at Colombo, 1518. Antoni Miranda, head of maritime affairs. What Alvarenga does in the Maldives. Lopes Brit, second Caretaker of Colombo, 1520. Builds the fortifications strong and firm. Caught in the utmost danger. Is prepared and makes a new treaty, 1524. The fort of Colombo broken up. A Moor from Malabar tries to get hold of the few Portuguese. But receives a sound beating. New fort built at Colombo. The young Prince Parea Bandara crowned in Lisbon in effigy, 1541. Is attacked by Raja Singa. He seizes Candi. The son of Fimala Lamantia sent by the Portuguese to Goa and baptized by Don Jan. Those of Candi put pressure on the Portuguese. They conquer the kingdom of Jaffanapatnam. And deal with those of Candi. Appoint Don Phillippo Emperor and Don Jan as his Commander. And make an agreement against Raja Singa. Provided that Don Philippo and Don Jan submit to Portugal. Don Jan's hatred of Don Phillippo and the Portuguese. Raja Singa's attack frustrated. Portuguese fort at Ganoor. Their departure from Candi. Don Phillippo poisoned by Don Jan who drives out the Portuguese. Then those of Candi made him Emperor. Forcing them to deliver Ganoor to him. Raja Singa is driven to flight by Don Jan. Tramples on a bamboo out of spite and dies. How he is accused of various cruelties. Janiere Bandara throws himself against Don Jan. Makes an agreement with the Portuguese. They obtain great reinforcements from Goa. Janiere's actions. Don Pedro's misconceived passion halted. Both of whom march to Candi with a large army. And drive Don

Jan from Walane. Don Pedro demands an oath of loyalty. The Cingalese want Donna Catherina as Queen. She is royally received, crowned and thereby everything is brought to peace. Don Pedro puts a big price on Don Jan's life. He comes as a beggar to Candi and raises a fire. The Portuguese conduct themselves lawlessly against the natives. Janiere seeks to marry the Queen. Don Pedro repulses this. He swears to wreak vengeance. He stirs up Don Jan against the Portuguese, offering him the kingdom. But everything is revealed. Thereupon the Portuguese decide to kill Janiere. Flight of the Cingalese. The Queen reflects on this evil. Don Jan sets the Cingalese against the Portuguese and crushes them pitifully. Don Pedro and the Queen captured. He too happens to die of his wounds. Don Jan conquers all Portuguese forts. Accepts the native kings in favour and marries the Queen. What he does next. Don Jeronimo D'Oviedo comes to Ceylon as Commander. Is put to flight by Don Jan and wounded. Correa goes over to Don Jan, becomes his Commander and, being defeated, is treacherously put to death. Don Jan's vengeance and his demand. The soldiers want to put Don D'Oviedo to death. Simon Correa's attack on Don Jan. Villainous deed of Manuel Dias, for which Don Jan makes him great Modeliaar. And the captured Portuguese killed.

It is now time for us to proceed to see when and under what circumstances the Portuguese came to Ceylon.[1]

First arrival of the Portuguese on this island

Their arrival on this island was not on purpose but happened very fortuitously.

The Viceroy of Goa, Francisco D'Almeida, sent his son, Don Laurens D'Almeida,[2] in 1505 with 9 ships to the Maldive Islands, to do as much damage as possible to the vessels of the Moors which passed there fleeing from Malacca and the Maldives to Arabia.[3] But, being blown by wind and storm, they came to land on the island of Ceylon and found themselves then the first of the Portuguese and Europeans on this island.

Laurens D'Almeida arrives, 1505

[1] Valentijn has relied heavily on Barros in this section. Barros, pp. 22–46.
[2] Dom Lourenço D'Almeida.
[3] Muslim merchants of Quilon had attacked the Portuguese and killed their Factor in this port. D'Almeida had bombarded Quilon on 1st November 1505 and was searching for Muslim vessels in reprisal.

It consisted then (so it is said) of 7 kingdoms though there was an Emperor over the entire island who then held his court in Colombo.[1]

In the Bay of Gale, and makes a treaty with the Emperor

Don Laurens had actually come to anchor in the Bay of Gabalican[2] (so say Osorius,[3] but of Gale, as Maffejus[4] says), where there was a separate king,[5] who sent him an ambassador in the name of the Emperor, who sought peace with him.[6]

He accepted this and allowed this treaty to be made by Pelagius Sousa[7] with the Emperor at Colombo, with this condition, that he should give to Emanuel, King of Portugal, an annual tribute of 250,000 pounds of cinnamon,[8] and that this King would then protect him against his enemies, and then planted there a marble stone on which stood carved the arms of the King of Portugal.[9]

The Emperor (as appears from the list of Emperors) was Rucculey Praccaram Bahu,[10] but he actually made that agreement with the King of Gale.[11]

1518 Alvarenga forces the Emperor to build a fort

In 1518 Lopes Suaar Alvarenga[12] went in September with 19 ships to Ceylon to build a fort there, according to the order of King Emanuel and following the permission granted by the Emperor of Ceylon. But the Emperor, regretting what he had allowed, did not want to permit this now, saying that he had

[1] In Kōttē, about 5 miles inland from Colombo.

[2] Early Portuguese writers referred to Galle as Gabaliquama.

[3] Jeronomio Osorio de Fonseca (1506–1580), Bishop of Silves. Author of *Cartas Portuguezas*.

[4] Petrus Maffaeus, S. J. (1535–1603). Author of *Historiarum Indicarum*. Coloniae Agrippinae, 1590.

[5] This 'separate king' was Vijayabāhu VII who ruled in Dondra in south Ceylon when Dharma Parākrama Bāhu ruled in Kōttē as 'Emperor'.

[6] For a discussion of the evidence on the first Portuguese landing in Ceylon, see Donald Ferguson, 'The Discovery of Ceylon by the Portuguese in 1506'. *Journal of the Royal Asiatic Society (Ceylon)*, XIX (1909), 284–400.

[7] Payo de Souza.

[8] Barros says 400 *bhars* cinnamon. See Barros pp. 22–5 for a more detailed account of this episode. Also Queyroz, I, 181.

[9] This was a padrão erected in Galle.

[10] Rucculē Parākrama Bāhu or Parākrama Bāhu VIII, ruled *c.* 1484–1509.

[11] This follows Barros, pp. 22–5. But Queyroz contradicts this. I, 177–83. Donald Ferguson supports the view that the Portuguese landed in Colombo and held negotiations with the King of Kōttē. Donald Ferguson, 'The Discovery of Ceylon by the Portuguese in 1506'. *Journal of the Royal Asiatic Society (Ceylon)*, XIX (1909), 284–400.

[12] Lopo Soarez de Albergaria, Governor of Portuguese India 1516–1518.

not granted permission for this to the Portuguese and slew some Portuguese who were working there.

Alvarenga, not being inclined to be appeased with words, and unable to tolerate that such a black Emperor should sneer at his King, attacked him immediately, crushed him mercilessly and forced him to accept a treaty on these conditions.[1]

1. It would be open to the Portuguese to build a fort in Colombo and Jan Sylveira[2] was made the first Caretaker of the fort there.

Joan Sylveira, first Caretaker at Colombo 1518

2. The Emperor should give King Emanuel annually a tribute of a certain number of precious stones, namely, 12 sapphire rings, 6 elephants and 120,000 pounds of cinnamon, which treaty should be confirmed by the Emperor and all the chiefs of the kingdom.[3]

As Alvarenga had appointed at this time a Caretaker over the fort, so also he appointed another, namely Antoni Miranda Azevedo,[4] as Head of maritime affairs, to oversee the four ships and the trade.

Antoni Miranda, Head of maritime affairs

We must note here that Alvarenga had made a treaty a short while earlier, or had renewed this treaty, with the King of the Maldive Islands, who was attacked by the Portuguese. Also it was the intention to build a strong fort there but this was stopped by the death of Joan Gomes in 1519.

What Alvarenga did in the Maldives

In 1520 Lopes Brit[5] succeeded Joan Sylveira at Colombo as second Caretaker there, who built and completed a new, strong and artistic fort in place of the former one which was of clay and stone. But the Portuguese after completing this became bolder, pestered the inhabitants now and then, whence further bitterness followed, to such an extent, that the Portuguese were put to death by the natives when they could get hold of them, which the Caretaker Brit[6] tolerated for some time. But later he struck back, fell on the Cingalese and put them to flight. Then they assembled together up to 20,000 men, surrounded the fort and besieged it for 5 months.

Lopes Brit, second Caretaker at Colombo
Builds a strong fort

The Caretaker Brit, a courageous man and in no way was it his fault that his people had got mixed up in this difficulty,

Comes to great danger

---

[1] Barros, pp. 38–45. Queyroz I, 189–95.   [2] João da Silveyra.
[3] Barros, p. 44.   [4] Antonio de Miranda D'Azevedo.
[5] Lopo de Brito.   [6] Brito.

sent a message to Cochin to inform the Viceroy there that he and his people were in the utmost danger.

Is ready and makes a new treaty

Thereupon the Viceroy sent Jacob Lopes Siqueira,[1] Alexis de Menezes[2] with a galleon and 50 Portuguese to help. Then the courageous Brit, pressed by hunger, effected a sally with 300 Portuguese, conquered the enemy's works and put them to flight, so that the Emperor was forced to sue for peace again, which was immediately granted to him because Brit knew that the lawlessness of his people had given the first occasion for these incidents. But he took care now that they conducted themselves better with the Cingalese.[3]

1524, the fort of Colombo demolished

In 1524 Emanuel, King of Portugal, decided to demolish the fort built in Colombo, for various reasons, through Ferdinand Gomes de Lima,[4] who left a Factor or manager of affairs, a secret writer and 15 Portuguese on the island.

A Moor from Malabar tries to get the few Portuguese in his hands

After he himself had left there, and as soon as a Moor of Calicut on the Malabar coast saw that very few Portuguese remained there, this Moor decided that he could easily take possession of it.[5] He left with 500 men and 4 vessels for Ceylon, came to anchor in the Bay of Colombo, and told the ruler that the Portuguese were besieged by all the Indian princes and that he was sent by the Emperor of Malabar to secure all the Portuguese who were there.

The Emperor of Cotta, taken aback at this, sought some delay, spoke with the Portuguese Factor on this and with the Secret Writer, who assured the ruler that it was an absolute lie and that he would discover the falsehood if he inquired about it. But as he found the contrary of what they had asserted, it was impossible that he could treat with them according to their desire.

But obtains a sound beating

Then this ruler dismissed the Moor, named Baleacen,[6] but he, being not satisfied, tried to force the Emperor to do this and get him in his power against his will. But he did this so badly that he went away humiliated since he received a sound beating.[7]

---

[1] Diogo Lopes de Sequeira.   [2] Alexio de Menesez.
[3] Barros, pp. 48–54.   [4] Fernão Gomez de Lemos.
[5] This Calicut Moor was Ali Hassan.   [6] Ali Hassan.
[7] Queyroz also describes this incident, I, 207–9.

Though the previous fort at Colombo had been demolished on the orders of King Emanuel (as we have said), later another fort had to be built here, as will appear to us subsequently, since Don Jan[1] had besieged them later in it. But when or by whom this was done we cannot say, since I have found nothing of it mentioned in the Portuguese writers.[2]

New fort built in Colombo

It is certain that meanwhile the succeeding Emperors of Ceylon lived with a good understanding with the kings of Portugal and that the Portuguese had their permanent residence at Colombo, siding always with the party of Emperor Darma Praccaram Bahu,[3] otherwise also called Aboe-Negabo Bandara.[4]

He ruled in 1536[5] and decided to place his grandson Parea Bandara,[6] son of Tribuloe Bandara[7] and of his only daughter, otherwise named Darmapalla[8] (though others call him Mahadassyn) under the protection of John III, King of Portugal, and to this end, to send two ambassadors with the image of this Prince and a gold crown to this king, requesting him that he be graciously pleased to put the crown on the head of the statue of this young Prince, as was done in 1541 with very great pomp and pageantry in the great hall of the Palace at Lisbon.[9]

The young Prince Parea Bandara crowned in effigy in Lisbon 1541

After the death of Aboe Negabo Bandara,[10] the young Prince took possession of the throne and dignity of his grandfather, but was attacked treacherously and with hostility by the youngest son of the king of Majadune[11] (or of the king of Sita-Vaca), Raja Singa, and pursued so closely that he was obliged to flee from Candi[12] (where he then held his court) to Colombo.

Is attacked by Raja Singa

[1] Vimala Dharma Sūrya I.
[2] The rebuilding of the Colombo fort happened in 1551.
[3] Dharma Parākrama Bāhu (1509–1528).
[4] Bhuvanēka Bāhu. This is not correct. Bhuvanēka Bāhu VII succeeded Dharma Parākrama Bāhu.
[5] This was Bhuvanēka Bāhu VII.   [6] Periya Bandāra.
[7] Tribulē Bandāra, also known as Vidiyē Bandāra by which name Valentijn has referred to him in the previous chapter.
[8] Dharmapāla.
[9] This repeats what is said in Chap. VI. See above pp. 235–6. Here Valentijn correctly says an image was sent to Lisbon, not the prince himself.
[10] Bhuvanēka Bāhu VII.   [11] Māyādunnē.   [12] Error for Kōttē.

He seizes Candi

Thereupon Raja Singa made himself master not only of the entire kingdom of Cotta but also of the kingdom of Candi, the lords and commoners were made slaves, and all the subjects treated with uncommon cruelty.

Fimala Lamantia's son sent to Goa by Portuguese and baptized by Don Jan

Previously we have come up to this point in our account of Raja Singa's dealings with those of Candi, but add here only to refresh the memory, that though Raja Singa had become master of Fimala Lamantia,[1] father of Don Jan,[2] by cunning, he did not get hold of his son since he was sent by the Portuguese to Colombo and from there to Goa to be instructed by the priests in the Roman religion and baptized as Don Jan, after Don Juan of Austria, brother of Philip II king of Castille and Portugal, and later was used further by the Portuguese, as we shall see.

Those of Candi conspire with the Portuguese

In the meanwhile, Raja Singa (who now called himself Fimala Darma Soria)[3] oppressed the Cingalese, by making them lift and carry entire blocks of earth from Candi to Sita-Vaca, to make many strongholds and forts for him, so that they decided to set the Portuguese against him, who were rather inclined to accept the request because it was the best means for them to get into Candi and thus make themselves masters of the whole island.

He conquers the Kingdom of Jaffanapatnam

After having considered this well, they saw that it was impossible for them to achieve this aim, before they were masters of Jaffanapatnam, and they sent first a powerful fleet thence under Don Andrea Furtado de Mendoza,[4] who surprisingly conquered that kingdom and forced the inhabitants to allow as many of the Portuguese as they thought good to march through their land to Candi; besides the king of Jaffanapatnam was obliged to give all imaginable help to further their aim.

And deals with those of Candi

Those of Candi, hearing, in the meanwhile, that the

[1] Valentijn is probably trying to say Vimala Dharma, but the person to whom he is referring is Vīrasundara. See above, Chapter VI, p. 254 n. 3.

[2] Dom João, the later Vimala Dharma Sūrya.

[3] This is a major error. Valentijn is confusing Rāja Sinha of Sitāvaka with Vimala Dharma Sūrya of Kandy.

[4] This was the second Portuguese expedition to Jaffna under Don Andre Furtado de Mendonza from Goa in 1591, to punish the king for his rebellion against Portuguese suzerainty. Queyroz II, 446.

Portuguese had conquered Jaffanapatnam, were at first very much afraid, since they had never so far dealt with the Portuguese. Don Andrea, realising this, decided to send to Candi a cousin of Donna Catharina (daughter of the lawful king Mahadassyn[1] whom Raja Singa had expelled and deposed from his throne), named Don Philipo,[2] and Don Jan[3] (both royal children of whom the first was a nephew, others say son, of the last king and thus a brother of Donna Catharina, and both educated in the Roman religion and baptized by the Portuguese), to quieten down the feelings that had arisen.

Not only did Don Andrea do this, he also decided to install Don Philippo as Emperor of Ceylon[4] and Don Jan[5] as his Commander as soon as he arrived there, and then to make a permanent treaty with those of Candi to attack Raja Singa together.

Raja Singa, suspecting this, marched courageously for Jaffanapatnam, not fearing those of Candi, as he had disarmed them earlier and forbidden them to keep any weapons in their houses. But they had, however, without his knowledge, provided themselves stealthily with new bows and arrows and hidden them in their houses. He intended to forestall the Portuguese and to be in Candi before them. But this was denied him and in the meanwhile the Portuguese arrived in Candi before him, crowned Don Philippo, appointed Don Jan at the same time as his Commander and made a firm treaty with those of Candi; but on an express condition that these two royal persons must swear on their faith in the presence of some persons that they would marry none other than Portuguese women and that they would be subject to and obey the King of Portugal, that those of Candi also should so promise and swear solemnly.

Don Jan, who had expected something more from the Portuguese according to their promises and had in no way

Don Phillip installed as Emperor and Don Jan as his Commander

And make a treaty against Raja Singa

Provided that Don Phillipo and Don Jan subject themselves to the Portuguese

Don Jan's hatred of Don Philippo and the Portuguese

[1] Karaliyaddē Bandāra of Kandy.　　[2] Dom Philip Yamasinha.

[3] Dom João, a twelve year old boy, not to be confused with the other and more famous Dom João (Konnapu Bandāra) who later became Vimala Dharma Sūrya, King of Kandy.

[4] Valentijn means King of Kandy.

[5] Dom João or Konnappu Bandāra who accompanied the expedition as commander of the native forces.

expected that Don Philippo would be crowned as Emperor, but on the contrary that he himself would be, was uncommonly hostile to Don Philippo on this, but even more inflamed against the Portuguese; but, as the time was still not ripe, he concealed his deathly hate against them, awaiting a better time to take revenge on both.

Raja Singa's attack rebuffed

In the meanwhile Candi, which Raja Singa had devastated very much, was fortified and brought into a better state for the new Emperor, Don Philippo. But Don Jan in the intervening time took counsel with a soothsayer as to how he could best get rid of Don Philippo and made him give him some poison.

Portuguese fort at Ganoor

At this time the Portuguese erected a stronghold at Ganoor,[1] to check Raja Singa further, also summoned more armed help from Manaar and brought the new Emperor Don Philippo first to his palace at Candi where he was received with much love by his subjects. Thereupon, most of the Portuguese departed from there, thinking that everything was now at peace and quiet, to deal with Raja Singa and deliver the Cingalese from all fear of him.

Their departure from Candi

Don Philippo poisoned by Don Jan who drives out the Portuguese

Don Jan, seeing, after the departure of most of the Portuguese from Candi, that it was now the right time for him, and not being able to wait till the poison taken in by Don Philippo could work, gave him another stronger dose, from which he died.[2]

After those of Candi had made him Emperor

Then he got very many people on his side, made them all kinds of great promises and made himself so loved by the Cingalese, that the Portuguese, seeing what he had in mind, immediately began to suspect him. They gave information to Manaar of the death of Don Philippo brought about by Don Jan, and of his further intentions, sending message upon message, with the request that Don Jan de Melo[3] should himself hasten to their relief or that otherwise Don Jan would cut off the pass and they would be put to the utmost danger.

Don Jan, occupying all the roads in the meanwhile and holding up all their messages, brought matters so far with the

[1] Gannōruva.

[2] From here the account follows very closely on Baldaeus Chaps. III–VIII (pp. 4–23). They have both used a common source.

[3] Captain João de Mello who had led the earlier expedition that put Don Philip on the throne.

Cingalese that those of Candi raised him to Emperor and gave him the new title of honour of Fimala Darma Soriya,[1] after his father, in the hope that he would avenge his death with so much more earnestness and would free them entirely from Raja Singa's tyranny which they had always feared.

As soon as he had become Emperor, not only did he openly deny the Portuguese who were in Ganoor his friendship, but he also ordered them, removing his mask entirely, to depart within 5 or 6 days from there, or he would put them to death, abusing them all as perjurers, traitors and deceivers, who sought only to make themselves masters of the land and the goods of the Cingalese, for which reason he did not desire that one of them should remain in his land.

Forcing them to give over Ganoor to him

The Portuguese not being in a position to oppose him, and seeing no relief, gave over this fort voluntarily and marched out with only their side-arms and without being able to take anything else with them.

The next day Don Jan de Melo arrived with his relief, but too late. Some Portuguese remained in Don Jan's service, letting themselves be used as traitors against their own people.

In the meanwhile, Raja Singa, King of Cita-Vaca, rapidly gathered together his forces and left with a large army and marched to Candi, with the intention of punishing both the inhabitants and also Don Jan as rebels.

Raja Singa

Don Jan, hearing this, and now deprived of the help of the Portuguese, was at first very agitated, the more so since he had learnt that Raja Singa's army had come into the Four Corlas. He speedily assembled together as many people as he could get together, marched against him where he was camped at Walane,[2] without fearing in any way the threats of Raja Singa, who let him know that he should take a lesson from his father or that he would otherwise tear him from limb to limb.[3] Whereupon Don Jan replied that if his father had been as careful as he was and had not trusted him, he would never have come to the misfortune of being mistreated by him in so treacherous a manner.

Don Jan driven to flight

Further, he let him know that however much he might be

---

[1] Vimala Dharma Sūrya.   [2] Balana.
[3] A reference to the fact that Rāja Sinha had killed his father.

on his guard, he would avenge his father's death, unless he gave himself over immediately. Over which message Raja Singa was so angry that he immediately gave orders to his commander to move.

He was much more upset when he heard that Don Jan, though much weaker than he, had had the courage to march up on him.

Then Don Jan himself appeared, now bearing two white umbrellas and a white shield above his head (all royal symbols), and attacked him with so much courage to the utmost surprise of Raja Singa, that even though Raja Singa himself was marching on him at the head of his body-guards, Don Jan drove him to flight after half an hour, in spite of his people being provided with very poor weapons (being nothing but arrows burned in the fire earlier which Don Jan had devised).

Trod out of spite on a bamboo and dies

Raja Singa Adassyn took this shameful defeat so much to heart, that he out of spite stamped his foot on a sharp bamboo which was on the way or standing on one side (others say on a thorn), and from this time on did not stand up, as he would not let his wound be treated, from which in a short time the fever came in and he died not long after, being 120 years old.[1]

How he regretted his cruelties

Before his death he regretted very much the various cruelties inflicted on those of Candi, but none so much as those he had later done to all the priests who were in his power.

He had then put to death his father, his uncle, his mother-in-law and his 3 legitimate brothers, he being only a bastard, and added many other cruelties which we briefly by-pass.

Having committed all this, he asked the priests of Daldowanse[2] whether there was hope of forgiveness of sins for such a man, to which the priests, without in any way fearing his anger, flatly said there was none.

He, who had not expected this in any way from them and had thought that they would have feared his power and rage

---

[1] Expanded version of what is briefly mentioned in Chapter VI above, p. 254. Baldaeus gives a similar account of his death p. 7.

[2] Dalada Māligawa, probably at Sītāvaca.

against his blood relations and given him a gentler reply, was so carried away by their indiscretion and disobedience (as he called it), that he put them all, except the high priest, into a house and burnt them there.[1]

Later he summoned some other priests of Paraneydeyo[2] to himself and asked them the same question. They, taking a warning from the death of the former priests, gave him a gentler reply, saying that for such a man there was no hope of forgiveness if he did not repent of his ways, but that if he had repentance for these committed atrocities, they could bring it about by their prayers for him that he should be suspended between heaven and earth and would be free of all temptation and torment of the devil.[3]

This put him at rest again in some way and he not only let them go alive but offered them much honour and great gifts which they would not accept. He begged of them not to think of the murder which he in his anger had committed on their colleagues, as they had forgiven him this also and then, not long after, he died.[4]

As soon as Don Jan heard that Raja Singa was dead, he assembled all his people to see by what means he could become master of the entire island. But Xavier Wandaar or (as others call him) Janiere Bandara,[5] secret writer of Raja Singa, threw himself against Don Jan, first stole all the treasures of Raja Singa and made a treaty with the Portuguese, since he saw that he could not carry on against Don Jan, delivering to them all the lands.

Janiere Bandara throws himself against Don Jan

---

[1] This cruel murder of the priests of Ganetenna by Rāja Sinha is recorded in another Sinhalese tradition. The reason appears to have been that these priests were involved in a conspiracy against him. P. E. Pieris, Ceylon. *The Portuguese Era* (Colombo, 1914), I, 400.

[2] Paranadeyō- literally, old gods, referring to the Brahmanic deities and tradition that had been grafted on to Buddhism.

[3] This refers to one of the Buddhist purgatories, derived from Hindu beliefs, a mild hell where those who are to be reborn on earth rest awhile awaiting their reincarnation.

[4] Similar version in Baldaeus pp. 7–8. *Rv*, being generally favourable to Rāja Sinha, does not record this incident.

[5] Jayavīra Bandāra who was Manamperi Mukavetti, a south Indian adventurer who took service under Māyādunnē and Rāja Sinha. See above Chap. VI, p. 245. He had defected to the Portuguese in 1593 and was given the title Jayavīra Bandāra (*Rv* pp. 80–3). Portuguese sources call him Janiere.

Makes a treaty with the Portuguese

The Portuguese, receiving hope by this of becoming masters of this island soon, informed the Viceroy immediately of Raja Singa's death and of the treaty made with Janiere, and requested a great relief force speedily to attack Don Jan and thus conquer the whole island for their King.

They get relief from Goa

Thereupon the Viceroy sent Don Pedro de Sousa[1] with 1250 white men, besides the mistices and blacks who were there.

Janiere's actions

Before his arrival, Janiere had already conquered all the lowlands through the assistance of those of Colombo and Gale, without Don Jan, who was in Walane and saw this with worried eyes, being able to prevent it, wherefore he began to have great fear, both of the army of the Portuguese and that of the Cingalese Princes who had risen up against him and had assembled already.

Don Pedro's wrong action stopped

Don Pedro, seeing in the meanwhile that the lowlands had been already conquered by another and that he thus, in his opinion, could not accomplish much more here, was on the point of returning. But he was stopped in this precipitate action by the other captains and, on being shown that Candi must be first conquered where the greatest treasures were to be taken, he was persuaded to remain behind.

Then he tried first to bring the lesser Princes under his control (which happened) and to subject gradually the Kings of the lowlands to himself, partly by friendly means and partly by force.

Both of whom march to Candi with a large army

While they were busy thus, Janiere brought a large army of 151086[2] men on foot, besides being provided with 75 war elephants, and 1000 without tusks, a great many coolies and porters and a great number of draught oxen.

Don Pedro's army consisted of 1474 white men, 1280 mistices, 1224 natives or Cingalese, 47 war elephants and 20000 oxen to carry baggage.[3]

---

[1] Pedro Lopez de Sousa. Author of a grand design to conquer the whole of Ceylon, make Dona Catharina the Queen and get her married to a Portuguese Fidalgo. Detailed account in Baldaeus, pp. 8–17 and Queyroz II, 476–96.

[2] A figure in agreement with Baldaeus (p. 9). Queyroz, more plausibly, has 15,000 (II, p. 481).

[3] All figures agree with Baldaeus, with the exception that Baldaeus has 19,900 oxen to Valentijn's 20,000 (p. 9).

With this army they marched together to Candi, but on the way they made 3 fortresses named Manikerowen,[1] Mapati[2] and Gannatari[3] for their security.

Don Jan, though only 30,000 or 40,000 men strong, brought together all his people against this strong force, which he courageously attacked twice. But the Portuguese attacking him for the third time with great fury, took the city of Walane, with a loss of 49 of theirs and 1500 others, but not without great opposition. Then they conquered the other lands easily, but could not become master of Dolleswagge.[4] *And drove Don Jan out of Walane and most other lands*

Don Jan had received such a beating and was so closely followed by the enemy, that he fled into the jungle with his Queen and had to subsist on wild herbs.

The Portuguese, having become masters of the land so far, desired that the Cingalese should take the oath of allegiance to the King of Portugal. But the people asked for Donna Catharina as Queen, who was at Manaar and was a daughter of the lawful Emperor Mahadassyn. *Don Pedro demands an oath of allegiance*

This proposal appeared to the Portuguese Commander Don Pedro de Souza as not a bad one, asking Janiere[5] (who was named King) his opinion on this, who also agreed, asserting that the Portuguese should not refuse him the marriage with this Princess, because of his demonstrated services, as it had been promised by them to him.[6] *The Cingalese request Donna Catharina as Queen*

Then a large body of troops was sent to fetch this future Queen from Manaar. When everything was ready for the expedition to Candi, and she was about to sit in the wonderfully decorated palanquin, the bamboo with which she was to be carried broke in pieces as they lifted it up.

This was a bad omen for the heathens and, though this Princess was a Christian, so much of this heathen superstitition remained with her that she would not set out. *She is taken regally*

It was explained to her with much reasoning that such a superstitition was unbecoming to a Christian, and that this

---

[1] Menikkadavara.   [2] Māpitigama.   [3] Ganetenna.
[4] Dolosbāgē.   [5] Jayavīra Bandāra.
[6] There is no other evidence that Jayavīra wanted to marry Catharina. D. W. Ferguson doubts this on the basis of Portuguese evidence. Couto, p. 402, n. 3.

breaking of the bamboo should not hinder the journey in the least, as they were fully responsible for her safe journey.[1]

On such earnest advice and after a new bamboo was inserted, she again sat in it and arrived in Candi 8 days after her departure.

Crowned

Don Pedro[2] went to meet her with all his chiefs and fidalgos, prostrated himself before her out of respect and wished her all conceivable blessings, for which she thanked him with a few words.

And everything brought to peace

The Kings, chiefs and all Cingalese nobles fell flat on their faces on the ground, honouring her in the Cingalese way, whereupon she sat in her palanquin from which she had alighted, and was accompanied to Candi by Don Pedro with a procession of chiefs, with the scattering of gold and silver money, and after three days' resting, was crowned very ceremoniously, the expenses of which it was said amounted to 19½ tons of gold,[3] which they received from Raja Singa's treasury.

After she was installed as Queen of the island with the general consent of the Cingalese and was raised to her father's throne, there was a general peace in the land, whereupon all the Kings and Princes returned to their lands.

Don Pedro sets a big price on Don Jan's life

Don Pedro de Sousa kept with him, apart from the Portuguese, 1700 to 1800 natives and mistices, and put a price of ten thousand pagodas[4] on Don Jan's life, who, not being afraid

He comes as a beggar to Candi and sets fires

of it, came now and then to Candi as a pauper, setting fire in the night to different parts of the city, without anyone being able to discover the culprit. For while they were busy putting out the fire on one side, he deftly started a new fire on another side.

The Portuguese behave in lawless manner against the natives

After everything was at peace regarding the natives, the character of the Portuguese again came to the fore, who,

---

[1] Both Valentijn and Baldaeus (pp. 9–10) mention this incident but not Queyroz. *Rv*, however, has a very different version. It says that the Portuguese took her to Kandy, thinking that in the event of her being married to King Vimala Dharma Sūrya (Dom Jõão) they would both join the Portuguese (p. 83). This seems to be an afterthought.

[2] Don Pedro Lopes de Sousa, Commander of the Portuguese expedition.

[3] 1,950,000 florins.

[4] A gold coin current in south India and Ceylon worth about 6 florins or 11 shillings.

beginning now to become lawless and wanton, did not hesi-
tate to hurt the susceptibilities of the natives in various places
and commit such crimes that they were forced to complain
over this to the Queen, who, still being very young, could
give them little comfort, upon which they decided to cut off
all supplies to the Portuguese.[1]

Don Pedro and King Janiere, observing this, took
measures against it, sending 2000 Cingalese and 1000 Portuguese to the principality of Oeva[2] and 2005 natives and 200
Portuguese to another quarter, named Laleluja,[3] to see if they
could obtain any rice.

They were reasonably well received everywhere, but imposed an unbearable burden on the natives everywhere,
robbing them not only of their goods, but also violating their
wives and daughters and killing some of those who opposed
them and setting fire to their villages. All of which embittered
the Cingalese so much that they agreed among themselves to
take revenge in time, if the Portuguese continued in this way.

In the meanwhile King Janiere Bandara sought from Don
Pedro the hand of Queen Donna Catharina in marriage, but
he refused this, claiming that he should write to his King
about it first and was not empowered to do this without his
permission.

Janiere seeks the Queen in marriage

Don Pedro first refuses this

Janiere, understanding very well this pretext, asked then
for his sister's daughter, but this was denied him also. Then
he became very angry with Don Pedro and asked him
haughtily if this was the reward for all his faithful services,
swearing that he would regret having denied him both these
requests.

He swears vengeance

Don Pedro, seeing the King so hot-tempered, made him
more irate by his reply, for he told him that he should not take
this refusal amiss, since he could not give a born Queen to a
commoner who had put himself forward as King.

Janiere, wounded by this deadly barb, but disguising his
feeling for the time, only said that he saw well what the

---

[1] This criticism of Portuguese behaviour shows that both Valentijn and
Baldaeus were using Sinhalese sources and not relying solely on Portuguese
accounts.
[2] Ūva.   [3] Haloluva.

Portuguese wanted and that they intended nothing but to put their feet on his neck, now that they had become masters of everything with his help. But this just would not turn out in all respects according to their thoughts. He did not dwell long on this matter but changed the subject to something else, as if he was not much concerned with it and as if he paid no more attention to it.

He conspires with Don Jan against the Portuguese

In the meanwhile he wrote a letter the same evening to Don Jan, who still hid in the jungle and watched for a suitable opportunity to avenge himself on the Portuguese, which would appear never better than now with this letter of Janiere.

He informed him in detail of what had occurred between him and Don Pedro, offered Don Jan the kingdom with the promise that he would play his part in this and asked only to be King of the lowlands under him.

Don Jan, who in no way had this in his thoughts, agreed completely however with what Janiere had proposed, and made a treaty with him in which they promised to get rid of the Portuguese completely and to kill all of them wherever they might be on this island.

Thereupon Don Jan made himself known everywhere to the people of Candi, incited those who were already embittered against the Portuguese even more and stirred them on further, seeing them cry out everywhere for revenge over their impositions, so that he could acquire the kingdom sooner, in the hope that they would themselves avenge this lawless people with much more certainty.

But everything is revealed

Then Janiere prepared himself gradually and also the people of Candi to execute this decision, taken with Don Jan, in its time. But they did not do this secretly, for it became known. Besides, the Portuguese intercepted various letters of Janiere to Don Jan, from which they discovered clearly what was being prepared for them and what reliance was to be placed on Janiere's honeyed words and on the hypocritical and, as it appeared, very patient Candians.

On which the Portuguese,

Don Pedro de Sousa, thus seeing this plot in its context, was very alarmed and saw clearly that if Janiere were refused the Queen in marriage any longer, he could be certain of nothing other than that he and his people would no longer be safe in this island.

After much deliberation over this in the great Portuguese council, the one for, the other against this marriage, and a third again for Don Jan's or Janiere's death, the majority felt that it was the safest for them speedily to put Janiere to death, and, in order to give this work a cover, he should be accused of intending to put to death both the Queen and Don Pedro, as proof of which one should forge some letters to be intercepted from which this would appear.

At a certain time then, when King Janiere came to talk with the Portuguese Commander Don Pedro, he asked this King to see his *cris*,[1] in order, as he claimed, to have one made in the same fashion decorated with precious stones.

Janiere, suspecting no evil, gave over his *cris* to Don Pedro who pretended to be struck with amazement over its beauty and requested the King in a pleasant way to be able to hold the inscribed end for some time.

He allowed Don Pedro this, but was immediately, as Don Pedro had given someone a sign, stabbed in the heart with a dagger and mercilessly murdered with many others in his company.

His guard, hearing this, cried out that there was danger and that their King was murdered. But this was to no purpose and, as what was done could not be undone, they all, except the King of Cotta, took immediately to flight.

The Portuguese informed the Queen speedily of Janiere's death. But they had no consolation from her, for, though young, she prophesied that this deed would lay the foundation for their fall and decline, as time also had taught, considering that the natives were set against the Portuguese much more than before and were embittered, seeing that if the King was treated thus, they could not expect better from them.[2]

Marginal notes: put Janiere to death

The Queen reflects on this evil

---

[1] *Keris* (Malay)—dagger.

[2] The murder of Jayavīra has been treated in detail by both Valentijn and Baldaeus. They attribute it to the ambition of Jayavīra and the oppressive behaviour of the Portuguese (Baldaeus, pp. 11–13). Baldaeus seems to have secured a good Sinhalese source and reproduces some plausible Sinhalese words. Queyroz's account concentrates on the 'treachery' of Jayavīra and considers this the sole cause of his assassination (Queyroz II, 479 ff). The *Rv* does

Don Jan incites
the Cingalese
against the
Portuguese

And attacks them
fiercely

Don Jan, in the meanwhile fishing in these troubled waters, and inciting the Cingalese in general against the Portuguese with more ground through this murder, assembled together a large army, marched to Candi and forced them to abandon the city as they feared for worse.

They fled from there to Fort Ganoor and sent a number of messages to Colombo to come to relieve them as otherwise they were lost. Many were taken captive by the Cingalese, to some of whom, out of revenge for the cruelties inflicted on their wives and daughters, they cut off the noses, ears and genitals and sent them back to let their companions know what they would expect from the Cingalese.[1]

The Portuguese, alarmed to the utmost over this, abandoned Ganoor and fled to Walane, burning everything behind them to escape more safely in the fire.

This happened in 1590 on a Sunday[2] and Don Jan, informed of their flight, besieged and attacked them with such fury that the Portuguese, surrounded and fighting very courageously in the utmost difficulties, were however entirely put to flight.

Don Pedro and
the Queen
captured

Besides very many of their people who were dead, there were many of importance taken captive, among whom was Don Pedro, with his son, the Queen Donna Catharina, and very many other captains of the Portuguese and the Cingalese who had been on the side of the Queen.

Don Pedro was badly wounded, from which he died on the third day after, commending his son[3] very dearly to Don Jan before his death, who promised to send him to Colombo immediately which he did, though many were surprised at this.

The Candians obtained much booty here of weapons and ammunition which was wonderfully useful to Don Jan.

Don Jan
conquers all
Portuguese forts

He followed up his victory and within a short time took all

not support the contention that Jayavīra was treacherous but attributes it to a ruse of Dom João (Vimala Dharma) who 'contrived to send a letter, purporting to come from Jayavira Bandara to King Vimaladharma Surya' (p. 84).

[1] This cruelty is also attested by *Rv* (p. 84).
[2] The actual date of this defeat was 6 October 1594, the battle of Danturē.
[3] Diogo de Sousa.

the fortresses of the Portuguese, except Colombo and Gale, under his control, some by force of weapons, though these cost lives, and some by agreement, which he handled very affably. Then all the surrounding Kings subjected themselves to him very humbly and came to meet him with many presents, prostrating themselves, honouring him with their hands above their heads in the most reverential manner and claiming to have done nothing against him except through compulsion of the Portuguese; on which he accepted them in his favour as he was assured that they had not served the Portuguese except by compulsion.

Accepts the native Kings in his favour

After Don Jan had made himself complete master of everything he decided to make the kingdom more secure and to take the Queen Donna Catharina, who was but 10 or 12 years old, in marriage.

And marries the Queen

He did this with much pomp and glory and the wedding lasted a hundred and ten days and cost 5005 pagodas,[1] along with the innumerable expenses specially undergone, the presents added up together amounted to nine hundred and sixty eight thousand seven hundred and fifty four pagodas (each then worth 6 Guilders).

Thereafter he fortified his land with three magnificent forts and built a new palace with firm bulwarks and many other beautiful buildings, where he made the Portuguese captives work daily as slaves, while their captured ensigns flew from the points and bulwarks as a sign of his victories.

What he did thereafter

After that Don Jan rested for some time, without being molested by the Portuguese whose wings were not a little clipped. But as soon as Goa received the news that Don Pedro had been so mercilessly beaten and had died of his wounds, the Viceroy decided to send Don Jeronimo de Oviedo (others call him d'Azevedo)[2] as Commander with a great army of Portuguese and other support troops.

Don Jeronimo D'Oviedo comes to Ceylon as Commander

He, having arrived here 3 or 4 years after Don Pedro's defeat,[3] initiated many crafty means to become again master of

---

[1] See p. 270 n. 4.
[2] Dom Jeronimo D'Azevedo who came to Ceylon as Captain-General in December 1594.
[3] In fact he arrived within two or three months of the defeat.

the island, to which purpose he spurred on many lords and princes of the lowlands, either by gifts or by force and out of fear, and again reconstructed many forts which had been demolished by Don Jan.

Is put to flight by Don Jan and wounded

Thereupon Don Jan assembled his people, marched against Don Jeronimo, who proceeded to Walane, having intended to conquer first Candi and then an impregnable fort in Trikenam[1] and to remain in Palugam.[2] But Don Jan saved him all this trouble, administered him an immediate blow which was severe, heavy and for long doubtful. But finally it fell to the disadvantage of the Portuguese, as Don Jan drove him to flight and followed him for 5 days to Colombo, where most of them however entered in good order, though Don Jeronimo had lost many of his captains and nobles and was badly wounded himself. And if the King of Cotta had not hidden him, he would certainly have fallen into Don Jan's hands.[3]

The Cingalese immediately repossessed the constructed works of the enemy and after that Don D'Oviedo did not accomplish much.

Correa defects to Don Jan. Is made Commander

About this time, Dominicus Correa,[4] who had been greatly wronged by the Portuguese, crossed over to Don Jan who made him a prince and Commander of an army, in place of a certain rebellious prince named Corke Bandara[5] whom he brought captive to Don Jan, whereupon he left for Gale. But

Defeated and murdered

he and his brother Simon Correa[6] were thoroughly beaten and Dominicus taken captive and was treacherously killed in Colombo, in spite of a pledged word, for which Don Jan

Don Jan's revenge and demand

threw many Portuguese before an elephant and cut off the noses, ears and genitals of others and sent them to Colombo, vigorously demanding his other prisoners or threatening to treat all the Portuguese thus.

[1] Trincomalee on the east coast.   [2] Palugama.

[3] This was Azevedo's expedition to Kandy of 1602–3 which had an initial success but ended in a disastrous defeat for the Portuguese. Queyroz describes it in detail (II, 588–601).

[4] Domingos Correa. Sinhalese called him Edirillerale after the title Edirille Bandāra which he took for himself. He was a Sinhalese nobleman, a Mudaliyār of the Seven Kōralēs, who rebelled against the Portuguese in November 1595. Queyroz describes this rebellion in detail, II, pp. 504–15.

[5] Unidentifiable. Mentioned by both Baldaeus and Valentijn.

[6] Simão Correa, brother of Domingos Correa.

The soldiers in Colombo, hearing this and seeing their comrades in so miserable a state, threatened to kill Don D'Oviedo, as the cause of all this, who was very anxious for his life. The soldiers, who rushed at him with their swords, would certainly have killed him while he loudly asked for pity from them, if the priests had not come between, with great danger to their own lives, and gave him thus the opportunity to hide himself.[1]

Shortly thereafter Simon Correa fled to Colombo, pretending to avenge his brother's death. He was well received by the Portuguese, was married there, became Governor of a large district,[2] and took up arms against Don Jan.

At this time there was a great Modeliaar in Candi named Manoel Dias,[3] who was formerly a servant of the Commander Don Pedro de Sousa and was now held in very good esteem by Don Jan.[4]

He, in order to deceive the Portuguese in masterly fashion, pretended to be running away from Don Jan, and came to Don Jeronimo D'Oviedo[5] on Easter day 1602, offering his help by various means to murder the Emperor Don Jan, as he claimed—a proposal which made him very welcome to the Portuguese, and the ground was prepared whereby everything he said was believed.

He was to go to Candi with 5 Portuguese (among whom were three captains Christiaan Jacob,[6] Alberto Primeiro, and Gaspar Pereyra),[7] pretending to be running away, so that he might murder the Emperor at an opportune moment, provided that Manoel would become Emperor of Candi after the execution of this deed.

He was given a large sum of money and he swore everything on a silver cross and marched to Walane and then to Colombo, as if he was again deserting.

Marginal notes:
- Portuguese soldiers want to kill Don D'Oviedo
- The Priests prevent this
- Simon Correa falls out with Don Jan
- Cunning deed of Manoel Dias

---

[1] D'Azevedo was notorious for his brutality and rudeness. Couto, p. 406.

[2] The Seven Kōralēs.   [3] Manuel Dias.

[4] Dias was a Portuguese soldier captured as a young boy during de Sousa's expedition to Kandy. He was brought up by Vimala Dharma and made a Mudaliyār. He rose to a high position in the Kandyan administration, featuring later in negotiations with the Dutch.

[5] D'Azevedo.   [6] Christiano Jacome, a Fleming.   [7] João Pereyra.

Having come to Candi, he informed the Emperor of everything, as also of the stationing of some Portuguese soldiers near Walane to overrun this fort after the Emperor's murder.

Don Jan himself left, to handle this matter correctly, with his best soldiers for Walane by night and hid himself there, while the dispatched Portuguese came there shortly after. They were received by Dias in a very friendly manner, but immediately they were brought before the Emperor at the point of the sharp Japanese knives which they had with them and were bound. Then those in the fort gave a signal shot, so that the other Portuguese would also approach there. But they did not come to the fort, as they were warned by a servant and had returned to Colombo very dejected, leaving behind all their weapons and baggage.[1]

This service brought Manoel Dias into so great an esteem with Don Jan that he made him his great Modeliaar[2] or chief nobleman and gave him many privileges, while he killed the Portuguese in a cruel manner and with the utmost torture, after a long imprisonment.

[1] This episode is also described by Queyroz, II, 569–74 and Baldaeus, p. 17.
[2] Mahāmudaliyār.

Eighth Chapter

[Arrival of the Dutch]

Spilbergen arrives in Ceylon 1602. First at Baticalo. He is very well received, and his further activities here. Writes, after the imprisonment of his people, an earnest letter to the King. Sends an envoy to the Emperor. He asks that Spilbergen should come to visit him. Guyon le Fort comes here. And Spilbergen goes to Candi. Guyon Le Fort's return. Spilbergen goes again to the Emperor and elsewhere. Vintana described. His account on the way, and in Candi. He offers the Emperor the friendship of the Prince of Orange. Whereupon he presents him all the pepper and cinnamon that is ready. Why there was no more. Candi described in respect of its temples. Information of Spilbergen to the Emperor on our religion. He presents him with a portrait of the Prince of Orange and describes the state of the country. Honour done to him further by the Emperor and his offer to build a castle. Gives Spilbergen letters to the States and the Prince of Orange. Makes him his ambassador. Then he leaves, presenting to the Emperor two musicians. Is looked for by Emmanuel Dias. Seizes a Portuguese galleon and presents it to the King. Receives some cinnamon and pepper. Guyon Le Fort goes to Candi with some people. His account there. Various other events. Spilbergen sails from Ceylon in September 1602.

Now it is time that we begin to speak of the Netherlanders: for it was about this time that the Dutch or rather the Zealanders[1] came to Ceylon for the first time.

[1] The voyage of Joris van Spilbergen was a venture of the province of Zealand. Before the formation of the United East India Company (V.O.C.) in March 1602, Holland and Zealand, the two main maritime provinces of the Netherlands, were sending fleets to the east organised on a provincial or municipal basis.

279

Spilbergen comes to Ceylon 1602

The courageous Admiral, Joris van Spilbergen,[1] sailed to the East Indies on 5 May 1601 from before the city of Camp-Vere[2] in the ships de Ram, het Schaap and 't Lam and arrived on 26 May 1602 near Cape Comorin with two of these ships, as the ship de Ram, of which Guyon Le Fort[3] was commander, had separated from him at the Cape of Good Hope on 24 December 1601.[4]

First to Baticalo

He first set his course to Point Gale, the south-westerly point of Ceylon, arriving on the 29th[5] before the first and second reefs. He found everywhere very good ground of about 20 fathoms and proceeded from there further to the river of Maticalo.[6] He first saw there an entrance, where there appeared to be a river, proceeded towards it and came there on the 30th; but he found that there was no river there but rather a large forest of coconut trees. Also he saw a village, where stood a pagoda, where he came to anchor and sent his boat to shore. Then those of the land came in a *prauw*[7] to speak to the people on the boat, who, on being asked where Matecalo was, gave the reply that it was still further north. They presented these natives with some knives which they had promised to give the people the previous day for bringing them to Maticalo, as they did on the 31st.

Then Spilbergen, the first Netherlander to appear in

---

[1] Famous Dutch navigator and explorer of the early 17th century. The second Netherlander to sail round the world. He was appointed Commander of this fleet to the East Indies dispatched by a Zealand Company of merchants under the patronage of Prince Maurice. He already had substantial seafaring experience behind him in North Sea waters. Subsequently he commanded other fleets to the east.

[2] Veere in Kamperland. Situated on the island of Walcheren in the province of Zealand.

[3] Vice-Admiral of the fleet. He had previously sailed to the east in Cornelis de Houtman's fleet in 1598.

[4] From this point on the account follows closely the published diary of Spilbergen's voyage: *t'Historiael Journal van tghene ghepasseert is van weghen dry Schepen . . . ghevaren wt Zeelandt van der Stadt Camp-Vere naer d'Oost-Indien onder t'beleyt van Ioris van Spilberghen, Generael* Anno 1601. This Journal has been published by the Linschoten Vereeniging as *De Reis van Spilbergen naar Ceylon, Atjeh en Bantam 1601–1604.* Uitgegeven door Dr. F. C. Wieder et al. ('s Gravenhage, 1933). [Subsequent citations are from this edition.]

[5] 29th May 1602.

[6] The present Batticaloa. Actually, a lagoon, with an island at the entrance.

[7] *Perahu* (Malay). A canoe or small vessel of hewn-out log.

Ceylon, sent a man overland to Baticalo[1] to speak to the King, Derma Jangadare,[2] while he came to the roads the same evening.

He found that there was an entrance here, where the natives built many ships. But he still saw no river, except one about 6 miles from there which was very dry and where there was hardly 5 or 6 feet of water.

The city Maticalo (or Baticalo) lay about 1 mile from this place where they lay at anchor.

On the 1st June some Cingalese came on board and brought an interpreter also who spoke Portuguese, who told him that there was enough pepper and cinnamon, but that the Modeliar[3] who administered the King's affairs there requested that the Admiral be pleased to come ashore to speak with him.

About this time there also returned the man whom he had sent to the King who also brought him news that he was very well received by this ruler.

He presented the Cingalese and their interpreter with some beautiful glasses and other pretty things, whereupon they went back to the shore.

On the 2nd, Spilbergen went with 3 or 4 men to the shore, where 5 elephants stood ready and showed him much honour by kneeling before him and in other ways and lifted up some Cingalese with their trunks and set them up on their bodies. These Ceylonese elephants were said to be the most intelligent of the entire Indies.[4]

Spilbergen, having come to the Modeliar, was received in a very friendly way and left again with the promise that he would go to visit the King of Baticalo on the next day.

He went there on the 3rd again to the shore and took not only various gifts to present to the King but also his musicians who knew how to play various musical instruments.

At this time there appeared a *prauw* with a nobleman on board, who came six to eight miles from the north, asking that they would come there with their ship. But those of Baticalo

---

[1] Valentijn is using both the forms Maticalo and Baticalo interchangeably.

[2] Probably a feudatory ruler or Vanniyār of Batticaloa. The name is unidentifiable. Spilbergen's ship journal has Dermuts Jangadare. *De Reis van Spilbergen* ... p. 39.

[3] *Mudaliyār* (Tam. and Sinh.).   [4] *De Reis van Spilbergen* ... p. 39.

were very much against this, as each was inclined to desire his own advantage from them and to hold them there.[1]

On the 4th, Admiral Spilbergen was advised that he should come to the king on the shore.

On the 5th Spilbergen again went ashore and came in the evening to the king, who was accompanied by 1000 armed men.[2]

After he had come back on board, he related with what honours he was received and led before the King by his most important courtiers.

The bodyguard of the King consisted of more than 600 men, who all stood with weapons drawn as he arrived, and the King welcomed the Admiral with a drawn sword. He gave the ruler very pretty presents and honoured him with a fine musical performance in which the King had great satisfaction. Then he had Spilbergen taken to the house of the Modeliar, where he and his people were very well received.

Further events there
The next day he was ordered to remain with his people in the house where they had placed him and in the evening he was brought before the King where he was strongly accused of being a Portuguese. But he made them understand, with much difficulty, that he was different, through which he obtained the freedom to go anywhere he pleased, while so far he had been held there as a Portuguese, and the next day he went back on board.

He remained in the evening on board, but sent some more presents through other people to the ruler to move him to friendship, to provide speedily his cargo which he was promised he should have in 15 days.

On the 6th Spilbergen went ashore again to visit the King, who now remained near the shore and from time to time, almost every hour, received more armed men. Spilbergen asked again for his cargo, whereupon the King replied that he hoped to have the greatest part in 5 days, requesting in the

---

[1] There were a number of feudatory rulers on the east coast of the island at this time owing some tenuous allegiance to the Sinhalese kings. This was probably another such Vanniyār chieftain north of Batticaloa.

[2] There is a quaint pictorial illustration of this meeting in *De Reis van Spilbergen...* p. 40.

meanwhile that the ship be unloaded and the goods brought ashore.

Now, many people and elephants, so it was said, had been sent to bring the cargo. But the Modeliar demanded furthermore that the ship should be brought to the shore, as they were accustomed to do with their vessels, a request which was not only unjust in itself but also for Spilbergen ground for suspicion of evil, being sure that they were out to deceive him and sought to win time to execute an attack against him, especially as he understood from some Moors[1] that there was little or no pepper and that it was not their practice to trade in it.[2]

Spilbergen, seeing that he was embroiled with these people, consented to everything that they asked, even to fetch the ship to the shore, only demanding some men and another pilot to help him carry this out.

They gave him one with some men, but permitted only Spilbergen to go back on board alone, holding all his other men against their will on land. They also demanded four other Portuguese in place of their people.

Spilbergen again said that he and his people were not Portuguese but Zealanders; however he left three of them on land, going with 11 Cingalese on board.

After they had come to the ship, he asked their help to shift some chests and packages in the hold. Eight of them entered the hold and he had the grating closed above their heads. Then he went with the interpreter and some other Cingalese to another place, showed them many costly goods and said to him: go now to the shore with these two men and tell the King that I will hold his 8 persons here till he sends my people back, and tell him also what expensive goods you have seen which are all for the King, but he must first deliver me pepper and cinnamon.

He wrote also a pleasant letter to the King, warning him to guard himself from the evil counsellors and inciters against him and his people, assuring him, if only the King would give

Writes, after holding his people captive

---

[1] Muslim traders who frequented the ports of the east coast.

[2] No pepper or cinnamon grew on the east coast and there was no trade in these articles in the ports of that region.

pepper and cinnamon, that he had abundant goods to pay him for these.

He also informed the King that the reason for holding the Cingalese on board was that it had been demanded of him so unreasonably to bring the ship and goods to the coast, without having shown him any cinnamon or pepper to pay for these.

It struck him as very strange that he and his people had been held as Portuguese against all evidence, from which it appeared as if they had intended to declare his ship and goods as forfeit on such a pretence as soon as it came to the shore.

Finally he said that if the King was inclined in future to deal with him uprightly, he was also on his side inclined to show the King all friendship. Then he sent them away with some presents, flying all his flags and pennants and firing all guns in honour of the King, though this honour alarmed the King very much.

On the same day the King sent a *prauw* with the interpreter who offered Spilbergen many refreshments in venison, chicken, butter and many kinds of fruits in the King's name, adding further that he might use his land everywhere to his satisfaction. Also he sent his three men back on board, requesting that he would not depart yet, as he would in a short time prepare his cargo and for his peace of mind would leave 3 or 4 Cingalese with him on board, apologizing profusely regarding the demand to bring the ship and goods to the shore, for he had no evil in his mind, requesting however that he would have patience as he was busy collecting pepper. Thereafter it appeared though that all this consisted of but good words without any consequence.

On the 7th he sent a sample of pepper which he praised very much and also some wax. But Spilbergen would not make an offer on so small a quantity.

On the 8th the King left the coast, as he saw that he could not reach his aim nor would his plan succeed.

On the 9th, having come to the shore for water, they understood from some people who spoke Portuguese that the King paid tribute to the Portuguese.[1]

[1] This seems highly doubtful. The Portuguese seized Trincomalee and fortified it in 1623 and Batticaloa in 1628. It is possible, however, that now and then

On the 10th, the King again promised him to deliver the cargo but it would be fetched from the Emperor of this island, that is from Don Jan (now called Fimala Darma Soeriya[1]), for which time and patience were necessary, offering to send some people with one of Spilbergen's commissioned agents there.

After Spilbergen had seen that there was an Emperor of Candi, he, being inclined to go there himself, demanded 5 Cingalese of the King of Baticalo on board as hostages whom he sent immediately. One of them was one of his Counsellors named Panneka,[2] besides which were 2 headmen or overseers of the military.

Then came again the elephants to the shore to fetch the Admiral, from where he was taken to the King of Baticalo who prepared his journey to Candi.

It was decided, as the way was very far and difficult as the King said, to send ahead an Agent with some presents. Then the Admiral came back on board on the 15th, awaiting what news the dispatched Agent should bring.

Sends an Agent to the Emperor

In the meanwhile, he exchanged daily many kinds of precious stones, such as Rubies, Topazes, Garnets, Spinel Rubies, Hyacinths, Sapphires (white and blue), Cat's eyes and Crystal, for one or another trinket, but these were themselves of little importance and of a small price, so that they had the heavier expenses on the presents which they continuously had to give the King of Maticalo.

The dispatched Agent returned on 3rd July with 2 ambassadors, and a letter from the Emperor to Spilbergen showed that this ruler had received and entertained him very well.

The names of the 2 ambassadors were Gonsalo Rodrigos and Melchior Rebecca[3] and the Emperor sent besides some

He asks that Spilbergen would come to visit him

Portuguese vessels called there and collected some tribute from the rulers of this area.

[1] Vimala Dharma Sūrya. This name is supplied by Valentijn. Spilbergen's Journal says 'great king of Kandy'.

[2] Pannikan, a south Indian name. Also the name of an elephant trainer. Possibly one of the officers, considering the number of elephants there.

[3] Probably two Portuguese who had taken up service with the king of Kandy.

presents of gold rings and of a large arrow, called Segonsios,[1] and held by him of great value and as a great sign of his favour. He also promised all friendship to the Admiral, promised him as much cargo as he could possibly order and requested that he would come to visit him in Candi.

Guyon Le Fort comes here

On this same evening Guyon Le Fort appeared here with the ship de Ram, separated on the 24th December near the Cape of Good Hope from the Admiral and not seen since, over which there was great rejoicing among them.

And Spilbergen goes to Candi

It was decided together that Spilbergen should undertake the journey to Candi, especially as he had the order of the Directors and of his Highness the Prince of Orange for this, with the offer of his friendship to the Emperor, to be a friend of his friends and an enemy of his enemies.

He left on the 6th, taking with him various presents and 10 of his men as companions on the journey, among whom were some who could play on one or another musical instrument very well.

In the meanwhile the ship de Ram came to anchor at the place where the Admiral was and fired some shots in honour of the Emperor's ambassadors. But as a certain piece of cannon was overloaded, it blew up, by which the constable was wounded and he died.

Guyon Le Fort's return

Guyon Le Fort, Vice-Admiral, had been with his ship in the Island of Madagascar and in St. Augustine Bay, where he had lost a mast and bowsprit in a storm, by which he was put in danger of life, ship and goods.

While the Admiral went to the Emperor, they exchanged some more precious stones and sent the boat to some other places to look for a better road, but found nothing better than where they lay.

Spilbergen again travels to the Emperor and elsewhere

On the 28th, Spilbergen came back on board from the Emperor of Candi, leaving Captain Jongerheld behind two days earlier, as he had become sick on the way and could not follow the train because of fatigue. He had left behind 3 elephants and 6 men for his service to help him on the way as much as possible, and he also arrived there on the last of the month.

[1] Unidentifiable. The word is as it appears in Spilbergen's Journal (p. 43).

After Spilbergen had left for the highlands on the 6th July he had first come to the King of Baticalo who had received him elegantly, presented him with some gold rings and provided him with elephants, men and palanquins to carry him, his goods and some of his people who could not walk.

This escort went with him up to the Emperor's land, being everywhere received very remarkably without any expense to them.

As soon as he had come into the Emperor's country a Modeliar came to meet him with drums and music, or with gong and *tifa*,[1] who brought him to a village where he was also well received and lodged in an apartment with a bedstead draped with white cloth (an honour which is done to all the important ambassadors).

The Admiral presented some gifts to the Viceroy[2] and his Modeliar, who asked in a friendly manner that Spilbergen should come to visit him on his return journey, promising him to offer all friendship at every time.

Then he proceeded on his journey and was brought to a village two miles from there where a certain queen, daughter of the abovenamed Viceroy who was now one of the wives of the Emperor of Candi, lived. Don Jan had gifted her this village but she had now left for the city of Vintana (or Bintene)[3] where Spilbergen arrived the following day.

As he approached the place, 6 Modeliars came to meet him, accompanied by many people, pipes, drums, and other musical instruments, who led him to the city and to the place where he would reside, where he also found his bedstead draped with linen.

He remained there two nights and found the abovenamed queen, who longed to see him, offering him, on his return journey, everything that there was in her land at his service. This city lies on the River of Trinkemale, also called Mawieleganga,[4] where very beautiful boats were made.

Besides a beautiful pagoda, previously described by us,[5] Vintana described

[1] An Ambonese word meaning a tall drum.
[2] Probably the Dissāva of that province.
[3] The city of Alutnuvara on the banks of the Mahāveli Ganga. Spilbergen's Journal has a sketch of this city (p. 44).
[4] Mahāveli Ganga.   [5] See above Chap. II, p. 153.

he saw here many more similar buildings and a monastery where he found monks clothed in yellow who went along the street with large umbrellas and with slaves.[1] They were bald on their heads, shaved without a topknot, and had paternosters in the hand and were continuously muttering to themselves. They were held in great esteem and were free of all work and impositions.[2]

The monastery, where they were, is like the monasteries of Roman Catholics, provided with many galleries, passages and many chapels, beautifully gilded and decorated with images of many men and women who, in their opinion, had lived holy lives.[3]

These engraved images were dressed up in gilded silver cloth and had lamps and wax candles burning before them day and night, standing on altars where there were large candlesticks which were held by engraved naked children. Every hour these monks entered these chapels to read their prayers and breviary. He also saw them celebrating their festival and going on procession along the street, where the high priest sat on an elephant, clothed with silver and gold, holding a gold staff with both hands above his head. Before him went many other monks in order, with much playing of horns, trumpets, cymbals and the clanging of bells, all of which gave a good harmony. Many lamps and torches were carried and also many men, women and maidens followed.[4]

The most beautiful maidens are accustomed to perform many wonderful and artistic dances, before the exit and entry of the procession, the upper half of the body being naked and their arms, hands, and ears decorated, half with gold and precious stones, and the lower part with beautiful embroidered cloth. These people were seen daily in the chapels of the pagodas prostrate and threw themselves down on the ground with both hands folded above their heads.[5]

[1] Each monk had a novitiate to attend to his wants.

[2] Valentijn is referring to the *pirivena* or monastery where monks and novitiates lived and spent their time in prayer and study.

[3] The images of Buddha and *Bodhisattvas*.

[4] A festival in a Buddhist temple called the *perahera*. Valentijn's description follows very close on Spilbergen's Journal (pp. 45–6).

[5] The attitude of worship assumed by the Buddhist laity.

Leaving Vintana, he came into the village of the Emperor's son which was still a day's journey from Candi. Here the Emperor sent his own palanquin (which was very expensive and prepared with painted cloth), with some elephants, after which Spilbergen sent back the other palanquins, people, etc. to Vintana.

His account on the way and of Candi

Every hour the King sent him people with provisions, fruits and wine from a grape vine which he himself had planted in Candi and which was as good as any wine grown in Portugal.

Coming to a river near the city of Candi, Spilbergen had to stay for about an hour attended by many Modeliars. Then the Emperor sent the highest Modeliar Emanuel Dias[1] of whom we have spoken much earlier, and many Portuguese who all had their ears cut off and served the King.

He was received in a very stately pavilion by them and led to Candi with 1000 armed soldiers and 8 standards flying, taken from the Portuguese, while a very loud sound of various musical instruments came out from everywhere.

So Spilbergen was taken past the Emperor's palace to his residence and there again many salvoes were fired to welcome him. He had Captain Jongerheld of Vlissingen with him and had three trumpeters go ahead, of whom one carried the colours or the Prince's flag,[2] after whom followed four other servants holding a silk Spanish or Portuguese flag, which flag he presented to the Emperor, in return for which the ruler presented him with another flag which he had taken from the Portuguese.

After he had arrived in his residence, he found everything most magnificent, prepared not in the Cingalese but in Portuguese style.[3] Also, Emanuel Dias remained there with him, with other Portuguese, till the Emperor sent him 3 horses in the afternoon very well equipped with saddles, so that he could come to visit him.

He then went to the King with some beautiful presents and

---

[1] Manuel Dias, Mahāmudaliyār of the King. See above Chap. VII, pp. 277–8.
[2] That is, of Prince Maurice of Orange.
[3] This reflects the Portuguese upbringing of the King of Kandy.

was very well received, while he spread out his gifts on a cloth and showed them to his heirs and princes.[1]

Don Jan or Fimala Darma Soeria[2] was clothed in white, showing outwardly in his countenance all that one could wish in a magnificent Prince. He walked a few times with Spilbergen back and forth in a large hall and gave him permission to return to his resthouse after they had spoken over some matters of importance, to rest there a little, as he had asserted that he was very tired, and then to speak further with him in the morning.

Before Spilbergen left he got his musicians to play vigorously which gave great satisfaction to the King.

He offers the Emperor the friendship of the Prince of Orange

The next day the ruler again sent him his horses to come to him. He went there again and was received very pleasantly and royally as earlier.

The Emperor spoke with him on the trade in cinnamon and pepper but demanded so much for it that Spilbergen thought it best to change the subject.

Then he is presented with all the pepper and cinnamon there

When Spilbergen wished to take leave, the Emperor asked what he would give for it,[3] to which the Admiral replied that he had not come for pepper or cinnamon but only to convey the compliments of his Highness the Prince of Orange and to offer his friendship and help where his Majesty might have need of it against his enemies, the Portuguese.

Why there was no more

The Emperor, hearing this, related it to all his chiefs and courtiers who accepted it with much satisfaction. Also the ruler took the Admiral in his arms, raised him off the ground out of affection and said: All the pepper and cinnamon, which I have ready, is presented to you. But there was in all no more than 3000 Flemish pounds. He excused himself however over this, saying that his arrival here had been so sudden and that formerly he had not engaged in any trade in cinnamon or pepper, but on the contrary had laid waste all the cinnamon and expressly forbidden the peeling of this, in order to do all harm to the Portuguese, his enemies, from which he could understand very easily the reason why he was not better provided.

[1] A picture of this audience is found in *Reis van Spilbergen* ... p. 46.
[2] Vimala Dharma Sūrya.   [3] That is, for the cinnamon and pepper.

It was not advisable for Spilbergen to remain there longer, as the eastern monsoon would begin to blow soon and the place where they lay anchored had a low coast.

In the meanwhile the Emperor showed him, as he spoke daily with the Admiral on all sorts of matters, armour, *morions*[1] and other weapons which he had captured from the Portuguese. He also showed him his valuable pagodas, with more then 4000 or 5000 wonderful carved images, some as high as masts, of which the beautiful towers were made of very expensive stones, artfully carved, with wonderful gilded arches, so that the adornment of these pagodas, in the beauty of the building, almost exceeded the Roman Catholic churches.

Candi described in respect of its pagodas

After Spilbergen had seen all this and had returned to the ruler, the Emperor asked him what he thought of his pagodas, whereupon he said that he cared more for living men than for dead images.

Also the ruler asked him if we did not also decorate our churches with the images of Mary, Paul, Peter and all other saints, as the Portuguese did, and if we also believed in Christ.[2] Spilbergen replied that we were Christians but not Roman Catholics nor like the Portuguese; that we had churches but with bare walls, without any images, and that we served God, the creator of heaven and earth, in our hearts.

Information of Spilbergen to the Emperor on our religion

The Emperor asked again if our God could not die, whereon it was shown to him that no mortal man could be like God, in order thus to show the ruler that all his images in his pagodas were in vain as they represented but deceased men, exhorting him not to have faith in them but in God; in this manner having spoken with the Emperor over various matters of religion, he took his farewell from the ruler.

The next day the ruler entertained him with a lavish feast, bringing him into a great hall covered with carpets and furnished with Spanish chairs and a table, where everything appeared to be in the Christian style. He also honoured him

---

[1] Of Spanish origin; visorless, high-crested helmets worn by footsoldiers in the 17th century.

[2] The king had been baptized a Catholic but he had now apostatized and was very knowledgeable in the Christian faith.

with a very elegant musical performance, conducted according to the style of the land.

Is presented with a picture of the Prince of Orange and the state of our lands described

Then Spilbergen presented the Emperor with the portrait of the Prince of Orange, on horseback in full armour, as he was painted at the Battle of Flanders on 2nd July 1600,[1] in which he was very greatly satisfied, the more as the Admiral narrated to him the details of this battle and the further events of our wars with the King of Spain.

Honour done to him by the Emperor and his offer to build a castle

In the 5 days that Spilbergen was with the Emperor, this war-loving and courageous ruler could not be satiated in learning from the Admiral of everything concerning our land. He also had the portrait of the Prince of Orange hung in the chamber where he regaled himself daily and took Spilbergen to the apartment of the Queen where she sat with their children, the Prince and the Princess all clothed in Christian style, an honour which, according to the custom of this land, was uncommonly great.[2]

He also offered the States General and his Princely Highness that they could build a castle in his land, where they pleased, adding with very strong emphasis: See, I, my Queen, Prince and Princess will carry the stones, lime and other building material on our shoulders, if the States General and the Prince desire to build a fort in my land.

Gives Spilbergen letter to States General and Prince

Makes him his Ambassador

Thereafter he left, presenting two musicians to the Emperor

He gave Spilbergen various letters for the States General and the Prince of Orange, making the Admiral his ambassador, to deal with their High Mightinesses and with his Highness in his name.

Spilbergen was also presented with choice gifts and various great titles of honour by the ruler who asked to be presented with two of his musicians, Hans Rempel and Erasmus Martsberger, who could play very well on all kinds of instruments, which he enjoyed so much that he later began to play them himself.

Also the Prince and Princess made Martsberger thereafter their secretary. He was very worthy and suitable for that, as he was reasonably well educated and had knowledge of various languages.

[1] Valentijn corrects the mistake in the Spilbergen Journal which has 1602.

[2] Inviting a visitor to the female apartments of the palace was a sign of intimacy and respect towards the visitor.

Also the Emperor, Prince and Princess began to learn Dutch, saying that Candi has now become Flanders.

Finally, Spilbergen took his leave of the ruler, who showed him also considerable honour on his return journey, giving him very large arrows called Sergonsios,[1] as proof of his trust, truth and eternal friendship, besides a large number of people, elephants and what further he needed for his journey.

He also presented him with a gilded umbrella with 4 or 5 slaves to serve him.

Thus came the courageous naval hero back on board, after he had travelled everywhere in Ceylon, freely, openly and inexpensively, wherever it pleased him.

The ruler sent him Emanuel Dias with some other Modeliars and 120 soldiers on the 5th August to look after the ships and to look for a better anchoring place with Spilbergen on his return. They again spoke over various matters which they agreed and swore between them. *Is accompanied by Emanuel Dias*

He showed the Modeliar also all honour, brought him on board with two well armed boats and treated him in a stately manner.

On the 8th, a Portuguese galliot with 46 men was captured by Spilbergen's barge which had only 14 men. The captain of the galliot, which was laden with some old arecanuts and some pepper and cinnamon, was named Antonio de Costa Montero. *Captures a Portuguese galliot which he presents to the Prince*

After Modeliar Dias had observed this, he now believed firmly that the Portuguese were our enemies. He immediately informed the Emperor of this, to whom Spilbergen presented this galliot with its cargo which gave great joy in Candi.

On the 9th, Emmanuel Dias departed with Gujon Le Fort and Count Filips[2] to see that the promised cinnamon would follow soon, which was sent shortly thereafter. It consisted of 60 canisters[3] cinnamon, 16 bales of pepper and 3 bales of *curcuma*[4] or Indian saffron. *Receives some pepper and cinnamon*

Gujon Le Fort, coming to Candi, was also very well received and was given some gold rings as a gift, as also was *Gujon Le Fort goes with some others to Candi*

---

[1] See p. 286 n. 1. Previously spelt as *Segonsios*.
[2] Spilbergen's Journal has Hertogh Philips.
[3] Boxes or baskets. In vogue in Ceylon from Portuguese 'canastra'.
[4] *Kumkum* (Hindi)—saffron.

Count Filips. They found some more cinnamon there but as this was not yet ready, they could not wait as the monsoon was setting in.

His action there

On the 11th, our people seized another *sampan*[1] with old arecanut, which Spilbergen presented to the King of Baticalo.

He had formerly given permission to the Admiral to attack the Portuguese, but now made much fuss that it was seized thus within his land. But he did this more for a good appearance to hoodwink the others than from a good heart for the Portuguese.

Various other happenings

On the 12th, they seized another with 20 men and on these 3 seized vessels were about 100 men, of whom some remained with us and some were sent to Candi. Also in the meanwhile, Antonio de Costa Montero ran away, through our bad surveillance for which a certain Claas Cales and others were punished.

On the 23rd, Houtepen, Constable in the ship de Ram, was shot to death by the careless loading of a piece of cannon, this being the second misfortune that befell the Constable of this ship by such a manner of handling.

On the 1st September 1602, Guyon Le Fort came back on board with his company from Candi, bringing with him letters and presents from the Emperor to the Admiral.

Spilbergen sails from Ceylon in September 1602

After Spilbergen had prepared everything for his journey and had seen by land the whole market in Baticalo, whether the Cingalese who were there to the number of 200, required anything from him or his people, he set sail on the 2nd from Baticalo, setting fire to the two captured *sampans* with arecanut, as they had no time to sell them.

Before his departure 2 of his men deserted, a Constable and a carpenter, and on the 3rd he sailed from there to Atchin.

[1] *Malay*—boat.

Ninth Chapter

[Portuguese, Dutch and Kandy]

A.D. 1602. Three Zeeland ships come to Baticalo. How Sebald de Weerd is received there. His second expedition to Baticalo, 1603, where he is murdered. What provocation was given for this. And how he was the cause of his own death. What followed then. Death of Emperor Don Jan, 1604. Further described. The Prince of Oeva puts himself up as Emperor. Cenuwieraat opposes this. Donna Catharina sets herself on the throne. The Portuguese try in vain to make a treaty with her. New attempts on the crown by the two abovenamed Princes. Death of the Prince of Oeva. What the Queen does then. Her marriage with Cenuwieraat, 1604. He tries to make a treaty with the Dutch. The twelve year truce, 1609. Letters of their High Mightinesses to this ruler. Brought by Marcellus de Boschhouwer to the Emperor in Candi, 1612. He enters into a treaty with us. Brief content of this agreement. Boschhouder asks to take leave. But the Emperor will not let him depart. He makes him Prince of Mingone, etc. Design of the Portuguese with a large army. Conquers Mingone. The death of the heir-apparent Mahastane, 1612. The King of Panama beheaded. The fort of Walane conquered by the Emperor. The Prince of Mingone does great damage to the Portuguese. He and the Prince of Oeva are appointed guardians of the children of the Empress. Death of the Queen. Sickness of the Emperor who chooses the two abovenamed Princes as guardians. Death of Gaal Heneraad. Military attack. Don Munno de Ferieram. Whose army is beaten. The Prince of Mingone persuades the Emperor to set aside the marriage with his step-daughter.

In 1602 the Zealand ships Vlissingen, der Goes (or de Gans) and Ziriczee came to anchor in Baticalo on the last day of the year, which they left in the beginning of 1603 for Atchin and anchored there on 17th January.[1]

They left the ship Ziriczee in Ceylon to wait for their Commissioner Sebald de Weerd who arrived in Ceylon on the 28th November, went on land with 15 men to Baticalo and was very well received with 6 elephants, and from there was led 36 to 40 miles inland to the Emperor of Candi, with 6 men.[2]

Shortly thereafter, Sebald de Weerd also appeared with the ship Zirczee[3] at Atchin from Ceylon, where he was shown much honour and friendship by the Emperor.

There he found letters of Admiral Spilbergen with Martsberger,[4] now appointed royal secretary, which were useful since they gave him a complete and accurate account of how he had to conduct himself at that court.

By further information from Holland it appeared that Sebald de Weerd was made Vice-Admiral under Warwyk on the Zealand ships by the Gentlemen Seventeen,[5] which was very necessary, as there was almost no order to be kept because each of the members of the commission and the marines wished to have a great say.

His second
journey to
Baticalo 1603
where he was
murdered on the
orders of the
Emperor

Then Sebald de Weerd left from Atchin for Ceylon on 3rd April 1603, a part of the way in the company of Admiral Spilbergen, from whom he took leave outside the islands of Poeloway[6] and Gommerspoel[7] and proceeded on his journey to Baticalo.

He had previously made a treaty with the Emperor but had

---

[1] This was part of a combined fleet of 14 ships under the command of Admiral Wybrand van Warwijck of which Sebald de Weert was Vice-Admiral. Three of the ships named here were from Zealand and left from there in March 1602.

[2] Presumably Sebald de Weert had arrived there before the rest of the fleet and proceeded to Kandy in November 1602.

[3] Previously spelt 'Ziriczee' by Valentijn.

[4] One of the two musicians from Spilbergen's embassy who had been left behind at Kandy at the King's request.

[5] The Directors of the newly formed United East India Company (V.O.C.).

[6] Pulo Weh, one of an archipelago of islands off the north headland of Sumatra.

[7] Known to the Portuguese and Dutch as Gamisspola and Gomerspoel, this was the island Klappa in the same archipelago.

gone to Atchin for more ships and now came here with them to give help to the ruler against the Portuguese.[1]

On the way he had taken 4 Portuguese vessels, of which the Modeliar Emanuel Dias, having received information, demanded some from de Weerd for his Emperor. But he excused himself as he had promised to set them free, without thinking about it.

What provocation was given for this

The Emperor who had first come to Vintana or Bintene and was to have remained there, came to Baticalo, after he received information of the seizing of the Portuguese vessels; but he was very angry with the Vice-Admiral because these Portuguese were again set free, especially as he understood from his ambassador, who had also come from Atchin,[2] that Sebald de Weerd had at all times shown himself to be a friend of the Portuguese and no friend of the Emperor, for he had treated him generally very contemptuously, the Portuguese being entertained with dignity at the head of the table at mealtime and he, the Emperor's ambassador, was placed at the lower end of the table, from which it appeared that he had no other intention than to deceive the Emperor and make himself master of his land by cunning. All these actions went entirely against the treaty made with the Emperor.

This ambassador also warned the Emperor to be on his guard, if Sebald de Weerd and the Dutch should invite him and his most important nobles to their ships with no other design than to become master of their person and the land.[3]

The Emperor, having heard this account of his ambassador with much relief, took counsel with his courtiers and chiefs whether, in view of this account's being very probable, and as the treaty had also been broken by de Weerd with the

[1] This could not have been a treaty but was probably a promise by the king to allow the Dutch to build a fort in Ceylon in return for assistance against the Portuguese. Valentijn is very brief about de Weert's first visit to Kandy. Details of his reception are to be found in his letter to his Admiral at Bantam in P. E. Pieris, *Some Documents Relating to the Rise of the Dutch Power in Ceylon 1602–1670* (London, 1929), pp. 27–33.

[2] A Kandyan official had accompanied de Weert when he had visited Batticaloa first and returned to the Commander of the fleet at Achin.

[3] Baldaeus, whose version of these events is substantially similar, goes further in asserting that the Kandyan ambassador was poisoning the mind of the king against the Dutch. Baldaeus, pp. 19–21.

liberation of the Portuguese, he should be trusted any more in future. They were of the opinion that they should try to entice Vice-Admiral de Weerd to Gale to attack the Portuguese there and that they should then see how he conducted himself there.

Then Sebald de Weerd appeared before the Emperor and requested, after he was received cautiously, that he would have the goodness to come to visit him on board and inspect his ships from within.

He had 300 armed men with him, but on the request of the ruler, he sent them to the ships, keeping only a few with him.

The Emperor, finding the account of his ambassador true in this matter, and concerned for any treachery, refused this, saying that his chiefs would not permit it.

De Weerd, seeing that his Majesty was not inclined to come on board, asked again that he should come to the coast to see the ships at a distance, saying that he had created a tent, covered with cloth for this purpose for his Majesty.

The Emperor again refused this, convinced now that there was something afoot, because he had requested this twice, though in different ways; all the more because his ambassador again cautioned him not a little against de Weerd and still warned him that he should be on his guard.[1]

How he was the cause of his own death

De Weerd, very disturbed over both these refusals of the Emperor, and being of a hasty and quick-tempered nature, said bluntly that if his Majesty was not pleased to come to him to the shore or to the ships he would not help him to fight against the Portuguese.

Then the Emperor became very angry, but controlling himself, said that de Weerd should sail to Gale in his ships,[2] according to his promise, as he himself had to leave for Candi

[1] The king, Vimala Dharma Sūrya, was deeply suspicious of all Europeans after his experiences with the Portuguese, and was still unsure of the distinction between the Dutch and the Portuguese. The liberation of Portuguese ships after their capture alarmed him greatly because this was not how he dealt with prisoners-of-war. Also, according to one report, he was hoping to exchange Portuguese prisoners for his son who was in Portuguese hands.

[2] Vimala Dharma was very anxious to capture one of the western ports and had set his heart on taking Galle.

and his Queen who would otherwise be alone, for his half brother Cenuwieraat Adassyn[1] had marched to the frontier.

Sebald de Weerd, who had drunk too much, said not only very inconsiderately but also very impertinently that the Queen would not lack men and he did not desire to leave for Gale before his Majesty visited the ships and had first done him this honour.

The first part of his reply was language that he could have used of nothing but a loose woman or a whore in a brothel, but which he used of the Queen; the second part strengthened the ruler now completely in his suspicion and in what his ambassador had assured him, namely that de Weerd had in his mind nothing other than to take him prisoner.

What followed then

The Emperor, also very impetuous, and aroused by his intemperate and haughty reply, rose up immediately and said in a seething anger to his men: *Mara isto can,* that is, bind this dog.[2]

Then he was attacked by 4 nobles who tried to bind him, but as de Weerd felt for his pistol and called for help from his people whom the Emperor had detained on shore, he was seized from behind by a lock of hair by a courtier and his head chopped off with a broad sword, and he fell dead on the ground.

None of the chiefs dared to tell this to the Emperor, as he had not given orders to kill him, but only to bind him; finally the Prince of Oeva emboldened himself to give him this information.

He was specially alarmed by this news, asking: why did you not bind him, as I ordered you? The Prince of Oeva said that this was impossible, as he had drawn his pistol and had gone

---

[1] Senerat Adasyn.

[2] Spilbergen's Journal, the main source for this account, gives the king's order as *matta esto can.* Both Valentijn's Portuguese and his translation are faulty. [*Matar* (Portuguese)—to kill; *Atar* (Portuguese)—to bind]. Furthermore, it is highly improbable that the king gave his Sinhalese attendants an order in Portuguese. Baldaeus reports that the king said in Sinhalese: *Banda lapa mebal* (p. 20). This seems more plausible and corresponds to what an order of this nature would have been in colloquial Sinhalese: *Bendapalla mẽ balla* (Bind this dog). It appears that, in the description of this incident, Baldaeus had access to a superior source not available to Valentijn.

beyond the state where others could master him except in this way.

Then the Emperor, seeing that it was not to be undone, now that he was dead, said that his following should also be put to death, so that they might receive a similar reward to their master's.

This was immediately executed, without anyone of those who came on land with de Weerd surviving, except a youth from Vlissingen named Isaak Plevier whom the Emperor kept in his service and a few who swam away.[1]

After this murder the Emperor went to Candi, and wrote a short Portuguese letter with these contents to the Captain of the ship: Que bebem vinho, naon he bon. Deos ha faze justicia. Se quisieres pas, pas, se quires guerra, guerra. That is: He who drinks wine is not good. God has done justice. If you desire peace, peace, and if you desire war, war.

After this incident Don Jan did not live long, but contracted a sickness which caused him an indescribable and insufferable burning of the body, so that he had continuously to lie in water that was so cold that one could not keep it in the mouth, without his feeling any coolness or comfort by it.

He attributed this often to the innocent Dutch whom he, on the occasion of this murder, had had killed, though they had not harmed him. But Sebald de Weerd, he said, had his reward and deserved it well.

The Emperor
Don Jan's death

During this sickness he had no peace and was not in a condition to concern himself with any state affairs, as his pain increased so strongly from time to time that he died of it in 1604.[2]

He left behind a son (as we have said before) named Mahastane Adassyn and 2 daughters Soeria Mahadassyn,[3] that is well beloved sun, and the other Cathan or Hantanne and (as

[1] Valentijn's account of this episode shows a balanced judgement and fairness to both sides, unlike some other Dutch accounts. See for example, Pieter Van Dam, Beschrijvinge van de Oost-Indische Companie ('s Gravenhage, 1932), Tweede Deel, 2, p. 247.

[2] The account of Vimala Dharma Sūrya's death is similar to that of Baldaeus (p. 21).

[3] Sūrya Mahadasyn.

others say) Hatane Adasyn[1] or well beloved peace, all of whom he begat on Donna Catharina.

At the end of this year, our Admiral Steven van der Hagen[2] came before Colombo, where he was fired on by the Portuguese.

The Emperor was of tall stature, medium of limbs, black in colour, very dignified in bearing and language, particularly crafty and clever, versed in all the tricks of the Portuguese at the time he was brought up in Goa, and a great and courageous war hero, who had performed wonders against the Portuguese.

He is described further

Just as he had accumulated much treasure in his lifetime, he had also, as an intelligent ruler with good judgement, carried out everywhere the improvement and strengthening of his land and built fortresses in many places where it was necessary and public rest-houses for the service of his subjects.

He was a Prince who had an admirable, exact order in everything and among his subjects, being respected and feared by everyone, by the strong justice that he administered without respect of persons, so that one heard of little disorder and few misdeeds in his kingdom, to which also has helped, not a little, his uncommon generosity towards all who deserved it.

As a great statesman, he had a good understanding with all Indian rulers whom he needed; but the Portuguese whom he knew thoroughly and whose aim he had grasped from the outset (as being not otherwise than to have tried to get him and his land under their control) he hated with an irreconcilable hatred, for which reason he also could not get away from them.

He was a Cingalese by birth but later was instructed in the fundamentals of the Roman religion which had given him a good understanding of the bad principles of the Cingalese religion; but while on the one side the deceitful dealing of the Portuguese with him, breaking their promises to him in the choice of Don Philippo[3] as Emperor, had instilled in him a

---

[1] Hantāna Adasyn.
[2] A prominent Admiral of the V.O.C.'s early fleets. He was responsible for the foundation of Dutch power in Amboina of which he was the first Dutch Governor.
[3] Don Philip Yamasinha.

great detestation of their religion, being convinced that he could not support it on good grounds as his friends had been treated so treacherously, and on the other side his political acumen demanded that, if he became Emperor and wished to remain at peace, he must necessarily declare himself for the religion of the heathen as practised by the Cingalese, however much he was convinced of the ludicrousness of these practices, so he, choosing the better of two evils, went over to the religion of the Cingalese, though only in appearance. But in time he moved on the right track so far that he finally sneered at all religions and later allowed each one of them their complete freedom.[1]

The Prince of Oeva puts himself forward as Emperor

After he was burnt to ashes with great pomp under a royal tower according to the custom of the land, there arose no small division among the chiefs over the crown, for the Prince of Oeva,[2] the most powerful among the Cingalese princes, put himself forward immediately as Emperor, which

Cenuwieraat opposes it

Cenuwieraat Adassyn,[3] the Emperor's half brother, with all his chiefs opposed, claiming that he was guarding the kingdom for his brother's son and protecting and supporting the right of this young Prince, though time will show that he only had in view his own advancement to the throne.

Donna Catharina sets herself on the throne

Donna Catharina, seeing in the meanwhile this stirring and activity for the throne, deeming herself next in line as mother and guardian of the young Emperor, set herself proudly on the throne, had some of the critics and ringleaders put to death and by this means brought everything speedily again to peace.

The Portuguese try, in vain, to make a treaty with her

The Portuguese, thinking that they had profited by the death of Don Jan, gave information of this immediately to the Viceroy of Goa, by whom steps were immediately taken to make a treaty with this Queen, to obtain a greater footing on that island and thus in time to become master of it. But the Queen rejected the request of the Viceroy.

---

[1] Valentijn's judgement of Vimala Dharma Sūrya is similar to Baldaeus' (p. 21) but is more graphic in capturing the personality of this fabulous Sinhalese monarch. He has also borrowed from Spilbergen's Journal where there is a garbled version of Sinhalese history from the time of Rāja Sinha I (pp. 54–65).

[2] Kuruvita Rāla. [3] Senerat.

As the Prince of Oeva and Cenuwieraat were making very many efforts for the crown, the Queen summoned the chiefs to the court, who all appeared there, except the two Princes. Thereupon they were declared traitors by public decrees of the great State Council and their goods confiscated. But Cenuwieraat later replied to this very well and, by the intercession of one or other nobleman, discovered a means to obtain forgiveness, whereupon they both appeared in court as formerly, but with a large following and without trusting each other in any way. New attempts of the two abovenamed Princes on the throne

The Prince of Oeva had intended to murder Cenuwieraat at the adjournment of the State Council, to marry the Queen and thus set himself on the throne. But Cenuwieraat was aware of this plan, armed himself secretly against it, was always on his guard, pretending as if he were a great friend of this Prince and had much esteem for him, while in the meantime he had planned with most of the nobles of the administration at the court to let no opportunity slip to get rid of him. Death of Prince of Oeva

They both came again to court, to take leave of the Queen. But while they were showing pleasantries to each other at the outer gate of the palace and each requested the other to enter first, finally the Prince of Oeva stepped forward as the older in years. Immediately he was stabbed by Cenuwieraat with the words: Lie there you false traitor. He then departed from the city with his people, while the followers of the Prince of Oeva fled crying treachery, treachery, by which cry many thought that the Queen was murdered, which had the effect of many others being killed. But as soon as she showed herself to the people, the uproar was stilled.

It was thought fit that this murder, committed by Cenuwieraad so boldly, right in front of the palace gate ought to be publicly punished. But the Queen, fearing for even greater uproar thereby, knew how to bring this affair under control, so that this unfortunate event was passed over asserting that the Prince of Oeva was put to death on her order. By this everything was again brought to peace, but the Queen hated this affair in her heart, intending to take revenge in time. What the Queen did

She changed her mind however when Cenuwieraat convinced her that he had done all this for her good.[1]

Her marriage to Cenuwieraat

Hereby not only did he make his peace with her, but ingratiated himself so deeply in the favour of the Queen that he obtained her as his consort. He was crowned in 1604 and on his installation named Camapati Mahadassyn.[2]

He tries to make a treaty with the Dutch

After this time he sought the friendship of the Dutch and entered into a treaty with them against the Portuguese. But some years later, namely in 1609, the Gentlemen of the States General of the United Netherlands concluded a truce for 12 years with the Archduke Albert and the Infanta of Spain, Isabella Clara Eugenia, with the declaration that it should include the Indies as well.[3]

Then the Gentlemen Seventeen tried, during this truce, to establish their power in the Indies by entering into treaties with Indian rulers, for which they also sought the approval of their High Mightinesses.[4]

Letters to the King

These letters were sent to the Indies by the yacht de Hazewind, of which Wemmer van Berchem[5] was head, and were confirmed by the letter of the same content dispatched there under the first Governor General of the Indies, Mr. Pieter Both,[6] and he was instructed by the States General to make firm treaties with all kings and princes to protect themselves thereby in the future against the treacherous attacks of the Portuguese.

Their Highnesses also sent letters, dated 15th September 1609, to Cenuwieraat, Emperor of Ceylon, to which was added one of 5th October of the same year by Prince Maurits of Nassau (both of which one can read in Baldaeus).[7]

[1] This whole account has been taken over directly from Baldaeus (pp. 22–3) who seems to have used a contemporary first-hand record of the events of that time in Kandy.

[2] Sāmapati—Lord of the Earth.

[3] Portugal was under the Spanish crown and the truce between the United Provinces of the Netherlands and Spain meant that the Dutch could not attack Portuguese possessions in the east.

[4] The States General.

[5] Came out east in 1610, and was the V.O.C.'s Director on the Coromandel Coast.

[6] Appointed first Governor General of the East Indies in 1609 with the power to enter into treaties and make war or peace with Asian rulers.

[7] Baldaeus, pp. 23–4. Similar letters were sent by Prince Maurice to a number of Asian rulers with whom the V.O.C. had dealings.

They contained nothing other than evidence of friendship, with the assurance that this truce was entered into with the Portuguese on no other conditions than what the King was given to understand and on our side we were inclined to continue to deal in all friendship with his Majesty, for which the necessary orders were given to the Governor General of the Indies.

These letters were sent with the *Onderkoopman* Marcellus de Boschhouwer,[1] by the ship Zwarte Leeuw that had come out under the command of Mr. Both from the Choromandel coast to Ceylon, where, having landed, he proceeded speedily on his journey to Candi and appeared on the 8th March 1612 before the Emperor Cenuwieraat who received him with much respect and entered into a treaty with us on the 11th May[2] of the same year.[3]

Brought to the Emperor in Candi 1612 by Marcellus de Boschhouwer

He enters into a treaty with us

The important provisions of this treaty which contained 33 articles consisted of the following:[4]

They should faithfully help each other against all enemies and especially against the Portuguese.

Brief contents

The Emperor permitted us to build a fortress at Cotiar, promised to provide the material necessary for it, and to put up a stone storehouse for our merchandise.

All matters of war to be decided together for which purpose there should always reside two Dutchmen in his army.

The ruler binds himself to deliver to the shore without cost all the goods which we buy from him and also to carry inland the goods bought by him from us. He should also help protect our goods, when our ships remain there, and demand no tolls at all from us.

We should be free to trade with the Cingalese freely everywhere in his land and he should deliver to us yearly as

[1] Came out east with Pieter Both in 1609 as *Onderkoopman* and was appointed to Coromandel. Later Valentijn spells his name Boschhouder.

[2] Actual date of the treaty was 11th March 1612. Both Valentijn and Baldaeus are wrong here.

[3] Details of this audience given by the king to Boschhouwer are in the latter's letter to the Directors, 28th March 1612. See Pieris, *Some Documents ...*, p. 38.

[4] These 33 articles are given in detail in Baldaeus pp. 26–7. The treaty actually contained 45 Articles.

L

much of the best cinnamon as was possible at a fixed price to be paid with money or goods and no Europeans except us, or without the knowledge of Their Highnesses,[1] are to be permitted to come into his land or to trade there, but all Indian people may do so.

Also his Majesty agreed to provide wood for the building of our ships at the coast and to release all prisoners. All former enmities on both sides are to be forgotten and all offenders are to be delivered, each to his own side, to be punished by the heads of his own people.

The Emperor should not sell pearls to any other than to us, as we are obliged to deliver all jewels, ornaments and rarities to his Majesty for payment.

The Emperor alone should mint money but this should not be above the price fixed by his Majesty and us together. Those minting false coins should be put to death and every three years the mint should be changed either to Candi or to our area.

After the expiry of 3 years the range of tolls should be fixed and then each should take half of it, as also of what is seized in Ceylon.

Beschhouder
seeks his leave

After the conclusion of this treaty, Boschhouder sought permission to leave for the coast with the elephants which he had received from his Majesty for the comptoir of Tegenapatnam[2] to give Mr. Joan van Wezik, the Superintendent at Paleacatte,[3] an account of what he had accomplished with the Emperor.

But the
Emperor will
not let him go

But the Emperor would not decide to let him go, especially as it was expressly stipulated in that agreement that his Majesty must consult with some Netherlanders on all matters.

Thus he had to remain, otherwise the Emperor would not hold himself to the treaty nor place any trust in his letters.

He makes him
Prince of
Mingone etc.

In the meanwhile he was provided by the King with many

[1] The Directors of the V.O.C.

[2] Devanampatnam on the Coromandel coast at the mouth of the Pennar River where the Dutch had a trading factory.

[3] Joan van Wezik was largely responsible for establishing Dutch trade in Coromandel. He was *Opperkoopman* at Masulipatnam in 1609 and in 1610 established the Company's residence at Paleacatte (or Pulicat). He held the position of Director of Coromandel from 1610–1612.

titles of honour and installed as Prince of Mingone,[1] Kukule Corle, Anaragiepura,[2] Miwitigal,[3] Lord of the order of the Golden Sun, President of the High Military Council, second in the secret Council and Admiral, and so esteemed by the Emperor that he did not even do the slightest thing without his advice or permission.

On the 20th June 1712,[4] the Portuguese marched to Cotiar with 1000 white troops and 3000 blacks, under Simon Correa,[5] by a secret road shown to them by a Candian, where they murdered the Netherlanders from Boschhouder's embassy remaining there, returning hastily to the Seven Corlas so that they might not be seized by the Emperor's people.

Attack of the Portuguese on his people

As soon as the Emperor heard this, he sent 5000 men under the Colonel Marasinga Atsile[6] and 2 prominent nobles to Cotiar,[7] who followed on the heels of the fleeing murderers, caught up with them near the Seven Corlas and cut down 23 of them, besides 600 natives, set fire to many villages and took much booty to Candi.

Revenged by the Emperor

The Emperor, being inclined to assemble a powerful army, called together all the states of the kingdom, and it was decided in this assembly to raise 50000 footmen, and with half of it under the Prince of Oeva to attack the city of Gale, and with the other under the Prince of Mingone to attack the fort of Walane and do the Portuguese all possible damage there first and then in Colombo which they should besiege with the entire army.

He attacks the Portuguese with a large army

In the meanwhile, the Portuguese also mobilised a large army and marched to Jaffanapatnam but were severely beaten there. However on their return to Colombo they seized the principality of Mingone[8] which was delivered to them without any resistance by the Modeliaar and effected a great

They conquer Mingone

---

[1] The title he was given was Mīgamuva Mahā Rāla. Mīgamuwa was the Sinhalese name of Nigombo.

[2] Anurādhapura.   [3] Nivitigala.   [4] Error for 1612.

[5] Simao Correa, brother of Domingo Correa; see above Chap. VII, p. 276.

[6] Amarasinha Achchila.

[7] Baldaeus gives their names as Mayndappo [Naidappu] and Vire Segre [Virasekara], p. 26.

[8] Probably the Seven Kōralēs.

slaughter there. The Modeliaar informed the Prince of this by letter, promising that he would expel the Portuguese from there as soon as he could, which the Prince encouraged him to do in all earnestness, declaring that he had been appalled by this event.

On the 22nd August 1612, the heir Mahestane,[1] son of Don Jan and Catharina, died. He was ill for only 6 days, not without suspicion of having been poisoned by his stepfather Cenuwieraad, formerly the champion of his right of succession, so that his oldest son Comara Singa Hastana[2] might follow him on the throne.[3]

The death of the heir Mahestane 1612

The death of this Prince alarmed all the Princes of the kingdom and the Queen to such an extent that on the day of his cremation, the day after his death, she fell senseless and had to be taken to another apartment. He was cremated with much pomp and honour with the carrying on of a great mourning and wailing at the grave.

The musicians and pipers went ahead and the body was set on a height of 7 stone steps, in the middle of which was a large hole filled with sandal and *agel*[4] wood and with many delightful and sweet smelling spices.

Also the bier was covered all round with similar wood and spices up to the height of a man. Then three pots of cinnamon oil and one pot of butter were poured into this hole which then remained burning for half an hour.

Above the hole was a royal canopy, built like a tower 7 feet high, which was decorated with costly gold cloth and was for the convenience of the highest lords while the funeral was going on.

The Prince of Mingone set fire to the wood when a great wailing was heard. After everything had been done and the Prince was cremated, the Emperor returned with all the chiefs to the palace to comfort the Queen.[5]

[1] Mahāstāna.

[2] Kumārasinha Astāna.

[3] *Rv* confirms this murder but says it happened by drowning and does not implicate Senarat. *Rv.* p. 86.

[4] *Ahil* (Tam.)—aloe wood.

[5] A very similar account in Baldaeus, p. 31. Baldaeus quotes from what appears to be a contemporary account but does not reveal the source.

In September it was said that the King of Panua[1] and of Cotiar[2] had joined the Portuguese. They were both summoned to the court and the latter sent his nephew on 4th October,[3] who absolved him completely; but the King of Panua did not appear.

He was then attacked by the Prince of Mingonne on 1st January 1613 with an army of 35000 men, forced to come to court, found guilty of high treason against the Emperor's life and beheaded; his relatives were thrown before elephants and their lands declared forfeit.[4]

Shortly thereafter the Emperor seized the fort of Walane from the Portuguese but he lost this again by the avariciousness for plunder of his people, which cost 125 men their lives.

The fort of Walane taken

In the month of March 1613, the Prince of Mingonne attacked the Portuguese with a fleet between Cape Comorin and Ceylon, seized some of their ships and returned with a booty of 6 tons of gold, after burning 2 ships, 3 brigantines and 20 barks which he had taken.[5]

The Prince of Mingonne does damage to the Portuguese

The Queen who was pregnant and in grief over the loss of her son summoned the Princes of Mingonne and Oeva in July after she became ill, spoke to them under oath on different matters of weight and made them guardians of her children. She had, since the death of the heir-apparent, taken almost no food in her body.

He and the Prince of Oeva appointed guardians of her children

As she felt that her death also was approaching fast, she summoned her 5 children, the heir-apparent Comara Singa Hastana,[6] Janier Hastana[7] and Lamait or Mahastane,[8] as also the Princesses Mahadassyn and Hantanna Adassyn, to herself, kissing them one by one, called the abovenamed two Princes[9] and delivered to them (as guardians) her children very touchingly.

Death of the Queen

[1] Pānama. Probably the Dissāva of Pānama.
[2] Kottiyār. Probably the Vanniyār of Kottiyār and Trincomalee.
[3] 1612.
[4] Baldaeus gives more details of this revolt by the Dissāva of Pānama, pp. 33–4.
[5] Baldaeus gives details of the Sinhalese fleet. It appears that it was largely manned by Ceylonese and commanded by Boschhouwer, the Prince of Mīgamuva, p. 35.
[6] Kumārasinha Astāna.   [7] Vijayapāla Astāna.   [8] Mahāstāna.
[9] That is, the Princes of Ūva and Mīgamuva.

Sickness of the Emperor

Thereafter, seeing the Emperor, she said, 'You are the cause of my death', which went deeply to his heart and finally caused a sickness, for he loved the Queen deeply.

She died, after much regret for her sins, and especially for her occasional practice of idolatory, on the 20th July 1613, 35 years old and was cremated on the 21st with great pomp at the same place where the funeral of her son was celebrated.

The abovenamed chosen as guardians

After the death of the Queen, the Emperor's sickness increased gradually, whereupon he called his State Council together and asked for two guardians among them to administer the kingdom on the minority of the heir-apparent, on which the Council chose the Princes of Mingonne and Oeva.

At first they refused this. But later the royal heir himself choosing them, they accepted it and the Council enacted a very precise act on 19th August by which all the kingdoms were handed over to these two Princes. To this the Emperor added an earnest recommendation to the Princes and Princesses, his children, to obey their guardians, as long as they should have authority over them.[1]

Gaal Heneraad's death

In the meanwhile the Prince of Mingonne marched with an army against the Portuguese, defeated on the way some people of the Modeliaar Gaal Heneraad,[2] on which occasion a letter was discovered from which it appeared that he (Gaal) had intended to murder the Princes and Princesses, along with their two guardians. It was also discovered that he had conspired with the Portuguese against the Emperor.

He was then summoned to court as if for discussions regarding matters of weight concerning the kingdom. He came on the 20th September to Candi, was received pleasantly first by the Prince of Mingonne. But later he was convicted of high treason and mercilessly put to death with many of his relatives (as Baldaeus has related in detail).[3]

Military events

In 1614 a battle took place between the Emperor (who had completely recovered) and the rebels. There were on both

[1] Baldaeus, pp. 38–9. The imperial edict of 19th August 1613 is quoted by Baldaeus in full.

[2] Senerat Mudaliyār, Dissāva of Harispattuva.

[3] Baldaeus, pp. 40–41, who gives a lot of detail on this entire episode.

sides about 4000 men. But the rebels fled to the Portuguese who, shortly thereafter, fell on the Emperor's army, slew about 500 men, and the Princes of Mingonne and Oeva were wounded, the former in his right leg and the other in his arm.

On the 14th March, in place of Don Jeronimo D'Oviedo[1] who was now the Viceroy of Goa, came the brother of the Count of Fere, Don Munno de Feriera,[2] to Colombo with 150 white soldiers and some mistices with orders to make peace with the Emperor as best he could.

Don Munno de Feriera here

On 3rd June he sent an ambassador, Don Francisco de Meneses, to Candi, but the Emperor broke up the whole negotiations on various strange preconditions and demands, fearing treachery on their side, and he departed with the business unfulfilled.[3]

Then the Portuguese marched up with an army of 25000 men to Candi but were beaten on 6th August by an army of the Emperor of 29000 men near Walane. They lost 214 men and the Emperor 700 men.

On the 29th, the Emperor proposed to marry his step-daughter but the Prince of Mingonne opposed it strongly, in spite of the Emperor's saying that he already had taken her to bed.

All the other chiefs permitted the King this marriage. But the Prince of Mingonne hurt his feelings to such an extent that the tears ran down his cheeks and he was completely persuaded to put this matter out of his thoughts.[4]

On 5th October, the Candians put to death 900 Portuguese who had been sent to Walane, as they were going to look for some provisions.

[1] Dom Jeronimo D'Azevedo.
[2] Dom Nuno Alvares Pereira, brother of Conde de Feyra. He became Captain-General in 1616.
[3] A letter with conditions of peace from the Captain General to the King dated 22nd February 1614 is reproduced in Baldaeus, pp. 42–3.
[4] Baldaeus, p. 43.

Tenth Chapter[1]

[Portuguese, Dutch and Kandy (contd.)]

Boschhouwer leaves for Bantam, 1615, and he is sent to the Fatherland. Comes into dispute with the Directors. Goes to Indies again in the service of the Danes. Dies on the journey. As a result Danish affairs here vanish into thin air. Gule Gedde informs the Emperor of his arrival. He declares that he gave no orders for this. Further dealings of Gule Gedde with the widow and their outcome. Gule Gedde's departure from Ceylon. The Portuguese build a fort in the Bay of Trikoenemale. What the Emperor does against this. Constantyn de Saa is severely defeated by the Cingalese. Cenuwieraat's death, 1632. His kingdom divided among his three sons. But Raja Singa sets himself up as Emperor on the throne. Seizes Oeva. The Portuguese make a deceitful peace with him. Raja Singa calls the Dutch to his help, 1636. Writes a letter to the Governor of Choromandel. Their Excellencies send some ships to Ceylon. A certain Captain, having come to Ceylon sends people to the Emperor to attack Baticalo. The Portuguese plunder Candi, defeated by Raja Singa. There they are all killed except 70. The Emperor sends Ambassadors to Westerwolt, whom the Portuguese put to flight. Coster in Ceylon. Westerwolt in Ceylon, conquers Baticalo. And installs Coster as head. Makes a treaty with the Emperor, 1638. Short contents of this. Some goods delivered by the Emperor in reduction of debt. He sends some ambassadors to Batavia. Colombo besieged by the Emperor. Trikoenmale taken by Mr. Caan in 1639. Nigumbo conquered by Mr. Lucassoon in 1640, but retaken by the Portuguese. Gale conquered in 1640 by Mr. Coster. He is the first Chief of Gale but shortly thereafter is mercilessly murdered. Succeeded by Mr.

[1] This chapter is very closely based on Baldaeus, Chap. 17, pp. 44–6, including 8 unnumbered pages after p. 44.

Thyssen as Superintendent. Two ambassadors from Goa seek truce. This follows.

Marcellus Boschhouder,[1] now having become such a great Prince, received permission from the Emperor in 1615, on his own request, to leave from Ceylon to Mazulipatnam[2] to request the promised help against the Portuguese, with full power to make such treaties with all princes and men as he judged necessary for the welfare of his Majesty.

To this end he took various letters and Commissions from the Emperor from which it appeared that he appointed him his ambassador and authorised agent with promise to uphold everything he did.

Then he departed on 9th May 1615, came to Mazulipatnam on 2nd June, where he found Mr. Hans de Haze[3] as head, who, because of the lack of ships, took him to Bantam to speak with the Governor General of the Indies, Gerard Reynst,[4] over the help requested against the Portuguese. But Mr. Reynst having died and matters concerning the war in the Moluccas and the expedition to Banda being not in such a state that any troop assistance could be sent against the Portuguese,[5] it was thought best to send Boschhouder, on his own request, to the Fatherland to present his Commission in person to the States General, the Prince of Orange and the Directors.

Boschhouder, having arrived in Holland, fell out with the Directors, as he was swollen with pride by illusion of his greatness and princely status, claiming that he should receive more honour than they, which finally carried him so far that, forgetting his service, honour and oath, he betook himself to

Boschhouwer leaves, 1615

Goes to the Fatherland

---

[1] See Chapter 9, p. 305 n. 1. Valentijn spells his name variously as Boschhouwer and Boschhouder.

[2] On the Coromandel coast where the Dutch had a trading factory.

[3] Was appointed inspector of the Company's factories in Coromandel in 1613 and was the chief at Masulipatnam and then at Paleacatte till 1619, with the title of Director of Coromandel.

[4] Succeeded Pieter Both as Governor General in 1614 and continued till 1615.

[5] The Dutch were at this time embroiled in a war in the Banda Islands. They had sent a fleet in 1615 to attack Pulo Wai, one of the spice islands, to prevent the islanders from trading with the English. This brought them into conflict with the English fleet that was protecting the islanders against the Dutch.

Denmark where he landed on 26th June 1617 and made a treaty which was confirmed by King Christian IV in Copenhagen on 30th March 1618.

He left that same year with a ship and a pursuit-ship again for the Indies, taking his wife (who called herself the Princess of Mingonne) and some families, along with a good number of soldiers, again to Ceylon.[1] But he happened to die on the journey, and the enlisted men mostly deserted as a result on the Choromandel coast, and some time thereafter his son also died and the entire venture came to nothing.

Whereby the Danish matters vanished in thin air

Boschhouder had received a ship and a pursuit-ship from King Christian on behalf of the Emperor, to which the then established East India Company in Copenhagen added 5 more ships which sailed out of the Sond under the command of a Danish nobleman, Gule Gedde.

They first arrived, after wandering for 22 months and after the loss of Boschhouder and many people, first in Ceylon in 1620, where some ships landed in the Bay of Baticalo and some in that of Cotiari,[2] but afterwards they all came together.

Gule Gedde informs the Emperor of his arrival

Gule Gedde informed the Emperor of his arrival and of the number of ships as well as of the death of the Prince of Mingonne.

Also he informed his Majesty that all the ships were built on his account, requesting to know further his Majesty's orders on this.

He declared that he gave no order on this

But the ruler, seeing with sorrow the death of this Prince, and seeing with much dismay the account of these ships put so high to his charge, declared never to have given the order for this and that he would have nothing to do with it as he could not or would not approve the actions of Boschhouder.

Further dealings of Gule Gedde

The Danes, not a little startled at this, had very great disputes with the Emperor's officials, but received nothing but good words in payment for their ships and other expenses. Therefore Gule Gedde put all this loss on the dead Boschhouder's account, whose body with that of his son, was still

---

[1] This was the Danish expedition to Ceylon under Ove Giedde. A translation of Giedde's Diary is found in *Journal of the Royal Asiatic Society. Ceylon Branch*, 37, 11 (1946), 49–118.

[2] Kottiyār.

lying on board, and declared all his goods forfeit to the King of Denmark.

Then he buried the father very poorly, but the son of the Prince of Mingonne very nobly because King Christian IV had stood at his baptism.

He left the widow of this Prince very few goods, though she, by connivance, had still something hidden, after which they proceeded to Candi with 3 chambermaids and an old servant maid, while he reported everything to his King.

The widow and her fortune

She remained there for about 7 years and was later taken to Tranquebar,[1] on the request of the Danish Admiral, Roeland Carpe,[2] with her entourage, with the permission of the Emperor.

After the women were sent to Candi, Gule Gedde departed from the Bay of Cotiar to Baticalo where he awaited the Emperor's decision.

Gule Gedde's departure from Ceylon

In the meanwhile, the men who still remained in the Bay of Trikoenmale absconded from a ship which was wrecked on a rock while sailing out, from where they landed in small vessels on the Choromandel coast and entered the service of the Dutch or the Portuguese.

Gule Gedde, having heard this with much regret and fearing worse to follow, left again for Denmark, to the great joy of the Portuguese, who built a fort from the stones and the remains of the most famous pagoda in Ceylon on the northwest point of the bay of Trikoenmale, to keep out all others from there, having begun this in 1622 and proceeding with it vigorously in stealth, though the Emperor, with whom they were now at peace, knew of it for some time.[3]

The Portuguese build a fort

They added another fort to this in Baticalo, after which the Emperor sent an army against them,[4] as they now had 7 forts on all parts of the island where one must enter and thus sought to cut off the Emperor from all trade with foreign people,

What the Emperor does against this

[1] The Danes had established a factory at Tranquebar on the Coromandel coast in 1620.

[2] Roelant Crape, Admiral of the Danish fleet that secured the cession of Tranquebar from the Nāyak of Tanjore.

[3] The Portuguese fortified Trincomalee in 1623.

[4] With the Portuguese fortification of Trincomalee and Batticaloa, the King broke the truce and war was resumed in 1630.

against which the Emperor along with some Cingalese whom he had in Colombo planned very secretly and skilfully, trying to bring the Governor of the Portuguese in Ceylon, Constantyn de Saa,[1] out into the open field.

Shortly thereafter, in August 1630, when Don Michiel de Noronha, Conde de Linhares, was Viceroy of Goa,[2] Constantyn de Saa came with a large army into the field against the Prince of Oeva, Comara Singa Hastana, eldest son of the Emperor Cenuwieraat (or Zenerat Adassyn),[3] who assisted loyally by his brothers, the Princes Visiapalla[4] and Mahastana (or Raja Singa), had brought together a powerful army.

Was defeated
severely by the
Cingalese

Constantyn de Saa plundered Oeva, not finding the army which he expected to find there, but intending to return, he obtained information that all the Cingalese wished to abandon him, as they indeed did on the march.

Then the 3 Princes attacked him, cut off his rear and slew very many of his people.

The courageous de Saa would himself have escaped, but a heavy rain fell, and his men being rendered unable as a result to use their weapons, the Cingalese fell on them with bow and arrows and, with their spears, drove the Portuguese to flight and one of the Cingalese deserters cut off de Saa's head and brought it on a drum to Raja Singa, as he was sitting in the river to wash himself.[5]

Death of
Cenuwieraat
1632

His kingdom
divided among
3 sons

But Raja Singa
sets himself as
Emperor on the
throne

Not long after, namely in 1632, the Emperor Cenuwieraat died. He had divided the kingdom among his three sons and given Oeva to the Prince Comara Singa Hastana, Matule to the Prince Visiapalla and Candi to the youngest Mahastane, later named Raja Singa Raja.

After the Emperor's death the youngest of his sons set himself as Emperor on the throne of his father with the title of

---

[1] Constantino de Sa de Noronha, Captain General of the Portuguese in Ceylon 1618–1622, 1622–1630.

[2] Dom Miguel de Noronha, Conde de Linhares, Viceroy of Goa 1629–1635.

[3] Senerat.

[4] Vijayapāla.

[5] This account refers to the rout of de Sa and his army in the Battle of Randenivela on 25th August 1630. A more detailed account of the battle is found in Baldaeus, unnumbered pp. 4–5 between pp. 44 and 45.

Raja Singa Adassyn or Raja Singa Rajoe (as he signed most of his letters).

The oldest[1] opposed this but Raja Singa pretended not to notice this, carrying on till this Prince died in 1637, whereupon he took Oeva to himself against the will of Prince Visiapalla. Seizes Oeva

After the death of the Prince of Oeva, Visiapalla was not friendly, as Raja Singa had taken everything to himself. But he was then made Prince of Oeva so that he, who was somewhat naive and silly, could not begin anything with the Portuguese and so that he might be sent further away. Finally he was captured, because he always wanted to deal with the Portuguese, which he eventually did do, for he deserted to them, going to Colombo, though he was very little esteemed by them.[2]

In February 1643[3] a *sampan*[4] appeared in Point Gale from the Choromandel coast, in which there were two Queens, daughters of the King of Carnatic, and as they could not land on Baticalo because of a strong wind, they arrived in Gale and there asked for a yacht to bring them again to Baticalo. There were also ambassadors with them, both Moors as well as a Cingalese, who said that they had searched for 3 years and spent between 4000 and 5000 Pagodas.[5] They were to marry Raja Singa, King of Candi, and we therefore lent them a yacht immediately and Raja Singa wrote that thereby a great service had been done to him by us and promised to repay us.[6]

In the meanwhile, the Portuguese having obtained new replacement in weapons, set themselves furiously against Raja Singa, taking a large piece of land in the Seven Corles. But shortly thereafter they were put to flight by this ruler and were driven from there, so that they had to return again to The Portuguese make a deceitful peace with him

[1] That is, Kumārasinha, Prince of Ūva.

[2] For the defection of Prince Vijayapāla and his subsequent treatment by the Portuguese, see P. E. Pieris, *Prince Vijaya Pala of Ceylon 1634–1654* (Colombo, 1927).

[3] Appears to be a mistake for February 1633.

[4] Malay. Boat or canoe.

[5] Presumably for a bride for Raja Sinha.

[6] This boat must have been intercepted by Dutch ships blockading Galle. Sinhalese kings brought their brides from south India. Baldaeus does not mention this.

Colombo. Therefore, seeing they could achieve nothing more, they thought it best to make peace with him.

They obtained a peace from him but broke it shortly after, as soon as they saw they could get some advantage thereby.

Raja Singa, observing from these Portuguese actions that he could never go along with them, took to dissembling for some time, planning in the meanwhile at the same time to call in the Dutch to Ceylon to his help.

He sent, on the 9th September 1636, through a Brahmin, a letter to our Governor on the Choromandel Coast, Mr. Carel Reynierson,[1] but he was detained by the Portuguese at Jaffanapatnam for six months with danger to his life and finally went over in a *sampan* and delivered it to the Governor, who directed the letter immediately to Batavia, to await the further orders of their Excellencies, who left this matter entirely to the Governor of Choromandel and gave him the order to investigate if we, like the Portuguese, could not obtain a share of the cinnamon.

Before the pursuit-ships de Valk, Voorburg, Kleen Hollandia and the frigate Ruttem had left for Choromandel, however, the Governor General, Mr. Antonio Van Diemen,[2] and his Council decided to discuss this matter first with the Captain, Jan Thysson Payart,[3] who had good knowledge of Ceylon since he had been a prisoner there.

After their Excellencies had heard him on the matter, they sent him to the Coast on 31st July 1637 with the *Koopman* Andries Helmond[4] and the ships, to use him for the execution of their plan in Ceylon.

He came there on 31st August where the Governor Mr. Reynerssoon read out to him the instruction of their Excellencies.

Then he departed on 21st October via Tegenapatnam[5] to

Marginalia:

Raja Singa calls the Dutch to his help, 1636

Writes a letter to the Governor of Choromandel

Their Excellencies send ships to Ceylon

Captain Jan Thysson Payart

Comes to Ceylon

---

[1] Karel Reynierz, Governor of Coromandel 1635–1638. Later became Governor General from 1650 to 1653.

[2] Governor General from 1636 to 1645.

[3] He was in Adam Westerwolt's fleet and was taken prisoner by the Portuguese. He was later chief at Batticaloa (1639) and Governor of Ceylon (1645).

[4] Koopman in the Company's service in Westerwolt's fleet.

[5] Devanampatnam on the Coromandel Coast.

Ceylon, came to anchor in Calmunai[1] (also called Calarme) five days later, sent two blacks from Tegenapatnam ashore, who made known to him in the night by a fire signal who had authority there.

Having found everything after his wish, the blacks were again brought on board by a *prauw*[2] and one of them was sent up with a letter to the Emperor with the promise that he should come back again within 16 days.

Along with him also came a Netherlander, the Emperor's Chamberlain (Jan Albertzoon of Embden, who had deserted from Mr. Caan),[3] who returned to the highlands in four days with commissioned deputies, coming the same evening to the Emperor who remained in a royal city across the River Mawieleganga,[4] where they obtained an audience with him by torchlight.

The ruler read the letter and, having seen from the deployment of the ships of the Dutch what wrong information the Portuguese had given of us, questioned them closely on our state and found that we were certainly a much more powerful people than they had given him to understand from time to time.

He spoke on the second day, after the deputies had rested, of the delivery of cinnamon and wax and also of the capture of Baticalo.

After they had spoken with him for 8 days in all, twice a day, they departed again with 3 imperial ambassadors who had to go to Goa.[5]

The Portuguese, hearing that the Dutch had spoken to the Emperor, and that they had decided to attack Baticalo together, were very upset. Some were of the opinion that they should immediately evacuate the place. But others who were more courageous felt that they ought to march to Candi and prevent the Emperor from uniting with the Dutch, a very

Marginal notes:

Sends people to the Emperor to attack Baticalo

The Portuguese plunder Candi

---

[1] Kalmunai, on the east coast of Ceylon near Batticaloa.

[2] *Perahu* (Malay)—Canoe.

[3] Antonio Caen, was in the Company's service in the east from 1614 to 1643, rising to the position of Councillor of the Indies.

[4] Alutnuvara, on the Mahāveli Ganga.

[5] To Westerwolt's fleet which was blockading Goa.

good counsel which was given by the founder of this fort, Damjao Bottado.[1]

They immediately assembled their men and marched with the Governor, Diego de Melo,[2] the abovementioned Bottado and others in March 1638 to the highlands.

Raja Singa, hearing this, evacuated the city with all his people, letting them plunder the place, which they did.

Are attacked by Raja Singa

Their lust having been satisfied, they marched to the Ganoeroe hill where they encamped with about 2300 whites, partly Portuguese and partly mistices, and 6000 blacks, to their utter undoing. For Raja Singa immediately had the road to Walane and other by-ways blocked by cutting large trees and all the Cingalese and coolies whom the Portuguese had with them deserted. Seeing this, they now perceived that it was too late and that it was all over with them. However they sent an Augustine and a Franciscan Monk to the Emperor, seeking to enter into a treaty with him so that they might go unobstructed to Colombo. But the Emperor gave them such a reply that they thought it best to remain there.

The Portuguese Governor de Melo, receiving no news, was in dire distress and asked Bottado, his Commander, what he, who had given this advice to march to Candi, would now advise in this utmost need. Whereupon Bottado gave this courageous reply:There is nothing else to do except to fight bravely and not to die unrevenged. With the first de Melo did not agree and for the last he had no desire.

All except 70 died

Raja Singa, in the meanwhile biding his time, fell on them during a heavy shower of rain with 5000 bowmen and as many spearmen and massacred them in such a way that none, except those whom the ruler was inclined to spare, escaped.

A great many heads were brought to him, as he watched the battle seated on a high platform under a large tree. They were piled together on top of each other like a high pyramid.

No more than 70 Portuguese remained alive who were taken captive. Thus the courageous Bottado and the cowardly

[1] Damiao Bottado, who had been left by de Sa as Captain of the Batticalao Fort.
[2] Diego de Mello de Castro, Captain General of Ceylon 1633–1635, 1636–1638.

de Melo gave their lives on this Ganeroe Hill which the Portuguese held in their memory for long after.[1]

In the meanwhile, the Emperor also sent 3 ambassadors with a letter dated 28th November 1637 to Mr. Adam Westerwold, our Admiral,[2] who attacked the Portuguese before Goa with his fleet on the 4th January 1638 in the presence of these ambassadors and drove them to flight, an event that we will describe later under the affairs of Malabar.[3] In this letter Raja Singa promised that if Westerwold conquered Baticalo, the city would be held by them both, a matter which was to come in handy for us as the Emperor later wished to keep it for himself alone.[4]

The Emperor sends Ambassadors to Mr. Westerwolt

He drives the Portuguese to flight

After this attack, the Admiral Westerwold decided to send the ships Texel, Amsterdam and den Dolfyn with 110 men and 70 soldiers to Ceylon under the Deputy Commander Willem Jacobszoon Coster[5] to inform the Emperor of our further force which was to come here in May and in the meanwhile to give some service in the besieging of this or that fort, all of which Westerwold confirmed to His Majesty by letter.

Coster in Ceylon

He departed on the 17th March from Goa and came before Trikoenmale on 2nd April.

In the meanwhile, the Emperor had assembled together much pepper, wax and cinnamon, on hearing which, the Portuguese wrote to his Majesty for whom he did this since this merchandise belonged to them alone. He replied: for the Dutch my friends, according to my promise and to spite you people.

Mr. Westerwold conquers Baticalo

Shortly thereafter they heard that the Emperor had left for the southern lands and marched with haste to Candi to

---

[1] The Battle of Gannoruva, 23–24 March 1638, a military disaster for the Portuguese as bad as the Battle of Randenivela (1630).

[2] Adam Westerwolt was in the Company's service from 1614 and held a number of offices in various comptoirs. In August 1637 he was appointed Commander of a fleet against the Portuguese in Goa.

[3] *Bechrijvinge van Malabar* in Deel v Stuk 2, pp. 27–31.

[4] This letter is summarised in Baldaeus, pp. 49 and Pieris, *Some Documents...*, pp. 55–6.

[5] Served the Company in the east as Koopman from 1634, rising to Chief of Batticaloa (1638), Vice-Commander and Commander of the fleet to Ceylon and first President of Ceylon (1640). He was killed in Ceylon in 1640 in an encounter with the Sinhalese.

plunder it. But the Emperor, receiving information of it, took them on and harassed them so relentlessly (as we have seen earlier, for this happened then) that only 70 Portuguese survived whom he took captive.[1]

As a sign of this victory he sent the sword of Don Diego de Melo as a gift to Mr. Westerwold.

Then the Deputy Commander William Jacobszoon Coster came to him, with whom he deliberated on attacking the fort of Baticalo.

In the meanwhile Adam Westerwold, Extraordinary Councillor of the Indies, having left Goa on 22nd April 1638, came with the ships Maastrigt, Harderwyk, Rotterdam, Vere and Kleen Enkhuisen, with 800 men before Baticalo, and landed the day after with his entire force and with 6 half cannons which were placed on batteries to cover our people, and to be brought over to this island 2 miles long where the fort stood.

This happened on 18th May with 500 men who, after firing for 4 hours with our guns, forced the enemy to hand over the fort of Baticalo and march out bag and baggage without weapons.

And installs Coster as Chief

Willem Jacobszoon Coster was appointed head with 100 Netherlanders.

Makes a treaty with the Emperor 1638

After this conquest, Mr. Westerwold, in the name of their High Mightinesses, Prince Frederik Henrik and of the East India Company, with the approval of the Governor General of Indies and his Council, made a treaty with the Emperor, consisting of 20 articles (which are published in Baldaeus),[2]

Its short contents

consisting especially that a firm friendship was to be maintained, each to receive a half share of the booty from all conquered forts, that the Dutch would provide all the arms and his Majesty all the remaining needs for their security, all soldiers to be paid, and a stronghold or stone house to be provided for the safety of the goods and war implements and for the row-boats and people for safety from the current, while the Dutch would provide them with weapons.[3]

[1] The Battle of Gannoruva. See above pp. 319–20.
[2] The treaty of 23 May 1638. Baldaeus, pp. 56–9.
[3] Here and in what follows Valentijn gives a summary of the main clauses of the treaty.

On matters of war they were to take counsel together. His Majesty agreed to provide these ships with the men, the munitions of war belonging to them and to supply the other ships and equipment, and to follow up with the supply of cinnamon, pepper, wax, cardamom, indigo, rice, etc. but not wild cinnamon.[1]

He permitted us the trade everywhere in his land free of duty. But none of his subjects might sell us any goods (see article 9) except his Majesty alone.[2] Also no other Europeans might trade with any one of his subjects or be permitted on the roads except the neighbours of Dauei[3] and Tanjore.[4]

For the expenses incurred His Majesty would send yearly to Batavia one or two shiploads of cinnamon, pepper, cardamom, indigo and wax and if there were more cargo it was to be paid with money or with goods to his Majesty.[5]

Also our merchants should be free to go everywhere in his land to buy goods, and draught animals were to be provided to them to transport the goods to our residence or to the coast. No goods might be delivered to others by the natives before the Dutch were supplied, otherwise the seizure of those goods was to be allowed.[6] No coin was to be issued of higher or lower value than would have been fixed by agreement.[7] The miscreants of each were to be handed over to the other and no dealings had with the enemy. Also all Catholic priests were to be expelled.[8] In ships conquered by the Dutch the cargo should be for them but the loss of their ships also should be on their own account.[9] Pieces of artillery lent out here and there on the forts should be brought again to the ships. Also all help was to be shown to each other's vessels.[10]

All of which articles were concluded on the 23rd May 1638 and signed by His Majesty, Mr. Westerwold and Coster.

---

[1] Article 8.   [2] Article 9.

[3] Baldaeus also has 'Dauei' (p. 57). They have both misread the handwriting of the manuscript copy of the treaty. The original says: *naburige uijt het landt van de Neij van Tansjouwer*. 'Neighbours from the land of the Nayak of Tanjore.' See *Corpus Diplomaticum*—I, 313.

[4] Article 10.   [5] Article 11.   [6] Article 12.
[7] Article 14.   [8] Article 17.   [9] Article 18.
[10] Article 19.

Some goods given by the Emperor in payment

Then the Emperor gave 400 bales[1] of cinnamon, 87 quintals[2] of wax and 3059 pounds of pepper in liquidation of his debts with the promise of delivery of more soon.

He sends some ambassadors to Batavia

In approval of the concluded treaty he sent 2 ambassadors with Mr. Westerwold and some presents to the Governor General, Mr. Van Diemen, and the Councillors of Netherlands Indies, who were very well received and sent back with some presents on the pursuit-ships Grypskerk, de Valk and Venlo.

Colombo besieged by the Emperor

Trinkoenmale conquered by Coster 1640[4]

The army of the Emperor, 20000 men strong, proceeded with the siege of Colombo which had been undertaken; moreover the Portuguese were also attacked by various land expeditions so that it was not to be seen on the arrival of Mr. Antoni Caan,[3] ordinary Councillor of the Indies, that they could hold out long, and he after his arrival conquered the fort of Trikoenmale on 1st May 1639.

Negumbo taken by Mr. Lucaszoon 1604[5]

And Nigumbo was taken by the Director General of the Indies, Mr. Philip Lucaszon,[6] on 9th February 1640, which gentleman, having left Ceylon in the flute Sandvoord, died on the way on 5th March and his body was taken ashore in Batavia on 21st where he was buried with great honour.

Retaken by Portuguese

We did not hold Nigumbo for long, however, for the Portuguese recaptured it in the same year on 8th November.

Shortly after, William Jacobszoon Coster appeared before the city of Gale on 8th March 1640, divided his troops in three divisions, though there was news that there were still 350 white men marching to the relief of the city, which our men attacked courageously on the 9th.

Gale captured by Coster 1640

The Emperor's men, loitering, did not arrive before the 11th at Belligamme which was 6 miles from Gale. But Coster, not waiting for them, and having received the ships, Haarlem, Middelburg and Breda on the 11th with 400 men to strengthen

[1] A bale is a measure of weight varying with the commodity weighed. In this context here it seems to be equivalent to about 170 Dutch pounds.

[2] A Portuguese weight. About 130 to 150 pounds.

[3] See p. 319 n. 3.

[4] The sub-heading does not tally with the text which says correctly that Antonio Caan captured Trincomalee.

[5] Misprint for 1640.

[6] Philip Lucas. In the Company's service in the east from 1618, rising from Assistant to Opperkoopman, Governor of Amboina (1628), Director General (1636).

him, prepared everything on the 20th[1] for a general assault and stormed the city on the 13th so courageously that he became master of it after an hour's fighting.

He was made the first head of this city. But as matters then required that he should go at once to Candi to put in necessary order various things which had been neglected, he undertook the journey thence. But having come there, he obtained nothing for all his just requests and it was a fruitless enterprise, as a result of which he became dejected and impatient and began to threaten the Courtiers, while he ought to have taken a lesson from the case of Sebald de Weert.[2]

To his threats he added fruitless insults, none of which the Cingalese were able to tolerate and immediately informed the Emperor who gave Coster permission to leave Candi but without showing him any sign of honour (as was customary).

First commander of Gale; but mercilessly murdered

He, having been led to Baticalo by some Cingalese, was shamefully murdered on the way in the village of Nilgal.[3]

This was an abominable deed of the Emperor, especially as Coster had handed over to him Trikoenmale and Baticalo, with all their inhabitants, as also the lands of Gale and Mature, conquered by him, with all their taxes, though he was in no way required to do this according to the treaty and the subsequent negotiations. He began from this time onwards to try to trifle with us, as he otherwise could have made us masters of Colombo, while on the contrary now the Portuguese were given the opportunity to re-establish themselves fully, so that there might be a situation to keep us busy, and he had not to fear us in the meanwhile.

After the death of Mr. Coster, Mr. Jan Thyszoon Payart (who sailed out in 1638 as captain with the ship Zwol) became the second head of Gale with the title of President. These two sailors, risen from the ranks, have laid the first foundations of our power in Ceylon and, as if reliving in themselves the

Succeeded by Mr. Thyszoon as President

---

[1] This is an error for 12th (March).

[2] Reference is to the murder of Sebald de Weert by the king's men in 1603.

[3] Nilgala. Valentijn is somewhat more objective than Baldaeus in describing the murder of Coster by the Sinhalese. It took place in August 1640.

image of the old Catten[1] and Batavians,[2] have begun this enterprise with great fame.

Ambassadors from Goa seek truce

In 1642 two ambassadors of the Viceroy of Goa appeared in Batavia, Diego Mendes de Britto and Gonsalvo Viloso de St. Joseph,[3] priest from the order of St. Francis, to inform their Excellencies that Don Jan, Count of Braganza,[4] and the whole of Portugal had broken away from the King of Spain and that he, having been raised as King of Portugal with the name of Jan IV, had sent an ambassador to their High Mightinesses[5] to enter into a firm treaty with them which he confirmed had now been effected.

On this ground the Viceroy, Count D'Aveiras,[6] had now sent them to request a truce according to their letters of credence.

This follows

In the meanwhile, their Excellencies obtained information on the 14th of February of this year that a 10 year truce had been made between Don Jan IV, King of Portugal, and Their High Mightinesses but, as the approval of the King had not yet followed, the Ambassadors were to be delayed for some time till it was brought to Batavia on the 8th October.

Then all hostilities were halted even in the Indies, though the Viceroy did not act in this matter in good faith in Ceylon, over which their Excellencies showed great regret and made written protest against it.

In the meanwhile various matters that happened both between the Commissary Boreel[7] and the Count D'Alveiras, as also further between His Excellency and Don Phillipo

[1] Chatti or Catti. A Germanic tribe that inhabited the country round the upper Weser. They were formidable opponents of the early Roman Empire but were eventually subdued.

[2] Batavi. Name given by Romans to the people who lived in that part of Holland between the Rhine and the Waal.

[3] Diego Mendes de Brito, a fidalgo, and Frei Gonçalo Veloso de St. Joseph, a Franciscan friar, were sent by the Portuguese Viceroy to Batavia to negotiate the extension to the east of the truce proclaimed in Europe.

[4] Dom João IV who ascended the throne of Portugal in 1640, after the Portuguese rebellion from Spain.

[5] The States General of the Netherlands.

[6] Dom João da Silva Tello, Conde de Aveiras, Viceroy of Goa 1641–1645.

[7] Pieter Boreel. Came out east as Extraordinary Councillor of the Indies in 1642 and was sent as emissary to the Portuguese in Goa and Ceylon to negotiate the terms of the truce.

Mascarenhas,[1] Governor of Ceylon, in 1642 and 1643, are passed over here for the reason that they are to be found in Baldaeus.[2]

[1] Dom Felipe Mascarenhas, Captain General of Ceylon 1640–1645.

[2] Baldaeus does not give an account of these events. His description is detailed up to the capture of Galle in March 1640 and then he passes quickly over the administrations of Thijssen, Maatsuycker and Kittensteyn and moves on to the siege of Colombo which he deals with in great detail (p. 61). He comes back several pages later to deal briefly with the events which Valentijn has related in detail (pp. 142–5).

Eleventh Chapter

[Portuguese–Dutch wars]

Mr. Caron as Commander to Ceylon, 1643. Negumbo conquered by Mr. Caron, 1644. Mr. Maatsuyker arrives at a treaty with the Viceroy. Becomes third head and Governor of Gale, 1646. Difficulties with Raja Singa. Subsequently everything is at peace. Our prisoners in Candi released, 1649. Letter of Mr. Maatsuyker to the Emperor.

Mr. Caron as Commander to Ceylon, 1634

While matters were so convulsed between both and we could not agree at all among each other, their Excellencies decided to send the Hon. Mr. François Caron,[1] Director General of Indies, as Commander and Admiral of our armed forces in Ceylon with a Commission signed 8th October 1643 to reconquer the fort of Nigombo from the Portuguese as soon as possible, and appointing Mr. Thyssoon[2] in his place, if his Excellency should happen to die.

Nigombo stormed by Mr. Caron, 1644

Mr. Caron in the meanwhile having arrived in Ceylon in the beginning of the year 1644, attacked Nigombo and took it by storm on 9th January (or as others have it 9th February).[3]

He fortified it with four earth bulkwarks, covered from outside all round with turf, and put in 500 men for its defence.

The Governor Mascarenhas[4] intended to reoccupy it after

---

[1] François Caron came out east in 1620 as a young Assistant and rose to *Onderkoopman, Koopman* and in 1641 to Extraordinary Councillor of the Indies and Commander of the Return Fleet. He returned to the east in 1642 as Ordinary Councillor and was made Director General in 1647. Valentijn is wrong in saying that he was Director General when he conquered Negombo.

[2] Joan Thijssen Payart. See Chapter 10, p. 318 n. 3.

[3] 9th January is correct.

[4] Dom Felippe Mascarenhas, Portuguese Captain General of Ceylon.

the departure of this gentleman. But he was mistaken and had to break off with ignominy and depart to Colombo, having been very badly defeated.

On the 10th November of this year Mr. Joan Maatsuyker,[1] Ordinary Councillor of Indies, entered into a firm treaty in Goa with Don Joan de Telles de Menezes, Count of Aveiras and Viceroy of the Indies,[2] (on which we speak in more detail under the heading of Malabar) in which among other things the disputes over the land boundary in Ceylon between the two nations were resolved, according to which everything was directed there in 1646.[3]

Mr. Maatsuyker concludes peace with Viceroy of Goa

In 1646 Mr. Joan Maatsuyker succeeded Mr. Joan Thyszoon Payart as third head and Governor of Gale (as appears in his letter of 30th April 1646 to Raja Singa).

Is third head and Governor of Gale, 1646

Just before this, Raja Singa inflicted on us in the Seven Corlas all possible damage, as he begrudged us this place, for under the Portuguese it was devastated not a little, while at the time of Thyssoon he was able to cultivate it, so that we entered into open war with this ruler.

This was later also the reason why Commander Adrian van der Stel[4] was surrounded by Raja Singa's men on 19th May the same year in the Seven Corles, put to death, his head cut off (which he sent to us in a silk cloth) and the number of 688 Netherlanders taken captive to Candi, as appears later in part from Mr. Maatsuyker's letter.[5]

Difficulties with Raja Singa

[1] An important officer in the history of the V.O.C. He was appointed Commander of the fleet against the Portuguese in Goa and Ceylon in July 1644. He was sent to Ceylon for the second time in February 1646 and made Governor in April, in which capacity he served till 1650. In 1650 he returned to Batavia and was made Director General and in 1653 Governor General which office he held till his death in 1678.

[2] Dom Joao de Silva Tello de Meneses, Conde de Aveiras.

[3] The treaty was signed on 10th November 1644. Text in *Corpus Diplomaticum Neerlando-Indicum* Ed. J. E. Heeres ('s-Gravenhage, 1907), I. 429–37.

[4] Came out east in 1623 as Assistant, was enslaved in Pegu in 1635 and freed a few years later. In 1639–1645 he was Commander in Mauritius and in 1642 at Madagascar and from there was transferred as Commander of the armed forces to Ceylon.

[5] Account of this battle in K. W. Goonewardena, *The Foundation of Dutch Power in Ceylon 1638–1658* (Amsterdam, 1958), pp. 113–14. The number of Dutch prisoners was 340.

Before this, Nicolaas Overschie,[1] head of Nigombo, had brought the Emperor's tame elephants beyond the borders of the Company, which embittered this ruler so much that he, gathering together all his forces, tried to take revenge on us, which he did indeed, forcing our men to surrender (though needlessly).

To settle all these matters, Mr. Maatsuyker wrote to the Emperor in his letter of 4th May 1646 that Mr. Thyssoon had done this without our orders and that he and Overschie were therefore relieved of their office and that he was appointed for this reason in the former's place here as Governor by Their Excellencies, informing his Majesty that the 4 elephants seized by Overschie had been called for and had already arrived to be sent along when his Imperial Majesty wanted the letter of Their Excellencies and the presents to be dispatched.[2]

On the 10th, his Excellency wrote again to the Emperor, that it had never been our intention to deprive his Majesty of his lands, but only to protect him against the Portuguese (who were only trying to cause a division between the Company and Raja Singa and that we tried to prevent this in every way) and to make his Majesty enjoy the fruits for the payment of our war expenses, but if his Majesty could do this himself, we were prepared to give them up. We also called God to witness that it had never been the intention to try for possession of these lands but only to give his Majesty assistance and for this to receive the fruits of his lands at a reasonable price, according to the contract made with Westerwolt, wishing that his Majesty would be pleased to name a place to resolve the differences.

In the meanwhile, the head of our troops, Mr. Adriaan van der Stel who had been sent with some men to Hegeri[3] (as one

---

[1] He was chief of the Company's factory in Persia as *Opperkoopman* in 1633–1638, member of the *Raad van Justitie* (Court of Justice) at Batavia from 1638. In 1645 he was appointed Commander of Negombo.

[2] These summaries of letters that passed between the Dutch and the King Rāja Sinha provided by Valentijn here are most valuable as in some cases they are the only extant record of such letters.

[3] Unidentifiable. The name of the place where van der Stel was defeated and killed was Pannara, a few miles inland from Negombo in the Seven Kōralēs.

can read in greater detail in Georg Andrieszoon, fol. 71)[1] was attacked by the Cingalese and put to death with all his men.

On this Mr. Maatsuyker wrote on the 20th from Gale to the Emperor: that he had heard with regret that Commander van der Stel, who had been sent at his Majesty's pleasure to bring away our men in an orderly manner, had been attacked by his Majesty's people and, because he, following the order given to him for the maintenance of peace, had not dared to defend himself suitably, had been killed with almost all his men and robbed of all the guns and baggage that he had with him. That our enemies would rejoice over this, that the difference between us had gone so far that his Majesty even put to death the men sent for his service. Therefore he asked that his Majesty be pleased to declare whether he was inclined to maintain the peace or not, though he hoped that his Majesty would be wiser and not seek war against those who rescued him from the might of his enemies and still had four fortresses in hand and the power to be of even greater service to him.

But Raja Singa, not willing to listen to this, proceeded to do all harm to us, not even withholding himself from killing our men.

This is seen clearly from the following letter written by Mr. Maatsuyker to the Emperor on 31st May 1646:

Letter of Mr. Joan Maatsuyker, Governor of Ceylon, to the all-powerful Emperor Raja Singa Rajoe.

Letter from Mr. Maatsuyker to the Emperor

Joan Maatsuyker, Governor on behalf of the Company in Ceylon, wishes your Majesty all imaginable blessings and prosperity.

Instead of receiving a reply from His Majesty to my former letters, we receive news daily that he has had our men, who were forbidden to act with hostility, killed near Nigumbo and shown all enmity.

Moreover his Majesty had his ambassadors in Colombo demand help from the Portuguese, from which is to be concluded that his Majesty, in spite of our giving just offer

---

[1] *De Beschryving der Reizen van Georg Andriesz door Adam Olearius . . . uitgegeven* (Amsterdam, 1670). Georg Andriesz was an officer of the Company and served in many of the factories in the 1640s.

of satisfaction, desires to come to a total war with the Company, for which reason we, following the right of all people, have decided on our side to oppose force with force.

For which purpose we have prepared 4 ships and some sloops to occupy Baticalo, Cotjaar and Trikoenmale and to take possession again of those places, previously wrested from the Portuguese.

While being busy with this, I have received his Majesty's letter of the 21st, in which he makes known his inclination to maintain the Contract made with Westerwolt which we also desire.

His Majesty is in some measure right in saying that we have taken possession of his lands unjustly.

No order was given for this, but the Governor Jan Thyszoon had himself conceived it best in order to take all the cinnamon. But over the expulsion of your Majesty's Dessave he will be later held responsible and censured for it.

The Council at Batavia, being prepared to transfer the aforementioned lands to your Majesty, has given this order for the reduction of the expenses. Let his Majesty be pleased to send his Dessaves. They shall be received according to their rank, with this condition that his Majesty shall order that all the cinnamon, along with the other fruits of his lands, shall be delivered to us according to the Contract in payment of our outstanding monies.

This payment can happen within a few years, if his Majesty be pleased to take the necessary trouble in that direction.

This they have said on the first point of dispute.[1]

Regarding Nigumbo, which his Majesty says is occupied by us against his wishes, his Majesty had expressly desired this by his letter of 16th February last year, in which it is mentioned that because of the truce with the Portuguese our occupation there should remain and should be maintained and paid for by his Majesty; it being not advisable to demolish this fort because the Portuguese would then immediately come to settle there again.

[1] This sentence is Valentijn's interspersed comment.

The new fortifications which we have made there can be again demolished at his Majesty's pleasure.

Nigumbo must be maintained at least for another year to see how the Portuguese conduct themselves in the truce, as they have as yet not given good evidence, seeing their unfaithfulness perpetrated in Brazil.[1] And as thus all matters of dispute with his Majesty are satisfied, it is not to be doubted that his Majesty will now abstain from all further enmity.

The lands must first be evacuated by all soldiers[2] or the inhabitants will run away and then no cinnamon will be peeled there from which the payment for the expense must come.

It is also trusted that his Majesty will return all our prisoners which must happen first if the peace is to be concluded.

His Majesty's reply is sought immediately that we may direct ourselves accordingly, protesting that in the absence of fulfilment as stated above, we shall not be responsible for the bloodshed, for we are prepared to give his Majesty suitable satisfaction in everything, in the hope that his Majesty will accept the peace.

Regarding the letter of the Councillors of Batavia and the presents, his Majesty shall be pleased to give order to receive these with honour, wishing further that God will protect his Majesty.

While remaining,
Your Majesty's Humble Servant,
Joan Maatsuyker.

On the 21st June he wrote to his Majesty thus:

His Majesty's letter of the 10th of this month has been received, but is found to be of another content than was expected.

His Majesty says that it is not right to seek the peace of

---

[1] The reference is to the settler rebellion in Pernambuco in Brazil in 1645. The rebellion was aided by the Portuguese monarch, João IV, and the Dutch were eventually defeated.

[2] That is, Kandyan soldiers.

Kings with threats of war. But neither is his Majesty so high, nor we so low that we may not speak the truth.

His Majesty did not speak thus in 1640 when he accepted us as the protectors of his kingdom.

It is no threat but a warning. We do not seek peace as weaklings but offer peace or, on refusal, a righteous war, being assured in conscience that we have no responsibility for it.

We are favourable to the handing back of Nigumbo and have even ordered this to be done. But in such a state as we now stand with his Majesty, this will not happen for eternity, as his Majesty must drive us out from there with force.

Till today not a *laryn*[1] has been paid for the expenses of the conquest of Nigumbo, why is its return being demanded unreasonably and in a manner unbecoming of such a King.

Our prisoners are not mentioned in his Majesty's letter and without their release we cannot come to peace.

Our proposal is, in order to maintain the peace and the treaty according to Westerwolt's Contract, provided his Majesty first releases our people and gives the order for the cinnamon, etc. to be delivered to us, on this happening to our satisfaction, we will hand over to his Majesty as superfluous the administration of these lands.[2]

The translation of their Excellencies' letter was enclosed for his Majesty's observation.

On the 11th September 1646 his Excellency wrote to the Emperor as follows:

According to the letters of our prisoners in Candi, we have failed to reply to his Majesty's letters, which is surprising as we have received no letter from his Majesty since our letter of 21st June, but have only heard from some deserters that his Majesty had broken camp at Caymel[3] and again returned to Candi.

---

[1] A silver coin current in Ceylon and south India, worth about 10 Dutch Stuivers.
[2] End of summary of letter.   [3] Kammala, about 7 miles north of Negombo.

God is our witness that we still try to maintain Westerwolt's Contract, provided that his Majesty does this likewise.

It appears that peace is mutually desired.

His Majesty desires the compulsory return of Nigumbo and we would like the assurance of the fulfilment of our war expenses.

To accommodate each other's position in some way, it will be best that we retain Nigumbo for a further 6 to 8 months, when an open war may easily break out between us and the Portuguese.

Also it will be best that his Majesty leave us in possession of these lands for another 2 to 3 years so that we can find our recompense in cinnamon for the expenses incurred by us and thus his Majesty's debt will also be reduced for a great part.

Also we will be able to see, in the meanwhile, what and how much Nigumbo's environs can produce.

After which time, his Majesty is assured, in the name of our Masters, that we will again put in his hands all the lands without keeping back anything, except only the fort of Gale.

If his Majesty accepts these conditions, he is asked to reply to this and to send some of our people here, and especially Nicholaus Loenius Schryver.[1]

On the 8th January 1647, Mr. Maatsuyker wrote to the King thus:

We have not received as yet any reply to our letters from His Majesty, though the law of peoples and kings always required a reply to letters back and forth.

The conditions offered by us are all too favourable to be thrown in the wind by His Majesty.

Therefore we believe that our former letter may not have come to his Majesty's hands or that his Majesty will have been misled by the whispering of our enemies.

In order to ascertain the truth, to have a firm understand-

[1] Probably, one of the Dutchmen taken prisoner at Anguruwatota.

ing of how his Majesty is inclined, it is decided to send *Koopman* Maarchalk[1] as Commissary.

If his Majesty is pleased to hear him, a passport is awaited for this purpose with the promise that, be it peace or war, he be left to return unhindered.

On the 11th August he wrote thus to his Majesty:

His Majesty's letter of the 12th July we have received on the 27th and have seen from it with regret his Majesty's protracted sickness, wishing that the recovered health of his Majesty may continue long.

The Commissary, who was referred to in our previous letter, will be sent soon via Baticalo.

I would myself come before his Majesty, if the orders of my Masters permitted it, this being considered superfluous for the religious and scrupulous maintenance of the Contract made with Westerwold.

The former troubles have not occurred through our fault nor is his Majesty to blame, rather false tongues and evil men are to blame whom his Majesty is asked not to believe easily, but to take into consideration the faithful services which we have shown to his crown, without expecting other rewards than the maintenance of the contract and friendship.

On the 21st August he wrote further:

Presently the Commissary, Laurens Maarschalk, leaves for Candi and will make known our good intention to his Majesty, and will treat further with his Majesty for the settlement of the disputes that have arisen, for which the conditions have been dictated to him which your Majesty will accept without doubt.

Later we will send more important ambassadors to confirm the mutual agreement and to authenticate it by oath. Let his Majesty be pleased to give trust to the said Commissary.

---

[1] Laurens de Maerschalk. Came out east in 1620 as Assistant, was promoted *Koopman* in 1621. Came out east in 1637 a second time as *Opperkoopman* and served in Ceylon.

On the 10th September his Excellency wrote again to this ruler as follows:

> We have received his Majesty's letter of the 29th August on the 7th of this month, and our ambassador left for Baticalo on the 23rd, hoping that he will speedily appear before his Majesty.
>
> Noting that his Majesty is being sought by the Portuguese for a peace and desires to hear of our decision on this, let his Majesty be pleased to act in such a way according to his interests as he thinks is beneficial to his kingdom. But our decision is to maintain the Contract made with Westerwolt, provided that his Majesty also does so.
>
> The reason why the Portuguese seek for peace is that they fear that they will come to war with us before long, in view of their untrustworthiness in Brazil. They imagine that they can hide under the shadow of peace with his Majesty but they will be deceived: For the contract cannot forbid us to do them damage according to our power, with this difference that the war which was carried on before this against them was in the name of his Majesty but now will be carried on in the name of the States General and that, consequently, what we come to conquer from them would be not for his Majesty but on our account, so that, on the conquest of Colombo your Majesty could not demand that place.
>
> Let his Majesty be pleased to consider this and, at the same time, how little trust is to be given to a nation which, during the peace, carried out a shameful treachery in Brazil.[1]
>
> With the arrival of the ships from Batavia, we will communicate the latest news to his Majesty.

Mr. Maatsuyker wrote another letter on the 25th March 1648 to this King, but obtained then and for long after no reply. But on the 10th September his Excellency wrote that, having waited now for eleven months fruitlessly for news of our Commissary, he had finally heard from the Portuguese that his Imperial Majesty had made peace with them so that

[1] See p. 333 n. 1.

they both might fight against us, which, if it was true, his Excellency requested that his Commissary be allowed to return. But from his Excellency's letter of 27th October to his Majesty, it appeared that it was a groundless lie of the Portuguese and that, on the contrary, his Majesty was of the intention to release our ambassador and prisoners in a short time and then to reply to his Excellency's letters, for which generous decision his Excellency was thankful to his Majesty, adding in a further letter that another embassy was to be sent in place of Mr. Maarshalk.

From his Excellency's letter of the 30th March 1649 from Nigumbo (all the others being from Gale) to the Emperor was to be judged clearly enough that the prospects were still not bright for the return of this ambassador, in order to make which proceed more easily his Excellency wrote to this King among other matters:

In Gale a horse has arrived worthy to be ridden by a King. His Majesty's order is sought to send it up. Some trifles and fruits are also being sent to his Majesty.[1]

He had also received a letter from his Majesty of the 9th of this month in which his Majesty's sickness was apparent, which he said he heard with much regret, but had also seen that his Dessave did us all damage and cut off all supplies while everything was open to the Portuguese.

On the 10th April his Excellency wrote from Nigumbo that he had been some days in Catagambale Corla[2] to examine how in the next monsoon the collection of cinnamon in these lands should be done, as no more cinnamon was to be found around Gale. But his Excellency declared that he had not seen any living men in his journey through Pittigal Corle and that he had come across an Apohamy with some lascarines in Madampe, who said straightaway that he was put there by his Imperial Majesty to prevent any Chalias[3] or other inhabitants who might come there from the Portuguese lands, as his Majesty desired that these lands should be laid waste so that we might then not receive any service from the inhabitants

---

[1] A Persian horse was imported and sent to the king with some other things as a gift.

[2] Katugampola Kōralē. [3] Cinnamon peelers.

nor receive the promised cinnamon, which ran directly against the Contract of Westerwold.

This Apohamy had also had much contact with the Portuguese and by night had stealthily run away with all his lascarines and fled to the Portuguese lands, perhaps out of fear of being punished by his Majesty. He promised that he would send him to his Majesty as soon as he seized him.

The Portuguese had for two continuous years peeled the cinnamon which properly belonged to us. But his Excellency said that this would be prevented by the despatch of an army, of which he would give his Majesty prior information, requesting further that he be pleased to give his ambassador a favourable farewell.

On the 10th April, he received a letter from his Majesty, to which his Excellency replied on the 20th from Nigumbo, with expression of his pleasure over his Majesty's recovery from his sickness. But he said that he had read with surprise that his Majesty had not desired that anything should be brought to the Nigumbo Fort as the occupation force was there against his Majesty's wish. His Excellency requested that his Majesty be pleased to read his letter of the 16th February 1645 once again, as he should clearly find there that this occupation was authorised and ordered to be there by his Majesty.

His Excellency also requested that his Majesty would give orders to his people to populate the Pittigal Corle again as before, so that we might thus receive cinnamon, without which we could not settle our account with his Majesty.

He thanked his Majesty also, both for the permission given to us to bring an army again into the land to protect the cinnamon peelers against attack by the Portuguese, as also for his Majesty's permitting our nation to go freely and openly through his lands, and also for promising us, in case of shipwreck, to give all possible help in all his ports. He wished that the order of the Lords and Masters[1] would permit him to kiss his Majesty's hand in person, when his Majesty would get a better opinion of us and soon the entire island would come under his authority (for which his Excellency longed) so that

[1] The Directors of the Company.

all our forces would be withdrawn all at once from Gale and Nigumbo.

It was particularly pleasing to his Excellency that the horse was agreeable to his Majesty, and his Excellency would send it across by the ordered Walauwe road. He requested also instead to be able to appoint a permanent ambassador at the court to oppose the calumnies of our enemies.

From his Excellency's letter of the 24th May 1649 it was seen that he had received a letter from his Majesty of the 28th April, from which it appeared that his Majesty was pleased to thank us for our faithful deeds done in his service. His Majesty was further informed that his Dessave of the Mature lands would be received with great honour by us. He requested, however, that the one who was already placed there in his Majesty's name, be confirmed by his Majesty as he did good service, and be appointed to that office.

The Chalias on this side annually performed what they were obliged to do and had delivered 600 to 700 Bhars[1] to us in 3 years, which was paid into and credited to his Majesty's account. He requested that his Majesty be pleased to let us enjoy this for so long till we are paid off.

The Persian horse was ready to be taken up, as soon as the persons, whom his Majesty wished to send for this purpose, were to appear. Also his Excellency thanked his Majesty for the permission to send another ambassador, which would happen as soon as the present ambassador appeared with his Majesty's reply and with news and conditions of peace.

Then the Emperor wrote to his Excellency on 12th May, sending him some presents for which his Excellency thanked his Majesty on the 7th July from Gale.

He now sent the Persian horse with a Dutch saddle, on which no man had sat before. If his Majesty ordered so, one still better would be sent. He requested again that our ambassador might receive his leave, to make which happen sooner, his Excellency sent, besides this horse, some other small presents with the request that his Majesty be pleased to accept these in gratitude.

---

[1] About 480 pounds a bhar when weighing cinnamon.

On the 15th July, the ambassador Maarschalk (about whom it had been written so many times) appeared at last with two important men of his Majesty with a letter of the 27th June, along with conditions of peace.

In these conditions, his Excellency balked at the 10th Article, regarding cinnamon, which gave us, with other nations, a share in it, not even to the value of half. Besides, it was expressly stipulated in our contract that we must have this alone, in which hope his Excellency had signed the conditions, on the approval of their Excellencies, as he had said in his letter of 8th August to his Majesty sent with his ambassador and two of our officers of importance, the one to swear to this and to return to us with his Majesty's decision and the other to remain at court.[1]

It appears here that his Majesty asked for a suitable writer, on which it was written to Batavia. But if his Majesty be pleased to use any one of our people in Candi, it would be agreeable to his Excellency, but he reminded his Majesty that they were bonded for no longer than 5 years.

He also thanked his Majesty that he had been pleased to appoint one of our nation (as he had earlier requested his Majesty) as Dessave of Mature.[2] Also he recommended for his Majesty's favour one Lambert Cambolt after the contract of the appointed Dessave should come to an end.

Our ambassadors would request his Majesty that he be pleased to let us keep Nigumbo till we should deliver Colombo to him, towards which we intended to do our best, as the Portuguese harmed us in every way and for which we sought his Majesty's help and decision.

His Excellency proposed to send the abovenamed Cambolt as Commissary to the Emperor. But as he became sick, one Burchard Cocx[3] was to go in his place with some trifles for his

[1] In the negotiations conducted by Maerschalk to enter into a revised treaty with the king, there was a difference on this crucial article on the question of whether the Dutch were to have an exclusive monopoly over all the cinnamon. This appeared so in the treaty of 1638 which Rāja Sinha wanted to change, requesting the freedom to sell cinnamon to anyone he wished. Eventually a compromise was agreed by which he could sell cinnamon to allies of the Dutch after his debts had been settled.

[2] The Dutch Dissāva of Mātara was Marcus Cassel.

[3] Burchard Cox, a Captain in the Company's armed force.

Majesty, with the request that his Majesty be pleased to give him his trust in everything and send him back shortly.

By his Excellency's letter of the 9th September from Gale, it appeared that his Majesty had sent, on the 8th August, a letter to his Excellency with a bag, a gold chain and an elephant with tusks, for which honour, as also for the esteem which he had for the Persian horse, his Majesty was heartily thanked. Also he requested that the cinnamon, peeled in the Seven Corles, might be delivered to us, promising further that everything that his Majesty requested would be provided for him as soon as possible, as already a machine to lift heavy things and some bars of native steel were being sent now.

On 16th November his Majesty wrote a letter to his Excellency and the Ambassador Cocx appeared on 3rd December with the articles of peace signed by his Majesty. Whereupon his Excellency replied to the King on the 27th, informing him that on that day Mr. Jacob van Kittensteyn[1] had landed from Batavia to take over the government from him.

With this Ambassador Cocx some prisoners also came over and the sick were to be brought in a vessel from Baticalo.

He thanked his Majesty for the breast jewel which he had sent his Excellency as a memento.

Regarding Nigumbo and the war with the Portuguese, his Excellency had not received a reply yet from Batavia.

On the 5th February 1650 it appears from his Excellency's letter to this King that he, in the end of the previous year, had sent Pieter Kieft[2] as Agent to his Majesty, from whose letter he noted that his Majesty was very dissatisfied with us, laying the responsibility on us for having broken the peace, called us about six times very disrespectfully *casta Hollandesa* (which had never happened before),[3] without discovering the reason

---

[1] Began service in the Company as Assistant in Surat in 1635 and was made *Koopman* in 1643. In 1649 he was appointed to Ceylon as President and in 1651 the post was raised to Governor.

[2] Pieter Keeft accompanied Captain Cox on his embassy to Kandy and stayed over there as Dutch representative at the capital. Keeft served as Assistant in Madura in south India and was promoted *Onderkoopman* in 1648.

[3] This derogatory reference to the Dutch as 'the Dutch caste' or 'tribe' is in Rāja Sinha's letter to Kieft of 12 January 1650. He was angry at the deceit of the

for his, except that his Majesty's Dessave Rampot[1] had inflamed him against us (as he believed), this being the last letter which Mr. Maatsuyker wrote to the Emperor, and in which he has demonstrated that our faithful services shown to his Majesty in no way deserved our being treated so disrespectfully, as now happened.

All of which shows us that, though the Emperor was now and then peevish and sullen towards us and to this Governor, he not only favoured us now and then, but that we also afterwards possessed in peace Nigumbo, Gale Corle and Mature under the administration of Mr. Maatsuyker, with the subordinate lands, peeled the cinnamon there, caught wild elephants and collected the other income of the land to the profit of the Company, without Raja Singa having opposed it in any manner, besides that he later quietened down so far that he went back inland with his people, without opposing the outer watchposts of the Portuguese, from which it may be guessed without foundation that there certainly existed a secret agreement between him and the Portuguese or at least an understanding to leave each other untroubled.

Yet, in subsequent times, everything was quiet again

This remained in the same state till Mr. Maatsuyker obtained the release of our prisoners from the Emperor in 1649 through an embassy to which some presents were added (as we have seen).[2]

Our prisoners in Candi released, 1649

In this manner (except for very few minor happenings), matters remained for about three years, after which again great changes occurred here.

Dutch in not handing over the Mātara Dissāvany to his Dissāva Rampot, after promising it while confirming the treaty.

[1] Rampoth Adigār, who was appointed Dissāva of Matāra by the king.

[2] The embassy of Captain Cox.

Twelfth Chapter

[Portuguese–Dutch wars (contd.)]

Mr. Kittensteyn succeeds Mr. Maatsuyker as President in Ceylon, 1650. Extract from the Instructions left by Mr. Maatsuyker to Mr. van Kittensteyn. In 1652 the Emperor declares himself with us against the Portuguese. Mr. van Kittensteyn succeeded by van der Meyden. Futile attack of the Portuguese on Nigumbo, 1654. Sea battle between us and them. Mr. van Goens destroys some galleons near Cape de Ramos. Mr. Hulft in Ceylon, 1655, conquers Caliture. Besieges Colombo. And is shot dead on the 10th April 1656 in front of this city. Which is taken in the same year by Mr. van der Meyden. Toetoecoryn taken by van der Laan, 1658. Manaar and Jaffanapatnam conquered by Mr. van der Meyden. And the Portuguese driven entirely from Ceylon. Raja Singa is enraged against us, which lasts till his death. Takes Cnocx prisoner, 1660. Representations of the Governor van der Meyden on the state of Ceylon. Mr. van der Meyden succeeds Mr. van Goens again as Governor here, 1661. Short Extract from the Instructions of the Commissioner van Goens to the Governor of Ceylon. Mr. van Goens succeeds Mr. van der Meyden again as Governor here, 1663.

After Mr. Maatsuyker had been here for 4 years, he was succeeded by Mr. Jacob van Kittensteyn of Delft, with the title of President at Gale in 1650.[1]

He handed over to him on the 27th February of the same

---

[1] See above Chapter XI, p. 342 n. 1. President, in the Company's hierarchy, was an office of lower status than Governor. In 1651 his rank was raised to Governor.

year the following Instructions, which will give us much light on Ceylonese affairs.[1]

* * * * *

Mr. van Kittensteyn, having seen from these Instructions that it was necessary to request the Emperor for a Dessave from our nation, wrote a letter on this on the 1st April 1650 from Gale to this ruler, with the request that his Majesty be pleased to appoint one of our nation to this office. He thanked his Majesty also for the cinnamon delivered, loaded in Chilauw in one of our ships (which, however, one must know to have happened only for form's sake, as he would rather have denied this to us) amounting to 41280 pounds or $137\frac{180}{300}$ Bahar,[2] which was set off to his Majesty's account, by which his Majesty was made to appear to be in a good mood. He sent via Baticalo in one of our ships a Toetoecoryn clock and a jack-screw, which ship would take with it the sick prisoners sent there by his Majesty.

On the 2nd April, he wrote again to his Majesty, strongly complaining about the Adigar Rampot[3] who, after the withdrawal of our field forces within Mature, had not scrupled to make an invasion into his Majesty's lands[4] and place his guard posts up to the villages of Creme[5] and Catoene,[6] after he had chased our guard from there, which his Excellency could not believe to have been his Majesty's orders, for which reason he was obliged to stop his evil ways,[7] as his Excellency had made him depart from the territory of Mature, trusting

[1] The full text of these instructions has been published in Dutch and in English translation. *Memoir of Joan Maatsuyker, 1650*, Ed. and Transl. by E. Reimers. Selections from the Dutch Records of the Ceylon Government, No. 1 (Colombo, 1927). Valentijn's extracts are not reproduced here.

[2] A *bahar* has been reckoned here at 300 Dutch pounds. Its usual value in this period, in weighing cinnamon, was 480 Dutch pounds. Valentijn himself, in his list of weights and measures, gives this valuation. See above Chapter III, p. 187.

[3] Appointed by the King as Dissáva of Mátara. See above Chapter XI, p. 343 n. 2.

[4] Occupied by the Dutch.

[5] Kiráma in the Mátara Province.

[6] Katuwana.

[7] That is, Rampot's.

that this was pleasing to his Majesty and that he would recall this man from there for our further peace.[1]

On the 23rd July his Excellency again wrote to this King,[2] that he had received his letters on the 3rd and 11th May and had already replied to them, that we had no other desire for the Mature lands than in so far as the interest of his Majesty required it, for we had the intention to follow the Contract of Westerwolt scrupulously.

He also said that he had been informed many times that his Majesty had entered into dealings with the Portuguese over matters which were disadvantageous to our state, that he did not wish to believe this in any way, but hoped to understand from his Majesty himself what the truth of this matter was.

Then Mr. van Kittensteyn received on the 6th September a letter of the 25th August from his Majesty,[3] to which his Excellency replied on the 17th,[4] having heard that his Majesty (who had left from Vintenne for Badule,[5] in the Kingdom of Oeva) had summoned the Dessave Rampot from the Mature lands to learn from him of the reasons for the dispute that had arisen between him and Mr. Maatsuyker, not doubting that his Majesty, after a correct account of the matter, would place this Rampot in the wrong. Also he informed his Majesty that the war between us and the Portuguese in Europe had begun over a year ago and, as soon as ships arrived from Batavia with some relief, his Excellency should give his Majesty further information of our intentions.[6]

On the 28th December he thanked his Majesty in a letter, written from Gale, for the help which his Majesty had given us (according to his letter of the 29th August to his Excellency) through his Dessave during the stay of the ship de Haan on the island of Calpentyn, as also for the release of the four

[1] The reference here is to the altercations between the Dutch and Adigār Rampot's forces in Mātara when Rampot went to take control of the lands captured from the Portuguese.

[2] Text of this letter in Pieris, *Some Documents* . . . , pp. 159–60.

[3] Text of this letter in Pieris, *Some Documents* . . . , pp. 160.

[4] 17th September 1650. Text in Pieris, *Some Documents* . . . , pp. 160–1.

[5] Badulla.

[6] The Dutch-Portuguese truce ended in 1652 and van Kittensteyn received orders to resume the war in June 1652.

persons sent by the chief of this vessel with messages to Nigumbo and detained by the Dessave of the Seven Corlas.

From the letter of the Commissary Pieter Kieft[1] it also appeared to his Excellency that his Majesty was inclined to come to the lowlands and to send Kieft ahead to deal with his Excellency over a matter of great importance and that in the meanwhile his Majesty would persevere in delivering to the Company yearly a good quantity of cinnamon and elephants.

And since his Majesty guarded very closely our people in Candi, so that they had very little freedom, a certain attendant of our Commissary Kieft who was weary of this, cleverly took to flight. But as soon as he came into our lands, he was taken captive, so that his Majesty might not take this amiss, which was caused by an all too strict captivity. On the contrary the abovementioned Kieft and his people should be given somewhat more freedom, as was done by all kings, and be permitted to write to us often.

Also his Excellency sent to his Majesty, as a token of his affection, 5 yards of red cloth, 10 yards of gold and silver lace, $2\frac{1}{2}$ yards of large silver lace, a cap with a beautiful feather, a flask of Dutch distilled water, a vat of Spanish wine, and some Dutch butter, apologising that because of the by-passing of the Suratte ship he could not offer anything else to his Majesty.

On the 4th March 1651, his Excellency informed his Majesty from Gale that a long expected present had arrived from Batavia, for which reason his Excellency requested that his Majesty be pleased to issue an order for the bringing up of this gift.

From his Excellency's letter of the 15th April to his Majesty from Gale, it appears that he sent his Majesty this substantial present through Lieutenant Frans Has[2] (also called Sas by others):

    1 shining gold chain.
    1 saddle, coated with silver gilt,

---

[1] He was staying in Kandy as Agent of the Dutch in the capital.
[2] The letters from Batavia refer to him as Ensign Frans Has. He went with four soldiers bearing these presents to Kandy in April and returned in August 1651.

beautifully embroidered and provided
with all its accoutrements.

1 bridle, also of silver gilt, consisting
of a head- breast- and rear-piece.

1 gold and silver embroidered quiver.

1 gold and silver embroidered bow.

15 gilt arrows and 2 bow strings.

He also requested that his Majesty be pleased to send down Jurriaan Bloem,[1] now in Candi, to be used by him, according to his Majesty's desire, to write letters to his Majesty in Portuguese, which request his Majesty (who in the meanwhile wrote again to his Excellency on the 23rd July and 5th August) granted to his Excellency, as he thanked his Majesty for it on the 16th September.

On the 15th November his Excellency blamed his Majesty in a pleasant way from Gale, over his arrogating to himself the name of God and wishing to be so named by us, his Excellency saying it was no wonder that the Portuguese, like the ambassadors of the Prince of Bengal, gave his Majesty agreeable and flattering titles of honour, as necessity forced them to do this.[2] Our Commissary Pieter Kieft would not go along with this with much reason, without the knowledge of his Excellency, nor agree to make any changes in this matter.

By his letter of the 6th February 1652 from Gale, he informed his Majesty of the departure of the Commissary Kieft to Batavia as his contract had expired as well as to make known verbally to their Excellencies his Majesty's good inclinations to us.

A doctor's medicine chest and all kinds of rare machines, and very costly medicines, as also two large exceptional caps and a bagpipe were sent from Batavia for his Majesty's amusement, which his Majesty looked forward to seeing, and they were sent to his Majesty on the 15th May.

On the 27th September his Excellency informed his Majesty

---

[1] Presumably one of the Dutch personnel detained by the king in Kandy and one who could write Portuguese.

[2] Rāja Sinha was now demanding that the Dutch address him as 'God our Lord' in their letters. A historian has referred to the 'excessive vanity' of his personality at this time (Goonewardena, *Foundation of Dutch Power*, p. 129).

of the death of the Commissary Kieft, requesting that his Majesty be pleased to send to his Excellency the goods left by him in Candi.

By this letter, it also appeared that the Portuguese ambassador, Don Jeronimo D'Asevedo,[1] had written to his Majesty and that he had replied to it, and his Majesty had sent this also to his Excellency, on which matter, in his Excellency's view, it was very strange that the Portuguese General had permitted the Ambassador to write to his Majesty over matters of state, which he believed to have happened from some pride and arrogance.

From the same letter it also appeared that it had displeased his Majesty very much that the Portuguese General let himself be called King of Malvane,[2] though he never had a right to it.

His Excellency thanked his Majesty further for the favour which he did us, showing that all our services were directed towards maintaining the Contract made with Westerwolt, confirming that his Majesty should try to make good our expenses with the merchandise available in his land.

On the 26th October, his Excellency wrote that he had received his Majesty's letter of the 5th September from Badule with an important gift and that the copy of the letter which his Majesty received from Goa from his brother the Prince Visiapalle[3] and had sent to his Excellency had been received, from which one forms strange ideas as to what the Portuguese might be intending now.

Also his Excellency informed his Majesty that we had already begun the war against the Portuguese on this island, and taken possession of the lands up to Caliture, since the enemy had left this fortress also to our benefit.[4]

Thus the proper time was now born to do his Majesty more faithful service and to avenge ourselves over the treachery

[1] Portuguese ambassador sent to Kandy to negotiate peace and wean the king away from the Dutch in 1646. He and his party were detained there for four years.

[2] Malvāna, to which the Portuguese shifted the capital in 1599.

[3] Vijayapāla who had defected to the Portuguese and was now living in Goa.

[4] Kittensteyn had resumed the war against the Portuguese in October 1652.

committed against our state in Brazil.[1] He requested further that his Majesty be pleased to uphold his intention to send a powerful force to Jaffanapatnam, Manaar and Saffragam, not doubting that this was being put into operation.

And as he had understood that the General had sent an ambassador to his Majesty from Colombo, he requested that his Majesty be pleased not to give him any trust or hearing, but to be mindful of our faithful services for all time.[2]

The Emperor declares himself with us against the Portuguese, 1652

Later it appeared from his Excellency's letter of the 9th November that his Majesty was inclined to take the field against the Portuguese along with us and had got his army to march out of Macucaravare[3] against them.

On 23rd December his Excellency wrote to this ruler that it appeared as if the Portuguese wished to bring the Prince Visiapalle, his Majesty's brother, from Goa to this island, to prevent which, his Excellency advised his Majesty to attack the seaports of Manaar, Calpentyn and Jaffanapatnam as much as possible, as we would try to do that for Colombo, where we already had taken one of their frigates with our cruisers. And seeing that his Majesty was inclined to come down with his force to Colombo, his Excellency praised this proposal but advised his Majesty rather not to come there now as this city could not be captured without bloodshed.

In the meanwhile the Portuguese deprived us of the post of Anguratotte[4] on the 8th January 1653 and, though Raja Singa drove the Portuguese back near Cottegore[5] and made them withdraw to Colombo, it is certain however that this would not have happened to us, if the Dessave of Saffragam had not warned us too late (as also happened with the Emperor), and, as the loss of this frontier post was known by us from his Majesty, Mr. van Kittensteyn did not fail to thank his Majesty heartily for this trustworthy warning (though it was no use to us) by letter of 15th January 1653 from Gale.

He added to this that the Portuguese have let it be rumoured

---

[1] The rebellion and capture of Pernambuco, see above Chapter XI, p. 333 n. 1.

[2] The reference is to the overtures made to the king by the Portuguese Captain General, Manuel Mascarenhas Homem.

[3] Menikkadavara.   [4] Anguruwatota.   [5] Kotuwēgoda.

that they are in alliance with the King, and are supplied by his Majesty from the lands of Saffragam and that they were disposed to attack us together, which, as his Excellency meant, even had some appearance of truth.

His Excellency having understood in the meanwhile that rumour ran of the Viceroy's arrival from Goa with the Prince Visiapalle to this land, with a force of men, he informed his Majesty on the 3rd March, that he had received his Majesty's letter of the 21st February and that he had already left for Colombo to prevent their entry, as he also for this purpose had sent 8 of our ships along the Malabar coast to sink them on the way and destroy them; taking the responsibility on himself further to conquer Colombo first as it had been fortified greatly in a few years and required greater force than he now had.

He was very happy that his Majesty was disposed to get our prisoners released from Colombo for which we had in hand various priests and others in exchange.

In the meanwhile the troops of his Majesty and our people had a happy encounter near Manaar without any loss of life on our side, over which Mr. Adriaan van der Meyden,[1] who had succeeded Mr. van Kittensteyn as Governor after an administration of 3 years, wrote a letter to his Majesty in this month from Caleture, showing his pleasure at the victory achieved by his Dessave in the Seven Corles on the Portuguese, and also thanked his Majesty for his present.

On the 18th March and 22nd April, Mr. van Kittensteyn wrote to his Majesty that he had learned with surprise that someone had informed his Majesty that he was disposed to leave the island without informing his Majesty, which his Excellency had never considered, as he now showed to the contrary by his letter.

Mr. van Kittensteyn succeeded by Mr. van der Meyden 1653

Also his Excellency said that we still stood by our word given regarding the Nigumbo Fortress and his Majesty did not have to doubt this in any way.

His Excellency advised his Majesty to build a Fort at

---

[1] In the Company's service as *Onderkoopman, Koopman* and head of the comptoir of Tegenapatnam. Came to Ceylon as second-in-command in 1652 and appointed Governor in October 1653.

Reygamwatte[1] to close in on Colombo and build all obstacles in order to besiege Colombo. He thanked his Majesty for his present and his Excellency also informed the Emperor that Ragimade Thevar,[2] Lord of Ramancoil,[3] had informed us through his ambassadors how he had endured insufferable affronts from time to time from the Portuguese and was inclined to offer us a helping hand against them with men and vessels to help conquer Manaar and Jaffanapatnam.

The 3 tame tigers, sent by his Majesty, he had received and wished that his Majesty might also tame the wild and arrogant nature of the Portuguese.

On the 12th May his Excellency sent his Majesty's ambassadors back, and also, on his Majesty's request, a bodyguard for his Majesty, consisting of an Ensign, a Sergeant, a Corporal of the navy, two Corporals, a drummer, and 23 soldiers whom he asked his Majesty to treat well, saying that he would be writing to Batavia for a higher officer and for an experienced physician, which last was sent to his Majesty with a letter of the 19th July, along with an ordinary Dutch saddle.

In the meanwhile, his Excellency received a letter from his Majesty of the 15th August, which was answered on the 2nd September in a letter which asked that his Majesty be pleased to resolve his dissatisfaction regarding Colombo in the best way.[4]

Also his Excellency declared that we had never had it in our thoughts to possess a foot of land belonging to his Majesty's Crown, much less Colombo after its conquest, whereas we would show to the contrary by adding it to his Majesty's Crown.

For his Majesty's account, which he had requested many times, it was written to Batavia, on which it should appear that all the expenses, apart from what had been received against it, have been appropriately entered (except for the expenses of the fleets which must still be received).[5]

[1] Raygamvatta, about 10 miles east of Colombo.
[2] Ragunātha Thēvar, ruler of Rāmnād.
[3] Rāmēsvaram, part of the Thevar's principality of Rāmnād.
[4] Rāja Sinha was angry that the Dutch had not combined with him to make an immediate assault on Colombo towards the end of 1653.
[5] The Dutch argument was that they were retaining the lands they conquered from the Portuguese until their expenses were paid by the king. The king kept asking them for a detailed statement of the expenses.

Also his Majesty sought our advice, as the Portuguese wished to come over to deliver in Candi the letters of their King and of the Viceroy of Goa.[1] But his Excellency was of the opinion that the letters were but fabrications to hoodwink his Majesty and that they must therefore be rejected.

It was discovered in the meanwhile that on the 10th May they had received a great relief force of 12 frigates and many soldiers in Colombo under the new Governor General, Don Francisco de Melo de Castro,[2] as the people had risen up against the old Governor Manoel Mascarenhas Homem and had taken him prisoner,[3] our cruisers, which had sailed just previously to the Bay of Gale, not preventing this.

Every day a vast relief force was expected from Batavia and then our Governor promised his Majesty that he would be ready to appear with our army before the gates of Colombo.

On the 25th October, Mr. van der Meyden informed his Majesty from Gale that Mr. van Kittensteyn had left for Batavia and that his Excellency was appointed as Governor in his place, wherefore his Excellency requested from his Majesty to be so recognised, adding further that we had conquered 3 English and a Portuguese ship in the Persian Gulf.

The letter of his Majesty of the 13th to Mr. van Kittensteyn was also received.

On the 17th November his Excellency wrote from Caliture that his Majesty's letter of the 2nd from his army camp at Ancarravanelle[4] had been received, and his Excellency now informed his Majesty that the Portuguese who lay with their army in the previous month at Gourbeville, Canasture,[5] Attapotti[6] and Cotagodde,[7] and also sometimes at Alauwa, had marched back from the highlands up to Malvane, and that they had mustered there 24 Instantias[8] or platoons of white

---

[1] A new Captain Major had arrived from Goa in May 1653 and he attempted to come to terms with Rāja Sinha.

[2] Dom Francisco de Mello de Castro arrived in Colombo as Captain General with a relief force in May 1653.

[3] Portuguese soldiers had mutinied against Manuel Mascarenhas Homem, the Captain General, on 30th November 1652 and a government under Captain Gaspar Figueira took control.

[4] Anakanvila. [5] Probably Kannatota.

[6] Atapitiya. [7] Kotagoda.

[8] Probably *Estancia* (Portuguese)—a platoon consisting of 30 to 38 soldiers.

353

troops who would pillage the Seven and Four Corles to procure provisions, but he promised to keep an unbreakably good understanding with his Majesty's Dessaves and to help him faithfully.

His Excellency also knew that great hopes had been given to his Majesty now and then for the conquest of Colombo but all this awaited the arrival of our great relief force from Holland and from Batavia which should not be delayed long.

Also he informed his Majesty that the Commissioner Rijklof van Goens[1] had left with 4 ships from Caliture to Suratte and that the Bay of Colombo was occupied by 3 of our ships, his Excellency being further pleased to hear that our soldiers, who were with his Majesty, gave great satisfaction.

In the meanwhile there occurred a skirmish between us and the Portuguese near Oedeware[2] in which we lost our Dessave, Sybrand Groes,[3] 2 Ensigns, 1 Corporal, 2 soldiers and 3 Javanese, and 20 Dutch and 8 Javanese wounded, besides a lascarine, of whom some died later of their wounds.

It was felt that the Ensign had killed 100 and wounded 50 and we should have fared better there if we could have crossed the spring where they lay to their advantage, which was the cause why we suffered so many dead and wounded. And the enemy retreated in good order through our lack of ammunition.

Futile attack of the Portuguese on Nigumbo, 1654

In the beginning of the year 1654, the Portuguese tried to overrun Nigumbo, after Raja Singa had returned to Candi with his exhausted army, but their attack failed.

Sea battle between us and them

The new Governor van der Meyden made an attack on 20th March to conquer Caliture but was prevented from achieving this for intervening reasons, letting himself proceed to Nigumbo with much more reason.

---

[1] One of the founders of the Dutch empire in the east. In 1653 he was appointed Commissioner and Commander-in-Chief of the Company's forces against the Portuguese in Ceylon and West Asia. He was later Governor of Ceylon in 1662–1663 and 1665–1675 and Governor General in 1685–1687.

[2] Uduwara.

[3] Came out east in 1649 as *Koopman* and served in Ceylon for 5 years, in Negombo (1650), Galle (1651) and later as Dissāva of Mātara.

In the meanwhile there occurred a naval battle between 3 of our pursuit-ships, de Windhond, de Rhinocer and de Dromedaris, and 5 galleons with 1000 men as the Portuguese force, in which they lost their Captain Major or General and many men, besides many wounded, by which they were forced to run into Colombo.

Van Goens destroys some galleons at Cape de Ramos

They also received no small loss from the Commissioner Ryklof van Goens when he, returning from Persia and Suratte, attacked and destroyed their galleons at Cape de Ramos[1] and released 20 of our Anguratote prisoners,[2] of which even the Emperor was informed on the 6th June by a letter of the Governor, through Lieutenant Frans Has.

On the 27th November, his Excellency sent a letter to his Majesty, through the *Koopman* Ysbrand Godsken,[3] with some remarkable horses and other beautiful rarities for the prince, his son, and also various intercepted letters of the enemy for his Majesty's satisfaction.

To this letter, his Majesty replied on 8th March 1655, through Godsken who had come to the lowlands with his Majesty's ambassadors. Then Mr. van der Meyden informed his Majesty on the 27th March that the Portuguese were supported by unfaithful subjects of his Majesty in the Seven and Four Corles, which made them so bold that they dared to come bursting even into the Candian frontier gates, which his Majesty must prevent as far as possible, and guard against their traps.

His Excellency expected the arrival of the great relief force from Batavia every hour.

On the 19th May his Excellency informed his Majesty that Major van der Laan[4] had heavily bombarded the Caliture fortress but that the enemy had markedly strengthened it and had been supported by 4 Instantias[5] (or Platoons) from

[1] This battle took place in western India opposite Vengurla. Cape Ramas is about 20 miles south of Goa.

[2] Dutch prisoners captured when the fort of Anguruwatota was taken by the Portuguese.

[3] Captain of the forces and later Commander at Galle 1656–1661. Subsequently became Commander of Malabar 1665–1667.

[4] Jan van der Laan, Captain of the armed forces, made Commander of Negombo in 1652.

[5] See p. 353 n. 8.

Colombo. Also there was a rumour that Caspar Figero[1] had unexpectedly attacked his Majesty's Dessave in Caticapale[2] but that his Majesty had defeated 3 or 4 Instantias shortly thereafter, of which his Excellency awaited further news and confirmation. And as some Portuguese frigates had shown themselves near our Bay, his Excellency had fitted out two pursuit-ships to follow them to Colombo, Jaffanapatnam, Manaar, Pambanan[3] or wherever they went.

On the 9th July his Excellency informed the Emperor of our victory over the Portuguese relief force before Gale and how his Majesty's ambassadors had witnessed it themselves, that our forces had chased a frigate on the Gunderas[4] coast on to the shore, two had been brought by the pursuit-ship de Leeuw into the Gale Bay, and their General of Colombo, Antoni de Sousa Coutinho,[5] had been forced to run outside with his 8 other frigates, whereby the Portuguese force had been put out of commission, besides which we had taken many Portuguese and blacks captive. However, according to the latest information, the enemy was still 12 or 15 Instantias strong within Caliture, but as soon as our great relief force landed, which was now on the way, his Excellency did not doubt that we should be in a position to drive them entirely out of the island, supported by his Majesty, and to put all the conquered cities in his Majesty's hands.

Great promises, of which however not much was to be expected, as long as our heavy expenses of war were not settled, to which his Majesty appeared to give little thought.

Thus now and then some skirmishes occurred of little importance between us and the Portuguese, or between them and the Emperor, whose people were badly defeated in January 1655,[6] whereupon he left for the highlands to sulk,

---

[1] Gaspar de Figueira de Serpe. A Portuguese soldier of mixed Portuguese-Sinhalese descent who was the leader of the mutiny against the Captain General Homem in 1652 and played a major role in the battle against the Kandyans.

[2] Kotikapola.

[3] Pāmban Āru.

[4] Gintota.

[5] Antonio de Sousa Coutinho, who was coming to Ceylon as Captain General when his fleet was attacked before Galle.

[6] Gaspar de Figueira's victory against the Kandyan Dissāva in the Seven Kōralēs.

but nothing of importance happened until after Mr. Gerard Hulft[1] appeared here.

This gentleman, Director General of the Indies, and being in the way of Mr. Maatsuyker, was by a fine Jesuit trick of this Governor General, prevailed upon to leave from Batavia as Commander for Ceylon, as we have shown in more detail in the life of Mr. Maatsuyker, under the subject of Batavia.[2]

This gentleman came to Ceylon in the year 1655, conquered the fort Caliture on the 15th October by treaty of which the articles and other details can be seen in Baldaeus, as also in what esteem this gentleman was with Raja Singa.[3]

On 9th November 1655 he attacked the city of Colombo with no less courage but on 10th April 1656, while going to inspect the works closely, and being too busy to guard himself against the fire from a gallery, as a result of some gunfire by the Portuguese, he was so unfortunate as to be struck by a rifle bullet at sundown, at which he died immediately,[4] though the Fort Kais[5] was conquered on the 28th.

A poem written by Mr. Vondel we see among his Poems on Portraits, Fol. 557.[6]

On the Noble Gentleman Geeraerd Hulft
First Councillor and Director-General of the East
Indies, Commander-in-Chief of the armed forces,
both on water and on land, sent to Ceylon and the
Coast of India.

The Commander-in-Chief HULFT, to reduce Lisbon's
power,

[1] From an influential family in Holland, came out east in 1654 to Batavia as Director General. Was appointed Commander of the fleet dispatched early in 1655 to capture Colombo.

[2] Here Valentijn expresses a contemporary belief that Maatsuyker was a crypto-Catholic and that he was in some way responsible for Hulft's death. He calls Maatsuyker a 'crafty, cunning fox' in his earlier description. Valentijn IV. 1, 297–301.

[3] Baldaeus, p. 63.

[4] Described in detail by Baldaeus, pp. 107–108.

[5] Kayts in north Ceylon. It was taken by the Dutch on 28th April 1658. Valentijn has skipped over a number of events.

[6] The famous Dutch poet of the 17th century, Joost van den Vondel (1587–1679), wrote a few poems in honour of Gerard Hulft. This poem was a memorial to him and was engraved at the foot of his painting done by Flink.

Came thus to storm Colombo, on the order of the
                                           Company,
The Sea-port yielded in the end, and to oppress the heart,
Stood breathless and ready on the point of surrender.
When a bullet struck him, at the peak of his life,
So died this Commander, standing in armour, like a hero.

Colombo captured by Mr. van der Meyden

After his death the Governor, van der Meyden, took over control as Commander, resuming the assault on Colombo on the 7th May, conquered the bulwark Victoria, then named St. Joan, and seized the city on 12th May by treaty, since which time it has been our chief comptoir.[1]

The Portuguese had occupied this city for about 150 years and were now finally driven out of it by our people, in spite of their having obtained a great relief force on 18th May 1655 with the new Governor, Antonio de Sousa Coutinho,[2] after a siege of 6 months and courageous resistance.

Toetocoryn by Major van der Laan

Manaar and Jaffanapatnam conquered

And the Portuguese driven from Ceylon

In 1658 the city of Toetocorin was conquered on the 1st February by Major van der Laan and the island of Manaar on the 22nd by van der Meyden and on the 22nd June the kingdom of Jaffanapatnam which was followed by the city of Nagapatnam in August[3] and thus the Portuguese were wiped out entirely from the island where they had settled so long, all of which conquests of the courageous Batavians, one after the other in Ceylon, Baldaeus has narrated for us in great detail, to which we refer the reader, in order not to be long-winded;[4] the more so as our aim mostly is to write of things which are not to be found elsewhere.

Raja Singa angered against us

In the meanwhile, Raja Singa, seeing that we would not hand over to him the cities conquered by us, according to his expectation and the promise of Hulft, as he claimed, began to be embittered against us not a little, and to do us all damage, which he persisted in for many years thereafter and up to the end of his life, showing himself at one time somewhat better than at another.

[1] Treaty reproduced in Baldaeus, pp. 123–5.

[2] Antonio de Sousa Coutinho became Captain General in August 1655.

[3] The capture of north Ceylon and the ports of South India are described by Baldaeus, pp. 147–60. He was an eye-witness to many of these events.

[4] Baldaeus is far more detailed on this last phase of the Dutch-Portuguese conflict, pp, 62–160.

In 1660 he took the old and young Cnox with some Englishmen captive, but the son escaped to us in 1679.[1]

In the same year, Mr. van der Meyden handed over the Governorship to the Commissioner Rijklof van Goens who had been previously with this title, though in the meanwhile he had gone to the Fatherland in 1655, but that these gentlemen were not at all friendly will appear from the letter of Mr. van Goens of 10th November and that he sent Mr. van der Meyden to Batavia, though their Excellencies sent him shortly thereafter back to Ceylon.[2]

In the meanwhile Mr. van der Meyden left for Batavia where his Excellency delivered to their Excellencies an exposition of the state of Ceylon from the beginning till we conquered it, which we have deemed it necessary to reproduce here as something rare, as it will shed a great deal of light for the reader on the affairs of Ceylon.[3]

Extract from a Short Exposition, how our officers from time to time obtained a footing in Ceylon and have taken this island from the Portuguese. Also how Raja Singa conducted himself, in the meanwhile, against us and the Portuguese and what profit (apart from the cinnamon which is peeled there) is to be found there in compensation for our expenses and other things, delivered to his Excellency the Governor General and Councillor of Netherlands Indies.

My Lords,

After King Emanuel of Portugal first discovered the East-Indian route round the Cape of Good Hope through Vasco

Exposition of the Governor van der Meyden on the state of Ceylon

[1] Robert Knox and his son were ship-wrecked in their ship 'Anne' on the Kottiyār coast in 1660. They were seized by the Kandyans and taken to Kandy. The father died in captivity but the son escaped after twenty years.

[2] Van Goens was Commissioner with supervisory powers when van der Meyden was Governor. They were in conflict with each other and van der Meyden was recalled to Batavia to answer charges made against him by the Commissioner van Goens in 1662.

[3] This report is a valuable summary of the establishment of Dutch power in Ceylon. Much of the material has already been incorporated by Valentijn in his description, but there are some supplementary facts. The language is even more cumbersome than that of Valentijn, with long sentences, parenthetical clauses and sub-clauses and an inability to handle the narrative with clarity.

Gama in 1697,[1] and had taken possession of all the best ports and bays, a hundred years later our united Netherlanders came to trade here and Admiral Joris van Spilbergen was before Baticalo in 1602 and had negotiations with the Emperor of Candi over a quantity of pepper and over the cinnamon, in order to receive these for a reasonable price, if possible, and then to come to take this away yearly. The next year Vice-Admiral Sebalt de Weerd also appeared here with 6 ships, but he was (God forfend) treacherously murdered with 50 Netherlanders on 1st May 1603; his Majesty denied responsibility because de Weerd had tried to force him to come on board or at least to the coast to see his ships, otherwise he would not help him to conquer Point Gale; though it was more probable that the Portuguese, with whom he was now again at peace, planned it thus to drive him entirely from Ceylon, though others put the responsibility on the Emperor's Ambassador, who had come over with de Weerd from Achin, and was treated by him rather worse than the Portuguese; they also think that out of revenge for the insult of having seated the Portuguese at mealtime at the higher end and him at the lower end, not only did he so incite the Emperor against him, but had even informed him that de Weerd plotted an attack and treachery against the Emperor's life and had no other reason than this to invite the Emperor so earnestly to his ship and to the shore.

However, both these nations were afterwards engaged in war again and, the Emperor Don Jan having died, Raja Singa's father Seneraad Adasseyn, having succeeded him, wrote many times to the coast and here for Dutch help and in 1612 one Marcellus Boschhouder was sent via Choromandel to Jakatra and even to the Fatherland. But the Directors still remembering afresh the murder of De Weerd and not believing too readily his fine promises, Boschhouder betook himself to the Danish King from whom he obtained some ships and soldiers to help the Ceylonese King against the Portuguese and he then set sail towards that place. But Boschhouder having died on the way, and the disunited Danish nobility having anchored with

[1] Error for 1497.

their ships near Sambanture,[1] they informed Seneraad Adasseyn of their arrival, who had some of their chiefs convey inland the widow and maidservants of Marcellus Bouschhouder, without compensating them to any great extent with cinnamon, pepper or in any other suitable manner, letting further the Danes sit idly with their ships and requirements, who finally as a fruitless matter after the loss of some of their best ships in the bad monsoon, departed to Choromandel very dissatisfied, though their General Rouland Carpe and many others had sought compensation many times from the Emperor Adasseyn[2] and from Raja Singa.[3]

In the meanwhile the now reigning Raja Singa (1636) wrote with great promises to Paliacatta[4] and to Batavia for help, which took one year on the way. Also their Excellencies from here had ordered that this Emperor should be enticed in every manner, which happened in the meanwhile through the gentleman Carel Reynierszoon's[5] good management with Jan Thysson, Adrian Helmond and myself, according to Raja Singa's own request, when we arrived here by the pursuit-ship, de Valk, in November 1637 about seven miles south of Baticalo, having sailed a good 25 German miles through his Majesty's territory up the river Mawieleganga into the province of Bintene, came to this Emperor who, being pleased at our arrival, narrated to us how the Portuguese General Diego de Mello de Castro,[6] having information in Colombo of his dealings with us, had written about this to his Majesty's brother the Prince of Mature.[7] Finally the Emperor released us with promise of sufficient payment for all expenses of the Company in harming the Portuguese in Ceylon, along with 3 Commissioners, and a letter to Admiral Adam Westerwold, whom we found with the offensive fleet before Goa and gave information of what happened between us and the Emperor.

In the meanwhile the dissatisfied Cingalese (who had been

---

[1] Sambanthurai, near Batticaloa.　　[2] King Senerat.

[3] Senerat's successor.　　[4] Paleacatte or Pulicat in Coromandel.

[5] Carel Reyniers, Governor of Coromandel 1636–1638 and later Governor General, 1650–1653.

[6] Portuguese Captain General of Ceylon 1636–1638.

[7] Error for Mātalē. The prince referred to is Vijayapāla, the brother of King Rāja Sinha whom the Portuguese were trying to win over.

incited by the Portuguese and were even appointed as Dessaves) incited their General and their most important and hot-tempered officers who, with their force of 400 whites and some 1000 blacks, marched up to Candi in 1638 to besiege the King's men in the highlands and bring him to submission, who then took flight to Candi and in the meanwhile surrounded the Portuguese army and, after various skirmishes with their commanders, many of them were slain and the rest taken prisoners.[1]

Whereupon the Commissioner left with the conspiring Dessaves for the lowlands and crossed some frontier posts. The Portuguese, by their marching too high up into the mountains, lost their Generals Don Nunho Alvares Pereira and Constantinus de Saa[2] under Senerat Adasseyn and Raja Singa.

Shortly thereafter Westerwold mastered the Fort of Baticalo in May[3] and made a contract with Raja Singa. He could then have easily conquered Trikoenmale (where there were hardly 50 soldiers) but it appeared that Raja first would have a trial of the Company's army in Baticalo.

In 1639 Mr. Antoni Caan conquered Trikoenmale. The Director General Philip Lucaszoon conquered the Fort Nigumbo on 9th February 1640 and on 13th March 1640 the President Willem Jacobszoon Coster stormed the city of Gale, without the King's men giving any help there except to share in plundering the booty as soon as there was no more danger. Whereby then (as all the might of the Portuguese up to the possessions of Gale was cleared away) Colombo was very poorly manned with citizens, weapons and soldiers, so that they hardly dared to come outside the gates, as a result of which Raja could easily have conquered the badly fortified city. But then considering that it was better to be caressed by two nations than to be dominated by one proud, far-famed nation, he let the Portuguese again catch their breath.

Coster, appearing in the meanwhile before him in Candi,

[1] The battle of Gannoruva at which the Captain General Diogo de Mello himself was killed (1638).

[2] Dom Nuno Alvares Pereira, Captain General 1616–1618 did not lose his life in battle in Ceylon; Dom Constantino de Sa was killed in 1622.

[3] 1638.

could obtain little for all his just requests for the Company, was fruitlessly held up for so long that he could not hold his anger any longer and began to speak boldly against the chiefs, to scold them and to threaten them, so that they complained to the Emperor, who thereon immediately gave Coster his leave and let him depart without any honour or station, letting him be treacherously murdered by his guides to Baticalo with four of his attendants. A poor reward for Coster's faithful services to the Emperor, to whom he had delivered Trikoenmale and all the lands and inhabitants of Gale and Mature, with their taxes, and had entrusted them to his agents and only demanded the cinnamon that had been peeled and was still being harvested to be supplied within Gale.

Then the Portuguese obtained assistance in that year from Goa, retook Nigumbo on 8th November 1640 and also besieged Gale, without our being assisted, however, by the Emperor according to promises, who at first abandoned all the lowlands and these were given over or vacated to our enemies again.

This lasted till 1644 (though Baticalo was also handed over to Raja and still more was offered to him by the Ambassador Pieter Boreel), when Mr. François Caron seized Nigumbo by storm again and strengthened it with 4 earthen strong-points and bulwarks and surrounded it outside with turf, keeping about 500 men on guard there. The Portuguese General, Don Philippo Mascarenhas,[1] intended to reconquer this place after the departure of the fleet to Gale, but this was denied to him, for by a sudden attack so many people were killed that he was forced to break off the siege with the remainder of his men and return again to Colombo.

In the meanwhile, Mr. Joan Maatsuyker came to Goa and concluded a contract of peace (for the demarcation of the boundary between the forces of the two sides) with the Viceroy, Joan de Telles de Meneses, Count of Aveyras, as desired by their Excellencies, the Principals, which was so accomplished that he, after the completion of this affair in 1646, returned here again. But Raja Singa, begrudging us the Seven Corles, allowed his pillaging thieves to devastate it now and

---

[1] Dom Philippe Mascarenhas, Captain General of Ceylon 1640–1645.

then, which the Portuguese encouraged eagerly, and it was brought so far by the Governor Joan Thyszoon that open war was declared against the King's men, after which Commander Nicolaas Jacobszoon Overschie of Nigumbo had Raja Singa's tame elephants from Hiriale, beyond the Company's frontiers, captured, over which his Majesty felt so offended that he gathered together all his forces and avenged himself on our army and people in the Seven Corles, who, not being able to defend themselves suitably and being without necessities and without defence, surrendered.[1]

However, with the return of Maatsuyker, Nigumbo, Gale Corle and the lands of Mature were well secured with their inhabitants, the cinnamon peeled and the wild elephants captured and all other income of the land gathered and Raja Singa quietened by friendly letters, who thereupon departed back to the highlands with his forces, without once bothering the Portuguese outposts (as if they had made sufficient promises of peace to each other before) and this continued until the end of 1648 before his Excellency could obtain the release of the remaining prisoners through some embassies from Candi.

Whereupon the Emperor (because of the peace) now intended to get the inhabitants of the Mature district under his authority. But that was so well controlled by his Excellency in the beginning of 1650 that Rampot, his Dessave, according to his own request, left Gale and Mature. Now this being bad for Raja, he however let it finally drag on without being upset about it, but with the beginning of the war against the Portuguese in the end of 1652, he again declared himself with us against his enemy, both because the Portuguese soldiers with some important citizens mutinied against their Captain General Manuel Mascarenhas Homem and imprisoned him, besides other reasons which moved his Majesty to this action.

These conspirators gathered a large force in Colombo, departed immediately with 800 whites and many more blacks to our post Anguratotte, which was handed over to them after 11 days' siege and the killing of some persons on the 8th January 1653, with 98 Netherlanders, 24 Javanese and more

---

[1] Already described by Valentijn. See above Chapter XI, pp. 330–1.

lascarines under condition of reasonable release, just as we on the same afternoon with about 300 soldiers and rather more natives went to their relief. This apparently would not have gone on well even though our people had not surrendered because they were more than ever so strong in their advantage in the narrow passes and surrounded our people so closely and, if the Portuguese had followed up their victory on our forces departing to Caleture, they should have done us even more harm than this.

Now when Raja Singa saw that our people at Anguratotte were in need, he made his Dessave attack the enemy quarter in Cottegore[1] and fell on their outposts up to the passes around Colombo, whereupon their Governor and Captain-General summoned the entire army from the Pasdum and Reygam Corla to Colombo and, after they had chased the King's forces from Colombo and from their bases, they led them to our outposts of Nigumbo, where they captured three white soldiers, and shortly thereafter went to occupy the Four and Seven Corles with their smartest soldiers for provisions, when Raja Singa came down with a large army from the Ouva side to Saffragam (the capital of the Five Corles), which the Portuguese Dessave lying in wait with some companies forced to retire up to Goerbeville, whereby we were better able to assist each other, and Gale Corle and Mature district were held entirely unencumbered.

In the meanwhile on 10th May, 12 frigates arrived before Colombo with another old General named Francisco de Melo de Castro, some new officers, soldiers and many more necessities from Goa, our cruisers having broken up their siege only two days before through bad weather (God forfend) and sailed to the Bay of Gale.

This armada strengthened the Portuguese in Colombo very much; however they did not set up any men against us, using them only for the strengthening of their army in the Four and Seven Corlas inland where they lay on their guard against the King's men, to free their cinnamon peelers and inhabitants which they also naturally achieved.

But Raja Singa, having observed that the Portuguese in

[1] Kotagoda.

Colombo were provided with supplies from Toetocoryn in September 1653, and that we in the first four ships (by which the old Governor Jacob van Kitenstein was permitted his release) had not obtained one soldier for the relief of those who had long sought it, nor received any by the end of October through the Commissioner Rijklof van Goens, who was headed for Persia and Suratte with four more ships, his Majesty retired with his people, whom he had brought to the lowlands and who were mostly fatigued, from around the Portuguese military posts in November, from Carvanello[1] and elsewhere through the Four and Seven Corlas to Candi again back to his rest.

Just as the Portuguese were released from this dreaded crowd, they advanced to attack us with their might again before Nigumbo and to obtain some advantage. But they, not doing much there, went in the beginning of 1654 back to Caleture, to the upper side of the river, and camped in Reygam and Pasdum Corle, from which they sent out their parties now and then through Pasdum Corle and Wielawitte Corle up to Pittigelle[2] and Alican[3] to secure the harvest and animals and to commit further robberies, which his Excellency Jan van der Laan tried to attack with advantage along our coast, and I with a few soldiers set out on the 20th March from Gale to Caleture, from which we on the 23rd March, with all our forces, searched for the advancing Portuguese army via Verberin[4] to Matu, Dova Dodan Godde[5] and Tiboen,[6] which we found on the 26th in the morning a half hour further on in a strong position ready for battle (there being a deep spring between both forces) where our people could not approach further, and after an hour's attacking they retired somewhat beyond gunshot to attract the Portuguese closer to us but they dared not approach us nor abandon the good pass, otherwise they would have been routed, having on their side more soldiers wounded and dead than on our side. Having rested and eaten at Tiboen with this company, we left for Caleture and they marched from the Company's district via the river to Colombo where they found for themselves a reinforcement of five

---

[1] Karavanella.　　[2] Pitigala.　　[3] Alutgama.
[4] Beruwela.　　[5] Matugama, Dodangoda.　　[6] Tebuwana.

galleons with 900 men. As I passed in the pursuit-ship Zeerob to make an inspection of Nigumbo on the 29th March before Colombo hardly a great cannon shot to sea, these galleons attacked three Company ships, de Windhond, Rhinocer and Drommedaris, driving them before Nigumbo reef, though, God be thanked, not one could be mastered. From there the Portuguese, because of the loss of their Captain Major and many more dead and wounded, returned to Colombo on 23rd March in the evening and our abovenamed ships were saved by the Nigumbo cannon, whose authorities supplied us by water and by land, so that with the 5 galleons about 1000 white men were landed for Ceylon from the Indian coast. I therefore returned to Caleture without being followed and it was unanimously decided by the Council to abandon Caleture and to assist Nigumbo as much as we could, which happened on the 1st April. But the enemy having been strengthened with many people, came from Galkisse again to occupy Caleture and camped at Alican, against which we, after being reinforced from the ships, and from Nigumbo, sent out 200 soldiers, 80 Javanese and a company of lascarines (not being able to spare any more) to protect our long-possessed lands, cinnamon peelers and the inhabitants as has generally happened (God be thanked). On the return of the fleet of the Commissioner Ryklof van Goens from Suratte in the end of April, it so happened on the 1st May that his Excellency destroyed 40 frigates before Atchaira[1] and all the 5 galleons off Cape de Ramos[2] (only two were sighted at first) and released 20 of our Anguratotte prisoners and set them ashore at Gale, as a result of which the Portuguese could send few people with frigates to Ceylon. Therefore from both sides and even from the King's, nothing exceptional could be accomplished till in July we brought out our army again somewhat strengthened up to Bentotte (right opposite the enemy, only the river being between both forces) where they intended on the 11th August to refresh themselves somewhat, there being but a few people remaining. But the Portuguese

---

[1] Unidentifiable. Could it be Jinjeera or Janjira, a few miles south of Bombay or Agashi to its north?
[2] Cape Ramas, about 20 miles south of Goa.

had lost their 30 white soldiers and some *thonys* so that their courage was very dampened. They summoned more from the Four Corlas so that the Portuguese along the upper side could fall on our land and stop the cinnamon and arecanut harvest and the elephant capture.

In the meanwhile we obtained on the 31st September, by the pursuit-ships Tortelduyf, Roodeleeuw and Cabbeljauw, a reinforcement of 50 soldiers, and on the 4th December with the pursuit-ship de Konyn a further 54 fresh soldiers who, with another 150 marines from the cargo ships through the Director Henrik van Gent,[1] which arrived on the 9th December 1654 off Gale for fresh water and other things on the way, altogether added to our strength in the army at Bentotte, where we on the 16th before daybreak passed unhindered across the river Alican, above both the armies on 20 rafts with 690 officers, soldiers, marines and Javanese and also more Cingalese. But we found in passing 300 selected white Portuguese, some toepasses and Cingalese, such hard and long opposition that most of our Cingalese took flight and His Excellency van der Laan, with 10 companies of soldiers, withdrew. After a while he again looked for and gathered them together and made them march to the coast when we first drove the enemy away and obtained his metal piece over a 1000 pounds' weight, who retired defending continuously with extraordinary courage for about a mile till the evening, leaving behind about 60 dead soldiers, besides having sent out many more wounded.

Likewise their army withdrew from the upper side of Malvane and Colombo while the King's men then followed. But the Portuguese, seeing that we did not concentrate any further on Caleture and all their people having been provided with good allowances, quickly marched inland in January 1635[2] again and a party of them attacked Raja's Dessave of the Four Corlas, and with the assistance landed from Jaffanapatnam and Manaar and many lascarines of the Dessave of Seven

---

[1] Served the Company in a number of factories: head of the factory at Jambi in Sumatra 1640–43, Malacca 1643–44, head of Palembang and Jambi 1644–48, Director of Surat 1654–57.

[2] Error for 1655.

Corlas who had fallen to them, they followed him up to the narrow passes of Candi and plundered the inhabitants, at which his Imperial Majesty was so angry that he assembled together most of his army and on 5th April he was attacked by the advance guard of the Captain Major Caspar Tigero[1] near Attapittin[2] and Cottacapales[3] palace, as a result of which his Majesty once again retired inland with the remaining people to Candi and remained sulking there. It went badly for the new General Antonio de Sousa Continho,[4] who with about 500 soldiers in 8 frigates was attacked so well by us shortly there-after on the 18th May off Gale that 2 frigates with all the people and the provisions laden were captured by the pursuit-ships de Leeuw and Konyn, 2 frigates were beached and the afore-mentioned General was chased up to Punto das Pedras[5] and only 2 or 3 frigates reached the Bay of Colombo. The General, with a reasonable convoy from Jaffanapatnam and Manaar, reached Colombo on the 7th August via Puttalam, Calpentyn and the Seven Corlas and was installed there. He inspected Caleture at once with the Captain Major Antonio Mendez d' Arangie,[6] whom he left camping there with about 300 brave soldiers and a similar number of blacks, and the Captain Major Gaspar Tigero was summoned with all his subordinate men from the upper side between both forces to the works.

In the meanwhile the Director Gerard Hulft and especially Major van der Laan (who had sufficient knowledge of it) neglected to send 2 or 3 pursuit-ships of the fleet from the point of Commerin[7] in the middle of September in front of Toetocoryn to besiege the enemy's provision stores within the islands. At the same time the Portuguese withdrew their people from Caleture, especially because they knew that his Excellency with such a great force of men and ships had landed before Nigumbo and had tried to harass them over Mutwal river. But this armada consisting of 20 frigates and other vessels with all necessities assembled from Jaffanapatnam and from the Indian coast sailed close in front of Nigumbo (our ships remaining at anchor there), all arriving safely within the

---

[1] Gaspar de Figueira de Serpe.   [2] Atapitiya.   [3] Kotikāpola.
[4] Antonio de Sousa de Coutinho.   [5] Point Pedro.
[6] Antonio Mendes Aranha.   [7] Cape Comorin.

Bay of Colombo when Mr. Hulft received news by the pursuit-ship from Wingurla that a new Viceroy had landed from Portugal with 3 galleons, a pursuit-ship and many men. Whereupon his Excellency proposed on the 25th to sail against them to meet them on their way near Mormagon[1] or the Aguada[2] or to await this relief force in ships at anchor off Colombo. But his Excellency fared better with 4 ships and a party of soldiers before Verberin where he joined up on the 28th with our army on Macoene[3] and the following day besieged Fort Caleture which we soon mastered through their lack of provisions, and subsequently the relief force of 600 to 700 whites and many more Cingalese directed here was utterly defeated on the 17th October before Colombo. And the following day this fortified city was very easily surrounded entirely when the King's forces also came down delighted from the land in strength to assist us, and helped in cutting and bringing the coconut trees to the batteries. But after the blowing of sufficient breaches and the unanimous resolution of all the Councillors to attack first on the Watergate, we lost (God forfend) in this storming about 300 white men with those remaining in the city, and received about as many wounded (besides the blacks). However with holding out, sapping, starving them out and the unfortunate death of the valiant Director General Hulft, of beloved memory (in the work on the gallery and the driving out of the Portuguese relief sent from Goa which lay surrounded by our pursuit-ships before Toetocoryn), they escaped on the 7th July by night with 15 light frigates from there behind the rocky reefs through Pambenaar[4] with about 500 soldiers to Jaffanapatnam, after which we, on 12th May 1656, seized Colombo by a reasonable treaty, but as soon as Raja Singa heard that, his Majesty desired out of envy immediately that Colombo and Nigumbo especially must be delivered to his Majesty's Dessaves according to the promises of his Excellency the Director General Hulft, whereupon we offered to him Nigumbo and the greater part of Colombo also to be

---

[1] Marmagao, on the outskirts of Goa.
[2] Agoada, at the entrance to the harbour of Goa.
[3] Maggona. [4] Pāmban Channel.

demolished. However his Majesty still remained unfriendly, erupting finally very unreasonably even to the seizing and slaying of our white soldiers and black inhabitants and the troubling of the lands possessed long by the Company, at which I requested at different times in writing that he be pleased to desist or that we would finally be forced to oppose it ourselves, as in fact happened on the 10th and 11th November with his expulsion and that of all his men from around Colombo and Regamwatte.

Also on the 20th we bade farewell to Major van der Laan, proceeding to Batavia via Gale in the pursuit-ships de Windhond and 't Haasje, which were richly laden for Gamron, and to Commander Adrian Roodhaas[1] in the war ships, de Dolfyn, 't Zeepaard, Vlissingen, de Schelvis, de Zeerob, de Romeyn and a further four more frigates all well mounted and provided with 612 men to join up with the fleet before Goa and to besiege this Bar when the northeastern monsoon broke.

In the meanwhile some came to us escaping from the woods and Raja Singa sent from Candi an important ambassador to Jaffanapatnam for assistance, whom the Portuguese (who smarted under their great loss) treated badly and asked if his shameful Majesty still wished to trouble them any more in the lowlands. But the Governor of Goa ordered that those of Jaffanapatnam should give a better hearing to the Cingalese chiefs and that they should try to move Raja to devotion to them in order to retake Colombo, Gale or Nigumbo and Seven Corlas. But we have not seen how far they have later had agreement with each other, though we have heard many great rumours but have seen little consequence of it, doing us no great injury within our limits nor hindrance in our cinnamon or arecanut harvest, elephant hunt and nothing against the collection of our other taxes.

On the 10th January the Admiral, Commissioner and Superintendent, Ryklof van Goens, arrived off Colombo in de Avondster from the Goan bar and the Indian coast with 260 soldiers, 160 marines and 30 Ambonese where we met his

---

[1] Adriaan Roothaas, naval commander under the Company who assisted van Goens in the naval battles against the Portuguese in south Asia. Later appointed Commander of Galle and acted as Governor in 1665.

Excellency with a further 450 soldiers, 340 lascarines and marines from the pursuit-ships ter Goes, de Avondster, Ter Veer, Manaar, Mosambyke, de Romeyn, de Boterbloem, Tayouan, de Caneelschiller and 't Waterpas, 2 sloops and 8 large *thonies*[1] provided with sufficient ammunition, etc. and where his Excellency van der Laan was to come ashore with 270 men with the pursuit-ship Naarden and the ship de Salamander and more people from around Toetocoryn, of which town his Excellency took possession on 1st February, and with all this force on the 20th we landed successfully against 600 Portuguese on the west side of Manaar and immediately they took flight, and on the following day Fort Manaar was delivered to us with 180 prisoners, both from there and from the woods.

On 1st March his Excellency marched with the army over land and rivers up to the Jaffanapatnam castle without marked opposition, where the Portuguese were immediately surrounded as also in the Fort Cays.[2] In the meanwhile Commander Roodhaas engaged in battle off Goa against 10 galleons of which one was burnt and the others chased under the castle, whereby they could not come to relieve Jaffanapatnam.

On the 27th April 1658 Mr. van Goens captured Fort Cays and on 22nd January[3] the castle of Jaffanapatnam, and on 1st August Nagapatnam in the Tansjouwer Province[4] was taken by Major van der Laan which the people of the Naik[5] opposed, but they were routed by Mr. van Goens, so that some hundreds of Malabars remained dead and many were wounded. Whereupon they agreed that our occupation should remain even as that of the Portuguese in Nagapatnam.

Thereupon his Excellency proceeded to Palleacatta and came after transacting business there to Jaffanapatnam, Manaar and Colombo, where he was welcomed on 3rd November and found everything in good order. Then he went to Malabar with the army and Mr. van Goens rapidly mastered Coylan.[6] Then he departed with his army to Cananoor where he obtained the order from your Excellency to stop the expedition

---

[1] *Thony* (Tam.)—one-masted boat.
[2] Kayts.
[3] Error for 22nd June. See Baldaeus, p. 158.
[4] Thanjavur or Tanjore.
[5] Nāyak, the ruler of Tanjore.
[6] Now called Quilon.

and immediately to send here 500 soldiers which happened on the 1st February 1695[1] with Ter Goes and Workom, and the Admiral left behind a moderate occupation force in Coylan. And we resolved that in the middle of February I should make the journey to Toetocoryn to enter into a contract with the great governor Barramalle Aple Pulle[2] or the Nayk of Madura, which was proceeded with but by the death of this Naik shortly before and the accession of a bastard son whom we did not trust at all, it was stopped, though however we remain living in friendship with him.

At the same time I paid a visit to Coilan which had been besieged by 3000 Portuguese and some thousand Nayrs[3] right up to the walls, so that the Council unanimously decided the place could not be held because of the bad weather.

We therefore embarked everything on the 14th by night and abandoned the place towards the end of this month with the people from Coilan and with the pursuit-ships, together about 300 men and in addition another 100 soldiers and 200 Ambonese and Javanese as well as toepasses and 400 lascarines. Then I went along the coast on the 14th May through the Seven Corlas to Calpentyn to relieve our men surrounded on Navi Cadu,[4] which was very well protected against some thousand of Raja's people and I relieved 60 soldiers and some lascarines from Navi Cadu and returned to Colombo after demolishing the gates and strengthening the church on the north point of Calpentyn on the 26th May. The King's men have since had no army within the Company's frontiers.

Then Mr. van Goens set out on the 25th January of this year[5] with the army from Ceylon to Malabar where his Excellency however found everything still unprepared and not in a state to begin anything.

In the meanwhile I, after having governed Ceylon for some more time, was relieved from here by his Excellency in the

[1] Error for 1659.
[2] Parimalappa Pillai, the chief minister of the Nāyak of Madura.
[3] Nairs, a high caste of Malabar from whom in this period the militia was drawn.
[4] Nāvatkādu, near Putalam.
[5] 1660.

same year and have come here to give your Excellencies a further report on matters which happened there.

In Batavia Castle on the 20th
September 1660
Your Excellency's Obedient Servant,
Adriaan van der Meyden.

Although this gentleman had left for Batavia he did not remain there long, however; but in the meanwhile he, being appointed Ordinary Councillor of Netherlands Indies, their Excellencies decided to send his Excellency in 1661 back here as Governor of Ceylon.

He did not appear here alone in this same year, but Mr. van Goens gave this government back to his Excellency and also besides, according to the order of Their Excellencies, gave these following Considerations, which shed much light on the affairs of Ceylon for the reader, in the way of Instructions.[1]

* * * * *

After the handing over of this government to Mr. van der Meyden, the Commissioner van Goens appears to have seriously promoted the affairs of the company in Malabar for a time (as we shall see elsewhere in what follows),[2] and in the meanwhile to have left Ceylon to the Governor's care entirely, who during his time brought reasonable peace up to 1663, except that he had various difficulties now and then with Raja Singa, when he handed over this government back to Mr. van Goens in the month of April at which time he also departed to Batavia from here.

[1] These Considerations have been published in English translation: *Instructions from the Governor-General and Council of India to the Governor of Ceylon, 1656–1665*. Transl. by Sophia Pieters (Colombo, 1908). Valentijn's extracts are not reproduced here.

[2] Vol. V, 2, *Beschrijvinge van Malabar*, pp. 1–48.

Bibliography

ABEYASINGHE, TIKIRI, *Portuguese rule in Ceylon 1594–1612*. Colombo, 1966.

ANDRIESZ, GEORG, *De Beschryving der Reizen van Georg Andriesz*, door Adam Olearius, in de Hoogduitsche Taal uitgegeven, en van J. H. Glazemaker vertaalt. T'Amsterdam, 1670.

ARASARATNAM, S. *Dutch power in Ceylon 1658–1687*. Amsterdam, 1958.

—— 'François Valentijn's description of Coromandel', *Professor K. A. Nilakanta Sastri Felicitation Volume*. Madras, 1971, pp. 1–10.

BALDAEUS, PHILIPPUS, *Beschrijving der Oost-Indische Kusten Malabar en Choromandel der selver aengrensende Koninckrijcken en Vorstendomme als oock het Keijserrijck Ceylon*. Amsterdam, 1972.

—— *A true and exact description of the great island Ceylon*. Maharagama, 1960 (*The Ceylon Historical Journal*, Vol. VIII).

BANDARANAYAKE, W. M. et al. *A Glossary of Sinhala and Tamil names of the plants of Sri Lanka*. Colombo, 1974 (*The Sri Lanka Forester*, New Series, Vol. XI, Nos. 3 & 4).

BARROW, SIR GEORGE, *Ceylon past and present*. London, 1857.

BARROS, JOÃO DE, *The history of Ceylon, from the earliest times to 1600 A.D. as related by João de Barros and Diogo do Couto*. Transl. and Ed. Donald Ferguson. Colombo, 1909 (*Journal of the Ceylon Branch of the Royal Asiatic Society*, Vol. XX, No. 60, 1908).

BLAGDEN, C. O., *European manuscripts in the India Office library*, Vol. 1, Mackenzie Collection, Part 1. Oxford, 1916.

BOETZELAER VAN ASPEREN EN DUBBELDAM, C. W. TH. BARON VAN, *De Protestantsche Kerk in Nederlandsch-Indie*. 's Gravenhage, 1947.

BOXER, C. R., 'Three Historians of Portuguese Asia'. *Boletim de Instituto Portugues de Hong Kong*, Macau, 1948.

—— 'Portuguese and Dutch Colonial rivalry, 1641–1661'. *Studia*, Revista semestral No. 2, Julho 1955, pp. 7–42.

—— 'An Introduction to João Ribeiro's "Historical Tragedy of the

Island of Ceylon", 1685'. *The Ceylon Historical Journal*, Vol. V, No. 3 (1953), pp. 234–255.

BOXER, C. R., 'Ceylon through Puritan eyes: Robert Knox in the kingdom of Kandy, 1660–1679'. *History Today*, Vol. 4 (10) (Oct. 1954), pp. 660–667.

CODRINGTON, H. W., *Ancient land tenure and revenue in Ceylon*, Colombo, 1938.

——— *A short history of Ceylon*. London, 1947, Revd. ed.

COOLHAAS, W. PH., *A Critical survey of studies on Dutch colonial history*. 's Gravenhage, 1960.

——— 'Dutch contribution to the historiography of colonial activity in the eighteenth and nineteenth centuries', D. G. E. Hall, *Ed. Historians of Southeast Asia*. London 1961, pp. 225–234.

COUTO, DIOGO DO, *The History of Ceylon, from the earliest times to 1600 A.D. as related by João de Barros and Diogo do Couto*. Transl. and Ed. Donald Ferguson. Colombo, 1909 (*Journal of the Ceylon Branch of the Royal Asiatic Society*, Vol. XX, No. 60).

DAM, PIETER VAN, *Beschryvinge van de Oost-Indische Compagnie*. Uitgegeven door Dr. F. W. Stapel. Rijks Geschiedkundige Publicatien, Nos. 63, 68, 74, 76, 83. 's Gravenhage, 1927–1939.

ENCYCLOPOEDIE VAN NEDERLANDSCH-INDIE, 8 vols. 's Gravenhage, Leiden, 1917–1939.

FERGUSON, D. W., 'Robert Knox's Sinhalese vocabulary'. *Journal of the Royal Asiatic Society (Ceylon)*, Vol. XIV, No. 47 (1896), pp. 155–201.

——— 'The discovery of Ceylon by the Portuguese in 1506'. *Journal of the Royal Asiatic Society (Ceylon)*, Vol. 19, No. 59 (1909), pp. 284–400.

GODEE MOLSBERGEN, E. C., *Geschiedenis van Nederlands Indie*, Vol. IV. Amsterdam, 1939.

GILBERT, WILLIAM H., 'The Sinhalese caste system of Central and Southern Ceylon'. *Journal of the Washington Academy of Sciences*, No. 135, Nos. 3 and 4 (March–April 1945), pp. 105–125.

GOONETILEKE, H. A. I., *A Bibliography of Ceylon*, 2 Vols. Zug, 1970.

GOONEWARDENA, K. W., *The Foundation of Dutch Power in Ceylon 1638–1658*. Amsterdam, 1958.

——— 'Dutch historical writing on South Asia', C. H. Philips, Ed. *Historians of India, Pakistan and Ceylon*. London, 1961, pp. 170–182.

GRAAF, H. J. DE, 'Aspects of Dutch Historical writings on colonial activities in Southeast Asia with special reference to the indigenous people during the sixteenth and seventeenth centuries', D. G. E. Hall, Ed. *Historians of Southeast Asia*. London, 1961, pp. 213–224.

HAAN, F. DE, *Priangan*. Batavia, Den Haag, 1910.

HARRISON, J. B. 'Five Portuguese historians', C. H. Philips, Ed. *Historians of India, Pakistan and Ceylon*. London, 1961, pp. 155–169.

HAVART, DANIEL, *Op- en Ondergang van Cormandel*. Amsterdam 1693.

HEERES, J. E. Ed. *Corpus Diplomaticum Neerlando-Indicum*, Vol. 1. 's Gravenhage, 1907.

HODENPIJL, A. K. A. GIJSBERTI, 'François Valentijns laatste verblijfsjaren in Indie'. *De Indische Gids*, Vol. 38 (1916), pp. 168–177.

KALFF, S., 'François Valentijn'. *De Indische Gids*, Vol. 22, Part II (1900), pp. 907–939.

KEULEN, GERARD VAN, *De Nieuwe Groote Ligtende Zee-fakkel*. Amsterdam, 1728, Tweede Boek.

KNIGHTON, WILLIAM, *History of Ceylon from the earliest period to the present time*. London, 1845.

KNOX, CAPTAIN ROBERT, *An historical relation of the island Ceylon, in the East-Indies*. London, 1681.

LINSCHOTEN, JAN HUYGEN VAN, *Itinerario Voyage ofte schipvaert . . . naer Oost ofte Portugaels Indien, 1579–1592*. Amsterdam, 1595–6.

The Mahāvamsa or The great chronicle of Ceylon, Transl. by Wilhelm Geiger. Colombo, 1950.

MAJUMDAR, R. C., *The classical accounts of India*. Calcutta, 1960.

McCRINDLE, JOHN W., *Ancient India as described in classical literature*. Westminster, 1901.

MOOIJ, J., *Bouwstoffen voor de Geschiedenis der Protestantsche Kerk in Nederlands-Indie*, Derde Deel. Batavia, 1931.

NICHOLAS, C. W., 'Historical topography of ancient and medieval Ceylon'. *Journal of the Royal Asiatic Society (Ceylon)*, New Series, Vol. VI, Special Number.

NICHOLAS, C. W. and S. PARANAVITANA, *A concise history of Ceylon*. Colombo, 1961.

Nieuw Nederlandsch Biographisch Woordenboek, Deel V. Leiden, 1921.

PHILALETHES, *History of Ceylon from the earliest period to the year 1815*. London, 1817.

PIERIS, P. E., *Ceylon, the Portuguese era, being a history of the island for the period 1505–1658*, 2 vols. Colombo, 1913–14.

—— Ed. *Some documents relating to the rise of the Dutch power in*

Ceylon, 1602–1670, from the translations at the India Office. London, 1929.

PIERIS, RALPH, *Sinhalese social organization.* Peradeniya, 1956.

PINKERTON, JOHN, *A collection of the best and more interesting voyages and travels in all parts of the world; many of which are now first translated into English,* Vol. XI. London, 1812.

PRIDHAM, CHARLES, *An historical, political and statistical account of Ceylon and its dependencies,* Vol. 1. London, 1849.

QUEYROZ, FATHER FERNAO DE, *The temporal and spiritual conquest of Ceylon.* Transl. by Fr. S. G. Perera, 3 vols. Colombo, 1930.

RAGHAVAN, M. D., *The Karava of Ceylon. Society and culture.* Colombo, 1961.

The Rājāvaliya or A historical narrative of Sinhalese kings from Vijaya to Vimala Dharma Surya II. Ed. by B. Gunasekara. Colombo, 1900.

RIBEIRO, JOÃO, *The Historical tragedy of Ceilan.* Transl. from the Portuguese by P. E. Pieris. Colombo, 1925.

ROGERIUS, ABRAHAM, *De Open-deure tot het Verborgen Heydendom,* 1651. Uitgegevan door W. Caland. Linschoten Vereeniging X 's Gravenhage, 1915.

Rumphius Gedenboek 1702–1902. Haarlem, 1902.

RYAN, BRYCE, *Caste in modern Ceylon.* New Brunswick, 1953.

SILVA, C. R. DE, *The Portuguese in Ceylon 1617–1638.* Colombo, 1972.

SMITH, WILLIAM, *Ed. Dictionary of Greek and Roman Geography.* London, 1857.

SPILBERGEN, IORIS VAN, *t'Historiael Journael/van tghene ghepasseert// is van weghen dry Schepen/ ghenaemt den Ram, Schaep ende het Lam/ ghe// varen wt Zeelandt vander Stadt Camp. Vere naer d'Oost-Indien/ onder t'beleyt// van Ioris van Spilbergen, General/* Anno 1601 [1604].

SPILBERGEN, *De Reis van Joris van Spilbergen naar Ceylon, Atjeh en Bantam 1601–1604,* Linschoten Vereeniging, XXXVIII. 's Gravenhage, 1933.

TENNENT, JAMES EMERSON, *Ceylon. An account of the island, physical, historical and topographical,* 2 vols., Fifth edition. London, 1860.

TROOSTENBURG DE BRUIJN, C. A. L. VAN, *Biographisch Woordenboek van Oost-Indische Predikanten.* Nijmegen, 1893.

University of Ceylon History of Ceylon, Vol. 1, Pt. 11. Colombo, 1960.

VALENTIJN, FRANÇOIS, *Oud en Nieuw Oost-Indien,* 5 Vols. in 8 books. Dordrecht, 1724–26.

—— *Deur der Waarheid.* Dordrecht, 1698.

—— *Van en Naar Indie*. Voorafgegeven door Busken Huets. Opniew Uitgegeven door, A. W. Stellwagen. 's Gravenhage, 1881.

—— *Description of the Cape of Good Hope, with matters concerning it*. Edited and annotated by Prof. P. Serton *et al*. Cape Town, 1971.

—— *François Valentijn's Oud en Nieuw Oost-Indien*. Uitgegeven door Mr. S. Keijzer. Amsterdam, 1862, 3 vols.

WERNDLY, S. H., *Maleische Spraak Kunst*. Amsterdam, 1736.

WHITEWAY, R. S., *The rise of the Portuguese power in India 1497–1550*. Westminster, 1899.

WICKREMASINGHE, D. M. DE Z., *Catalogue of the Sinhalese manuscripts in the British Museum*. London, 1900.

WINIUS, G. D., *The fatal history of Portuguese Ceylon*. Cambridge, Mass., 1971.

WIT, H. C. D. DE, *Ed. Rumphius memorial volume*. Baarn, 1959.

Index

Place names are listed in the index in the form appearing in the text. Their modern forms, wherever identifiable, are provided by the side, in italics, within parentheses.